ACS General Chemistry
Study Guide

ACS Exam Prep Secrets

Full-Length Practice Test

Detailed Answer Explanations

Includes Step- by-Step
Video Tutorials

Paperback
ISBN 13: 978-1-5167-2237-2
ISBN 10: 1-5167-2237-X

DEAR FUTURE EXAM SUCCESS STORY

First of all, **THANK YOU** for purchasing Mometrix study materials!

Second, congratulations! You are one of the few determined test-takers who are committed to doing whatever it takes to excel on your exam. **You have come to the right place.** We developed these study materials with one goal in mind: to deliver you the information you need in a format that's concise and easy to use.

In addition to optimizing your guide for the content of the test, we've outlined our recommended steps for breaking down the preparation process into small, attainable goals so you can make sure you stay on track.

We've also analyzed the entire test-taking process, identifying the most common pitfalls and showing how you can overcome them and be ready for any curveball the test throws you.

Standardized testing is one of the biggest obstacles on your road to success, which only increases the importance of doing well in the high-pressure, high-stakes environment of test day. Your results on this test could have a significant impact on your future, and this guide provides the information and practical advice to help you achieve your full potential on test day.

Your success is our success

We would love to hear from you! If you would like to share the story of your exam success or if you have any questions or comments in regard to our products, please contact us at **800-673-8175** or **support@mometrix.com**.

Thanks again for your business and we wish you continued success!

Sincerely,
The Mometrix Test Preparation Team

TABLE OF CONTENTS

Introduction

Thank you for purchasing this resource! You have made the choice to prepare yourself for a test that could have a huge impact on your future, and this guide is designed to help you be fully ready for test day. Obviously, it's important to have a solid understanding of the test material, but you also need to be prepared for the unique environment and stressors of the test, so that you can perform to the best of your abilities.

For this purpose, the first section that appears in this guide is the **Secret Keys**. We've devoted countless hours to meticulously researching what works and what doesn't, and we've boiled down our findings to the five most impactful steps you can take to improve your performance on the test. We start at the beginning with study planning and move through the preparation process, all the way to the testing strategies that will help you get the most out of what you know when you're finally sitting in front of the test.

We recommend that you start preparing for your test as far in advance as possible. However, if you've bought this guide as a last-minute study resource and only have a few days before your test, we recommend that you skip over the first two Secret Keys since they address a long-term study plan.

If you struggle with **test anxiety**, we strongly encourage you to check out our recommendations for how you can overcome it. Test anxiety is a formidable foe, but it can be beaten, and we want to make sure you have the tools you need to defeat it.

1

Secret Key #1 – Plan Big, Study Small

There's a lot riding on your performance. If you want to ace this test, you're going to need to keep your skills sharp and the material fresh in your mind. You need a plan that lets you review everything you need to know while still fitting in your schedule. We'll break this strategy down into three categories.

Information Organization

Start with the information you already have: the official test outline. From this, you can make a complete list of all the concepts you need to cover before the test. Organize these concepts into groups that can be studied together, and create a list of any related vocabulary you need to learn so you can brush up on any difficult terms. You'll want to keep this vocabulary list handy once you actually start studying since you may need to add to it along the way.

Time Management

Once you have your set of study concepts, decide how to spread them out over the time you have left before the test. Break your study plan into small, clear goals so you have a manageable task for each day and know exactly what you're doing. Then just focus on one small step at a time. When you manage your time this way, you don't need to spend hours at a time studying. Studying a small block of content for a short period each day helps you retain information better and avoid stressing over how much you have left to do. You can relax knowing that you have a plan to cover everything in time. In order for this strategy to be effective though, you have to start studying early and stick to your schedule. Avoid the exhaustion and futility that comes from last-minute cramming!

Study Environment

The environment you study in has a big impact on your learning. Studying in a coffee shop, while probably more enjoyable, is not likely to be as fruitful as studying in a quiet room. It's important to keep distractions to a minimum. You're only planning to study for a short block of time, so make the most of it. Don't pause to check your phone or get up to find a snack. It's also important to **avoid multitasking**. Research has consistently shown that multitasking will make your studying dramatically less effective. Your study area should also be comfortable and well-lit so you don't have the distraction of straining your eyes or sitting on an uncomfortable chair.

The time of day you study is also important. You want to be rested and alert. Don't wait until just before bedtime. Study when you'll be most likely to comprehend and remember. Even better, if you know what time of day your test will be, set that time aside for study. That way your brain will be used to working on that subject at that specific time and you'll have a better chance of recalling information.

Finally, it can be helpful to team up with others who are studying for the same test. Your actual studying should be done in as isolated an environment as possible, but the work of organizing the information and setting up the study plan can be divided up. In between study sessions, you can discuss with your teammates the concepts that you're all studying and quiz each other on the details. Just be sure that your teammates are as serious about the test as you are. If you find that your study time is being replaced with social time, you might need to find a new team.

2

Secret Key #2 – Make Your Studying Count

You're devoting a lot of time and effort to preparing for this test, so you want to be absolutely certain it will pay off. This means doing more than just reading the content and hoping you can remember it on test day. It's important to make every minute of study count. There are two main areas you can focus on to make your studying count:

Retention

It doesn't matter how much time you study if you can't remember the material. You need to make sure you are retaining the concepts. To check your retention of the information you're learning, try recalling it at later times with minimal prompting. Try carrying around flashcards and glance at one or two from time to time or ask a friend who's also studying for the test to quiz you.

To enhance your retention, look for ways to put the information into practice so that you can apply it rather than simply recalling it. If you're using the information in practical ways, it will be much easier to remember. Similarly, it helps to solidify a concept in your mind if you're not only reading it to yourself but also explaining it to someone else. Ask a friend to let you teach them about a concept you're a little shaky on (or speak aloud to an imaginary audience if necessary). As you try to summarize, define, give examples, and answer your friend's questions, you'll understand the concepts better and they will stay with you longer. Finally, step back for a big picture view and ask yourself how each piece of information fits with the whole subject. When you link the different concepts together and see them working together as a whole, it's easier to remember the individual components.

Finally, practice showing your work on any multi-step problems, even if you're just studying. Writing out each step you take to solve a problem will help solidify the process in your mind, and you'll be more likely to remember it during the test.

Modality

Modality simply refers to the means or method by which you study. Choosing a study modality that fits your own individual learning style is crucial. No two people learn best in exactly the same way, so it's important to know your strengths and use them to your advantage.

For example, if you learn best by visualization, focus on visualizing a concept in your mind and draw an image or a diagram. Try color-coding your notes, illustrating them, or creating symbols that will trigger your mind to recall a learned concept. If you learn best by hearing or discussing information, find a study partner who learns the same way or read aloud to yourself. Think about how to put the information in your own words. Imagine that you are giving a lecture on the topic and record yourself so you can listen to it later.

For any learning style, flashcards can be helpful. Organize the information so you can take advantage of spare moments to review. Underline key words or phrases. Use different colors for different categories. Mnemonic devices (such as creating a short list in which every item starts with the same letter) can also help with retention. Find what works best for you and use it to store the information in your mind most effectively and easily.

Secret Key #3 – Practice the Right Way

Your success on test day depends not only on how many hours you put into preparing, but also on whether you prepared the right way. It's good to check along the way to see if your studying is paying off. One of the most effective ways to do this is by taking practice tests to evaluate your progress. Practice tests are useful because they show exactly where you need to improve. Every time you take a practice test, pay special attention to these three groups of questions:

- The questions you got wrong
- The questions you had to guess on, even if you guessed right
- The questions you found difficult or slow to work through

This will show you exactly what your weak areas are, and where you need to devote more study time. Ask yourself why each of these questions gave you trouble. Was it because you didn't understand the material? Was it because you didn't remember the vocabulary? Do you need more repetitions on this type of question to build speed and confidence? Dig into those questions and figure out how you can strengthen your weak areas as you go back to review the material.

Additionally, many practice tests have a section explaining the answer choices. It can be tempting to read the explanation and think that you now have a good understanding of the concept. However, an explanation likely only covers part of the question's broader context. Even if the explanation makes sense, **go back and investigate** every concept related to the question until you're positive you have a thorough understanding.

As you go along, keep in mind that the practice test is just that: practice. Memorizing these questions and answers will not be very helpful on the actual test because it is unlikely to have any of the same exact questions. If you only know the right answers to the sample questions, you won't be prepared for the real thing. **Study the concepts** until you understand them fully, and then you'll be able to answer any question that shows up on the test.

It's important to wait on the practice tests until you're ready. If you take a test on your first day of study, you may be overwhelmed by the amount of material covered and how much you need to learn. Work up to it gradually.

On test day, you'll need to be prepared for answering questions, managing your time, and using the test-taking strategies you've learned. It's a lot to balance, like a mental marathon that will have a big impact on your future. Like training for a marathon, you'll need to start slowly and work your way up. When test day arrives, you'll be ready.

Start with the strategies you've read in the first two Secret Keys—plan your course and study in the way that works best for you. If you have time, consider using multiple study resources to get different approaches to the same concepts. It can be helpful to see difficult concepts from more than one angle. Then find a good source for practice tests. Many times, the test website will suggest potential study resources or provide sample tests.

Practice Test Strategy

When you're ready to start taking practice tests, follow this strategy:

UNTIMED AND OPEN-BOOK PRACTICE

Take the first test with no time constraints and with your notes and study guide handy. Take your time and focus on applying the strategies you've learned.

TIMED AND OPEN-BOOK PRACTICE

Take the second practice test open-book as well, but set a timer and practice pacing yourself to finish in time.

TIMED AND CLOSED-BOOK PRACTICE

Take any other practice tests as if it were test day. Set a timer and put away your study materials. Sit at a table or desk in a quiet room, imagine yourself at the testing center, and answer questions as quickly and accurately as possible.

Keep repeating timed and closed-book tests on a regular basis until you run out of practice tests or it's time for the actual test. Your mind will be ready for the schedule and stress of test day, and you'll be able to focus on recalling the material you've learned.

Secret Key #4 – Pace Yourself

Once you're fully prepared for the material on the test, your biggest challenge on test day will be managing your time. Just knowing that the clock is ticking can make you panic even if you have plenty of time left. Work on pacing yourself so you can build confidence against the time constraints of the exam. Pacing is a difficult skill to master, especially in a high-pressure environment, so **practice is vital**.

Set time expectations for your pace based on how much time is available. For example, if a section has 60 questions and the time limit is 30 minutes, you know you have to average 30 seconds or less per question in order to answer them all. Although 30 seconds is the hard limit, set 25 seconds per question as your goal, so you reserve extra time to spend on harder questions. When you budget extra time for the harder questions, you no longer have any reason to stress when those questions take longer to answer.

Don't let this time expectation distract you from working through the test at a calm, steady pace, but keep it in mind so you don't spend too much time on any one question. Recognize that taking extra time on one question you don't understand may keep you from answering two that you do understand later in the test. If your time limit for a question is up and you're still not sure of the answer, mark it and move on, and come back to it later if the time and the test format allow. If the testing format doesn't allow you to return to earlier questions, just make an educated guess; then put it out of your mind and move on.

On the easier questions, be careful not to rush. It may seem wise to hurry through them so you have more time for the challenging ones, but it's not worth missing one if you know the concept and just didn't take the time to read the question fully. Work efficiently but make sure you understand the question and have looked at all of the answer choices, since more than one may seem right at first.

Even if you're paying attention to the time, you may find yourself a little behind at some point. You should speed up to get back on track, but do so wisely. Don't panic; just take a few seconds less on each question until you're caught up. Don't guess without thinking, but do look through the answer choices and eliminate any you know are wrong. If you can get down to two choices, it is often worthwhile to guess from those. Once you've chosen an answer, move on and don't dwell on any that you skipped or had to hurry through. If a question was taking too long, chances are it was one of the harder ones, so you weren't as likely to get it right anyway.

On the other hand, if you find yourself getting ahead of schedule, it may be beneficial to slow down a little. The more quickly you work, the more likely you are to make a careless mistake that will affect your score. You've budgeted time for each question, so don't be afraid to spend that time. Practice an efficient but careful pace to get the most out of the time you have.

6

Secret Key #5 – Have a Plan for Guessing

When you're taking the test, you may find yourself stuck on a question. Some of the answer choices seem better than others, but you don't see the one answer choice that is obviously correct. What do you do?

The scenario described above is very common, yet most test takers have not effectively prepared for it. Developing and practicing a plan for guessing may be one of the single most effective uses of your time as you get ready for the exam.

In developing your plan for guessing, there are three questions to address:

- When should you start the guessing process?
- How should you narrow down the choices?
- Which answer should you choose?

When to Start the Guessing Process

Unless your plan for guessing is to select C every time (which, despite its merits, is not what we recommend), you need to leave yourself enough time to apply your answer elimination strategies. Since you have a limited amount of time for each question, that means that if you're going to give yourself the best shot at guessing correctly, you have to decide quickly whether or not you will guess.

Of course, the best-case scenario is that you don't have to guess at all, so first, see if you can answer the question based on your knowledge of the subject and basic reasoning skills. Focus on the key words in the question and try to jog your memory of related topics. Give yourself a chance to bring the knowledge to mind, but once you realize that you don't have (or you can't access) the knowledge you need to answer the question, it's time to start the guessing process.

It's almost always better to start the guessing process too early than too late. It only takes a few seconds to remember something and answer the question from knowledge. Carefully eliminating wrong answer choices takes longer. Plus, going through the process of eliminating answer choices can actually help jog your memory.

Summary: Start the guessing process as soon as you decide that you can't answer the question based on your knowledge.

How to Narrow Down the Choices

The next chapter in this book (**Test-Taking Strategies**) includes a wide range of strategies for how to approach questions and how to look for answer choices to eliminate. You will definitely want to read those carefully, practice them, and figure out which ones work best for you. Here though, we're going to address a mindset rather than a particular strategy.

Your chances of guessing an answer correctly depend on how many options you are choosing from.

How many choices you have	How likely you are to guess correctly
5	20%
4	25%
3	33%
2	50%
1	100%

You can see from this chart just how valuable it is to be able to eliminate incorrect answers and make an educated guess, but there are two things that many test takers do that cause them to miss out on the benefits of guessing:

- Accidentally eliminating the correct answer
- Selecting an answer based on an impression

We'll look at the first one here, and the second one in the next section.

To avoid accidentally eliminating the correct answer, we recommend a thought exercise called **the $5 challenge**. In this challenge, you only eliminate an answer choice from contention if you are willing to bet $5 on it being wrong. Why $5? Five dollars is a small but not insignificant amount of money. It's an amount you could afford to lose but wouldn't want to throw away. And while losing $5 once might not hurt too much, doing it twenty times will set you back $100. In the same way, each small decision you make—eliminating a choice here, guessing on a question there—won't by itself impact your score very much, but when you put them all together, they can make a big difference. By holding each answer choice elimination decision to a higher standard, you can reduce the risk of accidentally eliminating the correct answer.

The $5 challenge can also be applied in a positive sense: If you are willing to bet $5 that an answer choice *is* correct, go ahead and mark it as correct.

Summary: Only eliminate an answer choice if you are willing to bet $5 that it is wrong.

Which Answer to Choose

You're taking the test. You've run into a hard question and decided you'll have to guess. You've eliminated all the answer choices you're willing to bet $5 on. Now you have to pick an answer. Why do we even need to talk about this? Why can't you just pick whichever one you feel like when the time comes?

The answer to these questions is that if you don't come into the test with a plan, you'll rely on your impression to select an answer choice, and if you do that, you risk falling into a trap. The test writers know that everyone who takes their test will be guessing on some of the questions, so they intentionally write wrong answer choices to seem plausible. You still have to pick an answer though, and if the wrong answer choices are designed to look right, how can you ever be sure that you're not falling for their trap? The best solution we've found to this dilemma is to take the decision out of your hands entirely. Here is the process we recommend:

Once you've eliminated any choices that you are confident (willing to bet $5) are wrong, select the first remaining choice as your answer.

Whether you choose to select the first remaining choice, the second, or the last, the important thing is that you use some preselected standard. Using this approach guarantees that you will not be enticed into selecting an answer choice that looks right, because you are not basing your decision on how the answer choices look.

This is not meant to make you question your knowledge. Instead, it is to help you recognize the difference between your knowledge and your impressions. There's a huge difference between thinking an answer is right because of what you know, and thinking an answer is right because it looks or sounds like it should be right.

Summary: To ensure that your selection is appropriately random, make a predetermined selection from among all answer choices you have not eliminated.

Test-Taking Strategies

This section contains a list of test-taking strategies that you may find helpful as you work through the test. By taking what you know and applying logical thought, you can maximize your chances of answering any question correctly!

It is very important to realize that every question is different and every person is different: no single strategy will work on every question, and no single strategy will work for every person. That's why we've included all of them here, so you can try them out and determine which ones work best for different types of questions and which ones work best for you.

Question Strategies

READ CAREFULLY

Read the question and answer choices carefully. Don't miss the question because you misread the terms. You have plenty of time to read each question thoroughly and make sure you understand what is being asked. Yet a happy medium must be attained, so don't waste too much time. You must read carefully, but efficiently.

CONTEXTUAL CLUES

Look for contextual clues. If the question includes a word you are not familiar with, look at the immediate context for some indication of what the word might mean. Contextual clues can often give you all the information you need to decipher the meaning of an unfamiliar word. Even if you can't determine the meaning, you may be able to narrow down the possibilities enough to make a solid guess at the answer to the question.

PREFIXES

If you're having trouble with a word in the question or answer choices, try dissecting it. Take advantage of every clue that the word might include. Prefixes can be a huge help. Usually they allow you to determine a basic meaning. Pre- means before, post- means after, pro - is positive, de- is negative. From prefixes, you can get an idea of the general meaning of the word and try to put it into context.

HEDGE WORDS

Watch out for critical hedge words, such as *likely, may, can, sometimes, often, almost, mostly, usually, generally, rarely,* and *sometimes.* Question writers insert these hedge phrases to cover every possibility. Often an answer choice will be wrong simply because it leaves no room for exception. Be on guard for answer choices that have definitive words such as *exactly* and *always.*

SWITCHBACK WORDS

Stay alert for *switchbacks.* These are the words and phrases frequently used to alert you to shifts in thought. The most common switchback words are *but, although,* and *however.* Others include *nevertheless, on the other hand, even though, while, in spite of, despite, regardless of.* Switchback words are important to catch because they can change the direction of the question or an answer choice.

10

FACE VALUE

When in doubt, use common sense. Accept the situation in the problem at face value. Don't read too much into it. These problems will not require you to make wild assumptions. If you have to go beyond creativity and warp time or space in order to have an answer choice fit the question, then you should move on and consider the other answer choices. These are normal problems rooted in reality. The applicable relationship or explanation may not be readily apparent, but it is there for you to figure out. Use your common sense to interpret anything that isn't clear.

Answer Choice Strategies

ANSWER SELECTION

The most thorough way to pick an answer choice is to identify and eliminate wrong answers until only one is left, then confirm it is the correct answer. Sometimes an answer choice may immediately seem right, but be careful. The test writers will usually put more than one reasonable answer choice on each question, so take a second to read all of them and make sure that the other choices are not equally obvious. As long as you have time left, it is better to read every answer choice than to pick the first one that looks right without checking the others.

ANSWER CHOICE FAMILIES

An answer choice family consists of two (in rare cases, three) answer choices that are very similar in construction and cannot all be true at the same time. If you see two answer choices that are direct opposites or parallels, one of them is usually the correct answer. For instance, if one answer choice says that quantity x increases and another either says that quantity x decreases (opposite) or says that quantity y increases (parallel), then those answer choices would fall into the same family. An answer choice that doesn't match the construction of the answer choice family is more likely to be incorrect. Most questions will not have answer choice families, but when they do appear, you should be prepared to recognize them.

ELIMINATE ANSWERS

Eliminate answer choices as soon as you realize they are wrong, but make sure you consider all possibilities. If you are eliminating answer choices and realize that the last one you are left with is also wrong, don't panic. Start over and consider each choice again. There may be something you missed the first time that you will realize on the second pass.

AVOID FACT TRAPS

Don't be distracted by an answer choice that is factually true but doesn't answer the question. You are looking for the choice that answers the question. Stay focused on what the question is asking for so you don't accidentally pick an answer that is true but incorrect. Always go back to the question and make sure the answer choice you've selected actually answers the question and is not merely a true statement.

EXTREME STATEMENTS

In general, you should avoid answers that put forth extreme actions as standard practice or proclaim controversial ideas as established fact. An answer choice that states the "process should be used in certain situations, if..." is much more likely to be correct than one that states the "process should be discontinued completely." The first is a calm rational statement and doesn't even make a definitive, uncompromising stance, using a hedge word *if* to provide wiggle room, whereas the second choice is a radical idea and far more extreme.

BENCHMARK

As you read through the answer choices and you come across one that seems to answer the question well, mentally select that answer choice. This is not your final answer, but it's the one that will help you evaluate the other answer choices. The one that you selected is your benchmark or standard for judging each of the other answer choices. Every other answer choice must be compared to your benchmark. That choice is correct until proven otherwise by another answer choice beating it. If you find a better answer, then that one becomes your new benchmark. Once you've decided that no other choice answers the question as well as your benchmark, you have your final answer.

PREDICT THE ANSWER

Before you even start looking at the answer choices, it is often best to try to predict the answer. When you come up with the answer on your own, it is easier to avoid distractions and traps because you will know exactly what to look for. The right answer choice is unlikely to be word-for-word what you came up with, but it should be a close match. Even if you are confident that you have the right answer, you should still take the time to read each option before moving on.

General Strategies

TOUGH QUESTIONS

If you are stumped on a problem or it appears too hard or too difficult, don't waste time. Move on! Remember though, if you can quickly check for obviously incorrect answer choices, your chances of guessing correctly are greatly improved. Before you completely give up, at least try to knock out a couple of possible answers. Eliminate what you can and then guess at the remaining answer choices before moving on.

CHECK YOUR WORK

Since you will probably not know every term listed and the answer to every question, it is important that you get credit for the ones that you do know. Don't miss any questions through careless mistakes. If at all possible, try to take a second to look back over your answer selection and make sure you've selected the correct answer choice and haven't made a costly careless mistake (such as marking an answer choice that you didn't mean to mark). This quick double check should more than pay for itself in caught mistakes for the time it costs.

PACE YOURSELF

It's easy to be overwhelmed when you're looking at a page full of questions; your mind is confused and full of random thoughts, and the clock is ticking down faster than you would like. Calm down and maintain the pace that you have set for yourself. Especially as you get down to the last few minutes of the test, don't let the small numbers on the clock make you panic. As long as you are on track by monitoring your pace, you are guaranteed to have time for each question.

DON'T RUSH

It is very easy to make errors when you are in a hurry. Maintaining a fast pace in answering questions is pointless if it makes you miss questions that you would have gotten right otherwise. Test writers like to include distracting information and wrong answers that seem right. Taking a little extra time to avoid careless mistakes can make all the difference in your test score. Find a pace that allows you to be confident in the answers that you select.

KEEP MOVING

Panicking will not help you pass the test, so do your best to stay calm and keep moving. Taking deep breaths and going through the answer elimination steps you practiced can help to break through a stress barrier and keep your pace.

Final Notes

The combination of a solid foundation of content knowledge and the confidence that comes from practicing your plan for applying that knowledge is the key to maximizing your performance on test day. As your foundation of content knowledge is built up and strengthened, you'll find that the strategies included in this chapter become more and more effective in helping you quickly sift through the distractions and traps of the test to isolate the correct answer.

Now it's time to move on to the test content chapters of this book, but be sure to keep your goal in mind. As you read, think about how you will be able to apply this information on the test. If you've already seen sample questions for the test and you have an idea of the question format and style, try to come up with questions of your own that you can answer based on what you're reading. This will give you valuable practice applying your knowledge in the same ways you can expect to on test day.

Good luck and good studying!

Atoms

Historical Models of the Atom

ATOMIC MODELS AND THEORIES

There have been many theories regarding the **structure** of atoms and their particles. Part of the challenge in developing an understanding of matter is that atoms and their particles are too small to be seen. It is believed that the first conceptualization of the atom was developed by **Democritus** in 400 B.C. Some of the more notable models are the solid sphere or billiard ball model postulated by **John Dalton**, the plum pudding or raisin bun model by **J.J. Thomson**, the planetary or nuclear model by **Ernest Rutherford**, the Bohr or orbit model by **Niels Bohr**, and the electron cloud or quantum mechanical model by **Louis de Broglie** and **Erwin Schrodinger**. Rutherford directed the alpha scattering experiment that discounted the plum pudding model. The shortcoming of the Bohr model was the belief that electrons orbited in fixed rather than changing ecliptic orbits.

> **Review Video: Atomic Models**
> Visit mometrix.com/academy and enter code: 434851
>
> **Review Video: John Dalton**
> Visit mometrix.com/academy and enter code: 565627

THOMSON "PLUM PUDDING" MODEL

J.J. Thomson, the discoverer of the electron, suggested that the arrangement of protons and electrons within an atom could be approximated by dried fruit in a **plum pudding**. Thomson, whose discovery of the electron preceded that of the proton or neutron, hypothesized that an atom's electrons, the dried plums, were positioned uniformly inside the atom within a cloud of positive charge, the pudding. This model was later disproved.

RUTHERFORD SCATTERING

Ernest Rutherford concluded from the work of Geiger and Marsden that the majority of the mass was concentrated in a minute, positively charged region, the **nucleus**, which was surrounded by **electrons**. When a positive alpha particle approached close enough to the nucleus, it was strongly repelled, enough so that it had the ability to rebound at high angles. The small nucleus size explained the small number of alpha particles that were repelled in this fashion. The scattering led to development of the **planetary model of the atom**, which was further developed by Niels Bohr into what is now known as the Bohr model.

BOHR MODEL

Niels Bohr postulated that the electrons orbiting the nucleus must occupy discrete orbits. These discrete orbits also corresponded to discrete levels of energy and angular momentum. Consequently, the only way that electrons could move between orbits was by making nearly instantaneous jumps between them. These jumps, known as **quantum leaps**, are associated with the absorption or emission of a quantum of energy, known as a photon. If the electron is jumping to a higher energy state, a photon must be absorbed. Similarly, if the electron is dropping to a lower energy state, a photon must be emitted.

> **Review Video: Structure of Atoms**
> Visit mometrix.com/academy and enter code: 905932

Atomic Structure

ATOMIC NUMBER, ATOMIC WEIGHT

The three primary components of an atom are protons, neutrons, and electrons. Protons and neutrons are collectively called **nucleons** and form the nucleus of the atom; electrons orbit the nucleus at a distance—although they aren't really orbiting in the classical sense, like planets orbit a sun; rather, they are spread out in a probabilistic electron cloud. A neutral atom has the same number of electrons as protons; negative ions have more electrons; positive ions have fewer.

The atomic number of an atom is its number of protons. It is this that determines what element it is; carbon has an atomic number of six, so all carbon atoms have six protons. The mass number is the number of protons plus the number of neutrons. The number of electrons has no effect on the atomic number or the mass number. (The mass of an electron is only about $\frac{1}{1800}$ the mass of a proton or neutron.) The number of electrons does determine the charge of the atom or ion, but an atom can gain or lose electrons and change its charge without altering its atomic number or mass number.

The atomic weight of an atom is the mass of the atom in **atomic mass units (u or g/mol)**, defined as $\frac{1}{12}$ the mass of a carbon-12 atom (which contains six protons and six neutrons). Because the proton and the neutron have almost the same mass, the atomic weight is very close to the mass number—but because the protons and neutrons don't have exactly the same mass, and because the electrons also have some mass, they are not precisely equal. (There is also a little mass tied up in the binding energy of the atom.)

For the atomic weights of elements as given on a periodic table, however, there's a further factor to consider. The atomic weight of chlorine, for instance, is given as 35.45—much farther from an integral value than the slight differences in mass between protons and neutrons can account for. This is because the atomic weight given for each element in the periodic table is the average weight of the different isotopes of that element, weighted by their abundance in nature. Most chlorine atoms are chlorine-35, with some chlorine-37 and much smaller amounts of other isotopes; the weighted average of their weights comes out to 35.45.

NEUTRONS, PROTONS, ISOTOPES

An isotope of an element is an atom of that element with a particular number of neutrons. Two atoms of the same element are said to be different isotopes if their number of neutrons differs. A specific isotope is named in terms of the atomic number and mass number, either by stating the mass number after the element name or writing the atomic number to the lower left and the mass number to the upper right of the chemical symbol. An atom with six protons and eight neutrons, for instance, would be called carbon-14 or $^{14}_{6}\text{C}$.

Two isotopes of the same element differ in their mass, of course but often also in their stability. For example, carbon-12 and carbon-13 are stable; carbon-14 is radioactive with a half-life of 5,700 years (making it useful in carbon dating); carbon-15 is extremely radioactive with a half-life of only 2.45 seconds.

MASS SPECTROMETER

A mass spectrometer is a device used to separate molecules by mass. Although the spectrometer relies on the particles being charged, uncharged molecules can be separated by a mass spectrometer if they are first ionized. (Technically, the spectrometer separates particles by the mass-to-charge ratio, but it can often be assumed that the charges of most of the particles are the same.)

In a mass spectrometer, charged particles are first accelerated by a voltage that gives all the particles the same kinetic energy. The moving particles are then subjected to a magnetic field. Because the magnetic field deflects some particles more than others, particles of a specific mass (or mass-to-charge ratio) can be selected out. Specifically, the voltage accelerates the particles to an energy of $U = qV$; setting that equal to the kinetic energy gives $qV = \frac{1}{2}mv^2$, and hence $v = \sqrt{\frac{2qV}{m}}$. The magnetic field produces a force of qvB, deflecting the particle in a circular path; setting this equal to the centripetal force yields $qvB = \frac{mv^2}{r}$; putting in our previous formula for v and solving for the radius of the path gives $r = \frac{1}{B}\sqrt{2V\left(\frac{m}{q}\right)}$—the deflection depends on the mass-to-charge ratio.

ELECTRON VOLT

The electron volt, abbreviated eV, is a unit of energy equal to the change in potential energy of an electron when it moves across a potential difference of one volt. Because this change in potential energy is equal to $U_E = qV$, one electron volt is equal to the magnitude of the charge of an electron multiplied by one volt: $(1.602 \times 10^{-19} \text{ C})(1 \text{ V}) = 1.602 \times 10^{-19}$ J.

Although it is not an official metric unit, the electron volt is frequently used in atomic and nuclear physics. The energies involved in single atoms are inconveniently small numbers when expressed in Joules but have more manageable values when expressed in electron volts. For instance, the energy of a ground state electron in a hydrogen atom is -2.18×10^{-18} J, which is equal to –13.6 eV. For energies significantly larger than an electron volt but smaller than a joule, such as nuclear binding energies, units such as megaelectron-volts (MeV) and gigaelectron-volts (GeV) are commonly used.

Electronic Configuration

ORBITAL STRUCTURE OF HYDROGEN ATOM, PRINCIPAL QUANTUM NUMBER N, NUMBER OF ELECTRONS PER ORBITAL

According to quantum mechanics, each electron in an atom can be completely described by four quantum numbers. The values of these quantum numbers are important for the shapes of the electron orbitals, for the electron energies, and for other properties. Each quantum number is constrained to only a discrete set of possible values. The four quantum numbers and their possible values are the following:

- The **principal quantum number**, n, can be any positive integer. This is the only quantum number that can (in principle) have infinitely many possible values, although in practice it will seldom exceed 9 or 10.
- The **angular quantum number**, l, can be any integer between 0 and $n - 1$. Thus, if an electron has a principal quantum number of 1, $l = 0$; if $n = 2$, then l may be 0 or 1, and so on.
- The **magnetic quantum number**, m_l, can be any integer between $-l$ and $+l$. If $l = 0$, then $m_l = 0$; if $l = 1$, then m may be –1, 0, or +1, and so on.
- The **spin quantum number**, m_s, is always $+\frac{1}{2}$ or $-\frac{1}{2}$; it does not depend on the other quantum numbers.

The principal quantum number of a hydrogen atom, abbreviated n, is a number characterizing the potential energy of the single electron in the atom. The principal quantum number is always an integer greater than or equal to 1; the higher n, the higher the energy of the hydrogen atom. One of the basic principles of quantum mechanics—in fact, the one that gives the theory its name—is that the energy of atoms, among other quantities, is quantized; rather than being able to take on any value in a continuous range, it is restricted to a discontinuous set of possible values, or quanta. More specifically, if the potential energy of an atom in the lowest state, E_1, is appropriately defined at a certain negative value (-2.18×10^{-18} J for a hydrogen atom, or -13.6 eV), then the potential energy of the state with principal quantum number n is $E_n = \frac{E_1}{n^2}$. As usual with potential energy, it is only the difference in energy between states that really matters, so the assignment of a negative value to the energy is not physically problematic and is done for mathematical convenience.

An **atomic orbital** is a possible state that a pair of electrons can be in in an atom. Therefore, strictly speaking, there are at most only two electrons per orbital. However, the word "orbital" is sometimes used interchangeably with "shell" or "subshell," the former referring to the collection of electrons with the same principal quantum number n, the latter to electrons that also share the angular quantum number l. The subshells are successively symbolized by the letters s, p, d, and f; the s subshell contains only one orbital, the p three, the d five, and so on. The first shell contains only an s subshell and so only one orbital. The second contains an s and a p subshell for a total of $1 + 3 = 4$ orbitals. The third contains an s, p, and d, for $1 + 3 + 5 = 9$ orbitals, and so on through 16 and 25, and in general the nth subshell contains n^2 orbitals, and thus $2n^2$ electrons. Because the principal quantum number n corresponds to the energy level of the atom, it would also be correct to say that there are $2n^2$ electrons in each energy level of the hydrogen atom.

GEOMETRY

By solving Schrödinger's equation for a hydrogen atom, a set of wave functions is obtained. These wave functions, called **orbitals**, relate the distributions of electron probability density to space. Each orbital has discrete energy levels and shapes in electron distribution.

- The lowest energy orbital in the hydrogen atom is the $1s$ orbital. The $1s$ orbital has a sphere distribution of electron density. As the principal quantum number, n, increases, each orbital will have $(n-1)$ **nodes**, where the probability function goes to zero (the number of nodes also apply to other types of orbitals).
- The $2s$ orbital is also spherical, but it is larger in radius and has one node. The $2p$ orbital electron distributions are dumbbell-shaped.
- When $n = 2$, the values of quantum number m_l are –1, 0, and 1, creating three degenerate p orbitals, with different special orientations denoted as p_x, p_y, and p_z.
- When $n = 3$, m_l values are –2, –1, 0, 1, and 2. This creates five d orbitals. Four of these orbitals are shaped like four-leaf-clovers. The fifth orbital, d_{z^2}, has two lobes along the z-axis and a doughnut-shaped distribution in the xy plane.

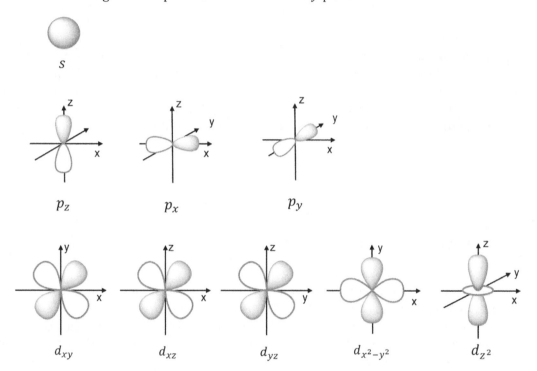

PAULI EXCLUSION PRINCIPLE

The Pauli Exclusion Principle is a principle in quantum mechanics named after the Austrian theoretical physicist Wolfgang Ernst Pauli, who discovered it. It states that for a certain class of particles called **fermions**, two such particles in the same system cannot be the same state at the same time. Photons, for example, are not fermions, and the Pauli Exclusion Principle does not apply to them. Protons, neutrons, and electrons, however, are all fermions, and it is in electrons that the consequences of the principle are most obvious—and in terms of which Pauli first formulated the principle.

It is the Pauli Exclusion Principle that limits the number of electrons per orbital and the number of orbitals per shell. Specifically, the Pauli Exclusion Principle states that no two electrons in an atom can have exactly the same quantum numbers. It is this fact that causes shells to be filled by particular numbers of electrons and that ultimately leads to the details of electron structure.

AUFBAU PRINCIPLE

The **Aufbau principle** is named from the German word for "building up," and it describes how electrons fill the energy levels or **shells of an atom**. In general, electrons will fill the $n = 1$ energy level before filling the $n = 2$ energy level, and electrons will fill the $n = 2$ energy level before filling the $n = 3$ energy level. The s subshell of an energy level will fill before the p subshell, which fills before the d and f subshells.

HUND'S RULE

Hund's rule describes how electrons fill the orbitals in a sublevel. Less energy is required for an electron to occupy an orbital alone than the energy needed for an electron to pair up with another electron in an orbital. Therefore, electrons will occupy each orbital in a subshell before electrons will begin to pair up in those orbitals. For example, in the $2p$ subshell, one electron will occupy each of the three orbitals before pairing begins. In the $3d$ subshell, one electron will occupy each of the five orbitals before pairing begins.

ORBITAL BOX DIAGRAM

The **orbital box diagram** is a visual representation of electron distributions in an atom. In this representation, the orbitals are drawn as boxes, while the electrons are indicated by half arrows. The electron's spin quantum number (m_s) can be positive, denoted by a half arrow pointing up (↑), or negative, denoted by a half arrow that is pointing down (↓). The diagram below shows the **electron configuration** of an oxygen atom at ground state, $1s^2 2s^2 2p^4$.

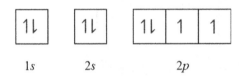

$$1s \qquad 2s \qquad 2p$$

To construct an orbital box diagram for an atom at ground state, these principles should be followed:

- The orbitals with lowest energy should be filled first; each orbital can have two electrons with opposite spin states (Aufbau Principle).
- The degenerate orbitals in the same subshell are filled first, each with one electron of the same spin state (Hund's Rule). Therefore, in the electron configuration of an oxygen atom the three degenerate $2p$ orbitals are filled in first, each with one electron spinning up, and the fourth electron is paired with another in the same subshell.
- No two electrons should have the same set of quantum numbers (Pauli Exclusion Principle).

ENERGY DIAGRAMS

An atom is in the **ground state** when the electrons are configured at the lowest energy level possible. In the hydrogen atom depicted below, the lowest energy configuration is $1s^1$—the electron is at its first allowed orbit and most negative energy possible ($n = 1$). When the electron absorbs a certain amount of energy, it gets promoted to another orbit ($n \geq 2$) with less negative energy (and a higher energy level), therefore the atom is in the **excited state**.

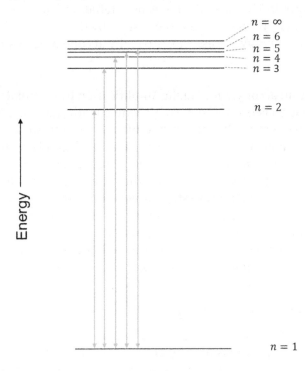

The energy levels are quantized, and an electron transition only absorbs or emits certain amounts of energy. In Bohr's hydrogen atom model, the energy for each allowed level is:

$$E = (-hcR_H)\left(\frac{1}{n^2}\right) = (-2.18 \times 10^{-18} \text{ J})\left(\frac{1}{n^2}\right)$$

In this equation, h is the Planck's constant, c is the speed of light, and R_H is the Rydberg constant. The value of n can be any positive integer (1, 2, 3, to infinity), and these correspond to an orbit. When an electron transitions from one orbit (n_i) to another (n_f), the energy change between the final energy level (E_f) and the initial energy level (E_i) is:

$$\Delta E = E_f - E_i = (-hcR_H)\left(\frac{1}{n_f^2} - \frac{1}{n_i^2}\right) = (-2.18 \times 10^{-18} J)\left(\frac{1}{n_f^2} - \frac{1}{n_i^2}\right)$$

Using $\Delta E = h\nu = \frac{hc}{\lambda}$, it is also possible to calculate for the frequency (ν) and wavelength (λ) associated with the energy change.

GROUND STATE AND EXCITED STATES

The ground state of an atom is the state with the lowest energy. In a ground-state atom, all the electrons are in the lowest-energy states possible, subject to the Pauli Exclusion Principle and the maximum number of electrons in an orbital. That is, no orbitals in a ground-state atom contain electrons unless all orbitals of lower energy are already full.

An atom that is not in the ground state is said to be in an excited state. An atom is in an excited state if there is at least one orbital that is not full despite at least one higher-energy orbital containing electrons.

An atom can change from its ground state to an excited state by one electron moving into an unoccupied, higher-energy state. This can occur if the atom is given energy by, for example, a high-energy photon colliding with it. The excited state is not stable, and an atom in an excited state will after some time spontaneously return to the ground state by the higher-energy electrons dropping back into unoccupied, lower-energy states. This is usually accompanied by emission of a photon.

LASERS

The word **laser** is actually an acronym for "Light Amplification by Stimulated Emission of Radiation". The laser radiation is produced in single wavelength (monochromatic), highly directional, and in-phase (coherent). Not all lasers emit visible light; some lasers emit radiation that falls in the infrared and ultraviolet region. Laser emissions are stimulated by inputting energy into the laser medium. Electrons are pumped into an excited state that is metastable, meaning that the excited electrons can maintain their state for only a short time. As more electrons are pumped into the metastable state (a process called **population inversion**), some will decay and emit photons, which stimulate other electrons in a chain-reaction. There are partial-reflecting mirrors installed in typical laser set-ups to return some of the emitted photons into the medium to help the stimulated emission continue. Because of their high directionality and intensity, lasers are useful in a wide variety of fields, including ophthalmological surgery, cancer removal, precision cutting, and welding hard materials.

ABSORPTION AND EMISSION LINE SPECTRA

Emission line spectra are produced by photons emitted as electrons in excited atoms drop back down to lower energy states. The atoms may be put into excited states by high temperatures or electrical currents. Each element or compound has a characteristic emission line spectrum that depends on its possible energy levels. Essentially, there is an emission line corresponding to each possible transition between energy levels—although some transitions are more likely than others, which means the corresponding emission lines will be accordingly more prominent. The frequency of the emission line can be determined by taking the difference in energies between the two energy levels and dividing by Planck's constant, h, 6.626×10^{-34} J $\cdot$ s.

For example, the emission spectrum of mercury vapor has a prominent blue line; this arises from an electron dropping from an excited energy level of 7.70 eV to a still excited but lower energy level of 4.87 eV.

$$\Delta E = 7.70 \text{ eV} - 4.87 \text{ eV } 2.83 \text{ eV} = 4.55 \times 10^{-19} \text{ J}$$

The frequency is this energy difference divided by Planck's constant.

$$f = \frac{\Delta E}{h} = 6.87 \times 10^{14} \text{ Hz}$$

The wavelength is the speed of light divided by the frequency.

$$\lambda = \frac{c}{f} = 4.36 \times 10^{-7} \text{ m}$$

This is 436 nm, which is in the blue range of visible light.

Absorption line spectra are produced by the absorption by a gas or other transparent medium of photons of particular frequencies from a continuous spectrum. When an atom or molecule absorbs a photon, the absorbed energy puts the particle into an excited state. It is not possible for the atom or molecule to partially absorb the photon; the photon must be absorbed completely or not at all.

22

This places a constraint on the frequencies of photons that can be absorbed: only the photons that have the exact amount of energy to raise the particle to an excited state can be absorbed. Therefore, the energies of photons in the absorption line spectrum correspond to differences in energy between the ground state and the possible excited states; from this energy, the frequency and wavelength of the photons can be determined from the relationships $E = hf$ and $c = \lambda f$.

Unlike the emission line spectrum, the absorption line spectrum does not include lines corresponding to transitions between different excited states. The time that a particle spends in an excited state before returning to its ground state is generally small enough that the chances of its being further excited by another photon while in that state are negligible.

Fluorescence is a phenomenon in which certain materials absorb light at one wavelength and emit light at a wavelength of a lower frequency (and therefore a lower energy). This occurs because each photon of the absorbed light excites an electron in an atom of the material, but rather than fall immediately to the ground state and emit a photon of the same energy as it absorbs, the electron first passes through an intermediate, lower-energy excited state, emitting a photon for each transition and therefore ultimately emitting two or more photons with a total energy equal to the energy of the single-incident photon.

The best-known examples of fluorescence involve materials that absorb ultraviolet light and emit light in the visible range. Because the initial ultraviolet light is not visible to the human eye, the materials when they emit visible light seem to glow. Fluorescent dyes and paints that seem to glow under "black light" (i.e., ultraviolet light) are used for decorative purposes and on amusement park rides as well as in security features on some bills and credit cards. Fluorescence also occurs in nature and even in some living things; many fish and other organisms exhibit biofluorescence.

WAVE BEHAVIORS OF MATTER

Light has both particle- and wave-like properties. Visible light is a part of the electromagnetic spectrum, which can be explained and mathematically represented by wave characteristics. However, as illustrated in the photoelectric effect experiment, there is always a minimum, quantized amount of light energy required to shine onto a metal surface to emit an electron from it. This indicates that light has discrete amounts of energy, which is particle-like behavior. Each of these particles in light are called **photons**. Like photons, all objects (such as electrons, neutrons, or even macroscopic matter like a tennis ball) possess wave-like characteristics, referred to as the **matter waves**. This concept was first proposed by the French physicist Louis de Broglie. The wavelength of matter waves depends on the mass, m, and the velocity, v, of a particle:

$$\lambda = \frac{h}{mv}$$

The h in the equation is Planck's constant, $h = 6.626 \times 10^{-34}$ J · s. If you substitute various values into the equation, you will see that wavelengths are only significant for incredibly small masses like electrons and other subatomic particles. Because of this wave-like behavior of a particle and the spatial extension associated with the waves, it is impossible to measure the momentum ($p = mv$) and the location of the particle precisely at the same time. This is Heisenberg's uncertainty principle.

FERROMAGNETISM, PARAMAGNETISM, AND DIAMAGNETISM

Ferromagnetism, paramagnetism, and diamagnetism all refer to a material's ability to be influenced by a magnetic field. **Ferromagnetism** is the type of magnetism present in familiar permanent magnets. Only a few materials are capable of ferromagnetism, including cobalt, nickel, and as the prefix *ferro-* implies, iron. In ferromagnetic materials, adjacent atoms tend to align so that their electrons' spins are in the same direction, causing their individual magnetic moments to build into a significant magnetic field. When the material is not magnetized, the atoms are aligned in parts of the material, called domains, but the magnetic fields of the domains point in different directions and cancel. It is when the domains line up and combine into one large domain that the object as a whole is said to be magnetized.

Paramagnetism and diamagnetism both apply to a broader range of materials but are much weaker effects. In **paramagnetic** materials, unpaired electrons are attracted by a magnetic field, and the rest of the atoms come with them. In **diamagnetic** materials, all electrons are paired, and an induced magnetic field causes the material to be repelled by a magnetic field. Aluminum and myoglobin are examples of paramagnetic materials; carbon and antimony are diamagnetic.

HEISENBERG UNCERTAINTY PRINCIPLE

The Heisenberg uncertainty principle states that the position and momentum of an object cannot simultaneously be known with arbitrarily high precision. Quantitatively, it states that $\Delta x \Delta p \geq \frac{h}{4\pi}$, where Δx is the uncertainty in the position, Δp is the uncertainty in the momentum, and h is Planck's constant, 6.626×10^{-34} J · s. This is often written $\Delta x \Delta p \geq \frac{\hbar}{2}$, where $\hbar$, the reduced Planck's constant, is defined as $\frac{h}{2\pi}$. Instead of position and momentum, the uncertainty principle can also be stated in terms of energy and time $\left(\Delta E \Delta t \geq \frac{\hbar}{2} \right)$ or certain other pairs of variables.

Although sometimes it is assumed that the uncertainty principle arises because in observing an object's position, one necessarily must disturb it, it is actually more fundamental than that—it is not just that the object's position and momentum can't be simultaneously measured; it is that—counterintuitively—a particle can't simultaneously have an exact position and momentum. Because Planck's constant is so small, the effects of the principle on macroscopic phenomena are negligible, but for objects on the atomic scale, it is significant. For instance, the Heisenberg uncertainty principle explains quantum tunneling, the ability of a particle to pass through a barrier that classically would be impermeable.

EFFECTIVE NUCLEAR CHARGE

The effective nuclear charge on an electron, Z_{eff}, is the effective net nuclear charge experienced by the electrons given the presence of other electrons in the atom. Because each electron is both attracted to the nucleus and repelled by the other electrons present, the electrical force from the other electrons effectively cancels much of the force from a like number of protons. The effective nuclear charge of an atom is therefore always less than the atomic number: $Z_{eff} < Z$ (except in the case of an atom or ion with only one electron). Calculating the exact effective nuclear charge is nontrivial, however, because it depends not only on the number of electrons but also on the shapes of the orbitals.

The effective nuclear charge has a number of ramifications. It affects the atomic binding energy, or ionization energy, as well as the atomic and ionic radius. It is also the reason that in an atom with multiple electrons, different orbitals with the same principal quantum number do not have the exact same energy and that at relatively high n, some of the orbitals fill in a different order than might be expected: for example, the $4s$ orbital has lower energy than the $3d$.

PHOTOELECTRIC EFFECT

The photoelectric effect is the phenomenon in which light shined on certain materials causes them to emit electrons. Although this can partly be explained by assuming that the energy of the light knocks electrons from the atom, there are several observed aspects of the phenomenon that this classically failed to explain. The photoelectric effect does not occur when the light's frequency is below a certain threshold, regardless of the intensity of the light. Likewise, the phenomenon can be prevented by applying a stopping voltage, but the necessary voltage depends only on the material and the frequency of the light, not on its intensity.

It was Albert Einstein who recognized that the photoelectric effect could be explained if light came in distinct quanta, now called **photons**, with an energy dependent on the light's frequency. The number of photons determined the intensity, but only if individual photons had sufficient energy would they be able to remove electrons from atoms. The recognition that light came in discrete quanta helped pave the way for the development of quantum mechanics. Although Einstein is most famous for his theory of relativity, it was for his work on the photoelectric effect that he won his Nobel Prize.

ELECTROMAGNETIC SPECTRUM

The **electromagnetic spectrum** is the range of all wavelengths and frequencies of known electromagnetic waves. Visible light occupies only a small portion of the electromagnetic spectrum. Some of the common classifications of electromagnetic waves are listed in the table below with their approximate frequency ranges.

Classification	Frequency (Hz)
Gamma Rays	$\sim 10^{19}$
X-Rays	$\sim 10^{17} - 10^{18}$
Ultraviolet	$\sim 10^{15} - 10^{16}$
Visible Light	$\sim 10^{14}$
Infra-red	$\sim 10^{11} - 10^{14}$
Microwaves	$\sim 10^{10} - 10^{11}$
Radio/TV	$\sim 10^{6} - 10^{9}$

Electromagnetic waves travel at the speed of light, $c = 3 \times 10^8$ m/s. To find the wavelength of any electromagnetic wave, simply divide c by the frequency. Visible light occupies a range of wavelengths from approximately 380 nm (violet) to 740 nm (red). The full spectrum of color can be found between these two wavelengths.

> **Review Video: Electromagnetic Spectrum**
> Visit mometrix.com/academy and enter code: 771761
>
> **Review Video: Light**
> Visit mometrix.com/academy and enter code: 900556

The Periodic Table

GROUPS AND PERIODS IN THE PERIODIC TABLE

A **group** is a vertical column of the periodic table. Elements in the same group have the same number of **valence electrons**. For the representative elements, the number of valence electrons is equal to the group number. Because of their equal valence electrons, elements in the same groups have similar physical and chemical properties. A period is a horizontal row of the periodic table. Atomic number increases from left to right across a row. The **period** of an element corresponds to the **highest energy level** of the electrons in the atoms of that element. The energy level increases from top to bottom down a group.

Group →	1	2	3	4	5	6	7	8	9	10	11	12	13	14	15	16	17	18
1	1 H																	2 He
2	3 Li	4 Be											5 B	6 C	7 N	8 O	9 F	10 Ne
3	11 Na	12 Mg											13 Al	14 Si	15 P	16 S	17 Cl	18 Ar
4	19 K	20 Ca	21 Sc	22 Ti	23 V	24 Cr	25 Mn	26 Fe	27 Co	28 Ni	29 Cu	30 Zn	31 Ga	32 Ge	33 As	34 Se	35 Br	36 Kr
5	37 Rb	38 Sr	39 Y	40 Zr	41 Nb	42 Mo	43 Tc	44 Ru	45 Rh	46 Pd	47 Ag	48 Cd	49 In	50 Sn	51 Sb	52 Te	53 I	54 Xe
6	55 Cs	56 Ba	*	72 Hf	73 Ta	74 W	75 Re	76 Os	77 Ir	78 Pt	79 Au	80 Hg	81 Tl	82 Pb	83 Bi	84 Po	85 At	86 Rn
7	87 Fr	88 Ra	**	104 Rf	105 Db	106 Sg	107 Bh	108 Hs	109 Mt	110 Ds	111 Rg	112 Cn	113 Nh	114 Fl	115 Mc	116 Lv	117 Ts	118 Og

*	57 La	58 Ce	59 Pr	60 Nd	61 Pm	62 Sm	63 Eu	64 Gd	65 Tb	66 Dy	67 Ho	68 Er	69 Tm	70 Yb	71 Lu
**	89 Ac	90 Th	91 Pa	92 U	93 Np	94 Pu	95 Am	96 Cm	97 Bk	98 Cf	99 Es	100 Fm	101 Md	102 No	103 Lr

> **Review Video: Periodic Table**
> Visit mometrix.com/academy and enter code: 154828

ATOMIC NUMBER AND ATOMIC MASS IN THE PERIODIC TABLE

The elements in the periodic table are arranged in order of **increasing atomic number** first left to right and then top to bottom across the periodic table. The **atomic number** represents the number of protons in the atoms of that element. Because of the increasing numbers of protons, the atomic mass typically also increases from left to right across a period and from top to bottom down a row. The **atomic mass** is a weighted average of all the naturally occurring isotopes of an element.

ATOMIC SYMBOLS

The **atomic symbol** for many elements is simply the first letter of the element name. For example, the atomic symbol for hydrogen is H, and the atomic symbol for carbon is C. The atomic symbol of other elements is the first two letters of the element name. For example, the atomic symbol for helium is He, and the atomic symbol for cobalt is Co. The atomic symbols of several elements are derived from Latin. For example, the atomic symbol for copper (Cu) is derived from *cuprum,* and

the atomic symbol for iron (Fe) is derived from *ferrum.* The atomic symbol for tungsten (W) is derived from the German word *wolfram.*

ARRANGEMENT OF METALS, NONMETALS, AND METALLOIDS IN THE PERIODIC TABLE

The **metals** are located on the left side and center of the periodic table, and the **nonmetals** are located on the right side of the periodic table. The **metalloids** or **semimetals** form a zigzag line between the metals and nonmetals as shown below. Metals include the alkali metals such as lithium, sodium, and potassium and the alkaline earth metals such as beryllium, magnesium, and calcium. Metals also include the transition metals such as iron, copper, and nickel and the inner transition metals such as thorium, uranium, and plutonium. Nonmetals include the chalcogens such as oxygen and sulfur, the halogens such as fluorine and chlorine, and the noble gases such as helium and argon. Carbon, nitrogen, and phosphorus are also nonmetals. Metalloids or semimetals include boron, silicon, germanium, antimony, and polonium.

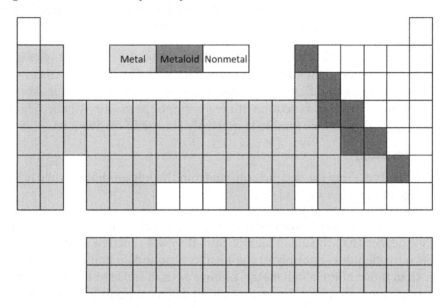

ARRANGEMENT OF TRANSITION ELEMENTS

The **transition elements** belong to one of two categories—transition metals or inner transition metals. The **transition metals** are located in the middle of the periodic table, and the inner transition metals are typically set off as two rows by themselves at the bottom of the periodic table. The transition metals correspond to the "*d* block" for orbital filling, and the inner transition metals correspond to the "*f* block" for orbital filling. Examples of transition metals include iron, copper, nickel, and zinc. The inner transition metals consist of the *lanthanide* or *rare-earth series*, which corresponds to the first row, and the *actinide series*, which corresponds to the second row of the inner transition metals. The *lanthanide series* includes lanthanum, cerium, and praseodymium. The *actinide series* includes actinium, uranium, and plutonium.

PHYSICAL PROPERTIES OF THE ELEMENTS IN RELATION TO THE PERIODIC TABLE

The **boiling point**, **melting point**, and **conductivity** of the elements depend partially on the number of valence electrons of the atoms of those elements. For the representative elements in groups 1A–8A, the number of valence electrons matches the group number. Because all of the elements in each individual group contain the same number of valence electrons, elements in the same groups tend to have similar boiling points, melting points, and conductivity. Boiling points and melting points tend to decrease moving down the column of groups 1A–4A and 8A but increase slightly moving down the column of groups 5A–7A.

CHEMICAL REACTIVITY IN RELATION TO THE PERIODIC TABLE

Atoms of elements in the same **group** or **family** of the periodic table tend to have **similar chemical properties** and **similar chemical reactions**. For example, the alkali metals, which form cations with a charge of +1, tend to react with water to form hydrogen gas and metal hydroxides. The alkaline earth metals, which form cations with a charge of +2, react with oxygen gas to form metal oxides. The halogens, which form anions with a charge of –1, are highly reactive and toxic. The noble gases are unreactive and never form compounds naturally.

ALKALI METALS

The alkali metals occupy the leftmost column of the periodic table, Group I. They include lithium, sodium, potassium, and so on; hydrogen, however, despite being usually positioned atop the leftmost column, is not conventionally included among the alkali metals.

The alkali metals all have a metallic luster and are soft enough to be easily cut with a knife. One of their most famous properties is their extremely high reactivity. The alkali metals even react with ordinary water, often bursting into flame on contact. Samples of alkali metals must be stored in oil to prevent their oxidation and their reaction with water vapor in the air. All alkali metals have a single valence electron and therefore tend to form singly charged positive ions.

ALKALINE EARTH METALS

The alkaline earth metals occupy the second column from the left on the periodic table. They include barium, magnesium, calcium, and so on.

The alkaline earth metals have a metallic luster and are relatively soft. They tend to react easily, although to a lesser degree than the alkali metals. Still, they are reactive enough that they are never found in nature as pure elements but only in chemical compounds. Their melting points and boiling points are higher than those of the alkali metals but lower than those of most other metals. All the alkaline earth metals have two valence electrons and therefore tend to form doubly charged positive ions.

HALOGENS

The halogens occupy the second column from the right on the periodic table. They include fluorine, chlorine, bromine, and so on. By convention, all the halogens are given names ending in -ine, and no other elements are, so you can tell from the name whether or not a particular element is a halogen.

The halogens are highly reactive elements, all of which can react with hydrogen to form acids. In their pure elemental state, halogens form diatomic molecules, although because of their reactivity, halogens are never found in their pure elemental state in nature. All of the halogens have seven valence electrons and therefore form singly charged negative ions.

NOBLE GASES

The noble gases occupy the rightmost column in the periodic table. Newly discovered noble gases are given names ending in -on, but this convention is relatively recent, so there are exceptions among some of the elements discovered earlier: helium is a noble gas but does not have a name ending in -on, whereas boron, carbon, and silicon have names ending in -on but are not noble gases.

The noble gases were formerly also called inert gases; both names come from the nonreactivity of these elements. Although it isn't true that they're completely inert—the noble gases can react with other elements and form compounds—their reactivity is extremely low, and they are almost always found in nature in their pure elemental form. As the name also implies, all known noble gases are in the gaseous state at room temperature, although their melting points increase with their atomic numbers.

TRANSITION METALS

By convention, the transition metals are usually considered to be the elements in groups III through XII of the periodic table, starting with the column topped by scandium (Sc) on the left and usually ending with the column topped by zinc (Zn) on the right. Sometimes the lanthanides and actinides, usually shown in separate rows below the rest of the table, are also included and called inner transition metals. The elements that are not transition metals are called main-group elements or representative elements.

As the name implies, the transition metals are all metals and have the properties shared by most metals: ductility, high electrical and thermal conductivity, and metallic luster. However, they differ from main-group metals in their high electronegativity, which allows them to form covalent compounds and to exist in several different **oxidation states**. For instance, beryllium, a main-group metal, always forms Be^{2+} ions. On the other hand, iron, a transition metal, can exist in a compound as Fe^{2+}, Fe^{3+}, or in any state from Fe^{2-} to Fe^{7+}.

METALS AND NONMETALS

Most of the elements in the periodic table are considered metals; the nonmetals occupy the upper right corner of the periodic table (plus hydrogen). Metals are characterized in their solid state by malleability and ductility—the former property referring to the fact that they can be reshaped by pressure or hammering, the latter by the fact that they can be stretched into thin wires. Nonmetals, on the other hand, tend to be brittle, cracking under stress or strain rather than reshaping. Metals are also good conductors of both heat and electricity, resulting from the fact that their outer electrons are relatively free to move between atoms. Nonmetals, in general, do not conduct heat or electricity well. Another characteristic of metals is their metallic luster—metals look shiny, whereas nonmetals tend to have a matte and dull appearance. Generally, metals have a higher density and higher melting and boiling points than nonmetals, although this is less reliable; there are metals with relatively low densities (such as lithium) and melting points (such as mercury) and nonmetals with high densities and melting points (such as carbon).

OXYGEN GROUP

The oxygen group is the third column from the right in the periodic table. The elements in the oxygen group are also sometimes called chalcogens. The uppermost element in the group is oxygen, hence the name; the group also includes sulfur, selenium, tellurium, and polonium.

All the elements in the oxygen group have six valence electrons, and the lighter elements in this group usually form doubly negative ions, such as O^{2-} and S^{2-}. Other oxidation states are possible, however, especially for the heavier elements in the group that have smaller electronegativities—polonium more often attains Po^{2+} or Po^{4+} states.

METALLOIDS

The metalloids are elements that lie between the metals and the nonmetals in the periodic table and have properties intermediate between the two. From lowest to highest atomic number, the metalloids include boron (B), silicon (Si), germanium (Ge), arsenic (As), antimony (Sb), tellurium (Te), polonium (Po), and astatine (At), although the last two are not always included. All the elements above and to the right of the metalloids are nonmetals; all the elements below and to the left of the metalloids are metals, with the exception of hydrogen.

Metalloids are solid at room temperature, and have a metallic luster, but are brittle and for the most part behave chemically like nonmetals. Perhaps their most useful property, however, is the ability of some metalloids to act as semiconductors—they can behave either as conductors or as insulators depending on certain conditions. This makes them very useful for various electronic applications and is the reason that computer chips, for example, contain silicon, a semiconductor metalloid.

VALENCE ELECTRONS

Valence electrons are the electrons in the outermost shell of an atom. For a main-group element, it is under normal circumstances solely the valence electrons that are involved in chemical reactions; therefore, it is the number of valence electrons in an atom that primarily determines its chemical properties. This is why elements in the same group have similar chemical properties: elements in the same group have the same number of valence electrons. All the alkali metals have one valence electron, all the halogens have seven, and so on. As a general rule of thumb, atoms will tend to gain or lose electrons in such a way as to be left with a full outer shell of eight valence electrons; this principle is known as the octet rule.

In transition metals, some of the electrons in inner shells can also participate in chemical reactions. The concept of valence electrons is therefore less well defined for transition metals than it is for main-group elements.

FIRST AND SECOND IONIZATION ENERGY

The ionization energy of an element is the amount of energy needed to ionize an atom of that element—that is, to remove an electron from the atom. More specifically, the energy required to remove one electron from a neutral atom is the first ionization energy, the energy required to remove another electron from an atom that has already lost an electron (a singly charged positive ion) is the second ionization energy, and so on; the nth ionization energy is the energy required to remove one electron from an atom that has already lost $n - 1$ electrons.

In general, the closer the outermost electron is to the nucleus, the harder it is to remove, and therefore the greater the ionization energy. This means that the ionization energy increases as the atomic radius decreases. Therefore, the ionization energy within a group tends to decrease as the atomic number increases because the heavier elements in a group have a larger atomic radius. However, across a period the atomic radius decreases from left to right, and therefore the ionization energy increases. So, the atomic energy of elements in the periodic table tends to increase from left to right and from down to up.

ELECTRON AFFINITY

Electron affinity is a measurement of the change in energy when an atom or molecule in the gaseous state gains an electron. Equivalently, the electron affinity can be defined as the amount of energy required to remove an electron from a singly charged negative ion. The larger the electron affinity, the more stable the negative ion.

Electron affinity tends to increase from left to right on the periodic table, although there is no clear trend within groups: electron affinity decreases from top to bottom within the alkali metals, for instance, but mostly increases from top to bottom within the alkaline earths. A few elements do not form negative ions at all or require energy to be added to give them an electron; the electron affinity of these elements is considered to be negative or zero. These elements include the noble gases as well as beryllium, nitrogen, magnesium, manganese, zinc, cadmium, and mercury.

ELECTRONEGATIVITY

Electronegativity is the tendency of an atom to attract electrons. Electronegativity is a unit-less quantity that is only meaningful in terms of the difference in electronegativity between two atoms. It is therefore necessary to decide on a reference point; by convention, the electronegativity of hydrogen is defined as 2.20, and the electronegativities of other atoms are derived based on this. Generally, when two atoms or molecules of different electronegativity interact, the atom that has a smaller electronegativity will tend to "donate" an electron to the atom with a larger electronegativity—or, in the case of a covalent bond, the shared electron will tend to be more closely associated with the latter atom.

Generally, among elements in the periodic table, electronegativity increases from left to right and decreases from top to bottom. (The noble gases are a special case, and because of their nonreactivity are often considered not to have electronegativity.) There are exceptions to these trends among the transition metals and in the boron and carbon groups; lead, for example, has a higher electronegativity than tin despite being positioned below it on the periodic table.

> **Review Video: Electronegativity**
> Visit mometrix.com/academy and enter code: 823348

ELECTRON SHELLS AND THE SIZES OF ATOMS

The sizes of atoms of elements in the periodic table tend to increase from top to bottom within a column, and to decrease from left to right within a row. The former trend is easy to understand; as one goes down a row in the periodic table, the atoms have added electron shells that must lie outside the inner shells possessed by the higher atoms and must therefore increase the atomic radius.

The latter trend, however, may be more counterintuitive; as one goes from left to right along a row in the periodic table, the atoms gain more protons and electrons, and one might therefore expect them to become larger, not smaller. The key to understanding the trend is that it is not the size of the nucleus that determines the size of the atom but the size of the electron clouds; as the number of protons increases without adding a new electron shell, the effective nuclear charge on the electrons in the outermost shell increases, pulling these outermost electrons closer to the nucleus.

ELECTRON SHELLS AND THE SIZES OF IONS

In general, negative ions are larger than the neutral atom, whereas positive ions are smaller. Furthermore, the greater the charge of the ion, the greater the difference in size from the neutral atom; for instance, a Ti^{4+} ion is smaller than a Ti^{3+} ion, which is smaller than a Ti^{2+} ion.

The reason for this difference has to do with the effective nuclear charge on the outermost electrons. As an atom gains electrons to become a negative ion, the effective nuclear charge on the outermost electrons decreases because the extra electron partially cancels it; this results in less force holding the electrons to the nucleus, so the electrons' distance from the nucleus is greater. As an atom loses electrons to become a positive ion, the opposite occurs; the effective nuclear charge increases, and the outermost electrons are bound more tightly to the nucleus.

An electron shell is a collection of electrons with the same energy level—the same value of the principal quantum number, n. Very roughly, an electron shell can be thought of as a layer of electrons surrounding an atom. A shell in turn consists of subshells of electrons with the same angular quantum number l. Each shell can hold only a certain maximum number of electrons; the greater the energy of the shell, the more subshells it has, and the more electrons it can hold. The

31

first shell holds up to 2 electrons, the second $2 + 6 = 8$, the third $2 + 6 + 10 = 18$, and so on. It is largely the electron shells that determine the arrangement of the atoms in the periodic table—each row of the periodic table has one more shell than the one above it.

Because each electron shell lies farther from the nucleus than the previous, the more electron shells an atom or ion possesses, the higher its radius. This is the reason that the atomic and ionic radii increase within a group as the atomic number increases.

Example Problems

Calculate energy related to electronic transitions using Bohr's H atom model for electronic transitions from $n = 6$ to $n = 2$ and from $n = 3$ to $n = 2$.

To start, note that in the Bohr model of a hydrogen atom, the absolute value of ΔE is used, as the wavelength cannot be negative. Now, plug in $n_f = 2$ and $n_i = 6$, and we get:

$$\Delta E = (-2.18 \times 10^{-18} \text{ J}) \left(\frac{1}{n_f{}^2} - \frac{1}{n_i{}^2} \right) = (-2.18 \times 10^{-18} \text{J}) \left(\frac{1}{2^2} - \frac{1}{6^2} \right) = -4.84 \times 10^{-19} \text{ J}$$

To find the wavelength, we use the following:

$$\Delta E = hf = \frac{hc}{\lambda}$$

$$\lambda = \frac{hc}{\Delta E}$$

$$\lambda = \frac{(6.62 \times 10^{-34} \text{ J} \cdot \text{s})(3.00 \times 10^8 \text{ m/s})}{4.84 \times 10^{-19} \text{ J}} \times \frac{1.00 \times 10^9 \text{ nm}}{1.00 \text{ m}} = 410 \text{ nm}$$

This emission is in the violet range of the visible spectrum. Applying the same calculations to the transition from $n_f = 2$ and $n_i = 3$:

$$\Delta E = (-2.18 \times 10^{-18} \text{ J}) \left(\frac{1}{2^2} - \frac{1}{3^2} \right) = -3.02 \times 10^{-19} \text{ J}$$

$$\lambda = \frac{(6.62 \times 10^{-34} \text{ J} \cdot \text{s})(3.00 \times 10^8 \text{ m/s})}{3.02 \times 10^{-19} \text{ J}} \times \frac{1.00 \times 10^9 \text{ nm}}{1.00 \text{ m}} = 656 \text{ nm}$$

This emission is in the red range of the visible spectrum.

Properties of Matter

Chemical and Physical Properties and Changes

CHEMICAL AND PHYSICAL PROPERTIES

Matter has both physical and chemical properties. **Physical properties** can be seen or observed without changing the identity or composition of matter. For example, the mass, volume, and density of a substance can be determined without permanently changing the sample. Other physical properties include color, boiling point, freezing point, solubility, odor, hardness, electrical conductivity, thermal conductivity, ductility, and malleability.

Chemical properties cannot be measured without changing the identity or composition of matter. Chemical properties describe how a substance reacts or changes to form a new substance. Examples of chemical properties include flammability, corrosivity, oxidation states, enthalpy of formation, and reactivity with other chemicals.

INTENSIVE AND EXTENSIVE PROPERTIES

Physical properties are categorized as either intensive or extensive. **Intensive properties** *do not* depend on the amount of matter or quantity of the sample. This means that intensive properties will not change if the sample size is increased or decreased. Intensive properties include color, hardness, melting point, boiling point, density, ductility, malleability, specific heat, temperature, concentration, and magnetization.

Extensive properties *do* depend on the amount of matter or quantity of the sample. Therefore, extensive properties do change if the sample size is increased or decreased. If the sample size is increased, the property increases. If the sample size is decreased, the property decreases. Extensive properties include volume, mass, weight, energy, entropy, number of moles, and electrical charge.

ATOMIC PROPERTIES OF NEUTRAL ATOMS, ANIONS, AND CATIONS

Neutral atoms have equal numbers of protons and electrons. **Cations** are positively-charged ions that are formed when atoms lose electrons in order to have a full outer shell of valence electrons. For example, the alkali metals sodium and potassium form the cations Na^+ and K^+, and the alkaline earth metals magnesium and calcium form the cations Mg^{2+} and Ca^{2+}.

Anions are negatively-charged ions that are formed when atoms gain electrons to fill their outer shell of valence electrons. For example, the halogens fluorine and chlorine form the anions F^- and Cl^-.

CHEMICAL AND PHYSICAL CHANGES

Physical changes do not produce new substances. The atoms or molecules may be rearranged, but no new substances are formed. **Phase changes** or changes of state such as melting, freezing, and sublimation are physical changes. For example, physical changes include the melting of ice, the boiling of water, sugar dissolving into water, and the crushing of a piece of chalk into a fine powder.

Chemical changes involve a **chemical reaction** and do produce new substances. When iron rusts, iron oxide is formed, indicating a chemical change. Other examples of chemical changes include baking a cake, burning wood, digesting food, and mixing an acid and a base.

Phase Transitions

STATES OF MATTER

The four states of matter are solid, liquid, gas, and plasma. **Solids** have a definite shape and a definite volume. Because solid particles are held in fairly rigid positions, solids are the least compressible of the four states of matter. **Liquids** have definite volumes but no definite shapes. Because their particles are free to slip and slide over each other, liquids take the shape of their containers, but they still remain fairly incompressible by natural means. **Gases** have no definite shape or volume. Because gas particles are free to move, they move away from each other to fill their containers. Gases are compressible. **Plasmas** are high-temperature, ionized gases that exist only under very high temperatures at which electrons are stripped away from their atoms.

> **Review Video: States of Matter**
> Visit mometrix.com/academy and enter code: 742449
>
> **Review Video: Properties of Liquids**
> Visit mometrix.com/academy and enter code: 802024
>
> **Review Video: States of Matter [Advanced]**
> Visit mometrix.com/academy and enter code: 298130

The following table shows similarities and differences between solids, liquids, and gases:

	Solid	Liquid	Gas
Shape	Fixed shape	No fixed shape (assumes shape of container)	No fixed shape (assumes shape of container)
Volume	Fixed	Fixed	Changes to assume shape of container
Fluidity	Does not flow easily	Flows easily	Flows easily
Compressibility	Hard to compress	Hard to compress	Compresses

SIX DIFFERENT TYPES OF PHASE CHANGE

A substance that is undergoing a change from a solid to a liquid is said to be melting. If this change occurs in the opposite direction, from liquid to solid, this change is called freezing. A liquid which is being converted to a gas is undergoing vaporization. The reverse of this process is known as condensation. Direct transitions from gas to solid and solid to gas are much less common in everyday life, but they can occur given the proper conditions. Solid to gas conversion is known as sublimation, while the reverse is called deposition.

> **Review Video: Chemical and Physical Properties of Matter**
> Visit mometrix.com/academy and enter code: 717349

PHASE DIAGRAM

A phase diagram is a diagram that shows the phase (solid, liquid, or gas) that a particular compound or element is in at different pressures and temperatures. It is conventionally drawn with pressure on the y-axis and temperature on the x-axis; lines on the diagram mark the boundaries of the regions in the diagram where the compound is in each phase. At points on these lines, the two phases are in equilibrium; the points on these lines at particular pressures mark the compound's freezing or boiling points at those pressures. The point where all three phases are in equilibrium is the triple point, the unique pressure and temperature where all three phases of the compound are in equilibrium.

For example, below is a phase diagram of water, with the triple point marked as well as the boiling and freezing points at atmospheric pressure:

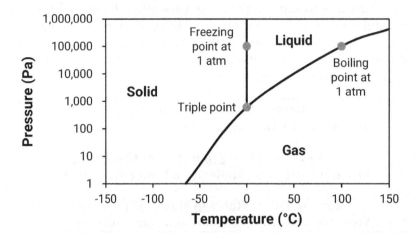

Note that in this diagram the pressure is given a logarithmic scale; this is common in phase diagrams to depict a wide range of pressures, but it is not required; phase diagrams can also be drawn with linear pressure scales.

CALCULATING PHASE TRANSITIONS
HEATING CURVE OF WATER FROM −40 °C TO 140 °C

In the first portion of the curve, the graph slants up and to the right as the ice is a solid that is increasing in temperature from −40 °C to 0 °C. In the second portion of the curve, the graph remains horizontal during the phase change from solid to liquid as the temperature remains constant at 0 °C. In the third portion of the curve, the graph slants up and to the right as the water now is in the liquid state and is increasing in temperature from 0 °C to 100 °C. In the fourth portion of the curve, the graph remains horizontal during the phase change from liquid to gas as the temperature remains at 100 °C. In the last portion of the curve, the graph slants up and to the right as water now is the gaseous state and the steam is increasing in temperature from 100 °C to 140 °C.

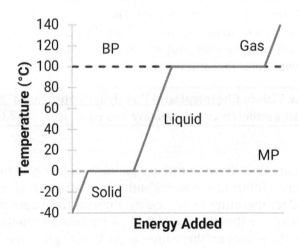

CALCULATING THE AMOUNT OF HEAT CORRESPONDING TO EACH PORTION OF A HEATING CURVE

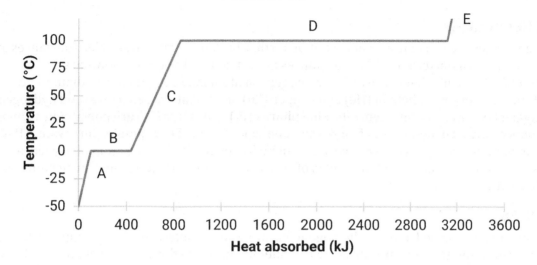

- For portion A, $Q = mc_{ice}\Delta T$, where Q is the amount of heat gained in joules, m is the mass of the ice in grams, c is the specific heat of ice, and ΔT is the change in temperature in degrees Celsius.
- For portion B, $Q = m\Delta H_{fus}$, where Q is the amount of heat gained in joules, m is the mass of the ice/water in grams, and ΔH_{fus} is the heat of fusion for water in joules per gram, $\frac{J}{g}$.
- For portion C, $Q = mc_{water}\Delta T$, where Q is the amount of heat gained in joules, m is the mass of the water in grams, c is the specific heat of water, and ΔT is the change in temperature in degrees Celsius.
- For portion D, $Q = m\Delta H_{vap}$, where Q is the amount of heat gained in joules, m is the mass of the water/steam in grams, and ΔH_{vap} is the heat of vaporization for water in joules per gram, $\frac{J}{g}$.
- For portion E, $Q = mc_{steam}\Delta T$, where Q is the amount of heat gained in joules, m is the mass of the steam in grams, c is the specific heat of steam, and ΔT is the change temperature in degrees Celsius.

Substances

PURE SUBSTANCES

Pure substances are substances that cannot be further broken down into simpler substances and still retain their characteristics. Pure substances are categorized as either **elements** or **compounds**. Elements that consist of only one type of atom may be monatomic, diatomic, or polyatomic. For example, helium (He) and copper (Cu) are monatomic elements, and hydrogen (H_2) and oxygen (O_2) are diatomic elements. Phosphorus (P_4) and sulfur (S_8) are polyatomic elements. Compounds consist of molecules of more than one type of atom. For example, pure water (H_2O) is made up of molecules consisting of two atoms of hydrogen bonded to one atom of oxygen, and glucose ($C_6H_{12}O_6$) is made up of molecules of six carbon atoms and twelve hydrogen atoms bonded together with six oxygen atoms.

MIXTURES

Mixtures can be classified as either homogeneous mixtures or heterogeneous mixtures. The molecules of **homogeneous mixtures** are distributed uniformly throughout the mixture, but the molecules of **heterogeneous mixtures** are not distributed uniformly throughout the mixture. Air is an example of a homogeneous mixture, and a pile of sand and rock is an example of a heterogeneous mixture. Solutions are homogeneous mixtures consisting of a **solute** (the substance that is dissolved) and a **solvent** (the substance doing the dissolving).

SUSPENSIONS

Suspensions are heterogeneous mixtures in which the particle size of the substance **suspended** is too large to be kept in suspension by Brownian motion. Once left undisturbed, suspensions will settle out to form layers. An example of a suspension is sand stirred into water. Left undisturbed, the sand will fall out of suspension and the water will form a layer on top of the sand.

MIXTURES WITH COMPOUNDS

Mixtures are similar to compounds in that they are produced when two or more substances are combined. However, there are some key differences as well. Compounds require a chemical combination of the constituent particles, while mixtures are simply the interspersion of particles. Unlike compounds, mixtures may be **separated** without a chemical change. A mixture retains the chemical properties of its constituent particles, while a compound acquires a new set of properties. Given compounds can exist only in specific ratios, while mixtures may be any ratio of the involved substances.

DENSITY

Density is the amount of mass in a substance or object per unit volume. It is usually abbreviated in science by the lowercase Greek letter rho, ρ. It is important to note that although this letter looks somewhat like a lowercase P, it is a different symbol, with a different meaning, and the two should not be confused, especially because there are some significant formulae (such as Bernoulli's equation) in which both symbols appear.

The units for density are the units of mass divided by the units of volume, so in SI units they are kg/m^3. Unlike mass and volume themselves, density is an intrinsic property, independent of the quantity of matter present. If you break a rock in two, the pieces have a smaller mass and volume than the original rock but the same density. Of course, for a gas, the density does depend on other properties, such as temperature and pressure; this is also true for liquids and solids but to a much smaller degree.

ABSOLUTE TEMPERATURE, (K) KELVIN SCALE

The size of 1 Kelvin is the same as the size of 1 degree Celsius; the only difference between the two scales is where the zero is: 0 °C corresponds to 273.15 K, so to convert from degrees Celsius to Kelvin, it is only necessary to add 273.15. Conversely, Kelvin can be converted to degrees Celsius by subtracting 273.15. For example, the typical room temperature of 25 °C corresponds to 298.15 K.

What makes the Kelvin scale particularly useful in science is the fact that 0 K corresponds to the absolute zero of temperature. Multiplying or dividing temperatures is only meaningful in such a scale; it doesn't make sense, for instance, to double a temperature expressed in degrees Celsius because doubling a negative temperature would result in a lower temperature (among other reasons). The Kelvin scale has no negative temperatures, and such an operation is entirely reasonable. In any calculation that involves multiplying or dividing by temperatures (such as some applications of the ideal gas law), the temperature must be expressed in Kelvins, not degrees Celsius. If only differences of temperature are involved, however, then the two scales are interchangeable.

Molarity

AVOGADRO'S NUMBER, MOLAR MASS, AND THE MOLE

Avogadro's number is equivalent to the number of atoms in 12 g of the carbon-12 isotope or the number of atoms in 1 mole of carbon-12. Avogadro's number is numerically equal to approximately 6.022×10^{23}. Just like a dozen eggs represents 12 eggs and a pair of shoes represents 2 shoes, Avogadro's number of atoms represents 6.022×10^{23} atoms. **Molar mass** is the mass of one mole of a substance in grams. The *mole* is Avogadro's number of anything. For example, 1 mole of carbon atoms is 6.022×10^{23} carbon atoms, and 1 mole of CCl_4 contains 6.022×10^{23} molecules of CCl_4.

> **Review Video: What is the Mole Concept?**
> Visit mometrix.com/academy and enter code: 593205

MOLAR VOLUME

Molar volume is the volume occupied by one mole of a substance: by definition, the number of molecules or atoms in one mole of a substance is Avogadro's number, about 6.022×10^{23}. Although the molar volume cannot be measured directly (you can't count 6.022×10^{23} atoms), it can be calculated from the molar mass and the mass density: $V_m = M/\rho$, where V_m is the molar volume, M is the molar mass, and ρ is the mass density. Because the mass density varies with temperature and pressure, so does the molar volume; it is therefore not correct to say that a particular substance has a specific molar volume but rather that it has a specific molar volume at some particular temperature and pressure.

For instance, nitrogen gas has a molar mass of 28.0135 g/mol and a mass density at 25 °C of 1.145 kg/m^3, or 0.001145 g/cm^3. This means that at 25 °C, nitrogen gas has a molar volume of $\frac{28.0135 \text{ g/mol}}{0.001145 \text{ g/cm}^3} = 24{,}470$ cm^3/mol, equivalent to 0.02447 m^3/mol or 24.47 L/mol.

CALCULATING AN EMPIRICAL FORMULA AND A MOLECULAR FORMULA OF A COMPOUND

To find the **empirical formula of a compound**, first, calculate the masses of each element in the compound based on the percent composition that is given. Then, convert these masses to moles by dividing by the molar masses of those elements. Next, divide these amounts in moles by the smallest calculated value in moles and round to the nearest tenth. These calculations provide the subscripts for each element in the empirical formula. To find the molecular formula, divide the actual molar mass of the compound by the molar mass of the empirical formula.

CALCULATING PERCENT COMPOSITION WHEN GIVEN THE MOLECULAR FORMULA

To find the **percent composition** when given the molecular formula, first find the molar mass of the compound. Next, find the percent contributed by each element of the compound by dividing the molar mass of the element (remembering to multiply through by the subscripts of the molecular formula) by the molar mass of the compound. Finally, check the calculations by totaling these individual percents of the elements to ensure their combined total is 100%. This may be slightly off if any of the numbers used were rounded.

Fluids and Liquids

SPECIFIC GRAVITY

The specific gravity of a fluid is the ratio of its density to the density of some reference substance—most commonly water for liquids or air for gases. More specifically, it is water at the temperature at which it is densest (about 4 °C) or air at room temperature (25 °C). Because specific gravity is a ratio between two quantities with the same units, the specific gravity itself is unit-less. For instance, the density of mercury is about 13,500 kg/m³, whereas the density of water is 1,000 kg/m³. This means mercury is 13.5 times as dense as water, so the specific gravity of mercury is 13.5.

UNITS OF PRESSURE

The units of pressure are pascals, abbreviated Pa, named after Blaise Pascal, a French mathematician and physicist also known for his contributions to the fields of probability theory and fluid flow. Because pressure is defined as force over area, the units of pressure must be equal to the units of force divided by the units of area: newtons divided by meters squared. So, $1 \text{ Pa} = 1 \text{ N/m}^2$. Because a newton is equal to a $\text{kg} \cdot \text{m/s}^2$, this can also be expressed in terms of fundamental units as $1 \text{ Pa} = 1 \text{ kg}/(\text{m} \cdot \text{s}^2)$. Some other common units of pressure include the following:

- **Atmospheres** (atm): one atmosphere is the (approximate) mean atmospheric pressure at sea level on Earth. It is defined as exactly 101,325 Pa.
- **Pounds per square inch** (psi): this is the standard unit of pressure in traditional avoirdupois (English) units, and although rarely used in science, is still often seen elsewhere: pressure in car tires, for instance, is usually measured in psi. Some equivalencies are that 1 psi is about 6890 Pa and 1 atm is about 14.70 psi.
- **Millimeters of mercury** (mmHg): this is a pressure scale based on the height of a column of mercury in a standard mercury barometer. Some equivalencies are that 1 mmHg is about 133.3 Pa and 1 atm is about 760 mmHg.

BUOYANCY

Any time that an object is immersed in a fluid, there is a buoyant force exerted on it that acts upward, against gravity. If the buoyant force is greater than the object's weight, the object floats; if less, the object sinks. If the buoyant force is equal to the object's weight, the object will neither float nor sink but remain at the same height within the fluid; this is called neutral buoyancy.

The buoyant force results from the difference in pressure on the top and bottom of the object. Because the hydrostatic pressure increases with depth, the pressure on the bottom of the object is slightly more than the pressure on the top of the object. This in turn means that the force on the bottom of the object will be slightly greater than the force on the top of the object, which results in an upward net force.

An object can float in a less dense liquid provided that the object displaces a weight of water greater than its own weight—which requires it to displace a greater volume of water than its own volume. This is possible if the object has a cavity or depression in it that increases its fluid displacement; metal boats can float because they are hollow, whereas a solid block of metal would sink.

For instance, consider a hemispherical shell of lead, 1.000 meter in diameter and 1 millimeter thick. Lead is much denser than water: 22,600 kg/m³ as opposed to 1,000 kg/m³ for water. The volume of the lead shell would be $\frac{1}{2}4\pi[(0.500 \text{ m})^3 - (0.499 \text{ m})^3)] = 0.0047 \text{ m}^3$; its weight would be $(0.0047 \text{ m}^3)(22,600 \text{ kg/m}^3)(9.80 \text{ m/s}^2) = 1,040 \text{ N}$. However, if it is placed in the water up to its rim, open side up, the volume of water it displaces is $\frac{1}{2}(4\pi(0.500\text{ m})^3) = 0.196\text{ m}^3$; the weight of water (and thus the buoyant force) is $(0.0196\text{ m}^3)(1{,}000\text{ kg/m}^3)(9.80\text{ m/s}^2) = 1{,}920\text{ N}$. The buoyant force is greater than the weight of the lead shell, so the shell would float!

HYDROSTATIC PRESSURE

The hydrostatic pressure within a fluid is the pressure exerted by a fluid at equilibrium. The hydrostatic pressure arises because of gravity; as gravity exerts a downward force on each part of the fluid, the fluid will therefore also exert a downward force on the fluid below it. This implies that the hydrostatic pressure increases with the depth in the fluid as there's more fluid above to press down.

To derive a formula for the hydrostatic pressure, consider a small cube of fluid a distance h below the surface, with an area of A on each face. Directly above the cube is a column of fluid with a height h and an area A, which means its volume is Ah. The mass of the column of fluid pressing down on the cube is the density times the volume, ρAh, and its weight—the force of gravity acting on the column—is its mass times gravity, ρAhg. The pressure on the small cube of fluid is the force exerted on its top surface divided by the area of that surface, $\frac{\rho Ahg}{A} = \rho gh$. So, the hydrostatic pressure at a depth h within a fluid is equal to ρgh.

PASCAL'S LAW

Pascal's Law states that a change in pressure exerted anywhere in an incompressible fluid in a closed container is propagated throughout the fluid. In other words, if the pressure of a fluid is increased at one point in the fluid, it increases everywhere in the fluid.

One of the best-known applications of Pascal's Law is hydraulics. Hydraulic brakes in a car, for instance, work because pushing down on the brake pedal exerts a pressure on the brake fluid below, and then that pressure is transmitted through the fluid to the brakes themselves, causing the brake pads to press against the rotor. A hydraulic lift works by a piston exerting a downward pressure on a fluid, and the pressure is then transmitted through the fluid to exert upward pressure elsewhere.

SURFACE TENSION

Surface tension is the tendency of the surface of a liquid to "stick together," as if the liquid were enclosed in a thin film or membrane. It is a consequence of the attractive forces between molecules of the liquid: because the molecules of the liquid are more strongly attracted to each other than they are to the molecules of the air or other surrounding gas, the molecules at the surface of the liquid are subject to a net inward force. Because of the relatively strong hydrogen bonds between water molecules, water has a higher surface tension than most liquids.

It is because of surface tension that small quantities of water and other liquids tend to form into rounded droplets rather than spreading evenly over a surface. Surface tension also can be sufficient to support small objects that are too dense to float because of the buoyant force—it is possible, with care, to place a paper clip such that it floats on a glass of water. Some small animals, such as water striders, are able to walk on the surface of water due to surface tension.

MERCURY BAROMETER

A mercury barometer in its simplest form consists of a tube closed at one end and filled with mercury inverted in an open container of mercury. The pressure of the surrounding air will press on the mercury in the open container; due to Pascal's Law, this pressure is propagated throughout the mercury. At equilibrium, the hydrostatic pressure due to the mercury column will precisely equal the atmospheric pressure of the surroundings, so the atmospheric pressure can be calculated from the height h of the column of mercury: $P_{atm} = \rho_{Hg}gh$.

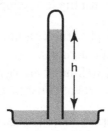

In principle, this would work the same with any incompressible liquid, not just mercury. In practice, mercury is chosen because of its high density. The higher the density of the fluid, the lower the height of the column, so for fluids of low density, the height becomes impractical. At normal atmospheric pressure, the column of mercury in a mercury barometer is about 76 centimeters high. A similar instrument using water would require a column more than 10 meters high!

VAPOR PRESSURE

Consider a substance in liquid phase that is captured in a container. The molecules at its surface may escape into the space above it and convert into the gas phase. This process is called **evaporation**, and the pressure that is attained by the gaseous vapor above the liquid is called the **vapor pressure**. Meanwhile, some escaped molecules near the surface can also be recaptured by the liquid. This process is called **condensing**. At some point, these two processes will reach a steady rate—the number of evaporating molecules is equal to the number of condensing ones. This state is called a **dynamic equilibrium**. In this state, there is a vapor pressure. A higher vapor pressure indicates that the liquid evaporates faster than those with lower vapor pressures. Those substances that readily evaporate are **volatile**. Temperature also affects the vapor pressure of a liquid—the vapor pressure increases as the temperature increases. The Clausius-Clapeyron equation describes the relationship between temperature and vapor pressure:

$$\ln P = \left(\frac{-\Delta H_{vap}}{R}\right)\left(\frac{1}{T}\right) + C$$

In this equation, P is the vapor pressure, ΔH_{vap} is the molar enthalpy of vaporization, R is the gas constant, T is the absolute temperature, and C is a constant. A plot of $\ln P$ against $\frac{1}{T}$ should demonstrate a linear relationship.

When the external pressure that is applied to the liquid surface becomes equal to its vapor pressure, the liquid boils. As the external pressure increases, the boiling point also increases. Boiling points recorded at 1 atm are defined as the **normal boiling points**.

Gases

IDEAL GAS

An ideal gas is a gas made up of particles with the following characteristics:

- Their volume is negligible compared to the volume of the container.
- They do not interact except during collisions.
- All collisions are perfectly elastic (no kinetic energy is lost).
- Between collisions, the particles travel at constant speed in straight lines.

Although an ideal gas is an abstract concept, and no real gases have exactly these characteristics, the ideal gas concept is useful because it allows certain calculations and predictions to be made about the gas's properties and behavior—and these predictions turn out to hold to a high level of precision for many real gases, even if they aren't exactly ideal. Essentially, a real gas behaves as an ideal gas to a very good approximation as long as its pressure isn't too high and its temperature isn't too low.

AVOGADRO'S LAW

Avogadro's Law states that at constant temperature and pressure, the volume of gas is proportional to the number of molecules or moles. That is, all else being equal, $V \propto n$, or $\frac{V_1}{n_1} = \frac{V_2}{n_2}$.

Avogadro's Law can be used to solve for an unknown volume or number of molecules or moles when the other is known and when both quantities are known at a different time. For instance, consider two chambers filled with gas at equal pressure and temperature. One chamber has a volume of 500 m^3, the other 200 m^3. If we are given that the larger chamber contains 20,000 mol of gas, we can use Avogadro's Law to determine the number of moles of gas in the smaller chamber.

$$\frac{500 \text{ m}^3}{20000 \text{ mol}} = \frac{200 \text{ m}^3}{n_2}$$
$$n_2 = 8{,}000 \text{ mol}$$

BOYLE'S LAW

Boyle's Law states that for a gas at constant temperature, the pressure of the gas is inversely proportional to the volume: all else being equal, $P \propto \frac{1}{V}$, or $P_1 V_1 = P_2 V_2$. It is named after the Irish chemist and physicist Robert William Boyle, who was among the first to define the modern study of chemistry.

Boyle's Law can be used to solve for an unknown pressure or volume, when the other is known and when both quantities are known at a different time. For instance, consider an air bubble deep under the ocean at a pressure of 20 atm. As it rises to the surface, the bubble will expand due to the decreased pressure. If the bubble initially has a volume of 1.0 cm^3, we can find its equivalent volume at the surface using Boyle's Law.

$$(20 \text{ atm})(1.0 \text{ cm}^3) = (1.0 \text{ atm})V_2$$
$$20 \text{ cm}^3 = V_2$$

> **Review Video: Boyle's Law**
> Visit mometrix.com/academy and enter code: 115757

44

CHARLES'S LAW

Charles's Law states that for a gas at constant pressure, the volume of the gas is proportional to the temperature: all else being equal, $V \propto T$, or $\frac{V_1}{T_1} = \frac{V_2}{T_2}$. The law is named after French physicist and inventor Jacques Alexandre César Charles, also known for his development of hydrogen balloons.

Charles's Law can be used to solve for an unknown volume or temperature, when the other is known and when both quantities are known at a different time. For instance, consider a balloon that at room temperature (25 °C) has a volume of 12.0 m^3. If the gas inside the balloon is heated, the balloon will expand. If the gas is heated to a temperature of 300 °C, we can find the balloon's new volume using Charles's Law,

$$\frac{12.0 \text{ m}^3}{298 \text{ K}} = \frac{V_2}{573 \text{ K}}$$
$$23.1 \text{ m}^3 = V_2$$

Note that we had to convert the temperatures from degrees Celsius into Kelvins—this is necessary whenever we're multiplying or dividing by temperatures.

IDEAL GAS LAW

The ideal gas law is an equation that relates the pressure, volume, temperature, and number of moles or molecules of an ideal gas. It combines Boyle's Law, Charles's Law, and Avogadro's Law, although each of these laws was originally separately determined on empirical grounds. Like these other laws, and like its name implies, the ideal gas law only holds exactly for a nonexistent ideal gas, but for most real gases it is a very good approximation.

The **ideal gas law** can be stated as $PV = nRT$, where P is the pressure of the gas, V is the volume, n is the number of moles, T is the temperature in Kelvin, and R is the ideal gas constant, equal to about 8.314 J/(mol · K) or 0.08205 (L · atm)/(mol · K), depending on the units used for pressure and volume.

The ideal gas law can be used to solve for the pressure, volume, temperature, or number of moles of gas if the other quantities are known. For instance, consider a room with a volume of 60.0 m^3 filled with air at 25 °C and a pressure of 1.000 atm = 1.013×10^5 Pa. We can use the ideal gas law to determine the number of moles of air in the room:

$$n = \frac{PV}{RT} = \frac{(1.013 \times 10^5 \text{ Pa})(60.0 \text{ m}^3)}{(8.314 \text{ J/(mol} \cdot \text{K))}(298 \text{ K})} = 2450 \text{ mol}$$

By definition, the particles of an ideal gas have negligible volume and do not interact except during collisions. The particles of a real gas, of course, do have some finite volume, and there are long-range forces between them, such as the van der Waals forces arising due to their charge distributions. The difference from ideal behavior is most notable at high pressures and low temperatures. At very high pressures, the effect of the volume of the particles may become important and $PV > nRT$, whereas at very low temperatures the intermolecular forces play a role and $PV < nRT$.

The Dutch physicist Johannes Diderik van der Waals derived a generalization of the ideal gas law that takes these features of a real gas into account: what is now called the **van der Waals equation**, $\left(P + \frac{an^2}{V^2}\right)(V - nb) = nRT$. Although still not exact, this equation gives closer results for real gases for a broad range of circumstances. Unfortunately, however, it relies on two constants, a and b, that are not universal and must be determined separately for each gas.

KINETIC MOLECULAR THEORY OF GASES
HEAT CAPACITY

Heat capacity is a measurement of the amount of heat that must be transferred to an object to raise its temperature by a specific amount (or, equivalently, the amount of heat that is released when its temperature lowers). It can be expressed as $C = \frac{Q}{\Delta T}$, where Q is the heat and ΔT the change in temperature. (Technically, the heat capacity itself varies slightly by temperature, so this equation isn't exactly valid, but it holds well for relatively small changes in temperature.) Because heat capacity depends on the amount of material, however, it is also useful to define the specific heat capacity, or **specific heat**, $c = \frac{C}{m} = \frac{Q}{m\Delta T}$. (Heat capacity is represented by an uppercase C, specific heat by a lower-case c.) The specific heat capacity depends only on the material and not on the quantity present.

Because heat has units of joules and temperature has units of Kelvins or degrees Celsius, the units of heat capacity are J/K or J/°C. For differences in temperature, Kelvins and degrees Celsius are interchangeable, so these two units are equivalent. Because $c = \frac{C}{m}$, the specific heat has units of J/(kg · K) or J/(kg · °C).

For a gas, the heat capacity is not a constant; it depends on what other quantities are changing. The ideal gas equation, $PV = nRT$, shows that temperature cannot change without affecting other properties of the gas; assuming that the amount of gas (the number of molecules) doesn't change, then either the pressure or the volume must change or both. The heat capacity depends on which of these is changing, and so a gas is said to have a heat capacity at constant pressure, C_P, and a heat capacity at constant volume, C_V.

These two heat capacities are not the same—the heat capacity at constant pressure is always higher than the heat capacity at constant volume because some energy is required to do work on the gas as it expands. However, for an ideal gas there is a simple relationship between the two. The derivation is a bit complicated, but it can be shown that for an ideal gas $C_P - C_V = nR$, where n is the number of moles of gas and R is the ideal gas constant.

BOLTZMANN'S CONSTANT

Boltzmann's constant, abbreviated k_B, is a constant that arises in multiple places in thermodynamics. It is named after Austrian physicist Ludwig Eduard Boltzmann, best known for his development of statistical mechanics. Boltzmann's constant is equal to about 1.38×10^{-23} J/K.

One place Boltzmann's constant arises is as the ratio of the ideal gas constant to Avogadro's number: $k_B = \frac{R}{N_A}$. In fact, by using the number of molecules instead of the number of moles, it is possible to rewrite the ideal gas law in terms of Boltzmann's constant instead of the ideal gas constant: $PV = Nk_BT$. This may be useful if you actually know (or want to determine) the number of molecules rather than the number of moles. Boltzmann's constant also turns up in the relationship of kinetic energy to temperature: the average kinetic energy of a molecule in a gas at temperature T is equal to $\frac{3}{2}k_BT$.

DEVIATION OF REAL GAS BEHAVIOR FROM IDEAL GAS LAW

The main property of an ideal gas that is affected by the number of atoms per molecule is the gas's heat capacity. It can be shown that the heat capacity of a gas at constant pressure is equal to $\frac{1}{2}nR$ for each degree of freedom of the gas particles—roughly, each direction in which the gas particles can meaningfully move or rotate. A single atom is spherically symmetrical, so rotations don't matter, but it can move along any of three axes, so it has three degrees of freedom: its heat capacity at constant pressure is therefore $\frac{3}{2}nR$. A diatomic molecule, on the other hand, has in addition two axes of rotation, so it has five total degrees of freedom and a heat capacity at constant pressure of $\frac{5}{2}nR$. (There's a sixth degree of freedom in the ability of the bond to change its length, but near room temperature it can be ignored due to energy limitations.) For an ideal gas $C_P = C_V + nR$, so we can also find the heat capacities at constant pressure: $\frac{5}{2}nR$ for a monatomic gas or $\frac{7}{2}nR$ for a diatomic. Once the molecules have more than two atoms, the degrees of freedom become more difficult to determine.

Most instruments that measure the pressure inside a container, including manometers, the gauges used to check tire pressures, and the sphygmomanometers doctors use to measure blood pressure, don't actually measure the total pressure. What they're really measuring is the difference in pressure between the inside of the container and the outside. Because this is the pressure read by gauges, this is called the gauge pressure.

Although the gauge pressure is often useful, at other times it is important to know not just the difference in pressure but the total pressure of the gas inside a container—for example, if one has to use that pressure to calculate some other property using the ideal gas law. This pressure is called the absolute pressure. There is a simple relationship between the two pressures: the absolute pressure is equal to the gauge pressure plus the atmospheric pressure.

For instance, if a gauge used to measure the pressure in a car's tire gives a reading of 32.5 psi, then the gauge pressure is 32.5 psi, but the absolute pressure is $P_{gauge} + P_{atm} = 32.5 \text{ psi} + 14.7 \text{ psi} = 47.2 \text{ psi}$.

DALTON'S LAW

The total pressure of mixing two or more ideal gases is equal to the sum of the partial pressure of each individual gas. If there are i total gases and each gas has the partial pressure denoted as P_1, P_2, P_3, ..., P_i, their total pressure, P_t, is then:

$$P_t = P_1 + P_2 + P_3 + \cdots + P_i$$

This relation is called **Dalton's law of partial pressures**. Since each gas in the mixture obeys the ideal gas law, the above equation can be rewritten into:

$$P_t = n_1\frac{RT}{V} + n_2\frac{RT}{V} + n_3\frac{RT}{V} + \cdots + n_i\frac{RT}{V} = n_t\frac{RT}{V}$$

where $n_1, n_2, n_3, ..., n_i$ are number of moles of each gas and n_t is the total number of moles of the gases.

At a given temperature and under constant volume, the ratio between the partial pressure of one gas and the total pressure of the gas mixture is:

$$\frac{P_1}{P_t} = \frac{n_1\left(\frac{RT}{V}\right)}{n_t\left(\frac{RT}{V}\right)} = \frac{n_1}{n_t}$$

Therefore, the ratio of the pressure is equal to the ratio of number of moles. The ratio of moles, $\frac{n_1}{n_t}$, is also called the **mole fraction** and is denoted as X. Rearranging the equation above, we obtain:

$$P_1 = \left(\frac{n_1}{n_t}\right)P_t = X_1 P_t$$

The partial pressure of one gas in the mixture is then the mole fraction of that gas times the total pressure.

Solids

PROPERTIES

Solids have definite shapes and volumes. **Crystalline solids** have well-ordered arrangements of constituents (ions, atoms, or molecules) in the three-dimensional space. Because of this ordered microscopic structure, these substances usually exhibit well defined crystalline shapes on the macroscopic level. Additionally, they have very distinct melting points. Table salt and sugar are good examples of crystalline solids in everyday life. In contrast, **amorphous solids** do not have well-ordered structures and usually do not display well-defined shapes. The lack of microscopic order means the strength of intermolecular interactions varies throughout the substance. Therefore, amorphous solids melt over a temperature range. Glass and wax are common amorphous solids.

CRYSTAL LATTICE AND STRUCTURE

Crystalline solids have highly ordered and repeated internal structures. The smallest repeating unit is called the **unit cell** of the crystal. The stacking of these units leads to the organized repeating three-dimensional structure, which is the **crystal lattice**. The particles, either ions or molecules, that make up the crystal structure are located on these points. These are called **lattice points**; each represents an identical environment in the crystal structure.

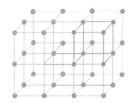

The unit cells are parallelepipeds; depending the length of the edges on the faces and the angles between the edges, seven crystal lattice systems are present. The cubic system is the simplest, with all edges having the same length and all angles between edges equal to 90°. Depending on the packing pattern of the ions, atoms, or molecules, there are three types of cubic unit cells:

- In **primitive cubic**, lattice points are only located at the corners.
- In **body-centered cubic**, lattice points are located at the center of the unit as well as all the corners.
- In **face-centered cubic**, lattice points are located at the center of all faces and corners.

Primitive cubic   Body-centered cubic   Face-centered cubic

COEFFICIENT OF EXPANSION

The coefficient of (thermal) expansion is a measurement of how much an object or substance expands as heat increases. For a solid, this increase can be measured either linearly or volumetrically. The linear coefficient of expansion, α, is defined as $\alpha = \frac{\Delta L}{L_0 \Delta T}$, where L_0 is the initial length of the object in question, ΔL is the change in length, and ΔT is the change in temperature. (This assumes that the coefficient is independent of temperature, but this is generally a good approximation.) For a liquid, with no fixed shape, only the volume coefficient of expansion is

49

meaningful; this is defined similarly but in terms of volume instead of length as $\beta = \frac{\Delta V}{V_0 \Delta T}$. For a solid, $\beta \approx 3\alpha$.

For example, the linear coefficient of expansion of steel is about 1.3×10^{-5} K^{-1}. This means that if a steel wheel with a diameter of 0.5 meters increases in temperature from 0 °C to 80 °C, its diameter changes by an amount equal to $\Delta L = \alpha L_0 \Delta T = (1.3 \times 10^{-15}$ K$^{-1})(0.5$ m$)(80$ K$) = 0.00052$ m or about half a millimeter. That may not sound like much, but for some high-precision instruments, such a small change may be significant.

Example Problems

Calculate the amount of heat required to change 100.0 g of ice at –10.0 °C to water at 10.0 °C. (Note that $\Delta H_{fus} = 334$ J/g, $c_{water} = 4.18$ J/(g · °C), and $c_{ice} = 2.06$ J/(g · °C).)

To calculate the amount of heat required to change 100.0 g of ice at –10.0 °C to water at 10.0 °C, it is necessary to calculate the heat required for each step along the way. Step 1 is to calculate the heat required to raise the temperature of the ice from –10.0 °C to 0.0 °C. Step 2 is to calculate the amount of heat required to melt the ice. Finally, step 3 is to calculate the amount of heat required to raise the temperature of the water from 0.0 °C to 10.0 °C.

For Q_1 and Q_3, the required equation is $Q = mc\Delta T$, and because Q_2 is a phase change, the required equation is $Q = m\Delta H_{fus}$.

$$Q_1 = (100.0 \text{ g})(2.06 \text{ J/(g} \cdot \text{°C)})\big(0.0\text{°C} - (-10.0\text{°C})\big) = 2{,}060 \text{ J}$$
$$Q_2 = m\Delta H_{fus} = (100.0 \text{ g})(334 \text{ J/g}) = 33{,}400 \text{ J}$$
$$Q_3 = (100.0 \text{ g})(4.18 \text{ J/(g} \cdot \text{°C)})(10.0 \text{ °C} - 0.0 \text{ °C}) = 4{,}180 \text{ J}$$
$$Q_1 + Q_2 + Q_3 = 2{,}060 \text{ J} + 33{,}400 \text{ J} + 4{,}180 \text{ J} = 39{,}640 \text{ J}$$

Calculate the amount of heat required to change 100.0 g of liquid water at 90.0 °C to steam at 110.0 °C. (Note that $\Delta H_{vap} = 2{,}260$ J/g, $c_{steam} = 1.86$ J/(g · °C), and $c_{water} = 4.18$ J/(g · °C).)

To calculate the amount of heat required to change 100.0 g of water at 90.0 °C to steam at 110.0 °C, it is necessary to calculate the heat required at each step along the way. Step 1 is to calculate the heat required to raise the temperature of the water from 90.0 °C to 100.0 °C. Step 2 is to calculate the amount of heat required to change the water to steam. Finally, step 3 is to calculate the amount of heat required to raise the temperature of the steam from 100.0 °C to 110.0 °C.

For Q_1 and Q_3, the required equation is $Q = mc\Delta T$, and because Q_3 is a phase change, the required equation is $Q = m\Delta H_{vap}$.

$$Q_1 = (100.0 \text{ g})(4.18 \text{ J/(g} \cdot \text{°C)})(100.0 \text{ °C} - 90.0 \text{ °C}) = 4{,}180 \text{ J}$$
$$Q_2 = m\Delta H_{vap} = (100.0 \text{ g})(2{,}260 \text{ J/g}) = 226{,}000 \text{ J}$$
$$Q_3 = (100.0 \text{ g})(1.86 \text{ J/(g} \cdot \text{°C)})(110.0\text{°C} - 100.0 \text{ °C}) = 1{,}860 \text{ J}$$
$$Q_1 + Q_2 + Q_3 = 4{,}180 \text{ J} + 226{,}000 \text{ J} + 1{,}860 \text{ J} = 233{,}040 \text{ J}$$

Explain how to determine the mass of 2.50 moles of O_2. (Note that $O = 16.0$ g/mol)

To convert from moles of O_2 to mass in grams of O_2, use the dimensional analysis method with the molar mass of O_2. The molar mass of O_2 is 2(16.0 g/mol) or 32.0 g/mol. This molar mass can be written as the conversion factor $\left(\frac{32.0 \text{ g } O_2}{\text{mol } O_2}\right)$. Then, using dimensional analysis, multiply $(2.50 \text{ mol } O_2)\left(\frac{32.0 \text{ g } O_2}{\text{mol } O_2}\right)$. The "mol O_2" cancels from the numerator of the first factor and the denominator of the second factor resulting in 80.0 g O_2.

Explain how to determine the number of moles of $C_{12}H_{22}O_{11}$ in 100.0 g of this substance. ($C = 12.0$ g/mol, $H = 1.0$ g/mol, and $O = 16.0$ g/mol)

To find the number of moles in a sample of $C_{12}H_{22}O_{11}$, first calculate the molar mass to be used in dimensional analysis. The molar mass of $C_{12}H_{22}O_{11}$:

$$\big(12(12.0) + 22(1.0) + 11(16.0)\big) \text{ g/mol} = (144.0 + 22.0 + 176.0) \text{ g/mol} = 342 \text{ g/mol}$$

This means that every mole of $C_{12}H_{22}O_{11}$ has a molar mass of 342 g. To convert from grams to moles, divide the mass of the substance by the molar mass:

$$\left(\frac{100.0 \text{ g}}{342 \text{ g/mol}}\right) = 0.292 \text{ mol}$$

Given the reaction $3H_2(g) + N_2(g) \rightarrow 2NH_3(g)$, determine how many grams of nitrogen gas are needed to produce 100.0 g of ammonia. ($N_2 = 28.0$ g/mol, $NH_3 = 17.0$ g/mol.)

One approach to working out this problem is to use the dimensional analysis method all the way through the work of the problem. Conversion factors using the molar masses of NH_3 and N_2 are used as well as a mole ratio from the balanced chemical equation. The approach is to convert from grams of NH_3 to moles of NH_3, then to convert moles of NH_3 to moles of N_2, and finally to convert the moles of N_2 to grams of N_2.

$$\left(\frac{100.0 \text{ g NH}_3}{1}\right)\left(\frac{1 \text{ mol NH}_3}{17.0 \text{ g}}\right)\left(\frac{1 \text{ mol N}_2}{2 \text{ mol NH}_3}\right)\left(\frac{28.0 \text{ g N}_2}{1 \text{ mol N}_2}\right) = 82.4 \text{ g N}_2$$

Review Video: Concept of a Mole Ratio
Visit mometrix.com/academy and enter code: 747963

Show how to find the empirical formula and the molecular formula for hydrogen peroxide given that it has a composition of 5.94% hydrogen and 94.1% oxygen. (The atomic mass for hydrogen is 1.008 u; the atomic mass of oxygen is 16.00 u.)

To find the empirical formula, calculate the masses of each element in hydrogen peroxide for a sample size of 100.0 g. Calculating 5.94% of 100.0 g yields 5.94 g of hydrogen. Calculating 94.1% of 100.0 g yields 94.1 g of oxygen. Next, convert the masses of these elements to moles. Multiplying $(5.94 \text{ g hydrogen})\left(\frac{\text{mol hydrogen}}{1.008 \text{ g}}\right) = 5.89$ mol hydrogen. Multiplying $(94.1 \text{ g oxygen})\left(\frac{\text{mol oxygen}}{16.00 \text{ g}}\right) = 5.88$ mol oxygen. Now, divide these amounts by the smallest value of moles that was calculated and round to the nearest tenth. For hydrogen, $\left(\frac{5.89}{5.88}\right) = 1.0$, and for oxygen, $\left(\frac{5.88}{5.88}\right) = 1.0$. These calculations are the subscripts for the empirical formula. Therefore, the empirical formula of hydrogen peroxide is HO. To find the molecular formula, find the molar mass of the empirical formula (HO) by adding $1.008 \text{ g} + 16.00 \text{ g} = 17.008 \text{ g}$. To perform the calculation, the molar mass of hydrogen peroxide would need to be given. If the problem states that the actual molar mass of hydrogen peroxide is 34.016 g, divide this molar mass by the molar mass of the empirical formula: $\frac{34.016}{17.008} = 2$. Multiply each subscript of the empirical formula by 2. The molecular formula for hydrogen peroxide is H_2O_2.

Explain how to find the percent composition of methane (CH₄). (The atomic mass of carbon is 12.01 u; the atomic mass of hydrogen is 1.008 u.)

To find the percent composition of methane, first find the molar mass of methane. The molar mass of methane is given by $12.01\text{ g} + 4(1.008\text{ g}) = 16.042\text{ g}$. Next, find the percent contributed by the carbon and the percent contributed by the hydrogen. For the carbon, $\%C = \frac{12.01\text{ g/mol}}{16.042\text{ g/mol}} \times 100\% =$ 74.87%. For the hydrogen, $\%H = \frac{4(1.008)\text{ g/mol}}{16.042\text{ g/mol}} \times 100\% = 25.13\%$. Finally, check to see that the total of the calculated percents is 100%. There may be a slight difference due to rounding. For methane, $74.87\% + 25.13\% = 100\%$.

A 5.0 L gas sample has a pressure of 1.0 standard atmosphere (atm). If the pressure is increased to 2.0 atm, find the new volume. Assume that the temperature is constant.

To find the new volume, use the equation associated with Boyle's law $P_i V_i = P_f V_f$. Solving the equation for the unknown V_f yields $V_f = \frac{P_i V_i}{P_f}$. Substituting in the given values $P_i = 1.0$ atm, $V_i = 5.0$ L, and $P_f = 2.0$ atm into the equation yields $V_f = \frac{(1.0\text{ atm})(5.0\text{ L})}{(2.0\text{ atm})} = 2.5$ L. This checks out because the pressure increased and the volume decreased. More specifically, because the pressure was doubled, the volume was reduced to one-half of the original volume.

A gas sample has a volume of 10.0 L at 200.0 K. Find its volume if the temperature is increased to 300.0 K.

To find the new volume, use the equation associated with Charles's law $\frac{V_i}{T_i} = \frac{V_f}{T_f}$. Solving the equation for the unknown V_f yields $V_f = \frac{T_f V_i}{T_i}$. Substituting the given values $V_i = 10.0$ L, $T_i = 200.0$ K, and $T_f = 300.0$ K into the equation yields $V_f = \frac{(300.0\text{ K})(10.0\text{ L})}{(200.0\text{ K})} = 15.0$ L. This checks because the temperature increased and the volume increased. Also, note that if the temperature had not been stated in Kelvin, it would have to be converted to Kelvin before substituting the values in to the equation.

Explain how to find the pressure that 0.500 mol of H₂(g) will exert on a 500.0 ml flask at 300.0 K.

To calculate the pressure that 0.500 mol of $H_2(g)$ will exert on a 500.0 mL flask at 300.0 K, use the ideal gas equation $PV = nRT$, where R is the ideal gas constant of $0.0821\ \frac{\text{L atm}}{\text{K mol}}$, P is the pressure in atmospheres, V is the volume in liters, n is the number of moles, and T is the temperature in Kelvin. Solving the ideal gas equation for P yields $P = \frac{nRT}{V}$. First, convert the 500.0 mL to 0.500 L. Substituting in $n = 0.500$ mol, $V = 0.500$ L, $T = 300.0$ K, and $R = 0.0821\ \frac{\text{L atm}}{\text{K mol}}$ yields:

$$P = \frac{(0.500\text{ mol})\left(0.0821\ \frac{\text{L atm}}{\text{K mol}}\right)(300.0\text{ K})}{(0.500\text{ L})} = 24.6\text{ atm}$$

Calculate the total pressure of a mixture of 15.0 g Ar, 6.5 g N_2, and 1.30 g H_2 gases in a cylinder that is 25.0 L in volume at 0 °C.

The number of moles for each gas is:

$$n_{Ar} = \frac{15.0\ g}{39.9\ g/mol} = 0.376\ mol, \quad n_{N_2} = \frac{6.5\ g}{28.0\ g/mol} = 0.232\ mol, \quad n_{H_2} = \frac{1.30\ g}{2.02\ g/mol} = 0.644\ mol$$

The partial pressure for each gas is:

$$P_{Ar} = n_{Ar}\frac{RT}{V} = (0.376\ mol)\frac{\left(0.0821\ \frac{L \cdot atm}{mol \cdot K}\right)(273\ K)}{25.0\ L} = 0.337\ atm$$

$$P_{N_2} = n_{N_2}\frac{RT}{V} = (0.232\ mol)\frac{\left(0.0821\ \frac{L \cdot atm}{mol \cdot K}\right)(273\ K)}{25.0\ L} = 0.207\ atm$$

$$P_{H_2} = n_{H_2}\frac{RT}{V} = (0.644\ mol)\frac{\left(0.0821\ \frac{L \cdot atm}{mol \cdot K}\right)(273\ K)}{25.0\ L} = 0.577\ atm$$

Therefore, the total number of moles of the gas mixture is:

$$P_t = P_{Ar} + P_{N_2} + P_{H_2} = 0.337\ atm + 0.207\ atm + 0.507\ atm = 1.12\ atm$$

We can cross-check this result by adding the number of mols for each gas first, then applying the ideal gas law:

$$n_t = n_{Ar} + n_{N_2} + n_{H_2} = 0.376\ mol + 0.232\ mol + 0.644\ mol = 1.252\ mol$$

The total pressure is:

$$P_t = n_t\frac{RT}{V} = (1.252\ mol)\frac{\left(0.0821\ \frac{L \cdot atm}{mol \cdot K}\right)(273\ K)}{25.0\ L} = 1.12\ atm$$

Bonding, Interactions, and Nomenclature

Bonding and Molecular Geometry

LEWIS ELECTRON DOT FORMULAS

A Lewis Electron Dot formula is a method of visually portraying the bonds between atoms in a molecule or ion and the positions of unbonded electron pairs. In a Lewis formula, each atom is represented by its chemical symbol; a line drawn between atoms represents a bond—with two lines for a double bond and three for a triple—and a dot represents an unbonded electron.

One method to derive Lewis structures starts with totaling the number of valence electrons in all the atoms. Then sum the electrons needed to surround each atom—usually eight for most atoms (the octet rule) and two for hydrogen. Total these electrons, subtract the valence electrons (and the charge, for an ion), and divide by two to find the number of bonds required. Find a way to place this many bonds between the atoms (which may involve some trial and error), and then place the remaining electrons to satisfy the octet rule.

For instance, formic acid is CH_2O_2. There are $4 + 2(1) + 2(6) = 18$ valence electrons; $8 + 2(2) + 2(8) = 28$; $(28 - 18) \div 2 = 5$. Five bonds are needed, which can be arranged as follows, with the additional electrons:

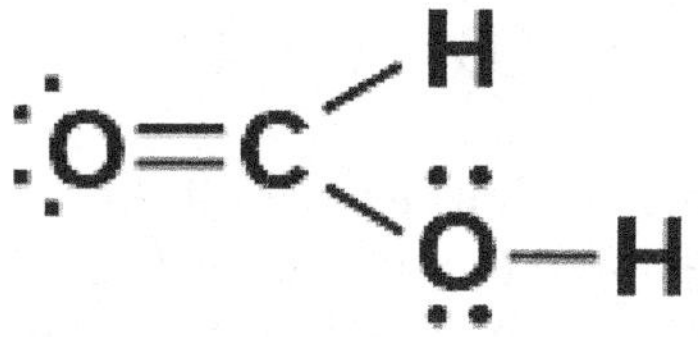

RESONANCE STRUCTURES

Sometimes when deriving a Lewis dot formula, it turns out that there is more than one possible way to arrange the bonds and electrons so that the necessary conditions are satisfied, without changing the overall structure of the molecule (which atoms are bonded to which other atoms). In this case, the molecule or ion is said to have resonance, and the different possible arrangements are called resonance structures. For example, consider the thiocyanate ion, CNS^-. There are four from C, five from N, six from S, and one from the charge for a total of sixteen valence electrons; $3(8) = 24$ are needed, so we need $(24 - 16) \div 2 = 4$ bonds. There are three ways to achieve this:

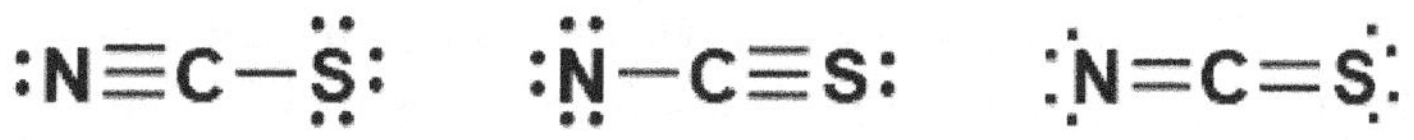

In this case, the third structure is the most accurate; the formal charges are minimized, and the most electronegative atom has the lowest formal charge. But often there is no preferred structure. For the carbonate ion CO_3^{2-}, we need $([4(8) + 2] - [4 + 3(6)]) \div 2 = 4$ bonds, leading to the following structure:

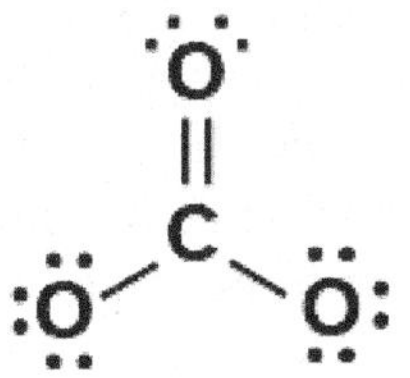

55

But there's no reason to choose any particular oxygen atom for the double bond; there are three resonant structures:

In practice, the ion's structure is a hybrid of all of these.

FORMAL CHARGE

To find the formal charge of an atom in a Lewis Electron Dot formula, take the number of valence electrons in a free atom of the element, subtract the number of unbonded electrons, and then subtract half the number of bonded electrons—which is equivalent to subtracting the number of bonds. The total of the formal charges of all the atoms is equal to zero for a neutral molecule or, for an ion, the charge of the ion. If there are multiple possible Lewis structures (resonances), the preferred structure is the one where the atoms have the smallest magnitudes of formal charges, and the most electronegative atom has the most negative formal charge.

$$Formal\ charge = valence\ electrons - bonds - bonded\ electrons$$

For example, consider carbon dioxide, which has three resonances:

In all three, the carbon atom has a formal charge of $4 - 0 - 4 = 0$. In the first, the oxygen on the left has a formal charge of $6 - 2 - 3 = +1$ and the oxygen on the right of $6 - 6 - 1 = -1$. In the second, these are reversed. In the third, both oxygen atoms have a formal charge of $6 - 4 - 2 = 0$, so the third is preferred.

LEWIS ACIDS AND BASES

The Lewis theory of acids and basis is named after American physical chemist Gilbert Newton Lewis, noted for his work in thermodynamics and chemical bonding. (This is the same Lewis who developed the Lewis Electron Dot formula.) A Lewis acid is a substance that can accept a pair of electrons. A Lewis base is a substance that can donate a pair of electrons. The Lewis definition of acids and bases further expands the concept beyond the Brønsted-Lowry definition, allowing consideration of chemicals as acids and bases that don't qualify under that theory. Any molecule or ion with an unshared pair of electrons can be a Lewis base, and any with an atom that requires one or more pairs of electrons to fill its valence shell can be a Lewis acid. This means that the H^+ ion qualifies as a Lewis acid because it needs a pair of electrons to fill its valence shell, but so do other molecules and ions, such as boron trifluoride, BF_3, in which the boron molecule has only six electrons in its valence shell.

FORMATION OF COVALENT BONDS

Unlike an ionic bond, in which one atom "donates" one or more electrons to another and then the two atoms are attracted to each other by their opposite charge, in a covalent bond two atoms share a pair of electrons. Covalent bonds usually occur between nonmetals; the elements in group 14 (carbon, silicon, etc.) are especially prone to form covalent bonds because their valence shells are half full: this makes it impractical to form an ionic bond as they would have to donate or accept four electrons.

It is possible for two atoms to share more than one pair of electrons. If they share two pairs of electrons, then there is said to be a double bond between them. If the atoms share three pairs of electrons, this is said to be a triple bond. Double bonds are shorter than single bonds—that is, the atoms are closer together—as well as stronger—and harder to break. Triple bonds are shorter and stronger still.

Lewis Electron Dot Formula Exceptions

One of the fundamental rules of creating Lewis Electron Dot formulas is the octet rule that each atom must be surrounded by eight electrons. Nevertheless, this rule has exceptions. The most common exception is that concerning hydrogen—unlike the heavier elements, hydrogen needs only two electrons to fill its valence shell, not eight. But exceptions sometimes occur, not including hydrogen as well. Most commonly, a compound will have too many electrons to make it possible to satisfy the octet rule, leaving one or more atoms with more than eight electrons surrounding them. Usually these excess electrons will surround the central atom. For instance, in thionyl chloride ($SOCl_2$), the sulfur atom has 10 electrons; in iodine pentafluoride (IF_5) the iodine atom has 12. Other compounds may have too few electrons; this is most common for compounds involving boron and beryllium. (These compounds generally act as Lewis acids.) In boron trichloride (BCl_3), the boron atom has only six electrons; in beryllium iodide (BeI_2) the beryllium has only four. Finally, some molecules contain an odd number of electrons, which makes it impossible to satisfy the octet rule; examples include nitrous oxide (NO) and chlorine dioxide (ClO_2).

Bond Enthalpy

Bond enthalpy (often denoted as $D(bond\ type)$) is defined as the enthalpy change when completely breaking one mole of a specific type of bond into atoms in gaseous phase. In the example below, the bond enthalpy, $D(H - Cl)$ is equal to breaking one mole of HCl into H and Cl atoms in gaseous phase:

$$H—\overset{..}{\underset{..}{Cl}}:_{(g)} \longrightarrow H\cdot_{(g)} + \cdot\overset{..}{\underset{..}{Cl}}:_{(g)}$$

Since energy is always absorbed to break chemical bonds, the bond enthalpy is always a positive value. The bond enthalpy values are associated with bond strength. In the $C—X$ (where X is halogen) bonds, as the halogen atom gets bigger, the bond length gets longer, resulting in less overlap between atoms and weaker bonds. So, the bond enthalpy ranks $C—F > C—Cl > C—Br > C—I$. Multiple bonds are shorter and share more electron densities than single bonds, so their bond enthalpies are typically higher. Therefore, the bond enthalpy increases as the bond order increases. The enthalpy for carbon-carbon bonds rank as follows.

$$(C - C) < (C = C) < (C \equiv C)$$

Partial Ionic Character
Role of Electronegativity in Determining Charge Distribution

Although electrons are shared between atoms in a covalent bond, they are not necessarily shared equally. Generally, the electron is more closely associated with the atom with higher electronegativity. If the two atoms have the same electronegativity, then the electron will be shared equally; thus, in a molecule of H_2 or O_2, the electrons in the covalent bonds are shared equally between both atoms. On the other hand, in hydrochloric acid (HCl), the chlorine has a much higher electronegativity than the hydrogen (3.16 vs. 2.20). The electron will thus be more closely associated with the chlorine atom, and although the atom as a whole will be neutrally charged, the chlorine atom will have a slight negative charge, whereas the hydrogen atom is slightly positive.

Similarly, because oxygen has a higher electronegativity than hydrogen (3.44 vs. 2.20), the oxygen atom in a molecule of water (H_2O) will have a slight negative charge, and the hydrogen atoms will have a slight positive charge. A covalent bond in which the electrons are shared unequally is called a polar covalent bond.

DIPOLE MOMENT

The dipole moment of a molecule is a measurement of the polarity of a molecule—the difference in charge between the ends. More specifically, the magnitude of the dipole moment of an atomic bond in a molecule is equal to the charge difference between the bonded atoms times the length of the bond. It is a vector quantity, pointing from the positive toward the negative charge. For a molecule with more than two atoms, the overall dipole moment can be found by adding together as vectors the dipole moments of each bond.

Polar molecules—molecules with nonzero dipole moments—tend to align themselves to electric fields and to other polar molecules and ions. This makes it possible to determine the dipole moment experimentally by measuring this alignment. For instance, a polar substance placed between the two charged plates of a parallel-plate capacitor will tend to align to the electric field of the capacitor and in doing so will alter the capacitance of the system; by measuring the capacitance, one can in principle derive the dipole moments of the particles.

A polar molecule is a molecule in which two sides of the molecule have opposite charges. A nonpolar molecule is a molecule in which in any orientation of the two sides of the molecule are equally charged. Equivalently, a polar molecule is a molecule with a nonzero dipole moment; a nonpolar molecule has a dipole moment of zero. Thus, for instance, H_2 is a polar molecule; the electrons are shared equally, and the dipole moment is zero. HF is polar; the hydrogen atom has a positive charge, and the fluorine negative.

Note that a molecule can be nonpolar even if the individual bonds are polar. For example, oxygen has a higher electronegativity than carbon, so in a carbon dioxide molecule, the oxygen atoms are slightly negative and the carbon atom positive. However, because the oxygen atoms are positioned symmetrically on either side of the carbon atom, the dipole moments of the bonds cancel, and the carbon dioxide molecule as a whole is nonpolar. The same is true of methane, CH_4, in which each bond is polar but the molecule has tetrahedral symmetry. It is not true, however, of molecules such as water and ammonia, which lack such symmetry and are polar.

MOLECULAR GEOMETRY
HYBRID ORBITALS sp, sp^2, AND sp^3 AND RESPECTIVE GEOMETRIES

Hybrid orbitals occur when atomic orbitals combine into new configurations to facilitate the pairing of electrons and the formation of bonds by orienting the electrons in such a way as to minimize the repulsive forces between them.

In a sp hybrid orbital, one s orbital mixes with one p orbital to form two sp orbitals. This often occurs in molecules that include a triple bond. Ethylene (C_2H_2) is an example of a simple molecule with sp orbitals: the $2s$ orbital of each carbon atom mixes with one of the $2p$ orbitals to form two sp orbitals, one of which bonds to the hydrogen atom and the other with the other carbon atom; and the remaining two $2p$ orbitals bond to the other carbon atom in pi bonds.

In a sp^2 hybrid orbital, one s orbital mixes with two p orbitals to form three hybrid orbitals. This often accompanies a double bond and occurs, for example, with the carbon atoms in ethene, C_2H_4. Finally, a sp^3 hybrid orbital mixes one s orbital and three p orbitals to form four symmetrically arranged hybrid orbitals; this occurs where bonds have tetrahedral symmetry, such as, for instance, in methane, CH_4.

VALENCE SHELL ELECTRON PAIR REPULSION AND THE PREDICTION OF SHAPES MOLECULES

Valence shell electron pair repulsion, or **VSEPR**, refers to the tendency of electrons around a given atom to arrange themselves in such a way as to put them maximally distant from each other, including both bonds and unpaired electrons. This can be used to predict the geometry of a molecule. The key to using this technique is to count the number of electron groups around the atom, which is sometimes called the VSEPR number. Any pair of unbonded electrons counts as one electron group; so does an unpaired electron; and so does a bond, regardless of its multiplicity (single, double, or triple). This VSEPR number determines how the electron groups are distributed: linear for 2, in an equilateral triangle for 3, tetrahedrally for 4, and so on. For example, the carbon in CO_2 has two (double) bonds and no unbonded electrons; its VSEPR number is 2. This means carbon dioxide is linear. On the other hand, the oxygen in water has two bonds plus two pairs of unbonded electrons for a VSEPR number of 4. Its electron groups are arranged tetrahedrally, with unbonded electron pairs on two corners of the tetrahedron and the bonded hydrogen atoms on the other two.

SHAPES

Linear—All diatomic molecules are linear molecules. Also, molecules with two bonding groups and two nonbonding pairs of electrons are linear. The bond angle measurement for linear molecules is 180°. Nitric oxide (also called nitrogen monoxide) is an example of a linear molecule.

Trigonal planar—For a trigonal planar molecule, the central atom has three bonding pairs of electrons and zero nonbonding pairs. These molecules are an exception to the octet rule. The bond angle measurement for trigonal planar molecules is 120°. Boron trifluoride (BF_3), which has has three bonding pairs and zero nonbonding pairs around the central atom, is an example of a trigonal planar molecule.

Angular—For an angular molecule, the central atom has two bonding pairs of electrons and one or two nonbonding pairs. The bond angle measurement for angular molecules is less than 120° if there is one nonbonding pair, and less than 109° if there are two. Oxygen difluoride (OF_2), which has two bonding pairs and two nonbonding pairs around the central angle, is an example of an angular molecule.

Tetrahedral—For a tetrahedral molecule, the central atom has four bonding pairs of electrons and zero nonbonding pairs. The bond angle measurement for tetrahedral molecules is 109.5°. Methane (CH_4), which has four bonding pairs and zero nonbonding pairs around the central angle, is an example of a tetrahedral molecule.

Trigonal pyramidal—For a trigonal pyramidal molecule, the central atom has three bonding pairs and one nonbonding pair. The bond angle measurement for trigonal pyramidal molecules is less than 109.5°. Ammonia (NH_3), which has three bonding pairs and one bonding pair around the central atom, is an example of a trigonal pyramidal molecule.

VALENCE BOND THEORY

The **valence-bond theory** is a model for describing the formation of chemical bonds between atoms through overlapping the atomic orbitals in their valence shell. The overlapped atomic orbitals contain a pair of electrons in opposite spin states that share the space between the two nuclei to form a **covalent bond**. As illustrated in the figure below, each hydrogen atom has an unpaired electron in its valance $1s$ shell. When the two atoms are infinitely far from each other, there is almost no interaction between them. Thus the potential energy approaches zero. As the atoms get closer and closer to each other, they start to interact and form overlapping regions of electron density between their nuclei, causing the total potential energy of the two to decrease. At the same time, the repulsion between the nuclei increases. The optimal distance between the two nuclei occurs as the balance of minimal potential energy with nuclei repulsion, which is defined as the **bond length**.

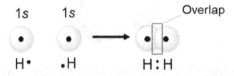

The overlap can also occur between other atomic orbitals. The following figure demonstrates the bond formation between two fluorine atoms by overlapping two $2p$ orbitals, forming one F_2 molecule. Since the orbitals overlap alongside the internuclear axis ("head-to-head"), the formed covalent bond is called the **σ-bond**.

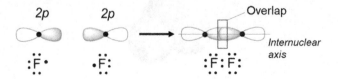

For the p orbitals, the overlap region may also occur above and below the internuclear axis (forming a "side-by-side" overlap region). In this case, the bond formed is called the **π-bond**.

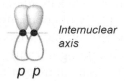

Internuclear axis

p p

MOLECULAR ORBITAL THEORY

When the overlap between the atomic orbitals forms a molecule, **molecular orbitals** are also formed. Each molecular orbital (MO) covers the entire molecule instead of localizing to just one atom. Like the atomic orbitals, each MO also contains a pair of electrons with opposite spin states. The constructively added wave functions from the atomic orbitals lead to molecular orbitals with lower energy, defined as **bonding molecular orbitals**. The destructively added wave functions lead to orbitals with higher energy levels, called **antibonding molecular orbitals**. Below is the MO diagram of an O_2 molecule. The σ_{2s}, σ_{2p}, and π_{2p} are bonding orbitals, while the σ_{2s}^*, σ_{2p}^*, and π_{2p}^* are antibonding orbitals.

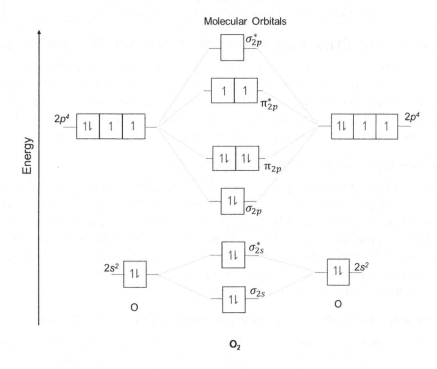

O_2

The **bond order** can be used to predict the stability of the formed covalent bonds:

$$bond\ order = \frac{1}{2}(bonding\ electrons - anti\text{-}bonding\ electrons)$$

The bond order of 1 refers to a single bond, a bond order of 2 refers to a double bond, and so on. Fraction bond orders, such as $\frac{1}{2}$ or $\frac{3}{2}$, are also possible when the difference between bonding and antibonding electrons is odd. When the bond order is zero, there is no bond formed between the atoms. In the case of an O_2 molecule, its bond order is: $\frac{1}{2}(8-4) = 2$, meaning a double bond is present in the O_2 molecule.

RIGIDITY IN MOLECULAR STRUCTURE

In general, single bonds are able to freely rotate, which may lead to some decrease in molecular rigidity. In some simple molecules, the rotation of a bond may not make a difference; rotating the bonds in a water molecule or a molecule of HF will not change the structure of the molecule at all. On the other hand, rotating the bond between oxygen atoms in a molecule of hydrogen peroxide, H_2O_2, will change the geometry of the molecule significantly. Double and triple bonds do not have this rotational freedom, so a molecule with many double or triple bonds will tend to be more rigid than a molecule of similar size with only single bonds.

PROPERTIES AFFECTED BY BONDING AND STRUCTURE

Bonding and structure determine whether a substance exists naturally as a solid, liquid, or gas. Properties that are affected by bonding and structure include boiling point, freezing point, and vapor pressure. Bonding and structure determine if a substance is soluble in water or in nonpolar solvents. Also affected are the viscosity of liquids and whether a solid material is hard or soft and whether or not a substance forms crystals or is amorphous. Bonding affects the conductivity of heat and electricity and whether a substance is a good insulator or conductor.

> **Review Video: Bonding and Structure**
> Visit mometrix.com/academy and enter code: 810110

AFFECT OF BONDING AND STRUCTURE ON BOILING POINTS AND MELTING POINTS

The types of bonds within molecules affect boiling and melting points. **Compounds with ionic bonds** typically have high melting and boiling points, whereas **compounds with covalent bonds** typically have low melting and boiling points. Intermolecular forces also affect these points. Substances with hydrogen bonds typically have high boiling and melting points. For example, hydrogen bonds are responsible for the high boiling and melting points of water.

AFFECT OF BONDING AND STRUCTURE ON SOLUBILITY

Bonding and structure affect **solubility**. The basic idea behind solubility is *like dissolves like.* This means that solutes with polar molecules typically dissolve in solvents with polar molecules. The polarity of the molecules is determined by the type of bonds and the arrangement of those bonds in the molecules. For example, both salt and table sugar (sucrose) dissolve in water because salt, table sugar, and water are polar molecules. Solutes with nonpolar molecules typically dissolve in solvents with nonpolar molecules. For example, a grease stain will not rinse out with water because water consists of polar molecules and grease is a nonpolar lipid.

AFFECT OF BONDING AND STRUCTURE ON EQUILIBRIUM VAPOR PRESSURE

Vapor pressure is related to the **boiling point** of a substance. The boiling point of a substance is the temperature at which the vapor pressure equals the atmospheric pressure. In general, as the vapor pressure increases, the boiling point decreases. Compounds with ionic bonds typically have high boiling points and low vapor pressures. Compounds with covalent bonds typically have low boiling points and high vapor pressures. Substances with the strongest intermolecular forces, hydrogen bonds, typically have high boiling points and low vapor pressures.

DRAWING THE STRUCTURAL FORMULA OF A MOLECULE

The structural formula of a molecule is a diagram that shows the atoms of the molecule and the bonds between them. Each atom is represented by its chemical symbol, and a line is drawn between bonded atoms—two lines for a double bond and three lines for a triple bond. Unlike a Lewis Electron Dot formula, the structural formula does not necessarily show unbonded electrons.

Common groups of atoms may be depicted as a unit rather than with their bonds; OH and CH_3 may appear in structural formulas in this way.

For complex organic molecules, the structural formula is often simplified by not explicitly representing carbon and hydrogen atoms. The carbon atoms are implied where the lines representing the bonds end and intersect, if no atom is explicitly shown there. Hydrogen atoms bonded to carbon atoms are omitted and can be inferred to exist wherever there are fewer than four bonds shown. This simplified structural formula is also called a skeletal formula.

As examples, shown below are the structural formulas for ammonia, NH_3, and acetaldehyde, C_2H_4O. The latter is shown in three ways: with all bonds shown, with the CH_3 compacted, and as a simplified (skeletal) formula.

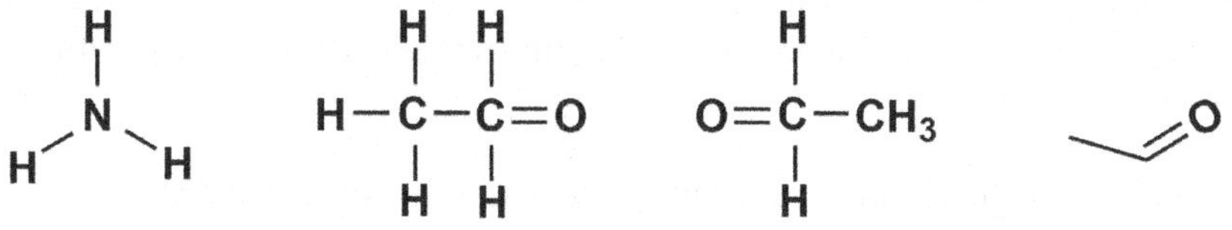

DELOCALIZED ELECTRONS

A delocalized electron is an electron that may pertain to a particular molecule or ion but is not associated with any one atom or bond. Because of their mobility, the presence of delocalized electrons tends to lead to greater electrical and thermal conductivity. Delocalized electrons are common in metals, which form metallic bonds in which the valence electrons move freely among the atoms in a sort of "electron sea" rather than remaining near one or two atoms. They also can occur under some circumstances, however, in other molecules. When a molecule or ion has two or more resonance structures, no one of which is highly favored over the others, this generally represents one or more electrons being delocalized to combine the resonance structures. One important example of such a structure is the benzene ring, which consists of a ring of six bonded carbon atoms. Although the benzene ring is sometimes depicted with alternating single and double bonds, a more accurate representation involves one electron from each carbon atom becoming delocalized and being free to move around the entire ring; each bond between atoms in the ring is not a "pure" single or double bond but something in between.

> **Review Video: Metallic Bonds**
> Visit mometrix.com/academy and enter code: 230855

STEREOCHEMISTRY OF COVALENTLY BONDED MOLECULES
ISOMERS

When two molecules have the same elements and the same number of atoms of each element, but have the atoms bonded together in different ways, they are said to be **structural isomers**. Structural isomers have the same molecular formula but different structural formulas. One of the simplest examples is C_2H_2O, which describes three different structural isomers: ethenone, ethynol, and oxirene. The structural formulas for these are depicted below:

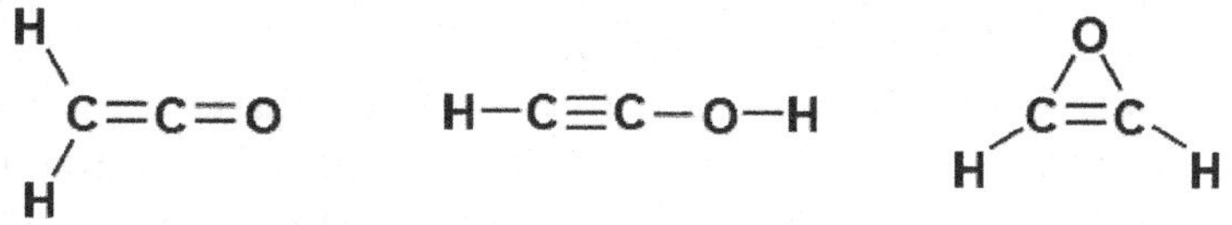

More complex organic molecules may have many more structural isomers. The molecular formula $C_6H_{12}O_6$, for instance, describes the sugars glucose and fructose but also hundreds more structural isomers with six carbon, twelve hydrogen, and six oxygen atoms (most of which have no simple names but are given complicated names like alpha-L-altropyranose and (2S,3R,4R,5S)-2,3,4,5,6-pentahydroxyhexanal).

Two molecules are **enantiomers** if they are mirror images of each other—not identical—so a symmetrical molecule would not be said to be an enantiomer of itself; the term only applies to **chiral molecules**. For example, the compound chlorofluoroiodomethane, CHClFI, exists in two different forms that are enantiomers. Both versions of the molecule are tetrahedral, with the carbon atom in the center and the hydrogen, chlorine, fluorine, and iodine atoms at the points of the tetrahedron. But there are two different ways of choosing the placement of the outer atoms that result in two different mirror-image molecules that cannot be rotated into each other. Despite their structural similarity, enantiomers may be very different in their interactions with biological systems.

There are, of course, much more complicated examples of enantiomers than chlorofluoroiodomethane. Amino acids, for example, are chiral—asymmetrical—and so each amino acid also has a corresponding mirror-image form. However, life on Earth uses almost exclusively only one form of each amino acid; their enantiomers are rarely found in nature.

In general, two molecules are **stereoisomers** if they have the same molecular and structural formulae, but they nevertheless differ in the orientation of the bonds and in their three-dimensional shapes. Enantiomers—different molecules that are mirror images of each other—are one kind of stereoisomer. Two molecules are **diastereoisomers** (or just diastereomers) if they are stereoisomers but not enantiomers—they differ in their three-dimensional structure but are not just mirror images. Diagrams of diastereomers are sometimes distinguished by drawing them in a sort of quasi-perspective, with black triangles representing bonds coming "out of the page" and dashed triangles representing bonds going "into the page."

For instance, 2,3-butanediol consists of a line of four carbon atoms, with an oxygen atom bonded to each of the middle two atoms, and hydrogen atoms filling all the remaining bonding locations. This chemical has three different stereoisomers, depicted below. (These are skeletal diagrams, so the carbon atoms and the hydrogen atoms bonded to them are implicit.)

Note that the two molecules on the right are enantiomers of each other, but they are both diastereoisomers of the molecule on the left (meso-2, 3-butanediol), which is symmetrical and has no enantiomer.

Two molecules are **cis/trans isomers** if they are stereoisomers that contain a chain of carbon atoms and that differ as to whether two like atoms or groups of atoms are on the same side (cis) or opposite sides (trans) of the central carbon chain. By definition, all cis/trans isomers are diastereoisomers, but not all diastereoisomers are cis/trans isomers. Note that in all cis/trans isomers, the carbon chain contains at least one double bond or ring structure; this is because parts of molecules can freely rotate around a single bond so that the same molecule can easily change between forms with like parts on the same or opposite side of the central carbon chain if it has only single bonds.

One simple compound that exhibits cis/trans isomerism is 1, 2-dichloroethene, a molecule with two carbon atoms connected by a double bond, and with one chlorine and one hydrogen atom connected to each carbon molecule. The cis and trans forms are shown symbolically below:

cis   trans

A slightly more complicated is 2-butene, a molecule consisting of four carbon atoms with a double bond between the center two and with hydrogen atoms filling the remaining bonding locales:

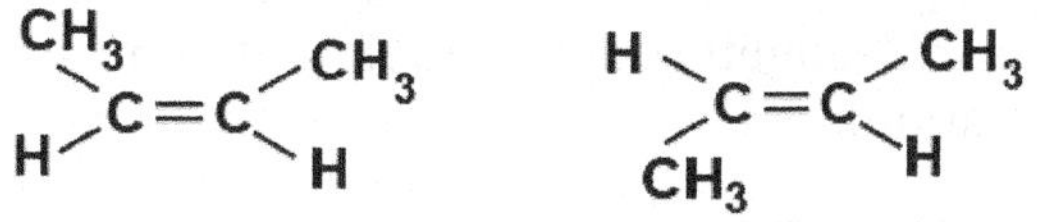

cis   trans

Two different molecular structures are **conformational isomers** if they have the same molecules with the same bonds (they are stereoisomers), but they can be converted between each other without breaking any bonds. In other words, the molecules are identical except for rotation around single bonds (double and triple bonds are more rigid and do not allow free rotation). However, this does not necessarily mean that the same molecule can freely change between conformational isomers; it may happen that only certain rotation angles are stable and that an energy barrier inhibits the molecule from readily changing from one stable state to another.

One simple molecule that has different conformational isomers is ethane, C_2H_6. The ends can be rotated about the single bond in the middle to form an **eclipsed** conformation, in which the hydrogens on each side are directly lined up with each other; a **staggered** conformation, in which the hydrogen atom on one side is in the middle of the gap between hydrogen atoms on the other or anywhere in between.

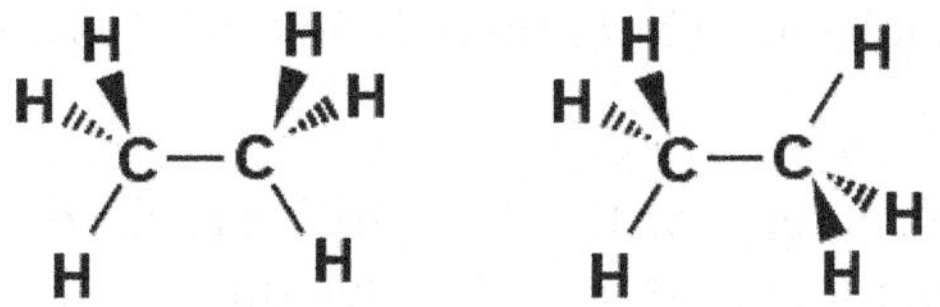

eclipsed   staggered

In practice, the staggered conformation is much more stable than the eclipsed, so ethane molecules will most often be found in or near this conformation.

POLARIZATION OF LIGHT, SPECIFIC ROTATION

A molecule is said to be optically active if the polarization direction of linearly polarized light is rotated when it passes through a substance composed of this molecule. Such molecules can be further classified based on which direction they rotate the light: molecules that rotate light clockwise are said to be dextrorotary; those that rotate light counterclockwise are levorotary.

65

Molecules are optically active only if they are chiral—that is, they are asymmetrical; they have a mirror image form. If a molecule is levorotary, its enantiomer—the mirror-image version—is dextrorotary and vice versa. An equal mixture of both enantiomers of a compound is said to be racemic and is not optically active because the rotation due to the levorotary and dextrorotary molecules tends to cancel out.

Specific rotation is a measurement of how much an optically active substance rotates linearly polarized light that passes through it. More specifically, it is a measurement of the angle by which the light rotates when it travels 1 decimeter (0.1 m) through a solution of the substance in question with a mass concentration of 1 gram per milliliter. The units of specific rotation are therefore degrees times milliliters (grams times decimeters) but are sometimes given in just degrees, the other units being implied.

The specific rotation of a substance can be measured by a device called a polarimeter, which measures the change in angle of polarization of light after it passes through a solution. Dividing this angle by the light's path length in decimeters and the solution's concentration in grams per milliliter yields the specific rotation.

ABSOLUTE AND RELATIVE CONFIGURATION

Absolute and relative configuration are terms that refer to the arrangement of atoms in chiral molecules—asymmetrical molecules that exist in two mirror-image forms, or enantiomers. The relative configuration of the molecule is its configuration relative to another molecule from which it can be produced. Historically, relative configuration was often stated relative to glyceraldehyde, a particular simple sugar which could be converted into many different compounds (without affecting the configuration of key parts of the molecule). The enantiomers were labeled with the prefix *D-* if they had the same configuration as the dextrorotary enantiomer of glyceraldehyde (which did not necessarily imply that the molecule in question was itself dextrorotary) and *L-* if they had the same configuration as levorotary glyceraldehyde. Absolute configuration refers to the precise known geometrical arrangement of the atoms, not relative to any other compounds.

ABSOLUTE AND RELATIVE CONFIGURATION: CONVENTIONS FOR WRITING THE R AND S FORMS

The enantiomers of a simple chiral molecule (i.e., the two mirror-image forms of an asymmetrical molecule) can be distinguished by calling one form the R form and one the S form. For a more complex molecule, this terminology can be applied not to a molecule as a whole but to each stereocenter—location in the molecule where there is an atom (usually carbon) with asymmetrical bonds.

To distinguish between the two, determine the "priority" of each constituent bonded to the central atom. The higher the atomic number of the atom bonded directly to the carbon, the higher the priority. If the atom immediately bonded is the same, follow the chain of atoms until you reach a difference. If there's still a tie, double bonds have higher priority than single bonds. Now, picture the lowest-priority constituent pointing away from you, and trace a circle through the others from highest to lowest priority. If this circle runs clockwise, it is an R form; if counterclockwise, it is L.

For instance, consider lactic acid:

Although this has three carbon atoms, only the central one is asymmetrical, so this is our stereocenter. The priority goes H < CH_4 < COOH < OH, so we have:

(R)-lactic acid   (S)-lactic acid

ABSOLUTE AND RELATIVE CONFIGURATION: CONVENTIONS FOR WRITING THE E AND Z FORMS

The E and Z terminology is used to distinguish stereoisomers with double bonds, based on the relative positions of the constituents on each side. When there are only two different constituents, they can be distinguished by calling the one with matching constituents on the same side of the central carbon chain cis and the other trans; with more than two constituents, however, these terms are ambiguous, and the E–Z terminology is used.

To distinguish between (E) and (Z) isomers, determine which constituent on each end has a higher "priority." The higher the atomic number of the atom directly connected to the double-bonded atom, the higher the priority; in case of a tie, consider the next atom out, and so on. If the higher priority constituents on each end are on the same side of the double bond, it is a (Z)-isomer; if not, it is an (E)-isomer.

For instance, consider the molecules tiglic acid and angelic acid: two chemicals that are (E) and (Z) isomers:

tiglic acid   angelic acid

CH_3 has a higher priority than H, but COOH has a higher priority than CH_3. So tiglic acid is the (E)-isomer, and angelic acid is the (Z)-isomer.

Intermolecular Interactions

HYDROGEN BONDING

Hydrogen bonding refers to an intermolecular force between two polar molecules arising because a hydrogen atom with a partial positive charge in one molecule is attracted to an atom in another molecule with a partial negative charge. Although hydrogen bonds are not as strong as molecular covalent bonds, the fact that they do cause the molecules to "stick together" better is responsible for increasing the boiling points and viscosities of the compounds in which hydrogen bonds occur. For example, water molecules form hydrogen bonds—between a hydrogen atom in one molecule and the oxygen atom in another—and it is this that gives water its relatively high boiling point and viscosity as well as allowing it to form an open lattice in the solid form that gives solid water (ice) its low density.

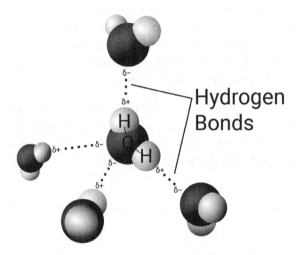

When two molecules form a hydrogen bond, due to a positively charged hydrogen atom in one molecule being attracted to a negatively charged atom in the other, the negatively charged atom that the hydrogen atom is attracted to is called the hydrogen bond acceptor, whereas the atom bonded to the hydrogen atom in the first molecule (not the hydrogen atom itself) is called the hydrogen bond donor. The hydrogen bond acceptor must have an unbonded electron pair for the hydrogen atom to be attracted to. Both the donor and the acceptor tend to be highly electronegative atoms—the acceptor because it is this electronegativity that results in the atom remaining negatively charged while part of a molecule, the donor because the electronegativity of the atom the hydrogen is bonded to results in the hydrogen atom being positively charged. Oxygen, nitrogen, and fluorine, due to their high electronegativities, are common as both hydrogen bond donors and hydrogen bond acceptors.

DIPOLE INTERACTIONS

A dipole-dipole interaction is an intermolecular force arising because of the attraction between the negative end of one polar molecule and the positive end of another. Generally, the more polar the molecules, the stronger this force, although dipole-dipole interactions are never as strong as covalent or ionic bonds. Hydrogen bonding is one kind of dipole-dipole interaction, but dipole-dipole interactions can occur between any polar compounds—molecules in which one end has a partial positive charge and one end has a slight negative charge. Dipole-dipole interactions play important parts in biological systems; for example, the shape of a protein is largely determined by the dipole-dipole interactions between its parts.

Van der Waals' Forces

London dispersion forces are weak forces that arise between molecules because of temporary polarization—even if a molecule is nonpolar, it may have a temporary dipole moment at a given time because the electrons happen to be at that time distributed more toward one side of the nucleus, and two molecules with such temporary dipole moments may be attracted to each other similarly to a dipole-dipole interaction. London dispersion forces and dipole-dipole interactions, the other main kind of intermolecular force, are collectively called **Van der Waals forces** (although sometimes this term is used to refer only to dispersion forces).

Although London dispersion forces can occur between any molecules, polar or nonpolar, they tend to be stronger between larger molecules and atoms than smaller ones and stronger in long, thin molecules than in more compact ones. That is because the larger the molecule or atom, and the less compact it is, the easier it is for the electrons to become displaced and for the molecule to become temporarily polar—this property is referred to as the molecule's polarizability.

Nomenclature

BINARY MOLECULAR COMPOUNDS

The names of binary molecular compounds follow this pattern:

prefix + first element name (space) prefix + root of second element name + -ide.

If a prefix ends with a or o and the element name begins with a or o, the first a or o of the prefix is dropped. For example, N_2O_5 is named dinitrogen pentoxide. The prefix *mono-* is usually dropped unless more than one binary compound may be formed from the two elements involved.

Binary Molecular Compounds			
#	Prefix	#	Prefix
1	mono-	6	hexa-
2	di-	7	hepta-
3	tri-	8	octa-
4	tetra-	9	nona-
5	penta-	10	deca-

NAMING BINARY IONIC COMPOUNDS

The names of binary ionic compounds follow this pattern: cation name (space) anion name.

The name of **simple cations** is usually the element name. For example, the K^+ cation is named potassium. Some cations exist in more than one form. In those cases, the charge of the ion follows the element as a Roman numeral in parentheses. For example, the Cu^+ ion is named copper(I) and the Cu^{2+} ion is named copper(II). **Simple anions** are named with the root of the element name followed by the suffix *-ide*. For example, the O^{2-} anion is named oxide, and the F^- ion is named fluoride. The following are some examples of names of binary ionic compounds: KI is named potassium iodide, and FeO is named iron(II) oxide.

NAMING ACIDS, BASES, AND SALTS

Acids are generally categorized as binary acids or oxyacids. **Binary acids** are named by the pattern: *hydro-* + root of element + *-ic* (space) acid. For example, HI is named hydroiodic acid, and HCl is named hydrochloric acid. One exception is that in hydrosulfuric acid (H_2S), the entire element name sulfur is used. The names of **oxyacids** depend on the endings of their polyatomic anions. If the polyatomic anions end in *-ate*, then the acid names end in *-ic*. If the anions end in *-ite*, the acid names end in *-ous*. The naming pattern for an oxyacid is as follows: anion root + ending (space) acid. For example, H_2CO_3 is named carbonic acid because the carbonate ion ends in *-ate*, and H_2SO_3 is named sulfurous acid because the sulfite ion ends in *-ite*.

Bases typically are ionic compounds with a hydroxide anion and are named following the conventions of naming ionic compounds. For example, NaOH is named sodium hydroxide and $Mg(OH)_2$ is named magnesium hydroxide.

Salts are ionic compounds with any cation except H^+ from an aqueous base and any anion except OH^- from an aqueous acid. Salts are named like regular ionic compounds with the name of the cation followed by the name of the anion. Examples of salts include sodium chloride (NaCl), potassium fluoride (KF), magnesium iodide (MgI_2), sodium acetate ($NaC_2H_3O_2$), and ammonium carbonate (($NH_4)_2CO_3$).

NAMING HYDRATES

Hydrates form from salts (ionic compounds) that attract water. Hydrates are named from their salt (ionic compound) name and the number of water molecules involved in the following pattern:

salt name (space) prefix + hydrate

For example, the name of $CuSO_4 \cdot 5H_2O$ is copper(II) sulfate pentahydrate, and the name of $CoCl_2 \cdot 6H_2O$ is cobalt(II) chloride hexahydrate.

Hydrates			
#	Prefix	#	Prefix
1	mono-	6	hexa-
2	di-	7	hepta-
3	tri-	8	octa-
4	tetra-	9	nona-
5	penta-	10	deca-

ANION AND CATION COMMON NAMES

A monatomic anion is named by the element of the atom with the suffix -*ide*. For example, a monatomic chlorine ion is called chloride, a monatomic iodine atom iodide, a monatomic sulfur ion sulfide, and so on.

With rare exceptions, the charge of a monatomic anion depends on its group. A halogen (group 17) has a charge of –1, an element in the oxygen group (group 16) has a charge of –2, and an element in group 15 has a charge of –3. Elements of other groups do not generally appear as monatomic anions. So, for instance, because iodine is a halogen, it has a charge of –1 and iodide is I^-; sulfur is in the oxygen group, so a sulfide ion is S^{2-}; because nitrogen is in group 15, a nitride ion is N^{3-}.

The prefixes *hypo-* and *per-* are used for oxyanions, which consist of one or more oxygen atoms and one atom of another element. For a given element, the most common such anion is named with the suffix -*ate* and the anion with one less oxygen atom with the suffix -*ite*. For some elements, however, there are more than two such ions, and in these cases the prefixes *hypo-* and *per-* are used for the additional anions. The prefix *per-* always accompanies the suffix -*ate* and identifies the anion with one more oxygen atom than the anion named with -*ate*. The prefix *hypo-* always accompanies the suffix -*ite* and identifies an anion with one fewer oxygen atom than the anion named with -*ite*.

The best-known anions using these prefixes are oxyanions of chlorine. Chlorine has four oxyanions: chlorate is ClO_3^-, chlorite is ClO_2^-, perchlorate is ClO_4^-, and hypochlorite is ClO^-. There are likewise four oxyanions of bromine: bromate is BrO_3^-, bromite is BrO_2^-, perbromate is BrO_4^-, and hypobromite is BrO^-. Iodine has the oxyanions iodate, IO_3^-; iodite, IO_2^-; periodate, IO_4^-; and hypoiodite, IO^-.

One of the most common types of anion is the oxyanion, consisting of one or more oxygen atoms and one atom of a different element. There are also some anions that are similar to oxyanions but with the addition of a hydrogen atom (and with one less negative charge). These anions are named by the name of the corresponding oxyanion preceded by hydrogen. For instance, CO_3^{2-} is carbonate, and HCO_3^- is hydrogen carbonate; PO_4^{3-} is phosphate, and HPO_4^{2-} is hydrogen phosphate; SO_4^{2-} is sulfate, and HSO_4^- is hydrogen phosphate. Hydrogen carbonate and hydrogen sulfate are also called bicarbonate and bisulfate, respectively.

The oxyanion may also have two hydrogen atoms added to it, in which case its name is preceded by dihydrogen. The only common example is dihydrogen phosphate, $H_2PO_4^-$.

As the prefix *di-* implies, the dichromate ion includes two chromium atoms. The suffix *-ate* is the same suffix used for oxyanions, and like an oxyanion, dichromate includes a number of oxygen atoms. Unfortunately, there's nothing in the name of the ion to specify exactly how many oxygen atoms it contains, or its charge, so those may have to be memorized. The dichromate ion is $Cr_2O_7^{2-}$.

The prefix *thio-* is applied to anions that are similar to oxyanions but have one of the oxygen atoms replaced by a sulfur ion. Cyanate is OCN^-, which is the cyanide ion, CN^-, with the addition of an oxygen atom. In thiocyanate, that oxygen atom is replaced by sulfur to make SCN^-. Sulfate is SO_4^{2-}; although it already contains a sulfur atom, in thiosulfate, one of the oxygen atoms is replaced by an additional sulfur atom to make $S_2O_3^{2-}$.

The suffixes *-ate* and *-ite* are used for oxyanions, a common class of polyatomic ions that combine one or more oxygen atoms with one atom of a different element. These ions are generally named after the non-oxygen atom, with the suffix *-ate* or *-ite*. Different anions exist with the same element but with different oxidation values and different numbers of oxygen atoms. They are distinguished by the suffixes: the most common such ion, or the one considered in some sense the more fundamental, gets the suffix *-ate*, whereas an anion with the same element but one less oxygen atom gets the *-ite* suffix.

Polyatomic cations are in general less common and less numerous than polyatomic anions (at least in terms of relatively simple ions, one can construct arbitrarily many complex examples of both). One important polyatomic cation, however, is ammonium, NH_4^+. Chemicals including ammonium include ammonium chloride, commonly used as in fertilizers; ammonium nitrate, used in fertilizers and explosives; and ammonium carbonate, used as a leavening agent (although today largely replaced by sodium bicarbonate).

Another important polyatomic cation is hydronium, H_3O^+, which is notable as one of the products of the dissociation of water: $2\ H_2O \rightleftharpoons H_3O^+ + OH^-$. Despite its importance in the chemistry of water, hydronium is not a component of any common stable compounds.

One other relatively common polyatomic cation is the mercury (I) ion, Hg_2^{2+}. This ion is found in compounds including mercury (I) chloride, also known as calomel, and is used in electrochemistry, and mercury (I) iodide, formerly used as a medicine despite its (then unrecognized) toxicity.

There are other polyatomic cations, but they are much less common. They include phosphonium $\left(PH_4^+\right)$, arsonium $\left(AsH_4^+\right)$, methanium $\left(CH_5^+\right)$, and tropylium $\left(C_7H_7^+\right)$.

As monatomic ions, metals are most likely to be cations, whereas nonmetals are most likely to be anions. This is because metals in general have only a few electrons in their outer shells, so they can most easily obtain full valence shells by donating electrons, turning them into positive ions. Nonmetals, on the other hand, have mostly filled valence shells, so they can most easily fill their valence shells by gaining electrons. (Carbon and silicon are exceptions because their valence shells are half full, but these elements do not commonly occur as monatomic ions.)

Hydrogen can be either a cation or an anion because it can fill its valence shell either by gaining one electron or by losing one electron. Most often it is a cation (as in hydrochloric acid, HCl, or hydrofluoric acid, HF), but it can also bond with a metal with a lower electronegativity to become an anion (as in lithium hydride, LiH).

There is, unfortunately, no easy way to tell from the name how many oxygen atoms a particular ion has, so it is useful to memorize some common ions. Some of the most important such anions include the following:

Carbonate	$CO_3{}^{2-}$
Nitrate	$NO_3{}^{-}$
Nitrite	$NO_2{}^{-}$
Phosphate	$PO_4{}^{3-}$
Sulfate	$SO_4{}^{2-}$
Sulfite	$SO_3{}^{2-}$

FORMULAS AND CHARGES FOR FAMILIAR IONS

Hydroxide is OH^-. Hydroxide ions are found in many strong bases including sodium hydroxide and potassium hydroxide as well as in water.

Cyanide is CN^-. Cyanide salts such as sodium cyanide are noted for their high toxicity.

Acetate is $C_2H_3O_2{}^-$. This organic anion is found in acetic acid, the main component of vinegar as well as in fatty acids and many other organic compounds.

Peroxide is $O_2{}^-$. Many peroxide compounds are used as bleaching agents. The simplest common peroxide compound is hydrogen peroxide, H_2O_2, used as a household disinfectant.

HYDRATION

Hydration refers to the addition of water to a chemical species. Although other reactions with water are sometimes called by this name, one common phenomenon referred to as hydration involves water molecules surrounding an ion or a polar molecule to form a hydration shell. The water molecules are attracted to the ion or molecule because the water molecules are themselves slightly polar—the oxygen atom slightly positive and the hydrogen atoms slightly negative—so the oxygen atoms in water are attracted to positive ions or to the positive ends of polar molecules, and the hydrogen atoms are attracted to negative ions or the negative ends of polar molecules.

Hydration helps polar molecules dissolve in water; when sodium chloride dissociates in water, for instance, the water molecules surrounding the ions help disperse them through the solution. Hydration also plays an important role in the functioning of proteins; the water molecules surrounding parts of the proteins affect their shapes.

Example Problems

Determine the typical bonding behavior of the following elements:

- Hydrogen
- Oxygen
- Nitrogen
- Carbon
- Fluorine
- Chlorine
- Silicon
- Phosphorus
- Sulfur

Hydrogen only has a single electron and needs one more electron to fill its valence shell, so it generally makes only one bond in a molecule.

Oxygen is in group 16 and has six valence electrons. It needs two more to fill its valence shell, so it will typically make two bonds, counting multiplicity—that is, it will make two single bonds or one double bond.

Nitrogen is in group 15 and has five valence electrons. It needs three more to fill its valence shell, so it will typically make three bonds, counting multiplicity—that is, it can make three single bonds, or one single bond and two double bonds, or one triple bond. It can form up to four bonds in some circumstances.

Carbon is in group 14 and has four valence electrons. It needs four more to fill its valence shell, so it will typically make four bonds, counting multiplicity. It is the fact that carbon makes so many bonds, and can bond in so many ways (four single, two double, one single and one triple, etc.) that enables it to form into complex organic molecules and form the foundation of life on Earth.

Fluorine and **chlorine** are both halogens in group 17. They have seven electrons in their valence shells and need one more to fill their shells; they therefore generally form one bond.

Silicon is in group 14, along with carbon; like carbon, it has four valence electrons, and needs four more to fill its valence shell, and so typically makes four bonds, counting multiplicity (i.e., counting a double bond as two bonds and a triple bond as three—although silicon rarely forms double or triple bonds). The bonds formed by silicon are weaker than those formed by carbon, however, and it isn't quite as versatile in the molecules it can make up.

Phosphorus is in group 15; it has five valence electrons and needs another three electrons to fill its valence shell. It often forms three bonds but can form up to five bonds—the reason nitrogen, in the same group, can't form as many bonds is simply because phosphorus is larger and can fit more atoms around it.

Sulfur is in group 16 and needs two electrons to fill its valence shell, but although it often forms two bonds, it can form anywhere from two to six.

Determine the name of the following compounds:

- N_2O_4
- S_2F_{10}
- Fe_2O_3
- $CuCl_2$

N_2O_4 is a binary molecular compound. Using the prefixes *di-* for 2 and *tetra-* for 4, this compound is named dinitrogen tetroxide. (Note that the entire element name is retained for the cation, but the root plus *-ide* is used for the anion name.)

S_2F_{10} is a binary molecular compound. Using the prefixes *di-* for 2 and *deca-* for 10, this compound is named disulfur decafluoride.

Fe_2O_3 is a binary ionic compound. Iron forms two types of cations Fe^{2+} and Fe^{3+}, but because the anion is O^{2-}, this must be the Fe^{3+} ion in order to balance the charges. This compound is named iron(III) oxide.

$CuCl_2$ is a binary ionic compound. Copper forms two types of cations Cu^+ and Cu^{2+}, but because the anion is Cl^-, this must be the Cu^{2+} ion in order to balance the charges. This compound is named copper(II) chloride.

Solutions, Reactions, and Stoichiometry

Solubility

DILUTE AND CONCENTRATED

The terms **dilute** and **concentrated** have opposite meanings. In a solution, the **solute** is dissolved in the **solvent**. The more solute that is dissolved, the more concentrated is the solution. The less solute that is dissolved, the less concentrated and the more dilute is the solution. The terms are often associated with the preparation of a stock solution for a laboratory experiment. Stock solutions are typically ordered in a concentrated solution. To prepare for use in a chemistry lab, the stock solutions are diluted to the appropriate molarity by adding a specific amount of solvent such as water to a specific amount of stock solution.

SATURATED, UNSATURATED, AND SUPERSATURATED

The terms *saturated, unsaturated,* and *supersaturated* are associated with solutions. In a **solution**, a **solute** is added to a **solvent**. In a saturated solution, the solute is added to the solvent until no more solute is able to dissolve. The undissolved solute will settle down to the bottom of the beaker. A solution is considered unsaturated as long as more solute is able to go into solution under ordinary conditions. The solubility of solids in liquids typically increases as temperature increases. If the temperature of a solution is increased as the solute is being added, more solute than is normally possible may go into solution, forming a supersaturated solution.

MIXTURE, SOLUTION, AND COLLOID

A **mixture** is made of two or more substances that are combined in various proportions. The exact proportion of the constituents is the defining characteristic of any mixture. There are two types of mixtures: homogeneous and heterogeneous. **Homogeneous** means that the mixture's composition and properties are uniform throughout. Conversely, **heterogeneous** means that the mixture's composition and properties are not uniform throughout.

A **solution** is a homogeneous mixture of substances that cannot be separated by filtration or centrifugation. Solutions are made by dissolving one or more solutes into a solvent. For example, in an aqueous glucose solution, glucose is the solute and water is the solvent. If there is more than one liquid present in the solution, then the most prevalent liquid is considered the solvent. The exact mechanism of dissolving varies depending on the mixture, but the result is always individual solute ions or molecules surrounded by solvent molecules. The proportion of solute to solvent for a particular solution is its **concentration**.

A **colloid** is a heterogeneous mixture in which small particles (<1 micrometer) are suspended, but not dissolved, in a liquid. As such, they can be separated by centrifugation. A commonplace example of a colloid is milk.

> **Review Video: <u>Solutions</u>**
> Visit mometrix.com/academy and enter code: 995937

UNITS OF CONCENTRATION

Molarity, molality, and normality are all measures of the concentration of a solution, but they are measured in different ways. **Molarity** (abbreviated M) is a measurement of the number of atoms or molecules of solute by volume of the solution; it has units of moles per liter. **Molality** (abbreviated m) is a measurement of the number of atoms or molecules of solute by mass of the solution; it has units of moles per kilogram.

Normality (abbreviated N) is a measurement of concentration that is used for acids. It measures the number of H^+ ions—of donatable protons—per liter of solution. For monoprotic acids, which only donate one proton per molecule, the normality is equal to the molarity. For polyprotic atoms, which donate multiple protons per molecule, the normality is equal to the molarity times the number of protons potentially donated by each atom. For example, sulfuric acid, H_2SO_4, is diprotic; it can donate up to two protons per molecule. The normality of a sulfuric acid solution is therefore double its molarity.

CALCULATING MOLE FRACTION, PARTS PER MILLION, PARTS PER BILLION, AND PERCENT BY MASS OR VOLUME

Concentrations can be measured in mole fractions, parts per million, parts per billion, and percent by mass or volume. **Mole fraction** (χ) is calculated by dividing the number of moles of one component by the total number of moles of all of the components of the solution. **Parts per million** (ppm) is calculated by dividing the mass of the solute in grams by the mass of the solvent and solute in grams and then multiplying the quotient by 1,000,000 ppm. **Parts per billion** (ppb) is calculated similarly, except the quotient is multiplied by 1,000,000,000 ppb. **Percent concentration** can be calculated by mass or by volume by dividing the mass or volume of the solute by the mass or volume of the solution. This quotient is a decimal that can be converted to a percent by multiplying by 100.

CALCULATING THE MOLARITY OF 100.0 G OF CaCl₂ IN 500.0 ML OF SOLUTION.

To use the formula molarity, you can make the necessary conversions from grams $CaCl_2$ to moles $CaCl_2$ and from 500.0 mL to liters using dimensional analysis. An alternate method of working this problem would be doing the conversions first and then substituting those values directly into the equation. Using the method of dimensional analysis and substituting the given information into the equation yields molarity $= \frac{100.0 \text{ grams CaCl}_2}{500.0 \text{ mL of solution}}$. Adding the necessary conversions using dimensional analysis yields:

$$\text{molarity} = \left(\frac{100.0 \text{ g CaCl}_2}{500.0 \text{ mL of solution}}\right)\left(\frac{\text{mol CaCl}_2}{110.98 \text{ g}}\right)\left(\frac{1,000 \text{ mL}}{\text{L}}\right) = 1.802 \text{ M}$$

PREPARING A DILUTE SOLUTION FROM A STOCK SOLUTION

In order to prepare a **dilute solution** from a **stock solution**, the molarity and the needed volume of the diluted solution as well as the molarity of the stock solution must be known. The volume of the stock solution to be diluted can be calculated using the formula $V_{stock}M_{stock} = V_{dilute}M_{dilute}$, where V_{stock} is the unknown variable, M_{stock} is the molarity of the stock solution, V_{dilute} is the needed volume of the dilute solution, and M_{dilute} is the needed molarity of the dilute solution. Solving this formula for V_{stock} yields $V_{stock} = \frac{V_{dilute}M_{dilute}}{M_{stock}}$. Then, dilute the calculated amount of stock solution (V_{stock}) to the total volume required of the diluted solution.

SOLUBILITY PRODUCT CONSTANT

The solubility product constant, K_{sp}, is a constant that relates to the equilibrium conditions for the concentrations of ions in a slightly soluble ionic compound. It is a special case of the general equilibrium constant K_{eq}. For an arbitrary ionic compound $A_m C_n$ with anion A and cation C, the equilibrium condition is $K_{sp} = [A]^m [C]^n$. (The original compound $A_m C_n$ does not contribute to the equilibrium condition because of its solid state; the concentrations of solids and liquids do not change in a reaction, so they do not appear in the equilibrium equation.)

If an ion is present from sources other than the dissolved chemical, the solubility product constant can be used to find out how much of the other ion is present. For example, consider calcium fluoride; CaF_2. K_{sp} for calcium fluoride is 3.45×10^{-11}. If all the calcium and fluoride ions in a solution come from dissolved CaF_2, then there must be twice as many fluoride ions as calcium. Set the number of calcium ions to x and solve.

$$K_{sp} = (x)(2x)^2$$
$$K_{sp} = 4x^3$$
$$\sqrt[3]{\frac{K_{sp}}{4}} = x$$
$$\sqrt[3]{\frac{3.45 \times 10^{-11}}{4}} = x$$
$$2.05 \times 10^{-4} = x$$

This must also be the moles per liter of the calcium fluoride that it dissolved; multiplying by the molar mass of CaF_2 gives a solubility of 0.016 g/mol.

The mass percent of a solution is a ratio of the mass of the solute in a solution to the total mass of the solution. Molarity is a measurement of the moles of solute to the volume of the solution in moles per liter. You can convert mass percent to molarity by first dividing by the molar mass to convert the mass of solution to moles and then multiplying by the density of the solution to convert the mass of solute to liters. To convert molarity to mass percent, just do the reverse.

For example, suppose you have a 4.00 M solution of NaCl, with a density of 1150 kg/m^3. The molar mass of sodium chloride is 58.443 g/mol, so the mass percent of this solution is:

$$\frac{(4.00 \text{ mol/L})(0.058443 \text{ kg/mol})}{(1150 \text{ kg/m}^3)(0.001 \text{ m}^3/\text{L})} \times 100\% = 20.3\%$$

Parts per million, sometimes abbreviated ppm, is a unit that is sometimes used for very dilute solutions when the concentration expressed in traditional units like molarity or mass percent would be an inconveniently small number. It literally refers to the number of grams of solute per million grams of solution. One ppm is therefore equal to 0.0001% as a mass percent. For an aqueous solution, which if sufficiently dilute will have essentially the same density as water, 1 g/mL; 1 ppm = 1 mg/L.

For even more dilute solutions, other, similar units are sometimes used such as parts per billion (ppb), parts per trillion (ppt), and so on.

SOLUBILITY OF IONIC COMPOUNDS IN WATER

If an ionic compound is soluble in water, the cations and anions will separate from each other when combined with water. In general, the rule for solubility is "like dissolves like." However, some ionic compounds are not soluble in water because the forces joining the ions are stronger than the intermolecular forces between the ions and the water molecules.

Soluble Ionic Compounds		Important Exceptions
Compounds containing	NO_3^-	None
	$C_2H_3O_2^-$	None
	Cl^-	Compounds of Ag^+, Hg_2^{2+}, Pb^{2+}
	Br^-	Compounds of Ag^+, Hg_2^{2+}, Pb^{2+}
	I^-	Compounds of Ag^+, Hg_2^{2+}, Pb^{2+}
	SO_4^{2-}	Compounds of Sr^{2+}, Ba^{2+}, Hg_2^{2+}, Pb^{2+}

Insoluble Ionic Compounds		Important Exceptions
Compounds containing	S^{2-}	Compounds of NH_4^+, the alkali metal cations, and Ca^{2+}, Sr^{2+}, and Ba^{2+}
	CO_3^{2-}	Compounds of NH_4^+, the alkali metal cations
	PO_4^{3-}	Compounds of NH_4^+, the alkali metal cations
	OH^-	Compounds of the alkali metal cations, and Ca^{2+}, Sr^{2+}, and Ba^{2+}

COMMON-ION EFFECT

The common-ion effect refers to the fact that a slightly soluble ionic compound will become less soluble in a solution that contains one of the same ions as the compound. For example, calcium carbonate ($CaCO_3$) already has a low solubility in water, but in a solution of potassium carbonate (K_2CO_3), its solubility is even lower because the calcium carbonate and the potassium carbonate share the carbonate ion in common. The common ion effect follows from the solubility equilibrium condition that the product of the concentrations of the ions is constant. Therefore, an increase in the concentration of one ion must result in a decrease of the other; this is only possible if some ions combine to precipitate the solid compound. The effect is a special case of Le Châtelier's Principle.

The common-ion effect is useful in preparing laboratory separations because it can be used to precipitate out a desired compound from a solution by adding another compound that shares an ion with it. For instance, sodium chloride (NaCl) can be precipitated out of saltwater by the addition of hydrochloric acid (HCl).

COMPLEX ION FORMATION

A complex ion is an ion consisting of a metal ion surrounded by other molecules or ions referred to as ligands. Each ligand acts as a Lewis base, donating one or more pairs of electrons to the metal ion at the center. Common ligands include water, ammonia (NH_3), hydroxide (OH^-), cyanide (CN^-) and various halide ions (Cl^-, F^-, etc.) For instance, two ammonia molecules bonded to a central silver (I) ion would form the complex ion $[Ag(NH_3)_2]^+$. The nomenclature of complex atoms is itself somewhat complex, including prefixes for the number of each ligand, followed by prefixes for the ligands, ending with the name of the metal. $[Ag(NH_3)_2]^+$, for example, would be called diamminesilver (I).

Complex ions are formed one ligand at a time. The central metal ion uses its empty orbitals to accept a pair of electrons from a ligand, and then the resultant single-ligand complex ion accepts a pair of electrons from another ligand, and so on. The maximum number of ligands depends on how many of the molecules or ions in question will fit around the metal ion. Six water molecules can fit around most metal ions, for instance, but only four chloride ions.

The formation constant K_f relates to the equilibrium condition for complex ions. It is arrived at the same way as any other chemical equilibrium constant: with the concentration of the product in the numerator—in this case, the complex ion—and the product of the concentrations of the reactants in the denominator—in this case, the separate metal ion and ligands (aside from water). For instance, for the complex ion $[Cu(NH_3)_4(H_2O)_2]^{2+}$—called tetraamminediaquacopper—the equilibrium condition would be $K_f = \frac{[Cu(NH_3)_4(H_2O)_2]^{2+}}{[Cu^{2+}][NH_3]^4}$.

The formation constant can be used as a measure of the stability of the complex ion: the higher K_f, the more stable the complex ion. Like other equilibrium constants, the formation constant can be used to determine an unknown concentration if other concentrations are known.

COMPLEX IONS AND SOLUBILITY

The formation of complex ions in a solution will tend to increase the solubility of a solute that shares an ion with the complex ion—whether it is the central metal ion or an ionic ligand. This is a consequence of Le Châtelier's Principle—the formation of the complex ion decreases the concentration of the ion in question; this shifts the equilibrium toward the formation of the ion, causing more of the solute to dissolve.

One application of this principle is in photography; some photographic film contains the photosensitive chemical silver bromide (AgBr), which can dissociate in the presence of light to form elemental silver and bromine. After the photograph is taken, the extra silver bromide must be removed. Silver bromide has a very low solubility, but that solubility can be increased dramatically by the use of a sodium thiosulfate ($Na_2S_2O_3$) solution—the thiosulfate ions react with silver ions to form the stable complex ion $[Ag(S_2O_3)_2]^{3-}$ (dithiosulfatoargentate [I]), removing free Ag^+ ions from the solution and therefore causing more AgBr to dissolve.

SOLUBILITY AND pH

The pH of a solution will not affect the solubility of all chemicals. In particular, the solubility of neutral salts will generally not be affected by the pH of a solution. However, the solubility of acidic or basic salts will be pH dependent.

A basic salt—the salt of a weak acid—will have a greater solubility the lower the pH of the solution. This is because the H_3O^+ ions in the acidic solution will react easily with the relatively strong basic anions of the salt. By Le Châtelier's Principle, the removal of these ions from the solution will shift the equilibrium toward the production of more such ions, leading to more of the salt dissolving. For similar reasons, an acidic salt—the salt of a weak base—will have a greater solubility the higher the pH of the solution.

EFFECT OF TEMPERATURE AND PRESSURE ON SOLUBILITY

Temperature and pressure affect **solubility**. For gas solutes in liquid solvents, increasing the **temperature** increases the kinetic energy causing more gas particles to escape the surface of the liquid solvents and therefore decreasing the solubility of the solutes. For most solid solutes in liquid solvents, increasing the temperature increases the solubility, as shown in this solubility curve for selected salts. For gas solutes in liquid solvents, increasing the **pressure** increases the solubility.

Increasing the pressure of liquid or solid solutes in liquid solvents has virtually no effect under normal conditions.

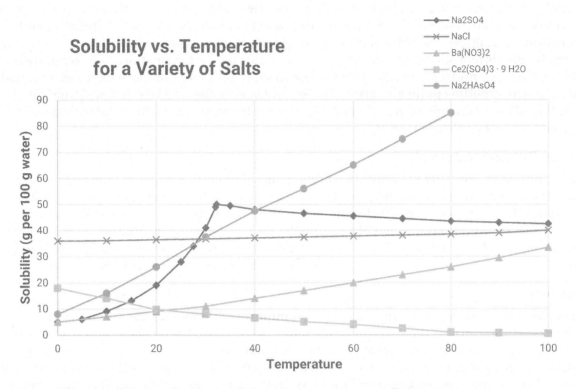

EFFECTS OF TEMPERATURE, SURFACE AREA, AGITATION, AND PRESSURE ON THE DISSOLUTION RATE

Temperature, pressure, surface area, and agitation affect the **dissolution rate**. Increasing the **temperature** increases the kinetic energy of the molecules, which increases the number of collisions with the solute particles. Increasing the **surface area** of contact by stirring (agitation) or crushing a solid solute also increases the dissolution rate and helps prevent recrystallization. Increasing the **pressure** will increase the dissolution rate for gas solutes in liquid solvents because the added pressure will make it more difficult for the gas to escape. Increasing the pressure will have virtually no effect on the dissolution rate for solid solutes in liquid solvents under normal conditions.

COLLIGATIVE PROPERTIES OF SOLUTIONS

FREEZING POINT DEPRESSION

Freezing point depression is a colligative property of solutions that depends only on the number of particles in solution, not on the identity of those particles. Adding a nonvolatile solute to a solution will lower the freezing point of that solution. This decrease in temperature is known as **freezing point depression.** Basically, the particles of the nonvolatile solute occupy spaces near the surface and block or inhibit the solvent particles from escaping from the surface of the solution. As fewer particles escape, the vapor pressure lowers. This decrease in vapor pressure causes a decrease in the freezing point known as freezing point depression. The amount of depression can be calculated from the equation $\Delta T_{FP} = mk_f$, where m is the molality of the solution and k_f is the molal freezing point constant for that particular solvent.

81

BOILING POINT ELEVATION

Boiling point elevation is a colligative property of solutions that depends only on the number of particles in solution, not on the identity of those particles. Adding a nonvolatile solute to a solution will raise the boiling point of that solution. This rise in temperature is known as **boiling point elevation**. Basically, the particles of the nonvolatile solute occupy spaces near the surface and block or inhibit the solvent particles from escaping from the surface of the solution. As fewer particles escape, the vapor pressure lowers. This decrease in vapor pressure causes an increase in the boiling point known as **boiling point elevation**. The amount of elevation can be calculated from the equation $\Delta T_{BP} = mk_b$, where m is the molality of the solution and k_b is the molal boiling point constant for that particular solvent.

VAPOR PRESSURE LOWERING

Vapor pressure lowering is a colligative property of solutions that depends only on the number of particles in solution, not on the identity of those particles. Adding a nonvolatile solute to a solution will lower the vapor pressure of that solution. Basically, the particles of the nonvolatile solute occupy spaces near the surface and block or inhibit the solvent particles from escaping from the surface of the solution. As fewer particles escape, the vapor pressure lowers. This decrease in vapor pressure causes an increase in the boiling point and a decrease in the freezing point.

OSMOSIS

Osmosis can be defined as diffusion through a **semipermeable membrane**. Typically, small solvent particles can pass through, but larger solute particles are too large to pass through. This means that osmosis is the net flow of solvent from a solution with a lower concentration to a solution with a higher concentration until a state of equilibrium is reached. The pressure that must be applied to the semipermeable membrane to stop the flow of solvent to reach this equilibrium state is called **osmotic pressure**. Osmotic pressure is a colligative property that depends on the number of nonvolatile solute particles, not the identity.

> **Review Video: Passive Transport: Diffusion and Osmosis**
> Visit mometrix.com/academy and enter code: 642038

Reactions and Stoichiometry

TYPES OF REACTIONS

One way to organize chemical reactions is to sort them into two categories: **oxidation/reduction reactions** (also called redox reactions) and **metathesis reactions** (which include acid/base reactions). Oxidation/reduction reactions can involve the transfer of one or more electrons, or they can occur as a result of the transfer of oxygen, hydrogen, or halogen atoms. The species that loses electrons is oxidized and is referred to as the reducing agent. The species that gains electrons is reduced and is referred to as the oxidizing agent. The element undergoing oxidation experiences an increase in its oxidation number, while the element undergoing reduction experiences a decrease in its oxidation number. **Single replacement reactions** are types of oxidation/reduction reactions. In a single replacement reaction, electrons are transferred from one chemical species to another. The transfer of electrons results in changes in the nature and charge of the species.

> **Review Video: Understanding Chemical Reactions**
> Visit mometrix.com/academy and enter code: 579876
>
> **Review Video: What is the Process of a Reaction?**
> Visit mometrix.com/academy and enter code: 808039

SINGLE SUBSTITUTION, DISPLACEMENT, AND REPLACEMENT REACTIONS

Single substitution, **displacement**, or **replacement reactions** are when one reactant is displaced by another to form the final product ($A + BC \rightarrow AB + C$). Single substitution reactions can be cationic or anionic. When a piece of copper (Cu) is placed into a solution of silver nitrate ($AgNO_3$), the solution turns blue. The copper appears to be replaced with a silvery-white material. The equation is $2AgNO_3 + Cu \rightarrow Cu(NO_3)_2 + 2Ag$. When this reaction takes place, the copper dissolves and the silver in the silver nitrate solution precipitates (becomes a solid), resulting in copper nitrate and silver. Copper and silver have switched places in the nitrate.

Double displacement, **double replacement**, **substitution**, **metathesis**, or **ion exchange reactions** are when ions or bonds are exchanged by two compounds to form different compounds ($AC + BD \rightarrow AD + BC$). An example of this is that silver nitrate and sodium chloride form two different products (silver chloride and sodium nitrate) when they react. The formula for this reaction is $AgNO_3 + NaCl \rightarrow AgCl + NaNO_3$.

> **Review Video: Single-Replacement Reactions**
> Visit mometrix.com/academy and enter code: 442975

COMBINATION AND DECOMPOSITION REACTIONS

Combination, or **synthesis**, **reactions**: In a combination reaction, two or more reactants combine to form a single product ($A + B \rightarrow AB$). These reactions are also called synthesis or **addition reactions**. An example is burning hydrogen in air to produce water. The equation is $2H_2(g) + O_2(g) \rightarrow 2H_2O(l)$. Another example is when water and sulfur trioxide react to form sulfuric acid. The equation is $H_2O + SO_3 \rightarrow H_2SO_4$.

Decomposition (or desynthesis, decombination, or deconstruction) reactions: In a decomposition reaction, a reactant is broken down into two or more products ($AB \rightarrow A + B$). These reactions are also called analysis reactions. **Thermal decomposition** is caused by heat. **Electrolytic**

83

decomposition is due to electricity. An example of this type of reaction is the decomposition of water into hydrogen and oxygen gas. The equation is $2H_2O \rightarrow 2H_2 + O_2$.

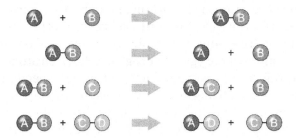

ACID/BASE REACTIONS

In **acid/base reactions**, an **acid** is a compound that can donate a proton, while a **base** is a compound that can accept a proton. In these types of reactions, the acid and base react to form a salt and water. When the proton is donated, the base becomes water and the remaining ions form a salt. One method of determining whether a reaction is an oxidation/reduction or a metathesis reaction is that the oxidation number of atoms does not change during a metathesis reaction.

ISOMERIZATION AND NEUTRALIZATION REACTIONS

Isomerization, or **rearrangement**, is the process of forming a compound's isomer. Within a compound, bonds are reformed. The reactant and product have the same molecular formula, but different structural formulas and different properties (A → B or A → A'). For example, butane (C_4H_{10}) is a hydrocarbon consisting of four carbon atoms in a straight chain. Heating it to 100° C or higher in the presence of a catalyst forms isobutane (methylpropane), which has a branched-chain structure. Boiling and freezing points are greatly different for butane and isobutane. A rearrangement reaction occurs within the molecule.

A **neutralization**, **acid-base**, or **proton transfer reaction** is when one compound acquires H^+ from another. These types of reactions are also usually double displacement reactions. The acid has an H^+ that is transferred to the base and neutralized to form a salt.

STOICHIOMETRY

Stoichiometry studies the quantities of substances in chemical reactions. In any chemical reaction, the conservation of mass is always obeyed; therefore, the chemical reactions are always balanced. Below is the combustion reaction of propane (C_3H_8), a very common fuel:

$$C_3H_8(g) + 5\,O_2(g) \rightarrow 3\,CO_2(g) + 4\,H_2O(g)$$

The same types of atoms (C, H, and O) in the **reactants** (propane and oxygen) and **products** (carbon dioxide and water) are equal in quantity. The numbers before each reactant and product that balances the quantity of atoms are called **coefficients**. The quantities of reactants and products are dealt with using **moles**; to convert mass into moles, divide it by the substance's molar mass:

$$moles = \frac{mass\ (g)}{molar\ mass\ (g/mol)}$$

In this sample reaction, 1 mole of propane needs 5 moles of O_2 to completely combust into 3 moles of CO_2 and 4 moles of water. For a 14.0 oz (400.0 g) cylinder of propane, there are $\frac{400.0\ g}{44.1\ g/mol} =$

84

9.070 mol of propane. In theory, it will produce 9.070 mol $\times 3 \times 44.01$ g/mol $= 1197$ g of CO_2 and 9.070 mol $\times 4 \times 18.01$ g/mol $= 653.4$ g of water. Since the propane is fully consumed in this reaction, it is called the **limiting reactant**. Often, we may consider that the quantity of O_2 in the surrounding environment to be in excess. Therefore, the O_2 can be referred to as the **excess reactant** in this case.

MOLECULAR WEIGHT

The molecular weight of a compound, also called molecular mass, is the mass of a single molecule of the compound, generally given in atomic mass units. It can be determined using the periodic table by looking up the atomic weight of each atom in the compound and adding them together. For example, sodium sulfate has the chemical formula Na_2SO_4: it contains two sodium atoms, one sulfur atom, and four oxygen atoms. The atomic weights of sodium, sulfur, and oxygen are 22.990 u, 32.065 u, and 15.999 u, respectively. The molecular weight of sodium sulfate is therefore each of these weights times the number of each atom present in the molecule.

$$2(22.990 \text{ u}) + 32.065 \text{ u} + 4(15.999 \text{ u}) = 142.04 \text{ u}$$

EMPIRICAL VERSUS MOLECULAR FORMULA

The **molecular formula** of a compound consists of the symbols for the elements in the compound, with a subscript indicating the number of atoms of that element if that number is greater than one. Water contains two hydrogen atoms and one oxygen atom, so its molecular formula is H_2O. Hydrogen peroxide contains two hydrogen atoms and two oxygen atoms, so its molecular formula is H_2O_2. Glucose molecules contains six carbon atoms; twelve hydrogen atoms; and six oxygen, so its formula is $C_6H_{12}O_6$.

The **empirical formula**, on the other hand, only gives the ratios of elements in the compound. If the numbers of atoms of each element have no common divisor, then the empirical and molecular formula are the same: thus, the empirical formula for water is still H_2O. Otherwise, the subscripts are reduced by their common divisor: the empirical formula for hydrogen peroxide is HO, and for glucose is CH_2O. Two compounds may have the same empirical formula but different molecular formulas: the molecular formula for ethylene is C_2H_4, propylene is C_3H_6, and butylene is C_4H_8, but all would have the same empirical formula of CH_2.

DESCRIPTION OF COMPOSITION BY PERCENT MASS

The percent mass of an element in a compound is the ratio of the mass of the element in question to the total mass of the compound, expressed as a percentage. For example, in water, H_2O, the mass of the hydrogen in each molecule is $2(1.008 \text{ u}) = 2.016$ u; the mass of the oxygen is 15.999 u; the total mass of the molecule is 2.016 u + 15.999 u = 18.015 u. The percent mass of hydrogen in the molecule is then 2.016 u ÷ 18.015 u = 0.1112 or 11.12%, and the percent mass of the oxygen is 15.999 u ÷ 18.015 u = 0.8881 or 88.81%. The chemical composition of water can therefore be said to be 11.12% hydrogen and 88.81% oxygen by mass.

The percent mass of the elements in a compound and the empirical formula are related—if the percent mass of each element is known, the empirical formula can be determined by dividing the percent mass of each element by the atomic mass of that element and finding the ratios of the results. The full molecular formula, however, cannot be found from the percent masses without more information.

AVOGADRO'S NUMBER

Avogadro's Number, abbreviated N_A, is the number of atoms or molecules in one mole of a substance. It is a constant equal to about 6.022×10^{23} mol^{-1}. Avogadro's Number is named after Italian physicist Lorenzo Romano Amedeo Carlo Avogadro, remembered for his contributions to molecular theory.

Avogadro's Number forms the basis of the definition of the mole, and it was not chosen arbitrarily. The number was originally defined as equal to the number of atoms in 1 gram of hydrogen and was later redefined as the number of atoms in 12 grams of carbon-12. As such, in addition to the number of atoms or molecules in a mole, Avogadro's Number is also the number of atomic mass units in 1 gram. Avogadro's Number is therefore useful in converting between microscopic and macroscopic units, including converting between moles and molecules or grams and atomic mass units.

OXIDATION NUMBER

The oxidation number of an atom in a compound is a measurement of its effective charge within the molecule. Essentially, the oxidation number is the number of electrons that have been removed from or (for a negative oxidation number) added to the atom in question. The more electronegative atom in a compound generally has a lower oxidation state.

The oxidation state of a monatomic ion is the charge of the ion; the oxidation state of a neutral pure element is zero (even if the element forms polyatomic molecules, such as H_2 or S_8). Some elements have consistent oxidation states: the oxidation state of alkali metals in compounds is always +1 and of alkaline earths always +2. Hydrogen usually has an oxidation state of +1, halogens of –1, and oxygen of –2, although there are exceptions.

The oxidation states of the atoms in a neutral molecule must add to zero and in a polyatomic ion must add to the charge of the ion. This often makes it possible to solve for the oxidation states of elements where the oxidation states are not consistent by plugging in the oxidation states of atoms that are known and solving for the unknowns.

Hydrogen atoms in a compound usually have an oxidation number of –1. However, this is not the case when the hydrogen is bonded to a metal (which has a lower electronegativity), such as in sodium hydride, NaH, or lithium aluminum hydride, $LiAlH_4$.

Oxygen atoms in a compound usually have an oxidation number of –2. However, there are two important exceptions. In the peroxide ion, O_2^{2-}, the ion as a whole has an oxidation number of –2, so each atom in the ion has an oxidation number of –1. This still holds when the ion is part of a compound, as in hydrogen peroxide, H_2O_2. The other exception is when the oxygen is bonded to fluorine. Fluorine is even more electronegative than oxygen, so in this case the fluorine will get a negative oxidation number, and the oxygen's oxidation number will be positive. In a molecule of oxygen difluoride, OF_2, the oxidation number of the oxygen atom is +2.

COMMON OXIDIZING AND REDUCING AGENTS

An oxidizing agent is an element or compound that takes electrons from another substance, causing it to be oxidized. A reducing agent is an element or compound that donates electrons to another compound, causing it to be reduced. Note that in an oxidation-reduction reaction, the oxidizing agent is itself reduced, whereas the reducing agent is oxidized.

Common oxidizing agents include oxygen, chlorine and other halogens, hydrogen peroxide, and sulfuric acid. Common reducing agents include hydrogen gas, sodium and other alkali metals, iron, and carbon monoxide.

DISPROPORTIONATION OF REACTION BY CHEMICAL EQUATIONS

A disproportionation reaction is a redox reaction in which the same chemical species is both oxidized and reduced: that is, some of the molecules of the compound are reduced, whereas others are oxidized. One well-known example of a disproportionation reaction is the decomposition of hydrogen peroxide: $2 H_2O_2 \rightarrow 2 H_2O + O_2$. Note that in the reactant, H_2O_2, the oxygen atoms have an oxidation number of –1. In the product H_2O, the oxygen atoms have an oxidation number of –2, meaning these atoms have been reduced. But in the other product, O_2, the oxygen atoms have an oxidation number of 0, meaning these atoms have been oxidized.

Other examples of disproportionation reactions are the disproportionation of copper(I) ions in solution, $2 Cu^+(aq) \rightarrow Cu(s) + Cu^{2+}(aq)$ (the oxidation number of the copper goes from +1 on the left to 0 and +2 on the right); the disproportionation of carbon monoxide, $2 CO \rightarrow C + CO_2$ (the oxidation number of the carbon goes from +2 to 0 and +4); and the disproportionation of mercury chloride, $Hg_2Cl_2 \rightarrow Hg + HgCl_2$ (the oxidation number of the mercury goes from +1 to 0 and +2).

CONVENTIONS FOR WRITING A CHEMICAL EQUATIONS

When writing a chemical equation, the reactants—the elements and compounds initially present before the reaction—go on the left, separated by plus signs, and the products—the elements and compounds produced in the reaction—go on the right, likewise separated. An arrow points from the reactants to the products. The relative number of particles of each reactant and product is shown by a number preceding them, such that the reaction is balanced—each element is represented in equal numbers on the left and right. Optionally, a parenthetical after each species can be written for its state: (s) for solid, (l) for liquid, (g) for gas, and (aq) for aqueous (in solution with water).

For example, take the reaction of sulfuric acid (H_2SO_4) with sodium hydroxide (NaOH) in solution to form water (H_2O) and sodium hydroxide (Na_2SO_4). The first two are the reactants, and the last two the products, so we would write $H_2SO_4 + NaOH \rightarrow H_2O + Na_2SO_4$. This, however, is not balanced; there are, for instance, three hydrogen atoms on the left but only two on the right. The full balanced equation, with states, would be $H_2SO_4(aq) + 2 NaOH(aq) \rightarrow 2 H_2O(l) + Na_2SO_4(aq)$.

BALANCING EQUATIONS

Balancing a chemical equation means putting the correct coefficient on each species in the reaction so that the total number of atoms of each element is the same on both sides of the equation. For complex equations, this may involve some trial and error, but there are some steps that make it easier. It is generally simplest to balance one element at a time and to start by balancing the elements that appear in the fewest species. One may end up with fractional coefficients; if this is the case, one can simply multiply all the coefficients by the lowest common denominator.

For instance, take the reaction $NH_3 + O_2 \rightarrow NO + H_2O$. H only appears in one compound on each side, so we can start there: $2 NH_3 + O_2 \rightarrow NO + 3 H_2O$. N, likewise, only appears in one compound on each side and can be balanced by writing 2 in front of NO. That leaves the oxygen. There are now five oxygen atoms on the right, so we need $\frac{5}{2}$ in front of the O_2 on the left. We can multiply all the coefficients by 2 to remove the fraction, giving finally $4 NH_3 + 5 O_2 \rightarrow 4 NO + 6 H_2O$.

REDOX EQUATIONS

Redox equation is short for **reduction-oxidation equation**, a chemical equation for a reaction involving the reduction of one element or compound and the oxidation of another. When balancing a redox equation, not just the number of atoms of each element on each side must match, but the total oxidation number of all the atoms must match on the left or right as well. Generally, this is done by separating the reaction into half-reactions for oxidation and reduction—adding electrons to the reactions as necessary—and then combining the two reactions such that the electrons cancel.

For instance, take the simple redox reaction $Fe^{3+} + Sn^{2+} \rightarrow Fe^{2+} + Sn^{4+}$. The number of atoms of each element on each side matches, but the oxidation numbers do not: we have a total of +5 on the left and +6 on the right. We first write the separate half-reactions $Fe^{3+} + e^- \rightarrow Fe^{2+}$ and $Sn^{2+} \rightarrow 2\,e^- + Sn^{4+}$. For the electrons to cancel when we combine the half-reactions, the first half-reaction must be multiplied by two. Our final balanced equation is then $2\,Fe^{3+} + Sn^{2+} \rightarrow 2\,Fe^{2+} + Sn^{4+}$, with a matching total oxidation number of +8 on each side.

> **Review Video: Oxidation-Reduction Reactions**
> Visit mometrix.com/academy and enter code: 317289

LIMITING REACTANTS

The limiting reactant is the reactant that determines how much of the product will be produced—essentially, it is the reactant that runs out first when the reaction takes place. The other reactants that remain after the limiting reactant has been expended are called excess reactants. One way to determine which reactant is the limiting reactant, given the quantities of each reactant, is to calculate how much of one of the products could be formed from each reactant (assuming that sufficient quantities of the other reactants are available). Whichever reactant yields the smallest amount of product is the limiting reactant.

For instance, consider the reaction $Si + 2\,NaOH + H_2O \rightarrow Na_2SiO_3 + 2\,H_2$. We have 20 grams of Si, 30 grams of NaOH, and 10 grams of H_2O. Dividing by the respective molecular masses, this means that we have 0.712 moles of Si, 0.750 moles of NaOH, and 0.555 moles of water. These would each be sufficient to produce, respectively, 0.712 moles, 0.375 moles, and 0.555 moles of Na_2SiO_3. Note that 0.375 moles, the amount produced by the NaOH, is smallest, so NaOH is the limiting reactant.

THEORETICAL YIELDS

The theoretical yield of a chemical product is the amount that would be produced if the maximum amount of the reactants reacted—that is, if all of the limiting reactant participated. The theoretical yield can be determined by identifying the limiting reactant and determining how much of the product it would produce based on the ratios of the coefficients in the chemical equation. For example, consider the reaction $Fe_2O_3 + 3\,C \rightarrow 3\,CO + 2\,Fe$, and suppose that we know that the limiting reactant is carbon, of which we have 500 grams; we want to determine the theoretical yield of iron. Five hundred grams of carbon is 41.6 moles; because there are two atoms of elemental iron produced for every three atoms of elemental carbon that reacts, this would produce $\frac{2}{3}(41.6\ \text{mol}) =$ 27.8 mol of iron, or 1.55 kg.

The experimental yield is the amount of product that is actually produced in a reaction and empirically measured. It is possible that not all the limiting reactant participates in the reaction—because other reactions occur or because the system reaches an equilibrium state. Therefore, the experimental yield may be (and generally is) less than the theoretical yield but never greater.

GRAVIMETRIC ANALYSIS

Gravimetric analysis is a commonly used method for analyzing the composition of a sample by measuring the mass of the products of interest. The products are usually obtained through separation processes or certain reactions.

- **Filtration** is where the sample is usually suspended in a solvent, then filtered through a porous pad, and the insoluble solid is collected as the **filtrate**. The remaining liquid is called the **mother liquor**; when needed, the solvent in the mother liquor can be removed by evaporation to obtain the species that was dissolved. After the solids are separated and recovered, the mass of each species can then be determined by weighing each of them on an analytical balance. In some cases, **precipitations reactions** are needed to allow certain components to precipitate chemically and get separated from the rest of the mother liquor.
- **Ignition** is also a commonly used technique in gravimetric reaction. It requires heating the sample to a high temperature until chemically converted to another known final product through a **combustion** or **decomposition** reaction. By determining the mass of the known final product, the mass of the original sample can be calculated through the **stoichiometry** of the known chemical reactions.

The precipitation reactions are useful methods for separating two or more substances with similar solubilities. By chemically converting one or more substances and changing the solubility of the resulting product(s), it becomes possible to separate the substances by their states. For example, we need to determine the iron element content in a 0.50 g sample of $FeCl_3$ (Iron(III) chloride) contaminated with NaCl. Since both are soluble in water, we may use this precipitation to separate the two, by add enough NaOH (sodium hydroxide) solution: $FeCl_3(aq) + 3\ NaOH(aq) \rightarrow Fe(OH)_3(s) + 3\ NaCl(aq)$. Although NaCl is produced in this reaction, we are interested in the iron content only. The reaction mixture is filtered and $Fe(OH)_3$ precipitate is collected as the filtrate (it is washed thoroughly with water to remove any NaCl residue, and thoroughly dried). In the end, 0.42 g of $Fe(OH)_3$ is collected. The mass of iron (by element) in the original sample is then:

$$\frac{0.42\ g}{106.87\ g/mol} \times 55.8\ g/mol = 0.22\ g$$

The mass percentage of iron in the sample is:

$$\frac{0.22\ g}{0.50\ g} \times 100\% = 44\%$$

If needed, the $FeCl_3$ can be recovered by adding HCl (hydrochloric acid) to $Fe(OH)_3$, following by removing the solvent water then thoroughly dried:

$$Fe(OH)_3(s) + 3\ HCl(aq) \rightarrow FeCl_3(aq) + 3\ H_2O(l)$$

PRECIPITATION REACTIONS

Precipitation reactions form insoluble products, called **precipitates**, by mixing two or more aqueous solutions. The **solubility** of a substance in a specific solvent determines how much of the substance can be dissolved into a given amount of the solvent. Generally, if a substance has a solubility of less than 0.01 mol/L, it is considered **insoluble**. Below are general solubility rules for common ionic compounds in water:

- Ionic compounds which are *soluble* in water:
  - Compounds with NO_3^- (nitrate), HCO_3^- (bicarbonate), and CH_3COO^- (acetate)

89

- o Compounds with halide ions (Cl^-, Br^-, and I^-), except those that contain Ag^+, Hg_2^{2+}, and Pb^{2+}
- o Compounds with SO_4^{2-} (sulfate), except those that contain Sr^{2+}, Ba^{2+}, Hg_2^{2+}, and Pb^{2+}
- o Compounds with alkali metal ions (Li^+, Na^+, K^+, Rb^+, and Cs^+) and NH_4^+ (ammonium ion)
- Ionic compounds which are *insoluble* in water:
  - o Compounds with PO_4^{3-} (phosphate) and CO_3^{2-} (carbonate), except those that also contain alkali metal ions and NH_4^+
  - o Compounds with S^{2-} (sulfide) and OH^- (hydroxide), except those that also contain alkali metal ions, some alkaline earth metal ions (Ca^{2+}, Sr^{2+}, Ba^{2+}), and NH_4^+

The most common type of precipitation reaction is the **metathesis (or double exchange) reaction**. In this type of reaction, the reactants exchange the ionic species that compose them in aqueous solutions:

$$AB + CD \rightarrow AD + CB$$

If one of the products AD or CB is insoluble in water, it will precipitate out from the solution. If both AD and CB are soluble, the precipitation reaction will not occur. It is the best to carefully check for the solubility of both the proposed product with the provided solubility rule to determine whether precipitations will form. For example, the reaction between KCl (potassium chloride) and $AgNO_3$ (silver nitrate) solution is:

$$KCl(aq) + AgNO_3(aq) \rightarrow KNO_3(aq) + AgCl(s)$$

One of the formed products, AgCl (silver chloride) is insoluble in water, which is consistent with the provided solubility rule. Therefore, there is a reaction between these two reactants. However, when mixing KCl and $NaNO_3$ (sodium nitrate) solution, the proposed reaction should be:

$$KCl(aq) + NaNO_3(aq) \rightarrow KNO_3(aq) + NaCl(aq)$$

Since both proposed products, KNO_3 and NaCl, are still soluble, no precipitation reaction will occur.

MOLECULAR, TOTAL, AND NET IONIC EQUATIONS

If a balanced chemical equation is written out with all the reactants and products in their complete molecular formula, it is called a **molecular equation**. Strong electrolytes completely dissociate in the solution in the ionic form; a written equation with strong electrolytes in reactants and products written in the complete dissociated form is called a **total (or complete) ionic equation**. However, not all the ionic species in the solution will participate in the chemical reaction. A written equation including only the active ions that participate in the reaction is a **net ionic equation**. The ions that did not take part in the reaction are referred to as **spectator ions**. For example, consider the chemical reaction between $Pb(NO_3)_2$ (lead nitrate) and Na_2SO_4 (sodium sulfate) in aqueous solution.

The molecular equation is:

$$Pb(NO_3)_2(aq) + Na_2SO_4(aq) \rightarrow PbSO_4(s) + 2\,NaNO_3(aq)$$

The total ionic equation is:

$$Pb^{2+}(aq) + 2\,NO_3^-(aq) + 2\,Na^+(aq) + SO_4^{2-}(aq) \rightarrow PbSO_4(s) + 2\,Na^+(aq) + 2\,NO_3^-(aq)$$

The NO_3^- and Na^+ did not take part in the reaction. The net ionic equation is then:

$$Pb^{2+}(aq) + SO_4^{2-}(aq) \rightarrow PbSO_4(s)$$

When writing a chemical reaction, first check to make sure there is actually a reaction occurring. This is usually indicated by forming a precipitation, gas, or a weak electrolyte. Then the written equation must be balanced; both the quantity of each element and total charges in the reactants and products should be equal. Next, the states of the reactants and products (whether they are gas, aqueous, liquid, or solid) should be indicated. If writing ionic equations, check and see if the reactants and substances are written in the correct dissociated form. Note that only strong electrolytes that are also soluble need to be written in the dissociated ionic form. Weak electrolytes such as water and acetic acid (CH_3COOH), as well as solid precipitations and gases, should remain in their molecular form, even in ionic equations. Lastly, for net ionic equations, make sure that no spectator ions are included. Consider the following molecular equation:

$$NiCl_2(aq) + 2\,AgNO_3(aq) \rightarrow 2\,AgCl(s) + Ni(NO_3)_2(aq)$$

The complete ionic equation for this is:

$$Ni^{2+}(aq) + 2\,Cl^-(aq) + 2\,Ag^+(aq) + 2\,NO_3^-(aq) \rightarrow 2\,AgCl(s) + Ni^{2+}(aq) + 2\,NO_3^-(aq)$$

The net ionic equation is:

$$Cl^-(aq) + Ag^+(aq) \rightarrow AgCl(s)$$

SOLUBILITY OF SOLIDS AND GASES, PARTICULARLY IN AQUEOUS SOLUTIONS

Temperature plays an important role in affecting the solubility of the gases and solids in aqueous solutions. In general, solid solutes will increase in solubility in water when temperature increases. For example, by increasing temperature from 20 °C to 50 °C, KNO_3 (potassium nitrate) will increase its solubility in water by about 3 times. There are very few exceptions such as $Ce_2(SO_4)_3$ (cerous sulfate), where solubility decreases as temperature increases. For gaseous solutes, solubility in water will decrease as temperature increases. When gently heating water, small gas bubbles will form on the side of the container as the solubility of air in water starts to decrease with heat. Pressure also affects the solubility of gaseous solutes. In fact, the solubility of the gas is directly proportional to the partial pressure of that gas above the solution. By increasing the pressure above the solvent, the solubility of the gas increases.

Example Problems

Given the following equation at standard temperature and pressure (STP): $4Fe(s) + 3O_2(g) \rightarrow 2Fe_2O_3(s)$, determine the volume of $O_2(g)$ needed to produce 10.0 mol of $Fe_2O_3(s)$.

One method to determine the volume of $O_2(g)$ needed to produce 10.0 mol of $Fe_2O_3(s)$ is to use dimensional analysis with the mole ratio for the balanced chemical equation. Because 3 mol of $O_2(g)$ produce 2 mol of $Fe_2O_3(s)$, the needed mole ratio is $\left(\frac{3 \text{ mol } O_2}{2 \text{ mol } Fe_2O_3}\right)$. Also, at STP, one mole of a gas has a volume of 22.4 L. This can be written as a conversion factor of $\left(\frac{22.4 \text{ L}}{1 \text{ mol } O_2}\right)$. Using dimensional analysis:

$$(10.0 \text{ mol } Fe_2O_3)\left(\frac{3 \text{ mol } O_2}{2 \text{ mol } Fe_2O_3}\right)\left(\frac{22.4 \text{ L}}{1 \text{ mol } O_2}\right) = 336 \text{ L}$$

Given the following equation at STP: $C_3H_8(l) + 5O_2(g) \rightarrow 3CO_2(g) + 4H_2O(g)$, determine the volume of $O_2(g)$ needed to burn 1.00 kg of $C_3H_8(l)$.

One method to determine the volume of $O_2(g)$ needed to burn 1.0 kg of $C_3H_8(l)$ is to use dimensional analysis with conversion factors for the molar mass, number of moles, and liters of gas at STP. The conversion factor for the molar mass of C_3H_8 can be written as $\left(\frac{1 \text{ mol } C_3H_8}{44.1 \text{ grams } C_3H_8}\right)$. Because 1 mol of $C_3H_8(l)$ requires 5 mol of $O_2(g)$, the needed mole ratio is $\left(\frac{5 \text{ mol } O_2}{1 \text{ mol } C_3H_8}\right)$.

Also, at STP, one mole of a gas has a volume of 22.4 L. This can be written as the conversion factor $\left(\frac{22.4 \text{ L}}{1 \text{ mol } O_2}\right)$. Using dimensional analysis:

$$(1.0 \text{ kg } C_3H_8)\left(\frac{1000 \text{ g}}{1 \text{ kg}}\right)\left(\frac{1 \text{ mol } C_3H_8}{44.1 \text{ g } C_3H_8}\right)\left(\frac{5 \text{ mol } O_2}{1 \text{ mol } C_3H_8}\right)\left(\frac{22.4 \text{ L } O_2}{1 \text{ mol } O_2}\right) = 2.54 \times 10^3 \text{ L } O_2$$

Given the following equation: $2Na(s) + Cl_2(g) \rightarrow 2NaCl(s)$, determine the amount in grams of $Na(s)$ needed to produce 500.0 g of $NaCl(s)$.

One method to determine the amount in grams of $Na(s)$ needed to produce 500.0 g of $NaCl(s)$ is to use dimensional analysis with conversion factors for the molar mass and number of moles. The conversion factor for the molar mass of NaCl can be written as $\left(\frac{1 \text{ mol } NaCl}{58.44 \text{ g } NaCl}\right)$. Because 2 mol of $Na(s)$ produce 2 mol of $NaCl(s)$, the needed mole ratio is $\left(\frac{2 \text{ mol } Na}{2 \text{ mol } NaCl}\right)$. The conversion factor for the molar mass of $Na(s)$ can be written as $\left(\frac{22.99 \text{ g } Na}{1 \text{ mol } Na}\right)$. Using dimensional analysis:

$$(500.0 \text{ g } NaCl)\left(\frac{1 \text{ mol } NaCl}{58.44 \text{ g } NaCl}\right)\left(\frac{2 \text{ mol } Na}{2 \text{ mol } NaCl}\right)\left(\frac{22.99 \text{ g } Na}{1 \text{ mol } Na}\right) = 196.7 \text{ g } Na(s)$$

Given the following equation at STP: $2Na(s) + Cl_2(g) \rightarrow 2NaCl(s)$, determine the volume of $Cl_2(g)$ needed to produce 1.00 kg of $NaCl(s)$.

One method to determine the volume of $Cl_2(g)$ needed to produce 1.00 kg of $NaCl(s)$ is to use dimensional analysis with conversion factors for the molar mass, number of moles, and liters of gas at STP. The conversion factor for the molar mass of NaCl can be written as $\left(\frac{1 \text{ mol } NaCl}{58.44 \text{ g } NaCl}\right)$. Because 1 mol of $Cl_2(g)$ produces 2 mol of NaCl(s), the needed mole ratio is $\left(\frac{1 \text{ mol } Cl_2}{2 \text{ mol NaCl}}\right)$. Also, at STP, one mole of a gas has a volume of 22.4 L. This can be written as a conversion factor $\left(\frac{22.4 \text{ L}}{1 \text{ mol } Cl_2}\right)$. Using dimensional analysis:

$$(1.00 \text{ kg NaCl})\left(\frac{1000 \text{ g}}{1 \text{ kg}}\right)\left(\frac{1 \text{ mol NaCl}}{58.44 \text{ g NaCl}}\right)\left(\frac{1 \text{ mol } Cl_2}{2 \text{ mol NaCl}}\right)\left(\frac{22.4 \text{ L } O_2}{1 \text{ mol } O_2}\right) = 191.65 \text{ L } Cl_2$$

This rounds up to 192 L because 191 L will not be enough.

Given that 100.0 g of $H_2(g)$ react with 350.0 g of $O_2(g)$, determine the limiting reactant and the amount of excess reactant that remains $2H_2(g) + O_2(g) \rightarrow 2H_2O(g)$.

To determine the limiting reactant, first determine the amount of H_2O that can be produced from each of the reactants:

$$(100.0 \text{ g } H_2)\left(\frac{1 \text{ mol } H_2}{2.016 \text{ g } H_2}\right)\left(\frac{2 \text{ mol } H_2O}{2 \text{ mol } H_2}\right)\left(\frac{18.016 \text{ g } H_2O}{1 \text{ mol } H_2O}\right) = 893.7 \text{ g } H_2O$$

$$(350.0 \text{ g } O_2)\left(\frac{1 \text{ mol } O_2}{32.00 \text{ g } O_2}\right)\left(\frac{2 \text{ mol } H_2O}{1 \text{ mol } O_2}\right)\left(\frac{18.016 \text{ g } H_2O}{1 \text{ mol } H_2O}\right) = 394.1 \text{ g } H_2O$$

Because O_2 produces the least amount of H_2O, O_2 is the limiting reagent. Therefore, H_2 is the reactant that is in excess. Calculating the amount of H_2 consumed in this reaction:

$$(350.0 \text{ g } O_2)\left(\frac{1 \text{ mol } O_2}{32.00 \text{ g } O_2}\right)\left(\frac{2 \text{ mol } H_2}{1 \text{ mol } O_2}\right)\left(\frac{2.016 \text{ g } H_2}{1 \text{ mol } H_2}\right) = 44.10 \text{ g } H_2 \ (consumed)$$

Subtracting this amount from the original amount yields the excess amount

$$100.0 \text{ g } H_2 - 44.10 \text{ g } H_2 = 55.91 \text{ g } H_2 \ (excess)$$

Find the percent yield in the following reaction if 200.0 g of solid $KClO_3$ produced 100.0 g of solid KCl: $2KClO_3(s) \rightarrow 2KCl(s) + 3O_2(g)$.

To calculate the percent yield if 200.0 g of solid $KClO_3$ produced 100.0 g of solid KCl, first calculate the theoretical yield of KCl or the maximum amount of KCl that can be produced.

Theoretical yield:

$$(200.0 \text{ g } KClO_3)\left(\frac{1 \text{ mol } KClO_3}{122.6 \text{ g } KClO_3}\right)\left(\frac{2 \text{ mol } KCl}{2 \text{ mol } KClO_3}\right)\left(\frac{74.55 \text{ g } KCl}{1 \text{ mol } KCl}\right) = 121.6 \text{ g } KCl$$

The formula to calculate percent yield is $\frac{\text{actual yield}}{\text{theoretical yield}} \times 100\%$. Substituting in the 100.0 g of KCl for the actual yield and the 121.6 g of KCl for the theoretical yield:

$$\frac{100.0 \text{ g}}{121.6 \text{ g}} \times 100\% = 82.24\%$$

Review Video: How to Calculate Percent Yield
Visit mometrix.com/academy and enter code: 565738

Write a balanced equation for the combustion of methane.

The molecular formula for methane is CH_4. For a combustion equation, the reactants are methane (CH_4) and oxygen gas (O_2). The products of this combustion reaction are water vapor (H_2O) and carbon dioxide (CO_2). Setting up the equation yields the following reaction:

$$CH_4(g) + O_2(g) \rightarrow CO_2(g) + H_2O(g)$$

This equation must still be balanced. Finally, the combustion of methane is given by the following reaction:

$$CH_4(g) + 2O_2(g) \rightarrow CO_2(g) + 2H_2O(g)$$

Review Video: Combustion
Visit mometrix.com/academy and enter code: 592219

Write a balanced equation for the neutralization of hydrochloric acid, HCl(aq), with sodium hydroxide, NaOH(aq).

In a neutralization reaction, an acid reacts with a base to form a salt and water. The salt forms from the cation of the base and the anion of the acid. The salt formed from these reactants is NaCl with the Na^+ from the base and the Cl^- from the acid. Water forms from the remaining H^+ and OH^- ions:

$$acid + base \rightarrow salt + water$$
$$HCl(aq) + NaOH(aq) \rightarrow NaCl(aq) + H_2O(l)$$

Write a balanced equation for the decomposition reaction of solid lithium carbonate (Li_2CO_3).

The general form for a decomposition reaction is $AB \rightarrow A + B$. However, this metal oxide has three elements and may at first not seem to fit the general form. When many metal carbonates are heated, they form the metal oxide and carbon dioxide gas. In this case, the products will also be compounds. In this decomposition reaction, when heated, solid lithium oxide decomposes to form solid lithium oxide and gaseous carbon dioxide:

$$Li_2CO_3(s) \overset{\Delta}{\rightarrow} LiO(s) + CO_2(g)$$

Write a balanced equation for the dehydration of ethanol.

Ethanol (C_2H_5OH) can be dehydrated to produce ethene (C_2H_4). The gaseous ethanol is passed over a hot aluminum oxide catalyst to produce ethene and water.

$$ethanol \xrightarrow{\text{aluminum oxide}} ethene + water$$

$$C_2H_5OH(g) \xrightarrow{Al_2O_3} C_2H_4(g) + H_2O(l)$$

This can also be shown in the form of condensed structural formulas:

$$CH_3CH_2OH \xrightarrow{Al_2O_3} H_2C = CH_2 + H_2O$$

Calculate the solubility of AgBr if the solubility product constant, K_{sp}, for AgBr is 4.9×10^{-13} at 25 °C.

The dissociation reaction for AgBr can be written as $AgBr(s) \leftrightarrow Ag^+(aq) + Br^-(aq)$. Because the dissociation of AgBr produces equal moles of Ag^+ and Br^- ions, the solubility is simply the concentration of the Ag^+ ions, $[Ag^+]$, or the concentration of the Br^- ions, $[Br^-]$. The solubility product constant for this reaction is given by $K_{sp} = [Ag^+][Br^-]$, but because $[Ag^+] = [Br^-]$, this can be written as $K_{sp} = [Ag^+]^2$. Substituting in the given value for K_{sp} yields $4.9 \times 10^{-13} = [Ag^+]^2$. Therefore, $[Ag^+] = 7.0 \times 10^{-7}$ M. Finally, the solubility of AgBr is 7.0×10^{-7} M.

Balance the following chemical equation involving an oxidation-reduction reaction:

$$Na + O_2 \rightarrow Na^+ + O^{2-}$$

In order to balance the equation $Na + O_2 \rightarrow Na^+ + O^{2-}$, first, write the individual half-reactions:

$$\text{oxidation: } Na \rightarrow Na^+ + e^-$$

$$\text{reduction: } O_2 + 4e^- \rightarrow 2O^{2-}$$

Next, balance the number of electrons by multiplying the oxidation half-reaction by 4:

$$\text{oxidation: } 4Na \rightarrow 4Na^+ + 4e^-$$

$$\text{reduction: } O_2 + 4e^- \rightarrow 2O^{2-}$$

Finally, cancel the electrons and combine the half-reactions into the net reaction:

$$4Na + O_2 \rightarrow 4Na^+ + 2O^{2-}$$

Write a balanced equation for the oxidation-reduction reaction of metallic zinc powder and aqueous copper(II) sulfate.

According to the activity series, zinc is more reactive than copper. Therefore, the zinc is oxidized, and the copper is reduced. Write the half-reactions:

$$\text{oxidation: } Zn \rightarrow Zn^{2+} + 2e^-$$

$$\text{reduction: } Cu^{2+} + 2e^- \rightarrow Cu$$

Cancel the electrons and combine the two half-reactions into the net equation:

$$Zn + Cu^{2+} \rightarrow Zn^{2+} + Cu$$

Finally, add the symbols to indicate the state of each reactant and product:

$$Zn(s) + Cu^{2+}(aq) \rightarrow Zn^{2+}(aq) + Cu(s)$$

Interestingly, this equation can also be written as the following single-displacement reaction:

$$Zn(s) + CuSO_4(aq) \rightarrow ZnSO_4(aq) + Cu(s)$$

This single-displacement reaction has the same net ionic equation after canceling out the spectator ions.

Write a balanced equation for the oxidation-reduction reaction of a piece of solid copper wire immersed in an aqueous solution of silver nitrate.

According to the activity series, copper is more reactive than silver. Therefore, the copper is oxidized, and the silver is reduced. Write the half-reactions:

$$\text{oxidation: } Cu \rightarrow Cu^{2+} + 2e^-$$

$$\text{reduction: } Ag^+ + e^- \rightarrow Ag$$

Multiply the reduction half-reaction by 2 to balance the number of electrons:

$$\text{oxidation: } Cu \rightarrow Cu^{2+} + 2e^-$$

$$\text{reduction: } 2Ag^+ + 2e^- \rightarrow 2Ag$$

Cancel the electrons and combine the two half-reactions into the net equation:

$$Cu + 2Ag^+ \rightarrow Cu^{2+} + 2Ag$$

Finally, add the symbols to indicate the state of each reactant and product:

$$Cu(s) + 2Ag^+(aq) \rightarrow Cu^{2+}(aq) + 2Ag(s)$$

Note that this equation is also classified as a single-displacement reaction:

$$Cu(s) + 2AgNO_3(aq) \rightarrow Cu(NO_3)_2(aq) + 2Ag(s)$$

This single-displacement reaction has the same net ionic equation after canceling out the spectator ions.

Kinetics and Equilibrium

Kinetics

REACTION RATE

The reaction rate of a chemical reaction is a measurement of what quantity of the reactants reacts per unit time. It is typically measured in units of $mol/(L \cdot s)$ so that a reaction rate, r, means that in each liter of the substance r moles of the reactants react each second.

For chemicals to react, their molecules must come into contact. Therefore, increasing the concentration of the reactants will increase the reaction rate—the higher the concentration of the reactants, the more likely it is for molecules of the reactants to meet each other. Temperature affects reaction rate for similar reasons; the higher the temperature, the faster the molecules are moving, and the more frequently molecules of the reactants will collide. For solid reactants, the shape of the solid may also affect things; the larger the surface area, the more molecules of the reactant are exposed and available to contact the other reactants. (This is why finely ground flour is highly flammable, and even aluminum dust may be flammable if the particles are small enough.) In general, however, reactants in the liquid or gas phases have higher reaction rates than solids. Furthermore, the reaction rate of a chemical reaction can be increased by the presence of a catalyst, another compound that facilitates the reaction without itself being consumed.

DEPENDENCE OF REACTION RATE UPON TEMPERATURE
ACTIVATION ENERGY

The activation energy of a chemical reaction is the minimum energy required for the reaction to proceed. Even if the total energy of the reactants is less than the total energy of the products, it takes some energy to break bonds in the reactants so that they can form new bonds and make the products; there is some initial energy needed to start, even if the compounds end up getting that energy back when the products are formed. Of course, the higher the temperature of the compound, the more kinetic energy its molecules have that can be used to overcome the activation energy, which is part of the reason that the reaction rate increases with temperature.

The activation energy is usually given not as the energy needed for one molecule of each reactant to react (or a number of molecules each to the stoichiometric coefficient of the compound in the balanced equation), but for a mole of the molecule (or a number of moles equal to the stoichiometric coefficient). The units of the activation energy are therefore equal to joules per mole or, more often, kilojoules per mole.

ACTIVATION ENERGY: ACTIVATED COMPLEX OR TRANSITION STATE

In a chemical reaction, the compounds do not change instantaneously from the reactants to the products but pass through a range of intermediate steps. These intermediate forms may have higher energies than either the initial reactants or the final products, which is why some activation energy is necessary to form them, and they may only exist for very brief periods of time before returning to a lower-energy state, either re-forming the reactants or becoming the products of the chemical reaction. These high-energy intermediate steps are known as activated complexes.

Of all the intermediate forms, there is one that has the highest energy. This form, which the molecules may pass through only briefly as they change from the reactants into the products, is

97

known as the transition state. It is this form that determines the activation energy of the reaction—it is the difference in energy between the transition state and the initial state of the molecules.

ACTIVATION ENERGY: INTERPRETATION OF ENERGY PROFILES

An energy profile is a representation of the energy that a chemical system goes through during a chemical reaction. The y-axis of the energy profile is the energy of the system (in any appropriate units, but because it is the shape of the energy profile that's important, the units are often omitted); the x-axis is the reaction coordinate, measuring progress of the reaction. (The x-axis is not given in concrete units such as time or concentration of reactants because the reactants may react at different rates, and the rate depends on concentration and other factors.) Usually, an energy profile shows the energy increasing gradually from its initial value to a maximum and then falling back to a lower energy again; multistep reactions may also show some local minima.

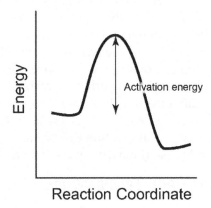

Several useful pieces of data can be drawn from the energy profile. Whether the final energy is higher or lower than the initial shows whether the reaction is endothermic or exothermic. The activation energy can be found as the difference between the maximum energy and the initial energy.

ARRHENIUS EQUATION

The Arrhenius equation is an equation showing the relationship between the reaction rate and the temperature. It is named after the Swedish scientist Svante August Arrhenius, who is credited as one of the founders of physical chemistry (and who also formulated the Arrhenius definition of acids and basis). The equation takes the form $k = Ae^{-\frac{E_a}{RT}}$, where A is a constant (which may be different for every reaction), E_a is the activation energy of the reaction, R is the ideal gas constant $(8.314 \text{ J}/(\text{mol} \cdot \text{K}))$, and T is the temperature in Kelvin.

Although it is not hard to see conceptually why the reaction rate increases with temperature, the Arrhenius equation quantifies the relationship and allows the calculation of the reaction rate at different temperatures as long as the relevant constants are known. The constant A, called the pre-exponential constant, is dependent on the frequency of collisions between molecules as well as their geometry but in practice is determined experimentally.

CATALYSTS

A catalyst is a compound that lowers the activation energy of a reaction and thus facilitates that reaction taking place without itself being expended in the reaction—it is said to catalyze the reaction. This may be because the catalyst does react in one step of a multistep reaction, but is then produced in another step, so that the total amount of the catalyst is unchanged. The highest activation energy of any step of the reaction involving the catalyst is smaller than the activation energy of the reaction without the catalyst, so the reaction can proceed at a greater rate.

For example, iron reacts with oxygen to form iron oxide (rust). However, the activation energy is high enough that this does not spontaneously occur at a noticeable rate when iron is exposed to oxygen. It does occur, however, in the presence of water because water acts as a catalyst to this reaction, lowering the activation energy. Important examples of catalysts in biological systems are enzymes, which ensure that metabolic processes occur at a high enough rate to sustain life.

> **Review Video: Catalysts**
> Visit mometrix.com/academy and enter code: 288189

KINETIC CONTROL VS. THERMODYNAMIC CONTROL OF A REACTION

In many cases, there is more than one set of products that could in principle be formed in a chemical reaction by a given set of reactants. Which products are formed depends on the rates of the related reactions as well as on the products' stability. A product produced by the reaction with the higher reaction rate (and generally the lower activation energy) is called a kinetic product. A product that is more stable (has the lower energy in its final form) is called a thermodynamic product.

Which products actually are formed in a given case, then, depends on which controlling factor becomes more important. At sufficiently low temperatures, there is not enough energy for the reaction forming the kinetic product to reverse despite its relative instability, so as this product has a faster reaction rate, it predominates, and the reaction is said to be under kinetic control. At higher temperatures, when the reaction forming the kinetic product can reverse, this limits the amount of those products that forms, and the thermodynamic product predominates; the reaction is said to be under thermodynamic control.

DEPENDENCE OF REACTION RATE ON CONCENTRATION OF REACTANTS

The **rate law** of a chemical reaction is an equation relating the reaction rate of a chemical reaction to the concentrations of its reactants. It generally (but not always) takes the form of a power law in which the reaction rate is equal to a reaction rate constant k times the product of the concentrations of the reactants, each raised to some exponent. These exponents are called the reaction orders of the associated reactants. That is, if a chemical reaction has reactants $R_1, R_2, R_3, ...,$ then its rate law is $r = k [R_1]^{x_1} [R_2]^{x_2} [R_3]^{x_3} ...,$ where x_n is the reaction order of the reactant R_n.

For example, for the reaction $2 NO + O_2 \rightarrow 2 NO_2$, the rate law is equal to $r = k[NO]^2[O_2]$, where k is about $7,100 \ L^2/(mol^2 \cdot s)$. (Note that whereas the reaction orders happen to be the same as the stoichiometric coefficients for this particular equation, this is not necessarily the case in general!) This means that if the concentration of NO is 0.02 mol/L and the concentration of O_2 is 0.1 mol/L, the reaction rate will be $r = (7100 \ L^2/(mol^2 \cdot s))(0.02 \ mol/L)^2(0.1 \ mol/L) = 0.284 \ mol/(L \cdot s)$.

The **reaction order** of a reactant in a chemical reaction is the exponent to which the concentration of that reactant is raised in the rate equation for the chemical reaction. For instance, the reaction $BrO_3^- + 5 Br^- + 6 H^+ \rightarrow 3 Br_2 + 3 H_2O$ has the rate law $r = k[BrO_3^-][Br^-][H^+]^2$—the reaction order of BrO_3^- and Br^- is 1, and the reaction order of Br_2 is 2. The overall reaction order of the equation is the sum of the individual reaction orders; for this equation, it would be $1 + 1 + 2 = 4$.

As shown in this example, unlike the exponents in a chemical equilibrium equation, the reaction orders of the reactants are not related to their coefficients in a balanced chemical equation. Rather, the reaction orders of the reactants must be determined experimentally. There is no straightforward way to figure out the reaction orders of the reactants just from the chemical equation.

There are some reactions with more complicated reaction laws and in which the reaction orders are not well defined. This may be because the presence of the product slows the reaction; for instance, the reaction $2 O_3 \rightarrow 3 O_2$ has rate law $r = k\frac{[O_3]^2}{[O_2]^3}$.

The **rate constant** of a chemical reaction is the proportionality factor between the reaction rate and the product of the concentrations of the reactants raised to the powers of their reaction orders. That is, it is the constant k in the rate law equation $r = k[R_1]^{x_1}[R_2]^{x_2}[R_3]^{x_3}$ .... Like the reaction orders, the rate constant must be determined experimentally. In practice, the rate constant of a reaction is not really a universal constant but depends on the temperature; rate constants are frequently given at a reference temperature of 298 K.

The units of k are chosen so that the reaction rate r has the appropriate units, usually mol/(L · s). This means the units of k are $L^{\Sigma x-1}/(mol^{\Sigma x-1} \cdot s)$, where Σx is the reaction order of the reaction, which is equal to the sum of the reaction orders of all the reactants. For instance, the reaction $2 ClO_2 + 2 OH^- \rightarrow ClO_3^- + ClO_2^- + H_2O$ has the rate law $r = k[ClO_2]^2[OH^-]$; the reaction order is $1 + 2 = 3$, and the rate constant must have units of $L^2/(mol^2 \cdot s)$.

DETERMINING A RATE LAW FROM PLOTS OF DATA

The graphical method for determining **integrated rate laws** uses plots of observed data that directly relate the time and reactant concentration. The integrated rate laws based on reaction orders are listed below:

- For zero order reactions, $[A]_t = [A]_0 - kt$, where $[A]_t$ is the concentration of a reactant at time t, $[A]_0$ is the initial concentration of the same reactant, and k is the rate constant. The plot of reactant concentration $[A]_t$ over time will be linear if a reaction is in zero order. The slope of the line is $-k$, and the y-intercept is the initial concentration $[A]_0$.
- For first order reactions, $\ln[A]_t = -kt + \ln[A]_0$. The plot of $\ln[A]_t$ over time will be linear if a reaction is in first order. The slope of the line is $-k$, and the y-intercept is $\ln[A]_0$.
- For second order reactions, $\frac{1}{[A]_t} = kt + \frac{1}{[A]_0}$. The plot of $\frac{1}{[A]_t}$ over time will be linear if a reaction is in second order. The slope of the line is $+k$, and the y-intercept is $\frac{1}{[A]_0}$.

METHOD OF INITIAL RATES

The rate laws need to be determined experimentally, as the stoichiometry of one chemical reaction is not directly related to the actual rate law. By varying the initial concentrations of reactants, any changes in the reaction rate are observed to determine the reaction order. For a typical reaction $A + B \rightarrow C + D$, a set of experiments are carried out:

Experiment	$[A]$ (M)	$[B]$ (M)	Initial Rate (M/s)
1	x	y	R_1
2	$2x$	y	R_2
3	x	$2y$	R_3

If changing the concentration of a reactant has no effect on the reaction rate, the reaction is zero order in that reactant. If doubling the concentration doubles the initial rate, the reaction is first order in that reactant. If the initial rate is increased to $2^2 = 4$ times after doubling the

100

concentration, the reaction is second order in that reactant. The rate law for a given reaction has the generic formula of: $k[A]^x[B]^y$. The reaction orders x and y can be obtained by comparing the change of initial concentration to the rate. After x and y are determined, they can be substituted into the rate law formula with any given set of concentrations and rate, and the resulting equation can be solved for the rate constant, k.

USING INTEGRATED RATE LAWS

The integrated rate law can be used to determine the reaction rate order with the graphical method, as previously demonstrated. The graphical method requires a set of data points (concentration vs. time); but if the reaction order, the initial concentration $[A]_0$, and the concentration $[A]_t$ at another time t are provided, the equilibrium constant k can be found using one of the following formulas:

- In zero-order reactions, $[A]_t = [A]_0 - kt$, so $k = \frac{[A]_0 - [A]_t}{t}$
- In first order reactions, $\ln[A]_t = -kt + \ln[A]_0$, so $k = \frac{\ln[A]_0 - \ln[A]_t}{t}$
- In second order reactions, $\frac{1}{[A]_t} = kt + \frac{1}{[A]_0}$, so $k = \frac{1/[A]_t - 1/[A]_0}{t}$

After the value of the equilibrium constant, k, is obtained, the concentration at any other time point can be solved by substituting k, t, and $[A]_0$ back into the original integrated rate law determined by the reaction order $[A]_t$.

To solve for the rate constant, the initial concentration $[A]_0$, the concentration $[A]_t$ at another time, and the time t need to be provided. Use the reaction $NO_2(g) + CO(g) \rightarrow CO_2(g) + NO(g)$ as an example. The reaction is a second order reaction that only depends on the concentration of NO_2 at lower temperature. The rate law for this reaction is rate $= k \times [NO_2]^2$. It is also known that the initial concentration, $[NO_2]_0$, is 0.0156 M, and at 60 second, the concentration of NO_2 is 5.96×10^{-3} M.

For second order reactions, the integrated rate law is $\frac{1}{[A]_t} = kt + \frac{1}{[A]_o}$. So,

$$k = \frac{1/[A]_t - 1/[A]_0}{t} = \frac{1/(0.00596 \text{ M}) - 1/(0.0156 \text{ M})}{60 \text{ s}} = 1.72 \text{ M}^{-1}\text{s}^{-1}$$

Now that both k and $[A]_0$ are known, we can solve for concentrations of NO_2 at any other point in time.

For instance, at 45 seconds:

$$\frac{1}{[A]_t} = (1.72 \text{ M}^{-1}\text{s}^{-1}) \times (45 \text{ s}) + \frac{1}{0.0156 \text{ M}}$$

$$\frac{1}{[A]_t} = 141.5 \text{ M}^{-1}$$

$$[A]_t = \frac{1}{141.5 \text{ M}^{-1}} = 7.06 \times 10^{-3} \text{ M}$$

REACTION HALF-LIFE

The **half-life** $(t_{1/2})$ for a reaction measures the amount of time that is needed for the reactant to decrease to one-half of its initial concentration. The half-life indicates how fast a reaction occurs. A longer half-life means that the reaction takes a longer time to consume half of the reactant, indicating a slower reaction. Shorter half-life, on the other hand, suggests that the reaction occurs more quickly. The equations for half-life regarding reaction order are derived from the integrated rate law.

- For zero-order reactions: $t_{1/2} = \frac{[A]_0}{2k}$, where the $[A]_0$ is the initial concentration of the same reactant, k is the rate constant, and t is reaction time.
- For first order reactions: $t_{1/2} = \frac{0.693}{k}$. The half-life for a first order reaction is independent of its initial concentration. If the reactant needs time interval T to decrease its concentration by half, the time interval for it to decrease by half again is also T. The cumulative series where the concentration of the reactant decreases by half takes time intervals of equal length.
- For second order reactions: $t_{1/2} = \frac{1}{k[A]_0}$.

COLLISON THEORY AND REACTION ENERGY DIAGRAMS

Collision theory models the occurrence of a chemical reaction as the result of collisions between molecules. Illustrated in the figure below, the hypothetical reaction $A + BCD_3 \rightleftharpoons AB + CD_3$ takes place after A collides with ABD_3. After the collision, the $B - C$ bond breaks, and a new bond $A - B$ forms, yielding the products AB and CD_3. Increasing the numbers of molecules (i.e., increasing the concentrations) can increase their chances of collisions.

| Before | Collision | After |

Not all collisions lead to actual chemical reactions. For reactions to occur, the molecules need to collide at the preferred orientation that is specific to the reaction. If, in the above reaction, the molecule A collides with BCD_3 at another angle (shown below), the $B - C$ bond does not break and the collision is ineffective. The new bond cannot be formed, and no products are yielded. The colliding molecules should also possess enough kinetic energy to overcome the energy barrier of bond cleavage. If not, the molecules only bounce off with each other without participating in the reaction.

| Before | Collision | After |

For reactions to occur, molecules must contain sufficient kinetic energy to produce effective collisions that lead to chemical reactions. When temperature increases, molecules move faster and their average kinetic energy becomes greater. The kinetic energy of the molecules follows the **Maxwell-Boltzmann distribution**. Illustrated in the figure below, each curve represents the molecular kinetic energy distribution at a certain temperature. The peak on each curve represents the *most probable speed*. With increasing temperature, a larger and larger fraction of molecules possess more than the minimum energy that is required to initiate effective collisions. Denoted as E_a, this minimum energy is called the **activation energy**, or **transition state**.

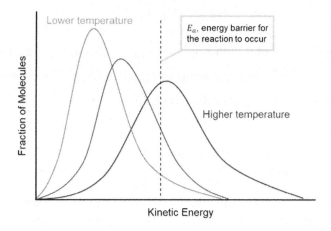

Maxwell–Boltzmann Distributions

The reaction energy profile for a hypothetical reaction $A + BCD_3 \rightleftharpoons AB + CD_3$ is shown on the figure below. When the collisions between the A and BCD_3 molecules occur, an intermediate $ABCD_3$ forms which sits at a much higher energy level. The energy barrier to form this intermediate is E_a. After the cleavage of $B - C$ bond and formation of the new bond $A - B$, the energy level drops to yield the final products. The energy difference between the products and reactants is the energy change of the reaction, ΔE. In this case, the products have lower potential energy than the reactants. Thus the sign of ΔE is negative for the forward reaction.

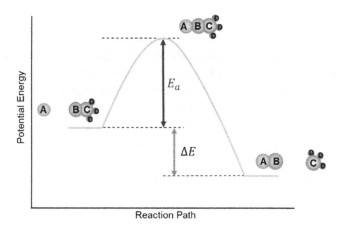

Reaction Energy Profile

CALCULATION OF ACTIVATION ENERGY FOR A REACTION

As temperature increases, a larger number of molecules possess enough kinetic energy for effective collision, which increases the equilibrium constant (k) for the reaction as a return. The activation energy (E_a) and k are related by the **Arrhenius Equation**, in non-linear relation:

$$k = Ae^{-E_a/RT}$$

The A is the **frequency factor** for effective collisions and is dependent on the temperature. R is the gas constant, and T is the absolute temperature in Kelvin. The natural log on both sides of this equation is taken:

$$\ln k = -\left(\frac{E_a}{R}\right)\frac{1}{T} + \ln A$$

Treating $\ln k$ as y and $\frac{1}{T}$ as x, the plot of $\ln k$ against $\frac{1}{T}$ generates a linear graph of the form $y = mx + b$, where the slope (m) is $-\left(\frac{E_a}{R}\right)$. Thus, the value of E_a is found by multiplying the slope by ($-R$). The y-intercept (b) of the line is $\ln A$, therefore A is equal to e^b.

REACTION MECHANISMS

Reaction mechanisms are a way of investigating how a chemical reaction occurs in detail. A balanced chemical equation describes the overall process of the reaction, but the true reaction happens step by step. These steps include breaking bonds, forming new bonds, or changing the position of the atoms. Each of these small steps are referred to as an **elementary reaction** or **process**. By adding elementary reactions together, they should yield an overall reaction that is equivalent to the balanced final equation. Some species are produced in one of the elementary steps, then are completely consumed in a later step. They do not appear on the final overall reaction; they are called the **intermediates**. The rate laws for elementary reactions are directly related to their molecularity.

- For a *unimolecular* elementary reaction, $A \rightarrow products$, its rate law is $k[A]$.
- For a *bimolecular* elementary reaction, $A + B \rightarrow products$, its rate law is $k[A][B]$.

Note that this direct relation between molecularity and rate law only applies to elementary reactions. The rate law of any overall chemical equation cannot be determined directly from their stoichiometry.

In most cases, chemical reactions occur in two or more elementary steps. Each of these steps or reactions has its own rate constant that usually differs from the others. One of the steps oftentimes takes place in a much slower manner than the others, and the slowest step then limits the rate for the entire reaction process. Therefore, this slowest step is the **rate-determining step**. For example, the reaction below occurs in two elementary steps:

$$O_3(g) + NO_2(g) \xrightarrow{k_1} NO_3(g) + O_2(g) \qquad (slow)$$

$$NO_3(g) + NO_2(g) \xrightarrow{k_2} N_2O_5(g) \qquad (fast)$$

$$O_3(g) + 2\,NO_2(g) \xrightarrow{k} N_2O_5(g) + O_2(g) \qquad (overall)$$

Note that the NO_3 that is generated in the first step gets consumed in the second step—it is the intermediate. Since the first step takes place much more slowly than the second step, the equilibrium constant k_2 is much greater than k_1. Therefore, the first step is the rate-determining step that determines the overall reaction rate: $k[O_3][NO_2]$.

In a two-step reaction with a relatively fast initial step, the overall rate law is determined by the second elemental reaction. However, as the second elemental reaction oftentimes involve the intermediates, it is very difficult to find the intermediates' concentrations. The rate law for the overall reaction then needs to be derived into an alternate form that does not include the intermediate. In the two-step reaction below:

$$H_2(g) + IBr(g) \underset{k_{-1}}{\overset{k_1}{\longleftrightarrow}} HI(g) + HBr(g) \qquad (fast)$$

$$HI(g) + IBr(g) \overset{k_2}{\longrightarrow} I_2(g) + HBr(g) \qquad (slow)$$

$$H_2(g) + 2\,IBr(g) \overset{k}{\longrightarrow} I_2(g) + 2\,HBr(g) \qquad (overall)$$

Since the second step is rate determining, the rate law is $k_2[HI][IBr]$. HI is the intermediate and its concentration is hard to measure. We can solve for it using the measurable concentrations of the reactant and final products. In the first step, the forward and reverse reaction have the same rates:

$$k_1[H_2][IBr] = k_{-1}[HI][HBr]$$

Solving for [HI], we get:

$$[HI] = \frac{k_1[H_2][IBr]}{k_{-1}[HBr]}$$

Then substitute this expression into the rate law:

$$rate = k_2[IBr][HI] = k_2[IBr] \times \frac{k_1[H_2][IBr]}{k_{-1}[HBr]}$$

The final expression for the rate law is:

$$rate = \left(\frac{k_1 k_2}{k_{-1}}\right)\frac{[H_2][IBr]}{[HBr]} = k\frac{[H_2][IBr]}{[HBr]}$$

Equilibrium

EQUILIBRIUM CONSTANT

The equilibrium expression is the constant K_{eq} that appears in the equilibrium expression $K_{eq} = \frac{[P_1]^{p_1}[P_2]^{p_2}\dots}{[R_1]^{r_1}[R_2]^{r_2}\dots}$, where $R_1, R_2, \dots$ are the reactants, $P_1, P_2, \dots$ the products, and r_n and p_n their respective stoichiometric coefficients. (Only gases and chemicals in solution are included in this equation; solid and liquid reactants and products are omitted.) A very large equilibrium constant implies that the products will predominate at equilibrium; a very small constant implies that the reactants will predominate.

The equilibrium constant can be used to determine an unknown concentration of a compound. For example, consider the reversible reaction $3\,H_2 + N_2 \rightleftharpoons 2\,NH_3$, which has an equilibrium constant at room temperature of 3.3×10^8, and suppose we know that at equilibrium the concentration of H_2 is 0.0050 M and of N_2 is 0.020 M. The equilibrium expression would be $K_{eq} = \frac{[NH_3]^2}{[H_2]^3[N_2]}$. This means we can find the concentration of NH_3 by solving for it in this equation:

$$[NH_3] = \left(K_{eq}[H_2]^3[N_2]\right)^{\frac{1}{2}}$$
$$= \left([3.3 \times 10^8][0.0050]^3[0.020]\right)^{\frac{1}{2}}$$
$$= 2.9\,M$$

Note that the concentration of the product (NH_3) is much larger than the concentrations of the reactants (H_2 and N_2); this is expected because $K_{eq} \gg 1$.

K_p AND K_c

For a typical reaction at equilibrium, where the forward and reverse reactions occur at the same rate, the law of mass action expresses the relations between the reactant and product concentrations:

$$a\,A + b\,B \rightleftharpoons c\,C + d\,D, \qquad K_c = \frac{[C]^c[D]^d}{[A]^a[B]^b}$$

The coefficients are $a, b, c,$ and d. A and B are reactants, while C and D are products. The equilibrium constant for concentrations, K_{eq} or K_c, is the value after substituting the equilibrium concentrations of the reactants and products into its equilibrium expression. For gaseous reactions, the equilibrium constant can also be expressed using the partial pressures of the reactants and products, denoted as K_p:

$$K_p = \frac{[P_C]^c[P_D]^d}{[P_A]^a[P_B]^b}$$

The relationship between K_p and K_c is $K_p = K_c(RT)^{\Delta n}$, where Δn is the change in the number of moles between reactants and products. In this example, $\Delta n = (c + d) - (a + b)$.

The numerical values of equilibrium constants indicate whether the reaction favors the reactants or products when the reaction reaches the equilibrium. If $K \gg 1$, it means that the forward reaction is favored, and more products are present at equilibrium. If $K \ll 1$, on the other hand, the reverse reaction is favored, and more reactants are present at equilibrium.

The concentrations of all products and reactants at equilibrium are related by their equilibrium constant expression. With given initial concentrations, it is possible to solve for the concentrations of the products through this correlation. For example, in the reaction between H_2 and I_2: $H_2(g) + I_2(g) \rightleftharpoons 2\,HI(g)$, we are given that the equilibrium constant K_c is 51 at 450 °C, and the reaction occurs in a 2.00 L vessel with 2.20 moles of H_2 and 4.60 moles of I_2 Therefore, the initial concentration for H_2 is: $\frac{2.20\ mol}{2.00\ L} = 1.10$ M, while the initial concentration of I_2 is: $\frac{4.60\ mol}{2.00\ L} = 2.30$ M. We may assume that at the equilibrium, x moles of H_2 are consumed. Based on the reaction stoichiometry, we also know that x moles of I_2 and $2x$ moles of HI are produced. The initial and changing concentrations are be listed in the table below:

	$H_2(g)$	$I_2(g)$	$2\,HI(g)$
Initial	1.10 M	2.30 M	0.000 M
Change	$(-x)$ M	$(-x)$ M	$(+2x)$ M
Equilibrium	$(1.10 - x)$ M	$(2.30 - x)$ M	$(2x)$ M

The equilibrium constant can be written as $K_c = \frac{[HI]^2}{[H_2][I_2]} = \frac{(2x)^2}{(1.10-x)(2.30-x)} = 51$. Expand this equation into the quadratic form, $4x^2 = 51(x^2 - 3.40x + 2.53)$, then rearrange and clear it into $47x^2 - 173.4x + 129.0 = 0$. The x can be solved using the quadratic equation with two possible values, 2.66 and 1.03. Since 2.66 exceeds the initial concentration for H_2, x should be 1.03 M. Plug this value into the relations above, the concentrations at equilibrium are: $[H_2] = (1.10 - 1.03)$ M = 0.07 M, $[I_2] = (2.30 - 1.03)$ M = 1.27 M, and $[HI] = (2 \times 1.03)$ M = 2.06 M.

APPLICATION OF LE CHÂTELIER'S PRINCIPLE

Le Châtelier's Principle states that a change in some property of a system in equilibrium will produce a shift in the equilibrium that counteracts the change. For example, if the concentration of one of the reactants is increased, the reaction will tend to proceed toward the right, using up some of the reactants and forming more of the product. A decrease in the concentration of a reactant (or an increase in the concentration of a product) will have the opposite effect. Increasing the pressure on a system of gases in equilibrium will shift the equilibrium toward the side of the reaction with fewer molecules. Increasing the temperature will shift the equilibrium toward the products, if the forward reaction is endothermic, or the reactants, if it is exothermic.

It is possible to take advantage of this principle to move a system's equilibrium in a desired direction. For instance, one step in the production of sulfuric acid involves the reversible reaction $2\,SO_2 + O_2 \rightleftharpoons 2\,SO_3$. This reaction can be made to proceed in the forward direction more efficiently by increasing the pressure or by adding oxygen. The reaction is also exothermic in the forward direction, so it works best at lower temperatures.

> **Review Video: Le Châtelier's Principle**
> Visit mometrix.com/academy and enter code: 360187

RELATIONSHIP OF THE EQUILIBRIUM CONSTANT AND ΔG°

The larger the equilibrium constant K_{eq} of a chemical reaction, the more the products will predominate, and the more the reaction will tend to proceed toward the right. The smaller K_{eq}, the more the reactants will predominate, and the more the reaction will tend to proceed toward the left. On the other hand, the reaction will tend to proceed in the direction that decreases the Gibbs free energy, so the larger the change in the free energy, ΔG, the more the equation will proceed toward the left, and the smaller ΔG, the more it will proceed toward the right. This suggests that the change in the Gibbs free energy and the equilibrium constant have an inverse relationship.

It is not, however, a simple matter of the two being inversely proportional (they can't be, because ΔG can be negative, and K_{eq} can't.) Rather, the relationship turns out to be logarithmic. The Gibbs free energy is equal to the negative product of the ideal gas constant $R = 8.314$ J/(mol · K), the temperature T in Kelvin, and the natural logarithm of the equilibrium constant: $\Delta G = -RT \ln K_{eq}$.

REACTION QUOTIENT OF A REACTION

A **reaction quotient** (Q) has the same format of the equilibrium constant expression. For the generic reaction $a\,A + b\,B \rightleftharpoons c\,C + d\,D$, the reaction quotient by concentration is $Q_c = \frac{[C]^c[D]^d}{[A]^a[B]^b}$, and the reaction quotient by partial pressure is $Q_p = \frac{[P_C]^c[P_D]^d}{[P_A]^a[P_B]^b}$ for gaseous reactions. The concentrations or partial pressures at any point of the reaction process may be substituted into this expression to obtain the reaction quotient at that given point (and recall that for the equilibrium constants, only the equilibrium concentrations/partial pressures should be used). The value of the obtained reaction quotient Q can then be compared to the value of the equilibrium constant so that the extent of the reaction can be seen. If, at a certain point in the reaction, the value of Q is greater than that of the equilibrium constant K, it indicates that the products are too concentrated and the reaction will proceed to the reactant side (reverse reaction predominates). If Q is less than K, it indicates that the reactants are in excess, and the reaction will proceed to the product side (forward reaction predominates). If Q is equal to K, it means the reaction is at equilibrium.

To determine the direction of a reaction at a given point, the concentrations of the reactants and products need to be known and substituted into the reaction quotient expression to obtain the numerical value of Q. The value can then be compared to that of the equilibrium constant K to determine in which direction the reaction will proceed. Consider the reaction $H_2(g) + I_2(g) \rightleftharpoons 2\,HI(g)$ occurring in a 5.00 L container at 450 °C ($K_c = 51$). At a point where 1.55 mol of H_2, 3.10 mol of I_2, and 4.21 mol of HI are present, then $[H_2] = \frac{1.55 \text{ mol}}{5.00 \text{ L}} = 0.310$ M, $[I_2] = \frac{3.10 \text{ mol}}{5.00 \text{ L}} = 0.620$ M, and $[HI] = \frac{4.21 \text{ mol}}{5.00 \text{ L}} = 0.842$ M. Substitute these values in the reaction quotient expression:

$$Q_c = \frac{[HI]^2}{[H_2][I_2]} = \frac{[0.842]^2}{[0.310][0.620]} = 3.69$$

Since the obtained Q_c is less than K_c, the reactants are in excess and more products need to be produced. The reaction will proceed in the forward direction.

Example Problems

Determine the rate law for the decomposition reaction of dinitrogen pentoxide (N_2O_5) in aqueous solution, $2\,N_2O_5(aq) \to 4\,NO_2(aq) + O_2(g)$, based on the given data points of time and concentrations of N_2O_5:

Time (s)	$[N_2O_5]$	$\ln[N_2O_5]$	$1/[N_2O_5]$
0	0.004714	−5.357	212.1
50	0.003143	−5.763	318.2
100	0.001689	−6.384	592.1
200	0.000897	−7.016	1,115
300	0.000391	−7.847	2,558

Plot each of the following over time: concentration ($[A]_t$), log of concentration ($\ln[A]_t$), and the reciprocal of concentration $\left(\frac{1}{[A]_t}\right)$. The three plots are:

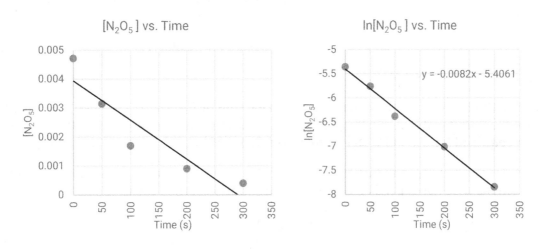

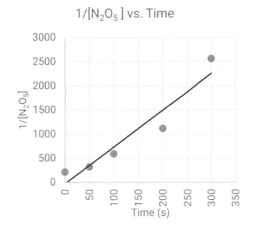

The plot of $\ln[N_2O_5]$ over time is linear, meaning that the reaction is first order in $[N_2O_5]$. The slope is equal to the negative of the rate constant k, thus $k = 8.2 \times 10^{-3}\ s^{-1}$. So, the rate of this first order reaction is:

$$rate = (8.2 \times 10^{-3}\ s^{-1}) \times [N_2O_5]$$

109

Determine the rate law and rate constant for the oxidation of NO, $2\,NO(g) + O_2(g) \rightarrow 2\,NO_2(g)$, based on the following experimental data:

Experiment	[NO] (M)	[O_2] (M)	Initial Rate (M/s)
1	0.15	0.15	1.35×10^{-3}
2	0.15	0.30	2.71×10^{-3}
3	0.30	0.15	5.41×10^{-3}

We see from experiments 1 and 2 that doubling the initial concentration of O_2 also doubles the initial reaction rate, so the reaction is first order in [O_2]. By comparing the experiments 1 and 3, however, we see that doubling the initial concentration of NO increases the initial rate by a factor of 4. The reaction is thus second order in [NO].

The rate law can now be written as: $rate = k[NO]^2[O_2]$.

Plugging in any set of concentration and initial rate data will allow to solve for k. For example, using experiment 2:

$$2.71 \times 10^{-3} \text{ M/s} = k(0.15 \text{ M})^2(0.30 \text{ M})$$

For this reaction, $k = 0.401 \text{ M}^{-2}\text{s}^{-1}$.

Determine the half-life for the decomposition reaction of $2\,N_2O_5(aq) \rightarrow 4\,NO_2(aq) + O_2(g)$ given that it is first order regarding [N_2O_5] and the rate constant, $k = 8.2 \times 10^{-3} \text{ s}^{-1}$. Find the time required for 0.8 M [N_2O_5] to decrease to 0.1 M [N_2O_5].

To determine the half-life of a reaction, determine the reaction order. Since the half-life of first order reactions does not depend on the initial concentration, its half-life is:

$$t_{1/2} = \frac{0.693}{k} \text{ s}$$
$$= \frac{0.693}{0.0082} \text{ s}$$
$$= 84.5 \text{ s}$$

To find the time required for 0.8 M [N_2O_5] to decrease to 0.1 M [N_2O_5], note that the result is $\frac{1}{8}$ of the initial concentration. This means that three half-lives have elapsed. In this case, $3 \times 84.5 \text{ s} = 253.5 \text{ s}$

Demonstrate how to calculate for the activation energy of a reaction given the following set of equilibrium constant and temperature data.

Temperature (°C)	$k\ (s^{-1})$
52.7	0.00139
61.9	0.00289
93.3	0.03465
114.2	0.17380

With a given set of experimentally measured equilibrium constants (k) and temperatures, calculate the values of the reciprocal of temperature and natural log of k. (Note that if the temperature data points are in Celsius, they should be converted to Kelvin.)

Temperature (°C)	$k\ (s^{-1})$	T (K)	$1/T$	$\ln k$
52.7	0.00139	325.85	0.003069	-6.58133
61.9	0.00289	335.05	0.002985	-5.84736
93.3	0.03465	366.45	0.002729	-3.36246
114.2	0.17380	387.35	0.002582	-1.74985

Next, construct a graph of $\ln k$ over $\frac{1}{T}$. Obtain the best-fit line from a graphing tool. This could be a spreadsheet or a calculator with graphing functions:

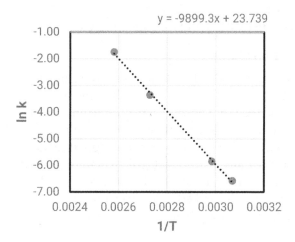

The slope of the linear function is -9,899.3, so:

$$E_a = (-9{,}899.3\ \text{K}) \times \left(-8.314\,\frac{\text{J}}{\text{mol} \cdot \text{K}}\right) \times \left(\frac{1\ \text{kJ}}{1000\ \text{J}}\right) = 82.30\ \text{kJ/mol}$$

Acids and Bases

Types and Reactions

DIFFERENCES BETWEEN ACIDS AND BASES

There are several differences between **acids** and **bases**. Acidic solutions tend to taste sour, whereas basic solutions tend to taste bitter. Dilute bases tend to feel slippery, whereas dilute acids feel like water. Active metals such as magnesium and zinc react with acids to produce hydrogen gas, but active metals usually do not react with bases. Acids and bases form electrolytes in aqueous solutions and conduct electricity. Acids turn blue litmus red, but bases turn red litmus blue. Acidic solutions have a pH of less than 7, whereas basic solutions have a pH of greater than 7.

> **Review Video: Properties of Acids and Bases**
> Visit mometrix.com/academy and enter code: 645283

ARRHENIUS ACID AND BASE

Arrhenius acids are substances that produce hydrogen ions (H^+) when dissolved in water to form aqueous solutions. Arrhenius bases are substances that produce hydroxide ions (OH^-) when dissolved in water to form aqueous solutions. The **Arrhenius concept** is limited to acids and bases in aqueous solutions and cannot be applied to other solids, liquids, and gases. Examples of Arrhenius acids include hydrochloric acid (HCl) and sulfuric acid (H_2SO_4). Examples of Arrhenius bases include sodium hydroxide (NaOH) and magnesium hydroxide ($Mg(OH)_2$).

BRØNSTED–LOWRY ACID AND BASE

The Brønsted–Lowry concept is based on the donation or the acceptance of a proton. According to the **Brønsted–Lowry concept**, an acid is a substance that donates one or more protons to another substance and a base is a substance that accepts a proton from another substance. The Brønsted–Lowry concept can be applied to substances other than aqueous solutions. This concept is much broader than the Arrhenius concept, which can only be applied to aqueous solutions. The Brønsted–Lowry concept states that a substance cannot act like an acid (donate its proton) unless another substance is available to act as a base (accept the donated proton). In this concept, water may act as either an acid or a base. Hydrochloric acid (HCl) is an example of a Brønsted–Lowry acid. Ammonia (NH_3) is an example of a Brønsted–Lowry base.

LEWIS ACID AND BASE

A **Lewis acid** is any substance that can accept a pair of nonbonding electrons. A **Lewis base** is any substance that can donate a pair of nonbonding electrons. According to the **Lewis theory**, all cations such as Mg^{2+} and Cu^{2+} are Lewis acids. Trigonal planar molecules, which are exceptions to the octet rule such as BF_3, are Lewis acids. Molecules such as CO_2 that have multiple bonds between two atoms that differ in electronegativities are Lewis acids, also. According to the Lewis theory, all anions such as OH^- are Lewis bases. Other examples of Lewis bases include trigonal pyramidal molecules such as ammonia, NH_3, and nonmetal oxides such as carbon monoxide, CO. Some compounds such as water, H_2O, can be either Lewis acids or bases.

CONJUGATE ACIDS AND BASES

In an acid-base reaction, under Brønsted-Lowry definitions, the acid donates a proton to the base, converting both the acid and the base into new compounds. In general, this reaction is reversible, which means that the new compound formed from the base can donate the proton it received, and

112

the new compound formed from the acid can accept a proton. This means the new compound formed from the base is an acid, and the new compound formed from the acid is a base. The base formed from an acid when it donates a proton is called its conjugate base; the acid formed from a base when it accepts a proton is called its conjugate acid. An acid or base together with its conjugate are known as a conjugate base pair. The stronger an acid, the weaker its conjugate base and vice versa.

For instance, hydrochloric acid, HCl, can donate a proton to become Cl^-, its conjugate base, but because HCl is a very strong acid, Cl^- is a very weak base. On the other end of the range, S^{2-} is a strong base by the Brønsted-Lowry definition; it can accept a proton to become HS^-, a very weak acid.

STRONG AND WEAK ACIDS AND BASES

The strength of an acid or base refers to how readily it donates or accepts a proton. A strong acid dissociates completely in water, with practically every molecule losing a proton. A weak acid only partially dissociates; the smaller the proportion of molecules that donate protons, the weaker the acid is said to be. Similarly, in a strong base, practically every molecule will accept a proton—in most cases because the base dissociates into a cation and a proton-accepting hydroxide ion. A weak base can accept a proton but does so less readily.

Common examples of strong acids are nitric acid (HNO_3), sulfuric acid (H_2SO_4), and hydrochloric acid (HCl). Weak acids include acetic acid (CH_3COOH), citric acid ($C_6H_8O_7$), and hydrofluoric acid (HF). Some strong bases include sodium hydroxide (NaOH), lithium hydroxide (LiOH), and potassium hydroxide (KOH). Weak bases include ammonia (NH_3), calcium carbonate ($CaCO_3$), and ammonium hydroxide (NH_4OH).

NEUTRALIZATION

Neutralization in chemistry refers to the reaction of an acid and a base to form a salt. In the case of Arrhenius bases—bases that include a hydroxide (OH^-) ion—the reaction also produces water. Despite the name, neutralization does not necessarily result in a neutral solution. The acid and base are said to be neutralized when no excess acid or base remains, but the resulting solution may be acidic, if it results from a strong acid and a weak base, or basic, if it results from a weak acid and a strong base.

For example, the strong acid hydrochloric acid and the strong base sodium hydroxide neutralize each other to form water and sodium chloride: $HCl + NaOH \rightarrow NaCl + H_2O$. (In this case, because HCl is a strong base and NaOH is a strong acid, the resulting solution is neutral.) Other neutralization reactions include $H_2SO_4 + 2 KOH \rightarrow K_2SO_4 + 2 H_2O$ and, for an example of a neutralization reaction involving Brønsted-Lowry acids and bases, $H^+ + NH_3 \rightarrow NH_4^+$.

IONIZATION OF WATER

pH is a measurement of the concentration of hydrogen ions in an aqueous solution and therefore of the solution's acidity. More specifically, it is equal to the negative logarithm base 10 of the ion concentration. Technically, free hydrogen ions in an aqueous solution tend to combine with water to form hydronium ions, H_3O^+, so it is really the concentration of hydronium ions, not free H^+ ions, that the pH measures. For example, if the molar concentration of H^+ (or H_3O^+) ions in a solution is 10^{-4}, then the solution's pH is $-\log_{10} 10^{-4} = 4$.

The pH of pure water is 7, which is considered neutral, neither acidic nor basic. Acidic substances have a lower pH; the pH of most orange juice is between 3.5 and 4, and the pH of white vinegar is about 2.4. Basic substances have a higher pH; the pH of baking soda is about 9, and the pH of strong drain cleaners can be about 14.

CALCULATION OF PH OF A SOLUTION

A salt is a compound (other than water) formed in a neutralization reaction between an acid and a base. When dissolved in water, a salt undergoes hydrolysis, reacting with the water to split into two products.

A salt of a weak base and a strong acid is called an acid salt. To find the pH, given the molarity of the salt and the base dissociation constant K_b of the base, you can find K_a for the conjugate acid and use it to solve for the concentration of H_3O^+ ions. For a basic salt of a strong base and weak acid, the procedure is similar but using K_b for the acid's conjugate base.

The salt of a strong acid and a strong base forms a neutral solution.

EQUILIBRIUM CONSTANTS K_A, K_B, PK_A, AND PK_B

K_a and K_b are the acid dissociation constant and the base dissociation constant, respectively. They are constants that relate to the equilibrium condition for the dissociation of a particular acid or base. The equilibrium condition for the dissociation of an acid HA with conjugate base A^- is $K_a = \frac{[H^+][A^-]}{[HA]}$; for a base B with conjugate acid HB^+, it is $K_b = \frac{[HB^+][OH^-]}{[B]}$. These constants can be used to determine the concentration of one of the chemical species involved if the concentrations of the others are known—in particular, they can be used to find the concentration of H^+ or OH^- and therefore the pH of the solution.

In practice, these concentrations are typically very small, so it is often more convenient to refer to logarithmic versions of these constants, pK_a and pK_b. These hold the same relation to K_a and K_b as pH does to the concentration of H^+ ions: $pK_a = -\log_{10} K_a$, and $pK_b = -\log_{10} K_b$.

For an acid and its conjugate base, $K_a \times K_b = 10^{-14}$ and $pK_a + pK_b = 14$.

BUFFERS

A buffer is a solution that resists changes in pH. A buffer's pH remains almost constant even after the addition of a strong acid or base (in relatively small amounts). Generally, a buffer solution contains either a weak acid and its conjugate base or a weak base and its conjugate acid. When a strong base is added to a solution containing a weak acid, the weak acid will tend to give up a proton to the base, changing it into its conjugate acid. Because there is no significant change in the concentration of hydronium ions in solution, there is little change in pH. Similarly, when a strong acid is added to a solution containing a weak base, the weak base will accept a proton from that acid, again tending to stabilize the concentration of hydronium ions and therefore the pH.

Buffer systems are present in the human body (and other organisms) because many enzymes and other chemicals only work well at certain pH ranges. Blood, for example, is a buffer solution (with carbonic acid, H_2CO_3, and its conjugate base) that remains at a pH of about 7.4. Buffers are also used in shampoos and detergents, in breweries, and in textile dyeing processes. Some examples of weak acids or bases used in buffer systems include acetic acid (CH_3COOH), ammonia (NH_3), citric acid ($C_6H_8O_7$), and monopotassium phosphate (KH_2PO_4).

> **Review Video: Buffer**
> Visit mometrix.com/academy and enter code: 389183

Titration

INDICATORS

An indicator is a substance that when added to a solution, changes color (or some other easily observable property) depending on the pH of the solution (or some other property not easily observed directly). One of the best-known indicators is litmus, a mixture of chemicals extracted from lichens that is red in acidic solutions and blue in basic. It is typically sold in the form of litmus paper, strips of paper impregnated with the chemical. Another class of indicators, anthocyanins, are found in red cabbage and certain other plants. Other widely used indicators include phenolphthalein, methyl orange, and bromothymol blue.

Indicators are useful in titration because they help the observer identify the moment at which the pH changes. Because different indicators differ in the range of pHs over which they change color, an appropriate indicator will be chosen for a given titration based on the pH of the expected change. Methyl orange, for instance, changes color at a low pH and phenolphthalein at a high pH; litmus and bromothymol blue both change color around neutral pH, although the range of pH for the color change of litmus is wider.

INTERPRETATION OF THE TITRATION CURVES

Titration is the process of slowly adding small amounts of a solution of known concentration—the titrant—to a known volume of solution of unknown concentration—the analyte—until some reaction occurs. The volume of titrant added can then be used to find the concentration of the analyte. One common type of titration is acid-base titration, in which the titrant is acidic and the analyte basic, or vice versa, and the looked-for reaction is neutralization.

The titration curve is a curve used in acid-base titration to chart how the pH of the solution changes as more titrant is added. The independent variable is the total volume of titrant added, and the dependent variable is the pH.

The equivalence point of a titration curve is the point of maximum slope. Generally, a titration curve will start out with a relatively shallow slope, then at some point the slope will sharply increase, only to level off again. The equivalence point is where the curve is at its steepest.

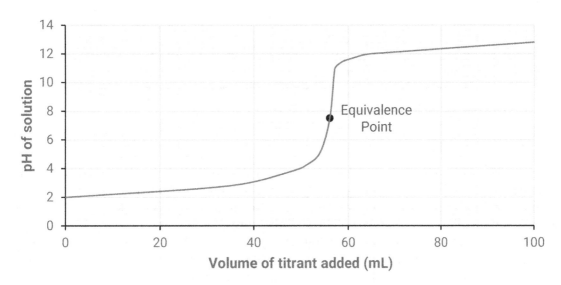

The equivalence point is important because it marks the moment where neutralization occurred. The slope of the titration curve of an acid-base titration indicates the rate of change of the pH of the solution as more titrant is added. It starts out shallow because when the solution is far from neutrality, adding small amounts of acid or base will have little effect. As the concentrations of acid and base become nearly equal, however, a small change in the amount of acid or base can have a large effect on pH, and the slope increases sharply. As the neutralization point is passed, and now the titrant is in excess, again a small increase in the amount of titrant has little effect on the pH, and the slope decreases again.

A monoprotic acid is an acid that can donate only a single proton or that has only a single H^+ ion. Monoprotic acids include hydrochloric acid, HCl; nitric acid, HNO_3; and acetic acid, $HC_2H_3O_2$. (Although acetic acid has four hydrogen atoms, three of them are part of the acetate anion and are not available for donation.) A polyprotic acid is one that has two or more protons or H^+ ions available for donation. Polyprotic acids include sulfuric acid, H_2SO_4; carbonic acid, H_2CO_3; and phosphoric acid, H_3PO_4.

Unlike a monoprotic acid, the titration curve of a polyprotic acid will have more than one equivalence point—the slope of the curve will become steeper and shallower several times. Specifically, it will have one equivalence point for each proton it can donate. This is because a polyprotic acid becomes a different acid when it donates a proton, and that acid has its own inflection point as well. For instance, when H_2SO_4 donates a proton, it becomes HSO_4^-, hydrogen sulfate, which is itself (weakly) acidic. The titration curve for H_2SO_4 shows both an equivalence point at which the H_2SO_4 itself is neutralized and then a second equivalence point where the HSO_4^- is neutralized.

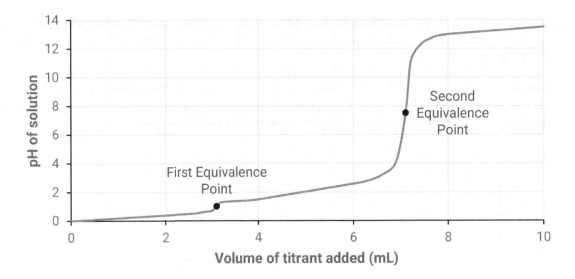

A titration curve with a strong acid or base will have a simple, well-defined sigmoid shape; the titration curve will rise or fall relatively slowly at the start, then become much steeper near the inflection point, and then return to a low rate of change. In the case of a weak acid or base, however, including a buffer solution, the shape will be slightly more complex. For a weak acid, at a pH below the equivalence point when the acid is of a higher concentration than the base, the solution will form a buffer, and the slope will become almost flat. Once the concentrations are nearly equalized, the slope will increase again, and the curve will reach an equivalence point as before. At the center of the flat region of the curve is the half-equivalence point, where half the acid has been converted to its conjugate base. At this point, the pH of the solution is equal to the pK_a for the weak acid.

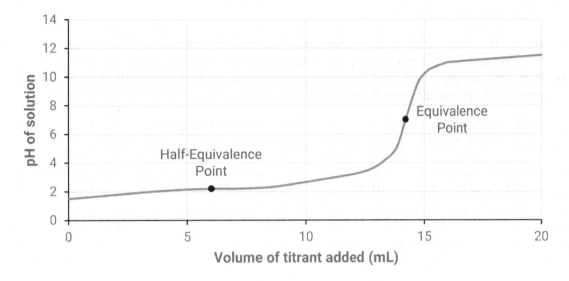

For a weak base, the situation is similar, except that the flat region of the curve and the half-equivalence point will be at a high pH, and at the equivalence point, the pH of the solution is equal to $(14 - pK_b)$.

REDOX TITRATION

A redox titration is a titration based not on a neutralization reaction as with acid-base titration but on a redox reaction. As with other titrations, small amounts of a substance of known concentration (the titrant) are added to a fixed volume of a substance of unknown concentration (the analyte). In a redox titration, the titrant is a reducing agent, and the analyte is an oxidizing agent, or vice versa.

In a redox titration curve, the independent variable is the amount of titrant added, and the dependent variable is the cell potential of the system. A redox titration curve starts out with a shallow slope, as the titrant is almost completely oxidized or reduced by the more abundant analyte, then becomes steeper as the concentrations of titrant and analyte near equality, and then becomes shallower again as the titrant becomes more abundant than the analyte. The point of steepest slope is the equivalence point, where the amount of reducing agent and balancing agent are just enough for each to react completely with the other.

> **Review Video: Titration**
> Visit mometrix.com/academy and enter code: 550131

Example Problems

Explain how the concentration of hydronium and hydroxide ions in an aqueous solution can be found given its pH, and vice versa.

The value of pH is equal to the negative log base 10 of the concentration of hydronium ions in an aqueous solution: $pH = -\log_{10}[H_3O^+]$. Turning this around to solve for the concentration of hydronium ions, we get $[H_3O^+] = 10^{-pH}$. For example, in a solution with a pH of 10, the molar concentration of hydronium ions is 10^{-10}.

The dissociation reaction of water is $2\,H_2O \to H_3O^+ + OH^-$. The equilibrium condition for this reaction is $K_{eq} = \frac{[H_3O^+][OH^-]}{[H_2O]^2}$. Because the number of the ions for typical solutions is very small in comparison to the number of neutral water molecules, we can treat $[H_2O]^2$ as being essentially constant and write $K_{eq}[H_2O]^2 = [H_3O^+][OH^-]$. The left-hand side of this equation can be written as a single constant K_w; at room temperature $Kw = 10^{-14}$, so the concentrations of hydronium and hydroxide ions must multiply to this number: $[H_3O^+][OH^-] = 10^{-14}$. Therefore, given either the concentration of hydronium ions or the concentration of hydroxide ions, you can find the other by dividing the known concentration into 10^{-14}. In the example with a concentration of hydronium ions of 10^{-10}, the concentration of hydroxide ions is $\frac{10^{-14}}{10^{-10}} = 10^{-4}$.

Explain what ions are present in pure water and in what concentrations.

Even in pure water, water molecules can spontaneously dissociate. Although this reaction is sometimes written as $H_2O \to H^+ + OH^-$, in practice free H^+ ions quickly join with other water molecules, so a more accurate rendition of the dissociation reaction is $2\,H_2O \to H_3O^+ + OH^-$. Therefore, pure water contains hydronium ions (H_3O^+) and hydroxide ions (OH^-).

The equilibrium condition for this dissociation reaction is $K_w = [H_3O^+][OH^-]$, where K_w is the water ionization constant, equal at room temperature to 10^{-14}. For pure water, because no other ions are present and the water as a whole is neutral, the concentrations of hydroxide and hydronium ions must be equal. We can then replace $[OH^-]$ in the equation by $[H_3O^+]$, and we get $K_w = [H_3O^+]^2$, so $[OH^-] = [H_3O^+] = \sqrt{K_w} = \sqrt{10^{-14}} = 10^{-7}$. In pure water, both hydroxide and hydronium ions are present at a concentration of 10^{-7} M.

Find the pH of a 2.00 M solution of potassium cyanide, KCN.

Because KOH is a strong base and HCN is a weak acid, KCN is a basic salt. K_a for HCN is 5.8×10^{-10}, so K_b for its conjugate base is $\frac{1.0 \times 10^{-14}}{5.8 \times 10^{-10}} = 1.7 \times 10^{-5}$. The equilibrium equation is $K_b = \frac{[HCN][OH^-]}{[CN^-]}$; we can set [HCN] and $[OH^-]$ (which must be equal) to x and solve it.

$$K_b = \frac{x^2}{[CN^-]}$$
$$x^2 = K_b[CN^-]$$
$$x = \sqrt{K_b[CN^-]}$$
$$= \sqrt{(1.7 \times 10^{-5})(2.00)}$$
$$= 0.0058 \text{ M}$$

Thus, the pH is $-\log_{10}\frac{1.0 \times 10^{-14}}{0.0058} = 11.8$.

Thermodynamics

Temperature, Heat, and the Laws of Thermodynamics

TEMPERATURE SCALES

Each of the temperature scales, Celsius and Fahrenheit, has a corresponding **absolute temperature scale**, Kelvin and Rankine, respectively. A temperature of zero Kelvin or zero Rankine is known as absolute zero, at which point there is **theoretically no atomic motion** or thermal energy. Kelvins and degrees Celsius are related by the equation, $T_K = T_C + 273.15$. Similarly, Rankines and degrees Fahrenheit are related as $T_R = T_F + 459.67$. From these relations, we can see that within both individual pairs of temperature scales, the magnitude of the unit is the same; that is, an increase of 1 °C is the same an increase of 1 K, while an increase of 1 °F equals an increase of 1 R. Converting from Fahrenheit to Celsius is slightly more complicated: $T_C = \frac{5}{9}(T_F - 32)$, or in reverse, $T_F = \frac{9}{5}T_C + 32$. From these equations, we can see that a change of one degree Celsius is greater than a change of one degree Fahrenheit.

HEAT AND TEMPERATURE

Heat, or **thermal energy**, is a measure of the kinetic energy of the atoms within a substance. Heat, being a form of energy, has SI units of joules, but is also commonly measured in calories. The amount of heat a substance contains is generally quantified as a temperature. Temperature has SI units of degrees Celsius, though degrees Fahrenheit are also widely used.

It is often useful to know how much heat is required to cause a certain amount of material to reach a desired temperature. Each material has a property called specific heat, which allows this calculation. To bring about a temperature increase ΔT to a mass m made of a material with specific heat c, the required heat input is found by the equation $Q = mc\Delta T$. This equation can also be used to calculate the amount of heat absorbed during a given temperature increase. The amount of heat required to raise the temperature of a gram of water by one degree Celsius, or one Kelvin, is one calorie, or 4.184 J. Thus, the specific heat of water is $1\frac{\text{cal}}{\text{g K}}$ or $4.184\frac{\text{J}}{\text{g K}}$.

It is important to note that since Kelvin and Celsius scales use the same unit size and the heat equation uses change in temperature, it is equally valid to use units of $\frac{\text{cal}}{\text{g °C}}$ or $\frac{\text{J}}{\text{g °C}}$.

HEAT TRANSFER

Heat transfer is the flow of thermal energy, which is measured by temperature. Heat will flow from warmer objects to cooler objects until an **equilibrium** is reached in which both objects are at the same temperature. Because the particles of warmer objects possess a higher kinetic energy than the particles of cooler objects, the particles of the warmer objects are vibrating more quickly and collide more often, transferring energy to the cooler objects in which the particles have less kinetic energy and are moving more slowly. Heat may be transferred by conduction, convection, or radiation. In **conduction**, heat is transferred by direct contact between two objects. In **convection**, heat is transferred by moving currents. In **radiation**, heat is transferred by electromagnetic waves.

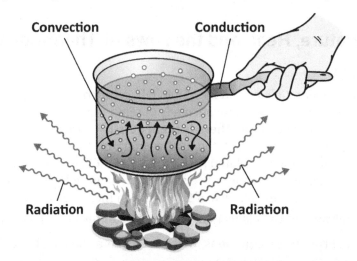

CONVECTION

Heat always flows from a region of higher temperature to a region of lower temperature. If two regions are at the same temperature, there is a thermal equilibrium between them and there will be no net heat transfer between them. Convection is a mode of heat transfer in which a surface in contact with a fluid experiences a heat flow. The heat rate for convection is given as $q = hA\Delta T$, where h is the convection coefficient, and q is the heat transferred per unit of time. The convection coefficient is dependent on a number of factors, including the configuration of the surface and the nature and velocity of the fluid. For complicated configurations, it often has to be determined experimentally.

Convection may be classified as either free or forced. In free convection, when a surface transfers heat to the surrounding air, the heated air becomes less dense and rises, allowing cooler air to descend and come into contact with the surface. Free convection may also be called natural convection. Forced convection in this example would involve forcibly cycling the air: for instance, with a fan. While this does generally require an additional input of work, the convection coefficient is always greater for forced convection.

CONDUCTION

Conduction is a form of heat transfer that requires contact. Since heat is a measure of kinetic energy, most commonly vibration, at the atomic level, it may be transferred from one location to another or one object to another by contact. The rate at which heat is transferred is proportional to the material's thermal conductivity k, cross-sectional area A, and temperature gradient $\frac{\Delta T}{\Delta x}$:

$$q = kA\left(\frac{\Delta T}{\Delta x}\right)$$

If two ends of a rod are each held at a constant temperature, the heat transfer through the rod will be given as $q = kA\left(\frac{T_H - T_L}{d}\right)$, where d is the length of the rod. The heat will flow from the hot end to the cold end. The thermal conductivity is generally given in units of $\frac{W}{m\,K}$. Metals are some of the best conductors, many having a thermal conductivity around 400 $\frac{W}{m\,K}$. The thermal conductivity of wood is very small, generally less than 0.5 $\frac{W}{m\,K}$. Diamond is extremely thermally conductive and may have a conductivity of over 2,000 $\frac{W}{m\,K}$. Although fluids also have thermal conductivity, they will tend to transfer heat primarily through convection.

RADIATION

Radiation heat transfer occurs via electromagnetic radiation between two bodies. Unlike conduction and convection, radiation requires no medium in which to take place. Indeed, the heat we receive from the sun is entirely radiation since it must pass through a vacuum to reach us. Every body at a temperature above absolute zero emits heat radiation at a rate of $q = e\sigma A T^4$, where e is the surface emissivity and σ is the Stefan-Boltzmann constant. The net radiation heat-transfer rate for a body is given by $q = e\sigma A(T^4 - T_0^4)$, where T_0 is the temperature of the surroundings. Emissivity, which has a value between 0 and 1, is a measure of how well a surface absorbs and emits radiation. Dark-colored surfaces tend to have high emissivity, while shiny or reflective surfaces have low emissivity. In the radiation heat-rate equation, it is important to remember to use absolute temperature units, since the temperature value is being raised to a power.

THERMODYNAMIC SYSTEM

A state function in thermodynamics is a quantity describing a thermodynamic system that depends only on the current state of the system and not on its history. If a state function changes, the magnitude of that change is entirely determined by the beginning and end states of the system, independent of the path it took between them. Pressure, volume, and temperature are all state functions; the current values of these properties of a system can be measured without requiring any knowledge of a system's past states. Other state functions include internal energy, entropy, enthalpy, and free energy. In contrast, non-state functions include work and heat. The work done by a system as it changes between two states very much depends on the path it takes; it cannot be calculated solely on the basis of the start and end states.

LAWS OF THERMODYNAMICS
ZEROTH LAW

The Zeroth Law of Thermodynamics states that two bodies both in thermal equilibrium with a third body are also in thermal equilibrium with each other. Two objects are in thermal equilibrium if they are in contact—or at least they are connected by some method that would allow heat to flow between them—but there is no net heat flow between the objects.

The importance of the Zeroth Law of Thermodynamics is that it establishes that temperature is a meaningful quantity. Two objects in thermal equilibrium can be defined as having the same temperature; two objects in thermal contact but not in thermal equilibrium have different temperatures. The Zeroth Law guarantees that this definition leads to no contradictions. In fact, sometimes the Zeroth Law is written directly in terms of temperature: systems in thermal equilibrium are at the same temperature.

FIRST LAW

The First Law of Thermodynamics states that the total energy of an isolated thermodynamic system is constant. For a non-isolated system, energy may be added or taken away from the system in the form of work or heat, but this means the system's internal energy will change by the same amount. The First Law is also written mathematically as $\Delta U = Q + W$, where ΔU is the change in internal energy of the system, Q is the heat added to the system, and W is the work done on the system. (Sometimes it is instead written in the form $\Delta U = Q - W$, in which case W represents the work done by the system.)

The First Law of Thermodynamics is essentially a restatement of the law of conservation of energy or at least an application of that law to thermodynamics. Among other things, it is the first law that proves the impossibility of perpetual motion machines that provide "free energy." Energy cannot be created arbitrarily; it can only be transferred between systems in the forms of work and heat.

PV DIAGRAM

A pV diagram is a diagram of a thermodynamic system in which the pressure is plotted on the y-axis and the volume on the x-axis. The thermodynamic state of a system is uniquely determined by these two variables, so any state variable pertaining to the system can be determined from its position on the diagram. Changes in thermodynamic state can be drawn as lines or curves on the pV diagram, representing all the states that the system passes through; changes in non-state functions can be determined from this curve. For instance, the work done by a system as it undergoes a change in state is equal to the area under the curve in a pV diagram.

As an example, the following pV diagram shows a thermodynamic cycle as a system undergoes first an isothermal (constant temperature) expansion, followed by an isobaric (constant pressure) compression, and finally an isochoric (constant volume) increase in pressure:

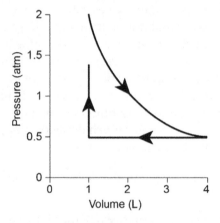

SECOND LAW

The Second Law of Thermodynamics states that the total entropy of an isolated system can never decrease. Over time, the disorder in an isolated system must increase or stay the same. Note that this refers only to isolated systems; the entropy of part of a system can decrease as long as there is an equal or greater increase to make up for it. For instance, the entropy of the water in a pond decreases when it freezes over in winter, but this is countered by an increase in the entropy of the air the water's heat escapes to.

There are several other statements of the law that are (not obviously) equivalent and that do not explicitly refer to entropy. For instance, it is equivalent to the statement that it is not possible for heat to flow from a colder to a warmer body without work being done on the system.

The Second Law of Thermodynamics has many consequences. It determines the maximum efficiency of a heat engine and demonstrates why some chemical reactions and other processes occur preferentially in one direction (because that direction increases entropy).

Review Video: Laws of Thermodynamics
Visit mometrix.com/academy and enter code: 253607

ENTROPY AS A MEASURE OF "DISORDER"

Entropy is, roughly speaking, a measurement of the "disorder" in a system. It can be defined more rigorously in terms of the number of possible states that are in a certain sense equivalent. (As a quantitative value, the entropy is conventionally abbreviated S.) As an analogy, if you have a number of coins on the ground, there's only one state in which they are all showing heads, so this is a low-entropy state; there are many states in which roughly equal numbers of coins are heads and tails, so this is a relatively high-entropy state. Entropy tends to increase with temperature, and thanks to the Second Law of Thermodynamics the entropy of a closed system increases (or at best remains constant) over time.

In general, gases have higher entropy than liquids, and liquids have higher entropy than solids. This follows, again roughly speaking, from the fact that as a compound passes from solid to liquid to gas, its molecules or atoms become less constrained, and there are more possible states for them to be in. Crystals have particularly low entropy.

HESS'S LAW

Hess's Law of Heat Summation states that if a chemical reaction can be broken down into smaller steps, then the total heat of the reaction is equal to the sum of the heats of reaction of each step. This can often be used to determine the heat of reaction of a particular chemical reaction if we have no feasible way to measure it directly but can find a way to break it down into sub-reactions with heats of reaction we know or can measure.

For instance, the heat of reaction of $2\,C + O_2 \rightarrow 2\,CO$ is not easy to measure directly, but we can measure those of the reactions $C + O_2 \rightarrow CO_2$ and $2\,CO + O_2 \rightarrow 2\,CO_2$. Doubling the first reaction and reversing the second, we can combine those into our original reaction:

$$2\,C + 2\,O_2 \rightarrow 2\,CO_2$$
$$2\,CO_2 \rightarrow 2\,CO + O_2$$
$$\cancel{2CO_2} + 2\,C + \cancel{2\,O_2} \rightarrow \cancel{2CO_2} + 2\,CO + \cancel{O_2}$$
$$2\,C + O_2 \rightarrow 2\,CO$$

The heat of reaction of $C + O_2 \rightarrow CO_2$ is –393 kJ/mol and the heat of reaction of $2\,CO + O_2 \rightarrow 2\,CO_2$ is –566 kJ/mol; therefore, the heat of reaction of $2\,C + O_2 \rightarrow 2\,CO$ is:

$$2(-393\,\text{kJ/mol}) - (-566\,\text{kJ/mol}) = -220\,\text{kJ/mol}$$

Practical Thermodynamics

FINDING THE SPECIFIC HEAT OF A SUBSTANCE WITH A CALORIMETER

The specific heat of a substance can be determined using a calorimeter. A known amount of the substance is heated to a known temperature. In the classroom setting, this can be accomplished by placing the metal in a loosely stoppered test tube and then placing the test tube in boiling water. The calorimeter is prepared by placing water of a known amount and temperature in the calorimeter. The heated metal is carefully placed into the water in the calorimeter. The temperature of the water is carefully monitored until it stops rising. The final temperature of the metal will be equal to the final temperature of the water. The heat lost by the metal equals the heat gained by the water as shown by the following equations:

$$Q_{lost\ by\ the\ metal} = Q_{gained\ by\ the\ water} - m_{metal}c_{metal}\Delta T_{metal} = m_{water}c_{water}\Delta T_{water}$$

where Q is the amount of heat lost or gained in joules, m is the mass in grams, c is the specific heat, and ΔT is the change in temperature $T_2 - T_1$ in degrees Celsius.

> **Review Video: Using a Calorimeter**
> Visit mometrix.com/academy and enter code: 703935

HEAT ENGINES AND THE CARNOT CYCLE

A **heat engine** is a mechanical device that **takes in heat energy** Q_H from a high-temperature region, uses that energy to **produce work** W, and then **expels heat** Q_C to a lower-temperature region. When the machine is operating at steady state, such that it does not change temperature, the first law of thermodynamics tells us that the net heat input is equal to the work achieved:

$$Q_H - Q_C = W$$

We can define the efficiency of a heat engine as the work received divided by the work put in, or $\eta = \frac{W}{Q_H}$. The rejected heat Q_C is not considered work received because it is not usable for work. The efficiency may also be calculated as $\eta = 1 - \frac{Q_C}{Q_H}$. From this, we can see that 100% efficiency can only be achieved if $Q_C = 0$. However, constructing a heat engine that expels no heat is impossible.

A **Carnot engine** is a heat engine that operates on the Carnot cycle, an ideal reversible gas cycle that consists of the following processes: high-temperature isothermal expansion, adiabatic expansion, low-temperature isothermal compression, and adiabatic compression. The efficiency of this ideal engine is given as $\eta = 1 - \frac{T_C}{T_H}$, where T_C and T_H are the low and high temperatures of the gas during the cycle. Carnot's theorem states that no heat engine operating between T_C and T_H can have a higher efficiency than that of the Carnot engine.

HEAT OF FUSION AND HEAT OF VAPORIZATION

The **heat of fusion** of a compound, abbreviated L_f, is the amount of heat released when a particular quantity of the compound changes from liquid to solid state—or, equivalently, the amount of heat required to change that quantity of the compound from solid to liquid. The **heat of vaporization**, L_v, is the amount of heat released when a particular quantity of the compound changes from gas to liquid state—or, equivalently, the amount of heat required to change that quantity of the compound from liquid to gas. Typically, in metric units, the quantity is taken to be 1 gram, and L_f and L_v are both measured in Joules per gram (J/g).

For instance, suppose we want to know the amount of heat required to convert 1.0 kilogram of ice into water vapor. This requires first melting the ice into water, then heating the water from 0 °C to 100 °C then vaporizing the water. Water has a heat of fusion of 334 J/g, a heat of vaporization of 2230 J/g, and a specific heat of 4.184 J/(g · °C); the total heat involved can be calculated as follows:

$$Q = mL_f + mC\Delta T + mL_v$$
$$= (1000 \text{ g})(334 \text{ J/g}) + (1000 \text{ g})\left(4.184 \frac{\text{J}}{\text{g} \cdot °C}\right)(100 \text{ °C}) + (1000 \text{ g})(2230 \text{ J/g})$$
$$= 2.98 \times 10^6 \text{ J} = 2,980 \text{ kJ}$$

Enthalpy, abbreviated H, is a measurement of the total energy of a thermodynamic system. Specifically, it is equal to the internal energy of the system plus the product of its pressure and volume: $H = U + PV$. (It should not be confused with entropy, which has a similar name but is an entirely different concept.)

During a process at constant pressure, the change in enthalpy (ΔH) is equal to either $\Delta U + P\Delta V$ or $\Delta U - W$, where W is the work done to or on the system (or $\Delta U + W$, where W is the work done by the system). The First Law of Thermodynamics says that $\Delta U = Q + W$; therefore, $\Delta U - W = Q$, and the change in enthalpy is equal to the heat added to the system. Because of this, the heat of reaction of a chemical process is also called its enthalpy of reaction; the two terms are equivalent because the heat added to the system is equal to its change in enthalpy.

LATTICE ENERGY

The **lattice energy** is the energy that is needed to completely break the ionic interactions in an ionic compound until gaseous ions are formed. This process requires a lot of energy, meaning that it is highly endothermic. As a result, the lattice energies are usually very positive in values. The values of lattice energy depend on the charges and sizes of the ionic species, with a given set of arrangement of ionic species, as the potential energy of two charged species is: $E = \frac{\kappa Q_1 Q_2}{d}$, where the κ is a constant, Q_1 and Q_2 are total charges, and d is the distance between the two species. When the total ionic charges are larger, the lattice energy gets higher. As the sizes of the ionic species increase, the lattice energy gets lower. For example, among the ionic compounds LiF, CsCl, and MgO, their lattice energy ranks: MgO > LiF > CsCl. Compound MgO is composed of Mg^{2+} and O^{2-}. Because the total charges are the greatest among the three compounds, the product of the charges affect the lattice energy the most. Therefore, its lattice energy is the highest among the three. The other two compounds, LiF and CsCl have the same total charge, but since Cs^+ and Cl^- are bigger than Li^+ and F^-, the longer distance between the ions decreases lattice energy. So, the lattice energy of LiF is greater than CsCl.

Lattice energy is calculated using the thermochemical **Born-Haber cycle**. For an ionic compound such as KCl(s) (potassium chloride, in solid phase), its heat of formation is:

$$K(s) + \frac{1}{2} Cl_2(g) \rightarrow KCl(s), \Delta H_f°[KCl(s)] = -436 \text{ kJ/mol}$$

There is an alternative, indirect route for the formation of KCl(s). This process involves the following steps:

- Formation of gaseous atoms:
  - Vaporization of potassium: $K(s) \rightarrow K(g), \Delta H_f°[K(g)] = 90.0 \text{ kJ/mol}$
  - Breaking the Cl − Cl bond: $\frac{1}{2} Cl_2(g) \rightarrow Cl(g), \Delta H_f°[Cl(g)] = 122 \text{ kJ/mol}$

- Potassium loses one electron. Chlorine gains the electron to form K^+ and Cl^- in gaseous phase:
  - First ionization energy of K: $K(g) \rightarrow K^+(g) + e^-$, $\Delta H = I_1(K) = 419$ kJ/mol
  - Electron affinity of Cl: $Cl(g) + e^- \rightarrow Cl^-(g)$, $\Delta H = E(Cl) = -349$ kJ/mol
- Formation of the KCl solid from the gaseous ion:
  - The enthalpy change is the reverse of the lattice energy: $K^+(g) + Cl^-(g) \rightarrow KCl(s)$, $\Delta H = -\Delta H_{lattice}$

Therefore, $\Delta H_f^\circ[KCl(s)]$ can be written as the sum of the above enthalpy changes:

$$\Delta H_f^\circ[KCl(s)] = \Delta H_f^\circ[K(g)] + \Delta H_f^\circ[Cl(g)] + I_1(K) + E(Cl) - \Delta H_{lattice}$$

Substitute the values and solve for $\Delta H_{lattice}$:

$$-436 \text{ kJ/mol} = 90.0 \text{ kJ/mol} + 122 \text{ kJ/mol} + 419 \text{ kJ/mol} - 349 \text{ kJ/mol} - \Delta H_{lattice}$$
$$-436 \text{ kJ/mol} = 282 \text{ kJ/mol} - \Delta H_{lattice}$$
$$718 \text{ kJ/mol} = \Delta H_{lattice}$$

The experimental lattice energy value is 701 kJ/mol, which is only slightly different from the calculated value. So, the Born-Haber cycle gives a good estimate for the lattice energy of ionic compounds.

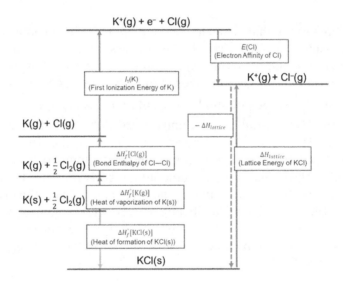

SPONTANEOUS REACTIONS

The Gibbs free energy of a system, abbreviated G, was originally defined by the American chemist and physicist Josiah Willard Gibbs, best known for his work on thermodynamics. Gibbs defined it as the amount of available energy in a chemical system, the energy that could be used to do useful work. Specifically, the Gibbs free energy is equal to the enthalpy of the system minus the product of the temperature and the entropy: $G = H - TS$.

A chemical reaction is said to be spontaneous if it occurs in nature when the reactants are present without any necessary input of energy. A reaction is spontaneous if and only if the total free energy of the reactants is greater than the total free energy of the products—that is, if ΔG of the reactants is negative. This was, in fact, what led Gibbs to formulate this concept in the first place; he was looking for a relatively simple criterion to determine whether or not a reaction would spontaneously occur.

PREDICTING THE SIGN OF THE ENTROPY CHANGE FOR A PROCESS

The number of particles involved in a process and their freedom of motion affect the entropy change. For example, in the reaction $2 SO_3(g) \rightarrow 2 SO_2(g) + O_2(g)$, two molecules of SO_3 as the reactant form three molecules of gases SO_2 and O_2. There is a net increase in the number of gas molecules, and the entropy for this system increases. The entropy of a system is also largely affected by the states of the substances in the system. The state of matter determines the degrees of freedom in motion—more freedom means more microstates for the particles become available, so the overall entropy increases. In the melting process of an ice cube, as the ice melts to become liquid water, the solid rigid structure in the ice cube is destroyed and the molecules are less restricted in their motion. Because of the decreased motion restriction, the molecules possess more microstates, and the total entropy of the liquid water is higher. The same goes for the vaporization process of the liquid water. As the liquid water gets heated and vaporizes, the molecules absorb energy and get more freedom in motion. The group of molecules in their gas phase also occupy more space, which contributes to the greater degrees of freedom and increased total entropy. The following factors generally contribute to the increase of overall entropy in a system:

- The increase in the total number of gas molecules.
- The formation of gas molecules from liquids or solids.
- The formation of liquids from solid, or the dissolution of solids to form solutions.

In the first reaction, $N_2F_4(g) \rightarrow 2 NF_2(g)$, there is no phase change during the reaction process, but there is a net increase in number of gas molecules after the reaction. Two molecules of NF_2 are the product, while only one molecule of N_2F_4 is the reactant. The increased number of gas molecules contribute to more microstates; therefore, the entropy is increased after the reaction.

For the second reaction, $Ba^{2+}(aq) + SO_4{}^{2-}(aq) \rightarrow BaSO_4(s)$, the Ba^{2+} and $SO_4{}^{2-}$ ions in the solution phase collide and form the precipitate $BaSO_4$ as the product. The degree of motion in the solid product is less than that contained in the ionic reactants, meaning that the solid product possesses less motion energy and gains a more ordered structure. Because of these, the entropy decreases after the reaction.

In the last reaction, $2 PbS(s) + 3 O_2(g) \rightarrow 2 PbO(s) + 2 SO_2(g)$, we may notice that two solid molecules of PbS are converted to another two molecules of PbO in the products, while three molecules of gaseous O_2 are converted to two molecules of gaseous SO_2. There is no net change in the number of solid molecules, so it is difficult to predict the entropy change based on the formation of new solid molecules. However, there is a net decrease in the gaseous molecules. Thus, the net entropy change for this reaction is decreasing.

CALCULATING THE VALUE OF ΔS FOR A CHEMICAL REACTION

The entropy changes in a system (ΔS) like a chemical reaction is the difference between the sum of entropies in the products and reactants. Under the standard states, the molar entropy of a substance is called the **standard molar entropy**, $S°$, with the unit of $\frac{J}{mol \cdot K}$. The $S°$ values for many substances can be found in scientific literature. Assuming there are m moles of reactants in total and n moles of products in total, the entropy changes for a chemical reaction system, $\Delta S°_{sys}$, is:

$$\Delta S°_{sys} = \sum nS°(\text{products}) - \sum mS°(\text{reactants})$$

The change in entropy of the reaction's surroundings depends on the amount of heat $\left(q_{sys}\right)$ that is transferred between the system and its surroundings. For **isothermal processes**, the change of entropy in the surroundings is:

$$\Delta S_{surr} = -\frac{q_{sys}}{T}$$

If a reaction occurs at standard conditions and is isobaric (at constant pressure), then q_{sys} is the enthalpy change for the reaction, ΔH_{sys}°. So, the entropy change in the surrounding becomes:

$$\Delta S_{surr}^{\circ} = -\frac{\Delta H_{sys}^{\circ}}{T}$$

The entropy change for the universe is:

$$\Delta S_{univ}^{\circ} = \Delta S_{surr}^{\circ} + \Delta S_{sys}^{\circ}$$

One example of a reversible process is the melting of ice at 0 °C (273 K) and 1 atm if the temperature and pressure are held constant. At this temperature and pressure, the amount of heat that is required to convert 1.00 mole of solid ice to liquid water is 6.01 kJ. This heat is absorbed from the surroundings to melt the ice in the system; therefore, this process is endothermic, $q > 0$. The entropy change for this system is:

$$\Delta S_{sys} = \frac{q_{sys}}{T} = \frac{6.01 \text{ kJ/mol}}{273 \text{ K}} \times \frac{1{,}000 \text{ J}}{1 \text{ kJ}} = +22.0 \text{ J/(mol} \cdot \text{K)}$$

The surroundings lose heat to the system, so $q_{surr} = -q_{sys}$. The entropy change in the surroundings is then:

$$\Delta S_{surr} = \frac{-q_{sys}}{T} = \frac{6.01 \text{ kJ/mol}}{273 \text{ K}} \times \frac{1{,}000 \text{ J}}{1 \text{ kJ}} = -22.0 \text{ J/(mol} \cdot \text{K)}$$

As we can see, the total change of entropy for this process at 273 K is $\Delta S_{univ} = \Delta S_{sys} + \Delta S_{surr} = 0$. Therefore, this process is reversible.

At 25 °C (298 K), the heat that is required to melt 1.00 mole of ice is the same, so the change in the entropy for the system is still $+22.0 \text{ J/(mol} \cdot \text{K)}$. However, the temperature in the surroundings is different, so the entropy change in the surroundings is:

$$\Delta S_{surr} = \frac{-q_{sys}}{T} = \frac{6.01 \text{ kJ/mol}}{298 \text{ K}} \times \frac{1{,}000 \text{ J}}{1 \text{ kJ}} = -20.2 \text{ J/(mol} \cdot \text{K)}$$

The total change of entropy in the universe is:

$$\Delta S_{univ} = \Delta S_{sys} + \Delta S_{surr} = (22.0 - 20.2) \text{ J/(mol} \cdot \text{K)} = +1.8 \text{ J/(mol} \cdot \text{K)}$$

The overall entropy change is positive. In most conditions, the melting of ice at room temperature and standard pressure is spontaneous and irreversible. We may conclude that for the spontaneous and irreversible processes, the overall entropy change in the universe always increases. This is one result of the second law of thermodynamics.

CALCULATING ΔG FOR A REACTION USING HESS'S LAW

In **Hess's Law**, the change of enthalpy (ΔH) for a reaction can be calculated by adding up the enthalpy changes of all individual steps. Enthalpy is a state function, which means that it is independent of the path from an initial state to its final state. Like enthalpy, free energy is a state function, so the calculation for ΔG has the same format as ΔH. For a reaction at standard conditions with m moles of reactants in total and n moles of products in total, the change in free energy, ΔG°, can be calculated from **standard free energy of formation** $\left(\Delta G_f^\circ\right)$ of the reactants and products. The ΔG_f° values of the substances can be found in reference literature, and ΔG° can be calculated as the difference between the sum of ΔG_f° for the products and the sum of ΔG_f° for the reactants:

$$\Delta G^\circ = \sum n \Delta G_f^\circ(\text{products}) - \sum m \Delta G_f^\circ(\text{reactants})$$

PREDICTING THE TEMPERATURE DEPENDENCE OF SPONTANEITY

The change in Gibbs free energy is directly related to the change in entropy for the universe:

$$\Delta G \propto -T\Delta S_{\text{univ}}$$

According to the second law of thermodynamics, for a process to occur spontaneously the change in the entropy must be positive. $\Delta S_{\text{univ}} > 0$. So $\Delta G < 0$ is true for a spontaneous process. $\Delta S_{\text{univ}} < 0$ and $\Delta G > 0$ is true for a non-spontaneous process. If a process is at its equilibrium, $\Delta S_{\text{univ}} = 0$ and $\Delta G = 0$.

The changes in the enthalpy, Gibbs free energy, and entropy are related by:

$$\Delta G = \Delta H - T\Delta S$$

The sign of ΔG depends on the signs of both ΔH and the $T\Delta S$ term. Their possible effects on determining the sign of ΔG can be summarized in the table below:

ΔH	ΔS	$-T\Delta S$	$\Delta G = \Delta H - T\Delta S$	Spontaneity
−	+	−	−	Always spontaneous
−	−	+	+ or −	At low T: The value of $-T\Delta S$ is small and positive. When add to ΔH, a negative ΔG is retained, so the process is spontaneous. At high T: The value of $-T\Delta S$ is large and positive. When added to ΔH, the ΔG becomes positive, so the process is non-spontaneous.
+	+	−	+ or −	At low T: the value of $-T\Delta S$ is small and negative. When add to ΔH, the ΔG is still positive, so the process is non-spontaneous. At high T: the value of $-T\Delta S$ is large and negative. When added to ΔH, it yields a negative ΔG, so the process is spontaneous.
+	−	+	+	Always non-spontaneous

For example, suppose that ΔH and ΔS do not change under different temperatures and predict the spontaneity of the ammonia synthesis reaction in Haber process:

$$N_2(g) + 3\,H_2(g) \rightleftharpoons 2\,NH_3(g), \Delta H° = -92.4 \text{ kJ/mol}$$

To determine the spontaneity of the reaction, i.e., the sign of ΔG, we first determine the sign of ΔS. Notice that the reaction has fewer molecules on the product side for the forward reaction and there is no phase change between the reactants and products. Therefore, entropy decreases in the forward direction, $\Delta S < 0$. Since both ΔS and ΔH are negative, the sign of ΔG depends on the temperature: $\Delta G = \Delta H - T\Delta S$. While the $-T\Delta S$ term is positive regardless of temperature, at low temperatures its numerical value is small. When added to the negative ΔH term, ΔG remains negative and $\Delta G < 0$. Therefore, this reaction is spontaneous at low temperatures. At high temperatures, the numerical value of the $-T\Delta S$ term is large. When added to the negative ΔH term, the large $-T\Delta S$ term leads to a positive ΔG, and $\Delta G > 0$. Therefore, this reaction is non-spontaneous at high temperatures. In practice, despite being non-spontaneous, this reaction is still carried out at high temperatures (usually around 450 °C) to increase the reaction rate. A catalyst is used to decrease the activation energy barrier, and high pressure is applied to push the reaction in the forward direction.

RELATING VALUES OF $\Delta G°$ AND EQUILIBRIUM COEFFICIENTS

The changes in the Gibbs free energy at non-standard conditions (ΔG) can be corrected from the standard free energy change ($\Delta G°$) by factoring in some adjustments:

$$\Delta G = \Delta G° + RT \ln Q$$

In this equation, R is the ideal-gas constant, T is the absolute temperature, and Q is the reaction quotient. Recall that under constant T and P, the change in the free energy is:

$$\Delta G = -T\Delta S_{\text{univ}}$$

For spontaneous forward reactions, $\Delta S_{\text{univ}} > 0$, so $\Delta G < 0$. In non-spontaneous forward reactions, $\Delta S_{\text{univ}} < 0$ and $\Delta G > 0$. However, their reverse reactions have reversed signs in ΔS_{univ} and ΔG, so the reverse reactions are favored. When ΔG is zero, the forward and reverse reactions occur at the same rate, so the overall reaction sits at equilibrium. Also, when a reaction is at equilibrium the reaction quotient Q is equal to K_{eq}. Substituting these values into the first equation, we have:

$$0 = \Delta G° + RT \ln K_{eq}$$

Rearranging the expression:

$$\Delta G° = -RT \ln K_{eq}$$

With this correlation, the equilibrium constant K_{eq} can be calculated from the standard free energy change $\Delta G°$ in the chemical reaction. Solving for K_{eq}, we get:

$$K_{eq} = e^{-\Delta G°/RT}$$

Example Problems

Explain how to calculate the amount of heat lost by a piece of copper with a mass of 100.0 g when it cools from 100.0 °C to 20.0 °C. The specific heat of copper is 0.380 J/(g · °C).

To calculate the amount of heat lost by a piece of copper with a mass of 100.0 g when it cools from 100.0 °C to 20.0 °C, use the equation $Q = mc\Delta T$, where Q is the amount of heat lost in joules, m is the mass of the copper in grams, c is the specific heat of copper, and ΔT is the change in temperature $(T_2 - T_1)$ in degrees Celsius. Substituting 100.0 g for m, 0.380 J/(g · °C) for c, 20.0 °C for T_2, and 100.0 °C for T_1 yields:

$$Q = (100.0 \text{ g})(0.380 \text{ J}/(g \cdot °C))\big((20.0 \text{ °C}) - (100.0 \text{ °C})\big) = -3{,}040 \text{ J}$$

The negative value confirms that heat was lost as the copper cooled.

Calculate the specific heat of an unknown metal under the following circumstances:

- In a calorimetry experiment, the specific heat of an unknown metal dropped 20.0 °C;
- The mass of the unknown metal is 100.0 g.
- The temperature of the water with a mass of 100.0 g in the calorimeter raised 1.00 °C; and
- The specific heat of water is 4.20 J/(g · °C).

The heat lost by the metal must equal the heat gained by the water as shown in the equation, $Q_{lost \ by \ metal} = Q_{gained \ by \ the \ water}$, where Q is the amount of heat lost or gained in joules. To calculate the specific heat of the metal, use $-m_{metal}c_{metal}\Delta T_{metal} = m_{water}c_{water}\Delta T_{water}$, where m is the mass of the metal or water in grams, c is the specific heat of the metal or water, and ΔT is the change in temperature $(T_2 - T_1)$ in degrees Celsius in the metal or water. Solving the equation for c_{metal} results in:

$$c_{metal} = -\frac{m_{water}c_{water}\Delta T_{water}}{m_{metal}\Delta T_{metal}}$$

Substituting in the given information yields:

$$c_{metal} = -\frac{(100.0 \text{ g})(4.20 \text{ J}/(g \cdot °C))(1.00 \text{ °C})}{(100.0 \text{ g})(20.0 \text{ °C})} = 0.21 \text{ J}/(g \cdot °C)$$

Calculate the $\Delta S°$ and $\Delta H°$ for the reaction $N_2(g) + O_2(g) \rightarrow 2 \text{ NO}(g)$ at 298 K, then calculate the $\Delta S°_{surr}$ and $\Delta S°_{univ}$ associated with this reaction.

Taking the values of $S°$ and $\Delta H°$ from reference literature, the standard entropy change for this reaction is:

$$\Delta S° = 2 \times S°[\text{NO}(g)] - (S°[\text{N}_2(g)] + S°[\text{O}_2(g)])$$
$$= 2 \times (210.62) - (191.5 + 205.0) \text{ J}/(\text{mol} \cdot K)$$
$$= +24.7 \text{ J}/(\text{mol} \cdot K)$$

The above value is also the entropy change of the system, $\Delta S°_{sys}$.

The standard enthalpy change, ΔH°_{sys}, is:

$$\Delta H^\circ = 2 \times \Delta H^\circ_f[NO(g)] - \left(\Delta H^\circ_f[N_2(g)] + \Delta H^\circ_f[O_2(g)]\right)$$
$$= 2 \times (90.37) - (0 + 0) \text{ kJ/mol}$$
$$= +180.7 \text{ kJ/mol}$$

The entropy changes in the surroundings, ΔS°_{surr}, is equal to:

$$\Delta S^\circ_{surr} = -\frac{\Delta H^\circ_{sys}}{T}$$
$$= -\frac{180.7 \text{ kJ/mol}}{298 \text{ K}}$$
$$= -0.607 \text{ kJ/(mol} \cdot \text{K)} = -60.7 \text{ J/(mol} \cdot \text{K)}$$

The entropy change for the universe is the sum of ΔS°_{surr} and ΔS°_{sys}:

$$\Delta S^\circ_{univ} = \Delta S^\circ_{surr} + \Delta S^\circ_{sys} = (-60.7 + 24.7) \text{ J/(mol} \cdot \text{K)} = -36.0 \text{ J/(mol} \cdot \text{K)}$$

Calculate the ΔG° for the reaction below at 298 K using the ΔG°_f for the reactants and products, then verify the calculated ΔG° with ΔH° and ΔS° values:

$$\mathbf{C_3H_8(g) + 5\,O_2(g) \rightarrow 3\,CO_2(g) + 4\,H_2O(l)}$$

Using the ΔG°_f values, the ΔG° for the reaction is:

$$\Delta G^\circ = \left(3 \times \Delta G^\circ_f[CO_2(g)] + 4 \times \Delta G^\circ_f[H_2O(l)]\right) - \left(\Delta G^\circ_f[C_3H_8(g)] + 5 \times \Delta G^\circ_f[O_2(g)]\right)$$
$$= \left(3 \times (-394.4) + 4 \times (-237.1)\right) - (-23.47 + 5 \times 0) \text{ kJ/mol}$$
$$= -2,108 \text{ kJ/mol}$$

The ΔG° value is also equal to $\Delta H^\circ - T\Delta S^\circ$. We may calculate for ΔS° and ΔH° using Hess's law, then verify the above result with this relation.

$$\Delta H^\circ = \left(3 \times \Delta H^\circ_f[CO_2(g)] + 4 \times \Delta H^\circ_f[H_2O(l)]\right) - \left(\Delta H^\circ_f[C_3H_8(g)] + 5 \times \Delta H^\circ_f[O_2(g)]\right)$$
$$= \left(3 \times (-393.5) + 4 \times (-285.8)\right) - (-103.9 + 5 \times 0) \text{ kJ/mol}$$
$$= -2,220 \text{ kJ/mol}$$

$$\Delta S^\circ = \left(3 \times S^\circ[CO_2(g)] + 4 \times S^\circ[H_2O(l)]\right) - \left(S^\circ[C_3H_8(g)] + 5 \times S^\circ[O_2(g)]\right)$$
$$= \left(3 \times (213.6) + 4 \times (69.91)\right) - \left(269.9 + 5 \times (205.0)\right) \text{ J/(mol} \cdot \text{K)}$$
$$= -347.5 \text{ J/(mol} \cdot \text{K)}$$

$$\Delta G^\circ = -2,220 \text{ kJ/mol} - \left((298 \text{ K})(-347.5 \text{ J/(mol} \cdot \text{K)})\left(\frac{1 \text{ kJ}}{1,000 \text{ J}}\right)\right) = -2,108 \text{ kJ/mol}$$

As shown above, the ΔG° values calculated with both methods are the same.

Calculate the $\Delta G°$ and K_{eq} of the Haber process $\left(N_2(g) + 3\,H_2(g) \rightleftharpoons 2\,NH_3(g)\right)$ using literature $\Delta G_f°$ values at 25.0 °C.

$$\Delta G_f°[NH_3(g)] = -16.66 \text{ kJ/mol}$$
$$\Delta G_f°[H_2(g)] = 0 \text{ kJ/mol}$$
$$\Delta G_f°[N_2(g)] = 0 \text{ kJ/mol}$$

Using the $\Delta G_f°$ values for $N_2(g)$, $H_2(g)$, and $NH_3(g)$, we get:

$$\Delta G° = \left(2 \times \Delta G_f°[NH_3(g)]\right) - \left(3 \times \Delta G_f°[H_2(g)] + \Delta G_f°[N_2(g)]\right)$$
$$= \left((2 \times (-16.66)) - (3 \times 0 + 0)\right) \text{ kJ/mol}$$
$$= -33.32 \text{ kJ/mol}$$

The value of $-\frac{\Delta G°}{RT}$, which is the exponent needed for calculating K_{eq}, is:

$$-\frac{\Delta G°}{RT} = -\frac{(-33.32 \text{ kJ/mol})}{(8.314 \text{ J/(mol} \cdot \text{K))}\left((273 + 25.0) \text{ K}\right)} \times \frac{1000 \text{ J}}{1 \text{ kJ}} = 13.4$$

Therefore, the value of K_{eq} is:

$$K_{eq} = e^{\frac{-\Delta G°}{RT}} = e^{13.4} = 6.92 \times 10^5$$

The value of K_{eq} at this temperature is very large, which means that the forward reaction (towards the direction of making ammonia) is favored.

Electrochemistry

Electrolytic Cell

ELECTROLYSIS

Electrolysis is the use of current to induce a chemical reaction that would not otherwise occur. For instance, passing a sufficiently strong current through pure water can split it into hydrogen and oxygen, $2 H_2O \rightarrow 2 H_2 + O_2$.

Electrolysis is used to purify metals, to deposit thin films of metal on other materials (electroplating), and to produce useful chemicals, including sodium hydroxide and potassium chlorate. The electrolysis of water also has applications; it is used to create hydrogen fuel and to produce breathable oxygen for the International Space Station.

ELECTROLYTE

An electrolyte is a substance that separates into positive and negative ions when dissolved in water. The resulting solution remains electrically neutral because the total charge of the positive ions equals the total charge of the negative ions, but the presence of the ions makes the solution electrically conductive.

One of the most familiar everyday electrolytes is table salt, sodium chloride (NaCl), which when dissolved in water separates into sodium cations (Na^+) and chlorine anions (Cl^-). Other common electrolytes include hydrochloric acid (HCl); sodium hydroxide, or lye (NaOH); and baking soda, or sodium bicarbonate ($NaHCO_3$). Electrolytes play an important role in the body; the charge they carry is important for the working of nerves and muscles and to regulate fluid balance.

ELECTRON FLOW; OXIDATION, AND REDUCTION AT THE ELECTRODES

In electrolysis, current is passed through an electrolytic substance to cause a chemical reaction to occur. The electrodes are the conductors that connect the substance to the rest of the circuit. The current flows from the voltage source to one electrode, called the **anode**, through the solution to another electrode, called the **cathode**, and back to the voltage source.

Because current is defined as the flow of positive charge, the direction that electrons travel through the circuit is opposite the current. The electrons, therefore, move from the anode into the voltage source and from the voltage source into the cathode. This means that the anode tends to accumulate a positive charge as electrons move from it and the cathode a negative charge as electrons move into it. Each electrode attracts from the solution ions of the opposite charge. Positive ions flow toward the cathode and negative toward the anode. Because of the excess of electrons at the cathode, the ions there tend to undergo reduction reactions, reacting with electrons and reducing their oxidation numbers. On the other hand, the ions at the anode tend to undergo oxidation reactions.

HALF-REACTIONS AND VOLTAIC CELLS

A **galvanic or voltaic cell** is a device that uses oxidation and reduction reactions in electrolytic solutions to produce electrical current. (There is no difference between a galvanic cell and a voltaic cell; these are two words for the same thing.) Electric batteries consist of one or more galvanic cells.

A voltaic cell consists of two electrodes of different metals in different solutions. The electrodes are connected by a wire, and the solutions are either separated by a permeable membrane or

134

connected by a "salt bridge" that allows some ions to flow between them and maintain the electrical neutrality of the solutions. The metals and solutions are chosen so that an oxidation reaction will occur at the electrode in one solution (the anode) and a reduction reaction will occur at the electrode in the other (the cathode). We refer therefore to the "half reaction" at each electrode. Essentially, as the metal atoms at the anode are oxidized, they release electrons that flow through the wire to the cathode, where they react to reduce metal ions at the cathode there. (Technically, single electrons don't make the entire circuit, but the effect is as if they did.)

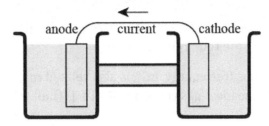

CALCULATING QUANTITIES IN ELECTROLYTIC CELLS

The quantity of charges is measured in coulombs (C), while the strength of the current is measured in amperes (A). One ampere is equal to the charges passing the same point in a circuit per second. So, the quantity of charges and current over a certain period are related by:

$$charge = current \times time$$

Written in units:

$$C = A \times s$$

Thus, one mole of electrons has a charge of 96,485 C, which is equal to 1 faraday. Dividing a quantity of charges by Faraday's constant generates the number of moles of electrons that are involved in the process:

$$moles\ of\ e^- = \frac{charge}{96,485\ C/mol}$$

The number of moles of electrons can then be related to the number of moles of the substances involved in an electrolytic cell. For example, in the electrolysis of molten $AlCl_3$, three electrons are needed to reduce one mole of Al^{3+}: $Al^{3+}(l) + 3\ e^- \longrightarrow Al(l)$. In this case, the number of moles of Al being produced is equal to the number of electrons divided by three. Lastly, the mass of the substances being produced or consumed is calculated by:

$$mass = (moles\ of\ the\ substance) \times (molar\ mass)$$

REDUCTION POTENTIALS AND CELL POTENTIALS

The reduction potential is a measurement of how strongly a particular chemical substance tends to acquire electrons and undergo a reduction reaction. It is measured in volts, the units of electrical potential. A substance with a much stronger reduction potential will tend to take electrons from a substance with a much weaker reduction potential, causing the latter to be oxidized.

The cell potential is the electrical potential produced by a galvanic cell. It is equal to the difference between the reduction potentials of the materials making up the two electrodes. In fact, because the reduction potential of a material can't readily be measured directly; it is generally cell potentials

135

that are used to determine reduction potentials, with the reduction potential of a "standard hydrogen electrode" defined as zero as a baseline.

RELATING VALUES OF $E°_{cell}$, $\Delta G°$, AND K_{eq}

When ΔG is negative and E_{cell} is positive, the redox reaction for the voltaic cell is spontaneous. The equation that relates $E°_{cell}$ and $\Delta G°$, both at standard conditions, is:

$$\Delta G° = -nFE°_{cell}$$

In this equation, F is Faraday's constant ($F = 96,485$ C/mol $= 96,485$ J/(V $\cdot$ mol)) and n is the number of electrons involved in the redox cell reaction.

The standard change in the Gibbs free energy, $\Delta G°$, is also related to the equilibrium constant K_{eq} by $\Delta G° = -RT \ln K_{eq}$, where R is the ideal-gas constant (8.314 J/(mol $\cdot$ K)) and T is absolute temperature in Kelvin.

Therefore, knowing the standard cell potential, $E°_{cell}$, means that both $\Delta G°$ and K_{eq} can be calculated.

CALCULATIONS USING CONCENTRATION CELLS

The **Nernst equation** is used to calculate for the cell potential under non-standard conditions:

$$E = E° - \frac{RT}{nF} \ln Q = E° - \frac{2.303\ RT}{nF} \log Q$$

The $E°$ is the standard cell potential, which is zero (since both electrodes have the same standard reduction potential). R is the ideal-gas constant, T is absolute temperature in Kelvin, F is the Faraday's constant, and n is the number of electrons. Quantity Q is the reaction quotient; both the natural log ($\ln Q$, where the base is e) and common log ($\log Q$, where the base is 10) can be used in this equation. In a concentration cell that is composed of M^+ metal solutions with different concentrations, its half-cell equations are:

- Anode: $M(s) \longrightarrow M^{n+}(aq, dilute) + ne^-$
- Cathode: $M^{n+}(aq, concentrated) + ne^- \longrightarrow M(s)$
- Overall: $M^{n+}(aq, concentrated) \longrightarrow M^{n+}(aq, dilute)$

A concentration cell operates until the concentration of both half-cells is the same. The oxidation occurs on the more dilute half-cell, as it needs to raise the concentration of M^+ in the cell solution to level the concentration on the other cell. Therefore, the reduction occurs on the more concentrated half-cell, as it needs to remove the of M^+ from the cell solution to reach the concentration of the other cell. The reaction quotient for the concentration cell is then:

$$Q = \frac{[M^{n+}]_{dilute}}{[M^{n+}]_{conctrated}}$$

Substituting the corresponding concentrations, the correct number of electrons for the redox cell reactions, the cell temperature, and the constants will yield the cell potential of the concentration cell.

Batteries

LEAD-STORAGE BATTERIES

A lead-storage battery is a galvanic cell in which the anode consists of lead, the cathode consists of lead dioxide (PbO_2), and the electrodes are surrounded by dilute sulfuric acid (H_2SO_4). Because both electrodes are immersed in the same electrolyte, it isn't necessary to have separate half-cells divided by a membrane or connected by a salt bridge. As the lead-storage battery discharges, the lead at the anode is oxidized and reacts with HSO_4^- ions in the solution to generate lead (II) sulfate ($PbSO_4$), while the lead dioxide at the cathode is reduced and reacts to also produce lead (II) sulfate. The full half-reactions are as follows:

- Anode: $Pb(s) + HSO_4^-(aq) \rightarrow PbSO_4(s) + H^+(aq) + 2\ e^-$
- Cathode: $PbO_2(s) + HSO_4^-(aq) + 3\ H^+(aq) + 2\ e^- \rightarrow PbSO_4(s) + 2\ H_2O(l)$

Lead-storage batteries are commonly used in cars. They have the advantage of being relatively lightweight and inexpensive and, importantly, of being rechargeable: because the lead sulfate generated in the redox reactions is not soluble, it remains available for reaction, and driving a current through the battery can reverse the discharge reactions and recharge its potential.

NICKEL-CADMIUM BATTERIES

A nickel-cadmium battery is a type of rechargeable battery commonly used in cordless power tools, although these batteries are becoming less common than they used to be as their place is being taken by nickel metal hydride batteries and lithium-ion batteries. They have the advantage over alkaline batteries and lead-storage batteries of delivering a more or less constant voltage over time rather than having their voltage decrease significantly as the battery is depleted.

A nickel-cadmium battery consists of galvanic cells with cadmium anodes and nickel oxide hydroxide $NiO(OH)$ cathodes. They are immersed in an alkaline electrolyte, commonly potassium hydroxide (KOH). The following are the half-reactions occurring at each electrode:

- Anode: $Cd(s) + 2\ OH^-(aq) \rightarrow Cd(OH)_2(s) + 2\ e^-$
- Cathode: $2NiO(OH)(s) + 2\ H_2O(l) + 2\ e^- \rightarrow 2\ Ni(OH)_2(s) + 2\ OH^-(aq)$

Because the electrolyte is not consumed in the net reaction, and because both the products cadmium hydroxide and nickel (II) hydroxide are insoluble in alkaline solutions, the battery is rechargeable; when a current is run through the battery, these reactions will occur in reverse.

Example Problems

Calculate the mass of magnesium metal produced over 1 day in the electrolysis of molten $MgCl_2$, assuming the current is 5.0 A.

The electrode reactions for this electrolytic cell are:

- Cathode: $Mg^{2+}(l) + 2\ e^- \longrightarrow Mg(l)$
- Anode: $2\ Cl^-(l) \longrightarrow Cl_2(g) + 2\ e^-$

The total charges for 5.0 A in one day are:

$$C = A \times s = (5.0\ A)(1.00\ day)\left(\frac{24.0\ h}{1.00\ day}\right)\left(\frac{60.0\ min}{1.00\ h}\right)\left(\frac{60.0\ sec}{1.00\ min}\right) = 4.32 \times 10^5\ C$$

The number of moles of electrons is:

$$\frac{C}{96{,}485 \text{ C/mol}} = \frac{4.32 \times 10^5 \text{ C}}{96{,}485 \text{ C/mol}} = 4.47 \text{ mol}$$

As is shown in the electrode reaction, two electrons are needed to reduce one mole of Mg^{2+}. Therefore, the number of moles of magnesium metal being produced is: $\frac{4.47 \text{ mol}}{2} = 2.24$ mol.

The mass of the produced magnesium metal is:

$$2.24 \text{ mol} \times 24.3 \text{ g/mol} = 54.4 \text{ g}$$

Calculate $E°_{cell}$, $\Delta G°$, and K_{eq} for a lead-acid battery, given that the overall reaction is:

$$\textbf{PbO}_2\textbf{(s)} + \textbf{Pb(s)} + \textbf{2 HSO}_4{}^-\textbf{(aq)} + \textbf{2 H}^+\textbf{(aq)} \rightarrow \textbf{2 PbSO}_4\textbf{(s)} + \textbf{2 H}_2\textbf{O(l)}$$

The reductive half-cell reaction for the cathode is:

$$PbO_2(s) + HSO_4{}^-(aq) + 3 H^+(aq) + 2 e^- \rightarrow PbSO_4(s) + 2 H_2O(l); \; E°_{red} = +1.685 \text{ V}$$

The oxidative half-cell reaction for the anode is:

$$Pb(s) + HSO_4{}^-(aq) \rightarrow PbSO_4(s) + H^+(aq) + 2 e^-; \; E°_{red} = -0.356 \text{ V}$$

So, the standard cell potential is:

$$\begin{aligned} E°_{cell} &= E°_{red}(\text{cathode}) - E°_{red}(\text{anode}) \\ &= +1.685 \text{ V} - (-0.356 \text{ V}) \\ &= +2.041 \text{ V} \end{aligned}$$

There are two electrons involved in the redox reactions, so the $\Delta G°$ is:

$$\begin{aligned} \Delta G° &= -nFE°_{cell} \\ &= -2 \times (96{,}485 \text{ J/(V} \cdot \text{mol)}) \times (+2.041 \text{ V}) \times \frac{1 \text{ kJ}}{1{,}000 \text{ J}} \\ &= -393.9 \text{ kJ/mol} \end{aligned}$$

The equilibrium constant K_{eq} is calculated from the $\Delta G°$:

$$\Delta G° = -RT \ln K_{eq}$$

$$-393.9 \frac{\text{kJ}}{\text{mol}} \times \frac{1000 \text{ J}}{1 \text{ kJ}} = -\left(8.314 \frac{\text{J}}{\text{(mol} \cdot \text{K)}}\right)(298 \text{ K}) \ln K_{eq}$$

$\ln K_{eq} = 159$, so $K_{eq} = e^{159} = 1.09 \times 10^{69}$. This reaction is highly spontaneous under standard conditions.

Calculate the cell potential for the concentration cell of Cu(s)|Cu²⁺(aq)(0.025 M) ‖ Cu²⁺(aq)(0.75 M)|Cu(s) at standard temperature and 273 K, and 330 K.

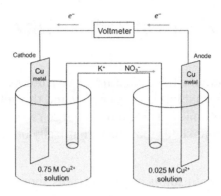

Recall that in the concentration cell, oxidation occurs in the half cell with the dilute solution, making it the anode of the cell. The electrons flow from the dilute side (the anode) to the concentrated side (the cathode). Meanwhile, the NO_3^- ions in the salt bridge move towards the anode to make up for the loss in the negative charge. The cell potential for this cell at the standard temperature (298 K) is:

$$E = E° - \frac{RT}{nF} \ln \frac{[Cu^{2+}]_{dilute}}{[Cu^{2+}]_{conctrated}} = 0 - \frac{(8.314 \text{ J/(mol·K)})(298 \text{ K})}{2(96,485 \text{ J/(V·mol)})} \ln \frac{0.025 \text{ M}}{0.75 \text{ M}} = 0.044 \text{ V}$$

At 273 K, the cell potential is:

$$0 - \frac{(8.314 \text{ J/(mol·K)})(273 \text{ K})}{2(96,485 \text{ J/(V·mol)})} \ln \frac{0.025 \text{ M}}{0.75 \text{ M}} = 0.040 \text{ V}$$

At 330 K, the cell potential is:

$$0 - \frac{(8.314 \text{ J/(mol·K)})(330 \text{ K})}{2(96,485 \text{ J/(V·mol)})} \ln \frac{0.025 \text{ M}}{0.75 \text{ M}} = 0.048 \text{ V}$$

Though the change is small, temperature does affect the cell potential of a concentration cell. As the temperature increase, the cell potential also increases.

Nuclear Chemistry

Basics of Radioactivity

RADIOACTIVITY

Radioisotopes, also known as radionuclides or radioactive isotopes, are atoms that have an unstable nucleus. This is a nucleus that has excess energy and the potential to make radiation particles within the nucleus (subatomic particles) or undergo radioactive decay, which can result in the emission of gamma rays. Radionuclides may occur naturally but can also be artificially produced.

Radioactive decay occurs when an unstable atomic nucleus spontaneously loses energy by emitting ionizing particles and radiation. Decay is a form of energy transfer, as energy is lost. It also results in different products. Before decay there is one type of atom, called the **parent nuclide**. After decay there are one or more different products, called the **daughter nuclide(s)**.

> **Review Video: Radioactivity**
> Visit mometrix.com/academy and enter code: 537142

Radioactive half-life is the time it takes for half of the radioactive nuclei in a sample to undergo radioactive decay. Radioactive decay rates are usually expressed in terms of half-lives. The different types of radioactivity lead to different decay paths, which transmute the nuclei into other chemical elements. **Decay products** (or daughter nuclides) make radioactive dating possible. **Decay chains** are a series of decays that result in different products. for example, uranium-238 is often found in granite. Its decay chain includes 14 daughter products. It eventually becomes a stable isotope of lead, which is why lead is often found with deposits of uranium ore. Its first half-life is equivalent to the approximate age of the earth, about 4.5 billion years. One of its products is radon, a radioactive gas. **Radiation** is when energy is emitted by one body and absorbed by another. Nuclear weapons, nuclear reactors, and radioactive substances are all examples of things that involve ionizing radiation. Acoustic and electromagnetic radiation are other types of radiation.

Stable, or non-radioactive, isotopes are those that have not been observed to decay. It is not known whether some stable isotopes may have such long decay times that observing decay is not possible. Currently, 80 elements have one or more stable isotopes. There are 256 known stable isotopes in total. Carbon, for example, has three isotopes. Two (carbon-12 and carbon-13) are stable and one (carbon-14) is radioactive.

Ionizing radiation is that which can cause an electron to detach from an atom. It occurs in radioactive reactions and comes in three types: alpha (α), beta (β), and gamma (γ). Alpha rays are positive, beta rays are negative, and gamma rays are neutral. **Alpha particles** are larger than beta particles and can cause severe damage if ingested. Because of their large mass, however, they can be stopped easily. Even paper can protect against this type of radiation. **Beta particles** can be beta-minus or beta-plus. Beta-minus particles contain an energetic electron, while beta-plus particles are emitted by positrons and can result in gamma photons. Beta particles can be stopped with thin metal. **Gamma rays** are a type of high energy electromagnetic radiation consisting of photons. Gamma radiation rids the decaying nucleus of excess energy after it has emitted either alpha or beta radiation. Gamma rays can cause serious damage when absorbed by living tissue, and it takes thick lead to stop them. Alpha, beta, and gamma radiation can also have positive applications.

Nuclear fission and nuclear fusion are similar in that they occur in the nucleus of an atom, can release great amounts of energy, and result in the formation of different elements (known as nuclear transmutation). They are different in that one breaks apart a nucleus and the other joins nuclei. **Nuclear fission** is the splitting of a large nucleus into smaller pieces. **Nuclear fusion** is the joining of two nuclei, which occurs under extreme temperatures and pressures. Fusion occurs naturally in stars, and is the process responsible for the release of great amounts of energy. When fusion occurs, many atomic nuclei with like charges are joined together, forming a heavier nucleus. When this occurs, energy can be absorbed and/or released.

Radioactive waste is a waste product that is considered dangerous because of either low levels or high levels of radioactivity. Radioactive waste could include discarded clothing that was used as protection against radiation or decay products of substances used to create electricity through nuclear fission. Small amounts of radioactive material can be ingested as a method of tracing how the body distributes certain elements. Other radioactive materials are used as light sources because they glow when heated. Uncontrolled radiation or even small amounts of radioactive material can cause sickness and cancer in humans. **Gamma wave radiation** is fast moving radiation that can cause cancer and damage genetic information by crashing into DNA molecules or other cells. Low-level radiation also occurs naturally. When related to everyday occurrences, radiation is measured in millirems per hour (mrem/hr). Humans can be exposed to radiation from stone used to build houses, cosmic rays from space, x-rays and other medical devices, and nuclear energy products.

BINDING ENERGY

The binding energy of a system in general is the energy required to separate a system into its component parts. In the case of an atom, the atomic binding energy is the energy required to separate the electrons from the atomic nucleus. Because the nth ionization energy of an atom is defined as the energy required to remove one electron after $n - 1$ have already been removed, the atomic binding energy can be thought of as the sum of the ionization energies of an atom for all possible values of n (up to the atom's atomic number).

The nuclear binding energy is the energy that would be required to completely separate the nucleus of the atom into isolated protons and neutrons. The nuclear binding energies are much larger than the atomic binding energies; the forces holding the atomic nucleus together are very large. For example, the atomic binding energy of a carbon-12 atom is about 7.85×10^{-17} J or 490 eV, whereas its nuclear binding energy is about 1.5×10^{-11}J or 92 MeV—almost a million times as great. This is why a nuclear fission reaction releases so much energy; a part of the nuclear binding energy is released.

CALCULATING RADIOACTIVE HALF-LIFE

The half-life of a radioactive material is the time it takes for half of the atoms in a sample to undergo radioactive decay. This does not mean that after two half-lives there is nothing left of the sample. Rather, after one half-life half of the original atoms have decayed, and after another half-life, half of the remaining atoms have decayed, which means that one-quarter of the original atoms remain. In general, the amount of a radioactive substance over time decays exponentially. The number of atoms of a radioactive sample remaining after a time t is equal to $N(t) = N_0 \left(\frac{1}{2}\right)^{t/t_{1/2}}$, where N_0 is the number of atoms originally present and $t_{1/2}$ is the half-life. This can be expressed in a base e exponential as $N(t) = N_0 e^{\ln 2(t/t_{1/2})}$.

For example, the radioactive isotope nitrogen-13 has a half-life of 9.965 minutes. This means that if you start with 100.0 moles of nitrogen-13, after one hour you would be left with 1.540 moles of the isotope that have not yet decayed.

$$(100.0 \text{ mol}) \left(\frac{1}{2}\right)^{(60 \text{ min})/(9.965 \text{ min})} = 1.540 \text{ moles}$$

ALPHA PARTICLES

Alpha particles are the products of **alpha decay**. They are identical to helium nuclei. Alpha particles consist of two protons and two neutrons. Because they have two protons but zero electrons, alpha particles have a net +2 charge. They are represented by the Greek letter alpha as α, α^{2+}, or $^4_2\alpha^{2+}$. Because they are identical to helium nuclei, they may also be written as He^{2+}, ^4_2He, or $^4_2He^{2+}$. Because alpha particles have a strong charge and travel slowly, they interact significantly with matter that they pass through and may therefore be stopped by a sheet of paper or a few inches of air. Alpha particles cannot penetrate the skin.

BETA PARTICLES

Beta particles are the products of **beta decay**. Beta particles may be high-speed electrons or high-speed positrons. These two forms of beta decay are designated by the Greek letter beta as β^- and β^+ or $^0_{-1}e$ and $^0_{+1}e$, respectively. Negative beta particles are created during radioactive decay when a neutron changes into a proton and an electron. Positive beta particles are created when a proton changes into a neutron and a positron. Beta particles have a greater penetrating ability than alpha particles. Beta particles can be stopped by thin plywood or metal or several feet of air.

GAMMA RADIATION

Gamma radiation (represented by the Greek letter gamma, γ) is released during **gamma decay**. Often, atoms that have just undergone alpha or beta decay then undergo gamma decay. An atom produced during alpha or beta decay may still be in an excited state. The atom then releases this energy in a burst of gamma rays as high-energy photons. Gamma radiation is part of the electromagnetic spectrum and consists of electromagnetic waves that travel at the speed of light with frequencies higher than x-rays. Because gamma radiation has no charge, it easily penetrates solid substances. Gamma decay is useful in medical procedures, including cancer treatment.

ENERGY, FREQUENCY, AND WAVELENGTH

The properties of energy, frequency, and wavelength can be used to describe electromagnetic waves. These properties also have a mathematic relationship between each other. Energy (E) is directly related to frequency (f) as given by $E = hf$, where h represents Planck's constant (6.626×10^{-34} J-s). As the frequency increases, the energy increases. For example, gamma rays, which have the highest frequency of the electromagnetic spectrum, also have the highest energy. The speed (v) of the wave is equal to the product of wavelength (λ) and frequency (f). Because the speed of light (c) is constant in a vacuum at 3.00×10^8 m/s, wavelength and frequency are inversely related. As wavelength decreases, frequency increases. For example, gamma rays have the shortest wavelength of the electromagnetic spectrum and the highest frequency.

Nuclear Reactions

TYPICAL FISSION REACTION

A typical fission reaction is the fission of uranium-235 from neutron bombardment:

$$^{235}_{92}\text{U} + ^{1}_{0}\text{n} \rightarrow ^{139}_{56}\text{Ba} + ^{94}_{36}\text{Kr} + 3[^{1}_{0}\text{n}]$$

The uranium-235 atom $\left(^{235}_{92}\text{U}\right)$ is bombarded by a neutron $\left(^{1}_{0}\text{n}\right)$. This neutron is absorbed, forcing the uranium-235 atom into an excited, unstable state. This excited, unstable uranium-235 atom splits into smaller more stable pieces, which consist of a barium-139 atom $\left(^{139}_{56}\text{Ba}\right)$, a krypton-94 atom $\left(^{94}_{36}\text{Kr}\right)$, and three neutrons $\left(^{1}_{0}\text{n}\right)$. These neutrons in turn may bombard other uranium-235 atoms causing the nuclear fission to continue.

Review Video: Reading Nuclear Equations
Visit mometrix.com/academy and enter code: 688890

NUCLEAR FUSION

Nuclear fusion is the process in which the nuclei of light, unstable atoms unite or fuse to form a heavier, more stable atom. Fusion requires extremely high temperatures and often pressures that force the atoms into a plasma state. In this high-energy state, the atoms collide frequently and are able to fuse together. In this process, some mass is lost and released as large quantities of energy. The Sun's heat and light are produced by a fusion reaction in the Sun's core of four hydrogen atoms fusing into a helium nucleus.

Review Video: Nuclear Fusion
Visit mometrix.com/academy and enter code: 381782

ALPHA EMISSION

In alpha emission, the parent nuclide splits into **two parts** consisting of the daughter nuclide and an alpha particle. The alpha particle is identical to a helium nucleus and consists of two protons and two neutrons as represented by $^{4}_{2}\text{He}$ or $^{4}_{2}\text{He}^{2+}$. The daughter nuclide has a mass number that is four less than the parent nuclide and an atomic number that is two less than the parent nuclide. An example of alpha emission is the decay of an uranimum-238 atom into a thorium-234 atom and an alpha particle as shown below:

$$^{238}_{92}\text{U} \rightarrow ^{234}_{90}\text{Th} + ^{4}_{2}\text{He}$$

POSITIVE AND NEGATIVE BETA DECAY

In **positive beta decay**, also known as **positron emission**, the parent nuclide splits into two parts consisting of the daughter nuclide and a positron. The positron is represented by $^{0}_{+1}\text{e}$ because its mass is negligible compared to a neutron or proton, and its charge is +1. The daughter nuclide has the same mass number as the parent nuclide and an atomic number of one less than the parent nuclide. An example of positive beta decay is when a carbon-11 atom splits into a boron-11 atom and a positron as given by the equation shown here:

$$^{11}_{6}\text{C} \rightarrow ^{11}_{5}\text{B} + ^{0}_{+1}\text{e}$$

In **negative beta decay**, also simply called **beta decay**, the parent nuclide splits into two parts consisting of the daughter nuclide and an electron. The electron is represented by $^{0}_{-1}\text{e}$ because its mass is negligible compared to a neutron or proton, and its charge is -1. An example of negative beta decay is when a carbon-14 atom splits into a nitrogen-14 atom and an electron as given by the following equation:

$$^{14}_{6}C \rightarrow \, ^{14}_{7}N + \, ^{0}_{-1}e$$

ELECTRON CAPTURE

In electron capture, an electron from an atom's own electron cloud impacts the atom's nucleus and causes a **decay reaction**. The parent nuclide absorbs the electron, and a proton is converted to a neutron. A neutrino is emitted from the nucleus. Gamma radiation is also emitted. The daughter nuclide has the same mass number as the parent nuclide, and the atomic number of the daughter nuclide is one lower that the atomic number of the parent nuclide. An example of electron capture is when a nitrogen-13 atom absorbs an electron and converts to a carbon-13 atom while emitting a neutrino ($^{0}_{0}\nu$) and gamma radiation (γ) as shown by the following equation:

$$^{13}_{7}N + \, ^{0}_{-1}e \rightarrow \, ^{13}_{6}C + \, ^{0}_{0}\nu + \gamma$$

TRANSMUTATION

Transmutation is a type of nuclear decay in which an atom is bombarded by **high-speed particles** to cause it to convert from one type of atom to another type of atom. Ernest Rutherford was the first to accomplish this with the transmutation of the nitrogen-14 atom into an oxygen-17 atom by bombardment with a beam of high-speed helium ions. In this transmutation, the helium-4 ion is also converted to a hydrogen-1 ion:

$$^{14}_{7}N + \, ^{4}_{2}He \rightarrow \, ^{17}_{8}O + \, ^{1}_{1}H$$

NEUTRON RADIATION

Neutron radiation is a type of transmutation that is used to create many isotopes that do not occur naturally. In neutron radiation, an atom is bombarded by high-speed neutrons ($^{1}_{0}n$) to cause nuclear decay. In neutron radiation, the daughter nuclide has a mass number one higher than the parent nuclide but the atomic number remains the same. The daughter is an atom of the same element as the parent nuclide but has one more neutron, which makes it a different isotope of that element. An example of neutron radiation is when a cobalt-59 atom is bombarded by a high-speed neutron and converts to a cobalt-60 atom as shown in the following equation:

$$^{59}_{27}Co + \, ^{1}_{0}n \rightarrow \, ^{60}_{27}Co$$

BALANCING A NUCLEAR REACTION

When balancing a nuclear reaction, two key principles must be applied. First, the **mass number must be conserved**. Second, the **atomic number must be conserved**. To determine the products formed, the mass numbers and atomic numbers of the particles emitted or absorbed must be known. Alpha decay emits alpha particles ($^{4}_{2}He$). Beta decay emits electrons ($^{0}_{-1}e$). Positron decay emits positrons ($^{0}_{+1}e$). Neutron radiation absorbs neutrons ($^{1}_{0}n$). In alpha decay, the mass number decreases by four, and the atomic number decreases by two. In negative beta decay, the mass number stays the same and the atomic number increases by one. In positive beta decay, the mass number stays the same and the atomic number decreases by one. In neutron radiation, the mass number increases by one and the atomic number stays the same.

Example Problems

Complete or balance the following nuclear reactions:

$$^{230}_{90}\text{Th} \rightarrow {}^{4}_{2}\text{He} + \underline{\quad}$$

$$^{40}_{19}\text{K} \rightarrow {}^{0}_{-1}\text{e} + \underline{\quad}$$

In the first reaction, thorium-230 under goes alpha decay and emits an alpha particle with a mass number of 4 and an atomic number of 2. Balancing the atomic numbers $(90 - 2)$ yields an atomic number of 88, which corresponds to radium. Balancing the mass numbers $(230 - 4)$ yields 226. Therefore, the missing product is $^{226}_{88}\text{Ra}$.

In the second reaction, potassium-40 undergoes beta decay and emits an electron with an assigned mass number of 0 and an assigned atomic number of -1. Balancing the atomic numbers $(19 - (-1))$ yields an atomic number of 20. Balancing the mass numbers $(40 - 0)$ yields a mass number of 40. Therefore, the missing product is $^{40}_{20}\text{Ca}$.

Safety, Math, and Data in the Laboratory

Safety and Equipment

FUME HOODS

Because of the potential safety hazards associated with chemistry lab experiments, such as fire from vapors and the inhalation of toxic fumes, a **fume hood** should be used in many instances. A fume hood carries away vapors from reagents or reactions. Equipment or reactions are placed as far back in the hood as practical to help enhance the collection of the fumes. The **glass safety shield** automatically closes to the appropriate height, and should be low enough to protect the face and body. The safety shield should only be raised to move equipment in and out of the hood. One should not climb inside a hood or stick one's head inside. All spills should be wiped up immediately and the glass should be cleaned if a splash occurs.

COMMON SAFETY HAZARDS

Some specific safety hazards possible in a chemistry lab include:

- **Fire**: Fire can be caused by volatile solvents such as ether, acetone, and benzene being kept in an open beaker or Erlenmeyer flask. Vapors can creep along the table and ignite if they reach a flame or spark. Solvents should be heated in a hood with a steam bath, not on a hot plate.
- **Explosion**: Heating or creating a reaction in a closed system can cause an explosion, resulting in flying glass and chemical splashes. The system should be vented to prevent this.
- **Chemical and thermal burns**: Many chemicals are corrosive to the skin and eyes.
- **Inhalation of toxic fumes**: Some compounds severely irritate membranes in the eyes, nose, throat, and lungs.
- **Absorption** of toxic chemicals such as dimethyl sulfoxide (DMSO) and nitrobenzene through the skin.
- **Ingestion** of toxic chemicals.

SAFETY GLOVES

There are many types of **gloves** available to help protect the skin from cuts, burns, and chemical splashes. There are many considerations to take into account when choosing a glove. For example, gloves that are highly protective may limit dexterity. Some gloves may not offer appropriate protection against a specific chemical. Other considerations include degradation rating, which indicates how effective a glove is when exposed to chemicals; breakthrough time, which indicates how quickly a chemical can break through the surface of the glove; and permeation rate, which indicates how quickly chemicals seep through after the initial breakthrough. Disposable latex, vinyl, or nitrile gloves are usually appropriate for most circumstances, and offer protection from incidental splashes and contact. Other types of gloves include butyl, neoprene, PVC, PVA, viton, silver shield, and natural rubber. Each offers its own type of protection, but may have drawbacks as

TYPES OF LABORATORY GLASSWARE

Two types of flasks are Erlenmeyer flasks and volumetric flasks. **Volumetric flasks** are used to accurately prepare a specific volume and concentration of solution. **Erlenmeyer flasks** can be used for mixing, transporting, and reacting, but are not appropriate for accurate measurements.

A **pipette** can be used to accurately measure small amounts of liquid. Liquid is drawn into the pipette through a bulb. The liquid measurement is read at the **meniscus**. There are also plastic disposable pipettes. A **repipette** is a hand-operated pump that dispenses solutions.

Beakers can be used to measure mass or dissolve a solvent into a solute. They do not measure volume as accurately as a volumetric flask, pipette, graduated cylinder, or burette.

Graduated cylinders are used for precise measurements and are considered more accurate than Erlenmeyer flasks or beakers. To read a graduated cylinder, it should be placed on a flat surface and read at eye level. The surface of a liquid in a graduated cylinder forms a lens-shaped curve. The measurement should be taken from the bottom of the curve. A ring may be placed at the top of tall, narrow cylinders to help avoid breakage if they are tipped over.

A **burette**, or buret, is a piece of lab glassware used to accurately dispense liquid. It looks similar to a narrow graduated cylinder, but includes a stopcock and tip. It may be filled with a funnel or pipette.

MICROSCOPES

There are different kinds of microscopes, but **optical** or **light microscopes** are the most commonly used in lab settings. Light and lenses are used to magnify and view samples. A specimen or sample is placed on a slide and the slide is placed on a stage with a hole in it. Light passes through the hole and illuminates the sample. The sample is magnified by lenses and viewed through the eyepiece. A simple microscope has one lens, while a typical compound microscope has three lenses. The light source can be room light redirected by a mirror or the microscope can have its own independent light source that passes through a condenser. In this case, there are diaphragms and filters to allow light intensity to be controlled. Optical microscopes also have coarse and fine adjustment knobs.

Other types of microscopes include **digital microscopes**, which use a camera and a monitor to allow viewing of the sample. **Scanning electron microscopes (SEMs)** provide greater detail of a sample in terms of the surface topography and can produce magnifications much greater than those possible with optical microscopes. The technology of an SEM is quite different from an optical microscope in that it does not rely on lenses to magnify objects, but uses samples placed in a chamber. In one type of SEM, a beam of electrons from an electron gun scans and actually interacts with the sample to produce an image.

Wet mount slides designed for use with a light microscope typically require a thin portion of the specimen to be placed on a standard glass slide. A drop of water is added and a cover slip or cover glass is placed on top. Air bubbles and fingerprints can make viewing difficult. Placing the cover slip at a 45-degree angle and allowing it to drop into place can help avoid the problem of air bubbles. A **cover slip** should always be used when viewing wet mount slides. The viewer should start with the objective in its lowest position and then fine focus. The microscope should be carried with two hands and stored with the low-power objective in the down position. **Lenses** should be cleaned with lens paper only. A **graticule slide** is marked with a grid line, and is useful for counting or estimating a quantity.

BALANCES

Balances such as triple-beam balances, spring balances, and electronic balances measure mass and force. An **electronic balance** is the most accurate, followed by a **triple-beam balance** and then a **spring balance**. One part of a **triple-beam balance** is the plate, which is where the item to be weighed is placed. There are also three beams that have hatch marks indicating amounts and hold the weights that rest in the notches. The front beam measures weights between 0 and 10 grams, the middle beam measures weights in 100 gram increments, and the far beam measures weights in 10 gram increments. The sum of the weight of each beam is the total weight of the object. A triple beam balance also includes a set screw to calibrate the equipment and a mark indicating the object and counterweights are in balance.

CHROMATOGRAPHY

Chromatography refers to a set of laboratory techniques used to separate or analyze **mixtures**. Mixtures are dissolved in their mobile phases. In the stationary or bonded phase, the desired component is separated from other molecules in the mixture. In chromatography, the analyte is the substance to be separated. **Preparative chromatography** refers to the type of chromatography that involves purifying a substance for further use rather than further analysis. **Analytical chromatography** involves analyzing the isolated substance. Other types of chromatography include column, planar, paper, thin layer, displacement, supercritical fluid, affinity, ion exchange, and size exclusion chromatography. Reversed phase, two-dimensional, simulated moving bed, pyrolysis, fast protein, counter current, and chiral are also types of chromatography. **Gas chromatography** refers to the separation technique in which the mobile phase of a substance is in gas form.

> **Review Video: Paper Chromatography**
> Visit mometrix.com/academy and enter code: 543963

CENTRIFUGES

A centrifuge is used to separate the components of a heterogeneous mixture (consisting of two or more compounds) by spinning it. The solid precipitate settles in the bottom of the container and the liquid component of the solution, called the **centrifugate**, is at the top. A well-known application of this process is using a centrifuge to separate blood cells and plasma. The heavier cells settle on the bottom of the test tube and the lighter plasma stays on top. Another example is using a salad spinner to help dry lettuce.

ELECTROPHORESIS, CALORIMETRY, AND TITRATION

- **Electrophoresis** is the separation of molecules based on electrical charge. This is possible because particles disbursed in a fluid usually carry electric charges on their surfaces. Molecules are pulled through the fluid toward the positive end if the molecules have a negative charge and are pulled through the fluid toward the negative end if the molecules have a positive charge.
- **Calorimetry** is used to determine the heat released or absorbed in a chemical reaction.
- **Titration** helps determine the precise endpoint of a reaction. With this information, the precise quantity of reactant in the titration flask can be determined. A burette is used to deliver the second reactant to the flask and an indicator or pH meter is used to detect the endpoint of the reaction.

Measurement Principles

PRECISION, ACCURACY, AND ERROR

Precision: How reliable and repeatable a measurement is. The more consistent the data is with repeated testing, the more precise it is. For example, hitting a target consistently in the same spot, which may or may not be the center of the target, is precision.

Accuracy: How close the data is to the correct data. For example, hitting a target consistently in the center area of the target, whether or not the hits are all in the same spot, is accuracy.

Note: it is possible for data to be precise without being accurate. If a scale is off balance, the data will be precise, but will not be accurate. For data to have precision and accuracy, it must be repeatable and correct.

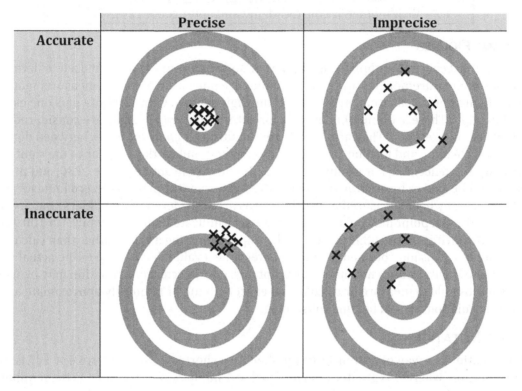

Approximate error: The amount of error in a physical measurement. Approximate error is often reported as the measurement, followed by the $\pm$ symbol and the amount of the approximate error.

Maximum possible error: Half the magnitude of the smallest unit used in the measurement. For example, if the unit of measurement is 1 centimeter, the maximum possible error is $\frac{1}{2}$ cm, written as ± 0.5 cm following the measurement. It is important to apply significant figures in reporting maximum possible error. Do not make the answer appear more accurate than the least accurate of your measurements.

> **Review Video: Precision, Accuracy, and Error**
> Visit mometrix.com/academy and enter code: 520377

ROUNDING AND ESTIMATION

Rounding is reducing the digits in a number while still trying to keep the value similar. The result will be less accurate but in a simpler form and easier to use. Whole numbers can be rounded to the nearest ten, hundred, or thousand.

When you are asked to estimate the solution to a problem, you will need to provide only an approximate figure or **estimation** for your answer. In this situation, you will need to round each number in the calculation to the level indicated (nearest hundred, nearest thousand, etc.) or to a level that makes sense for the numbers involved. When estimating a sum **all numbers must be rounded to the same level**. You cannot round one number to the nearest thousand while rounding another to the nearest hundred.

> **Review Video: Rounding and Estimation**
> Visit mometrix.com/academy and enter code: 126243

SIGNIFICANT FIGURES

The mathematical concept of **significant figures** or **significant digits** is often used to determine the accuracy of measurements or the level of confidence one has in a specific measurement. The significant figures of a measurement include all the digits known with certainty plus one estimated or uncertain digit. There are a number of rules for determining which digits are considered "important" or "interesting." They are: all non-zero digits are *significant*, zeros between digits are *significant*, and leading and trailing zeros are *not significant* unless they appear to the right of the non-zero digits in a decimal. For example, in 0.01230 the significant digits are 1230, and this number would be said to be accurate to the hundred-thousandths place. The zero indicates that the amount has actually been measured as 0. Other zeros are considered place holders, and are not important. A decimal point may be placed after zeros to indicate their importance (in 100. for example). **Estimating**, on the other hand, involves approximating a value rather than calculating the exact number. This may be used to quickly determine a value that is close to the actual number when complete accuracy does not matter or is not possible. In science, estimation may be used when it is impossible to measure or calculate an exact amount, or to quickly approximate an answer when true calculations would be time consuming.

SCIENTIFIC NOTATION

Scientific notation is a way of writing large numbers in a shorter form. The form $a \times 10^n$ is used in scientific notation, where a is greater than or equal to 1 but less than 10, and n is the number of places the decimal must move to get from the original number to a. Example: The number 230,400,000 is cumbersome to write. To write the value in scientific notation, place a decimal point between the first and second numbers, and include all digits through the last non-zero digit ($a = 2.304$). To find the appropriate power of 10, count the number of places the decimal point had to move ($n = 8$). The number is positive if the decimal moved to the left, and negative if it moved to the right. We can then write 230,400,000 as 2.304×10^8. If we look instead at the number 0.00002304, we have the same value for a, but this time the decimal moved 5 places to the right ($n = -5$). Thus, 0.00002304 can be written as 2.304×10^{-5}. Using this notation makes it simple to compare very large or very small numbers. By comparing exponents, it is easy to see that 3.28×10^4 is smaller than 1.51×10^5, because 4 is less than 5.

> **Review Video: Scientific Notation**
> Visit mometrix.com/academy and enter code: 976454

Units of Measurement

METRIC MEASUREMENT PREFIXES

Prefix	Meaning	Example
Giga-	One billion	1 *giga*watt is one billion watts
Mega-	One million	1 *mega*hertz is one million hertz
Kilo-	One thousand	1 *kilo*gram is one thousand grams
Deci-	One-tenth	1 *deci*meter is one-tenth of a meter
Centi-	One-hundredth	1 *centi*meter is one-hundredth of a meter
Milli-	One-thousandth	1 *milli*liter is one-thousandth of a liter
Micro-	One-millionth	1 *micro*gram is one-millionth of a gram

> **Review Video: Metric System Conversion - How the Metric System Works**
> Visit mometrix.com/academy and enter code: 163709

MEASUREMENT CONVERSION

When converting between units, the goal is to maintain the same meaning but change the way it is displayed. In order to go from a larger unit to a smaller unit, multiply the number of the known amount by the equivalent amount. When going from a smaller unit to a larger unit, divide the number of the known amount by the equivalent amount.

For complicated conversions, it may be helpful to set up conversion fractions. In these fractions, one fraction is the **conversion factor**. The other fraction has the unknown amount in the numerator. So, the known value is placed in the denominator. Sometimes, the second fraction has the known value from the problem in the numerator and the unknown in the denominator. Multiply the two fractions to get the converted measurement. Note that since the numerator and the denominator of the factor are equivalent, the value of the fraction is 1. That is why we can say that the result in the new units is equal to the result in the old units even though they have different numbers.

It can often be necessary to chain known conversion factors together. As an example, consider converting 512 square inches to square meters. We know that there are 2.54 centimeters in an inch and 100 centimeters in a meter, and we know we will need to square each of these factors to achieve the conversion we are looking for.

$$\frac{512 \text{ in}^2}{1} \times \left(\frac{2.54 \text{ cm}}{1 \text{ in}}\right)^2 \times \left(\frac{1 \text{ m}}{100 \text{ cm}}\right)^2 = \frac{512 \text{ in}^2}{1} \times \left(\frac{6.4516 \text{ cm}^2}{1 \text{ in}^2}\right) \times \left(\frac{1 \text{ m}^2}{10{,}000 \text{ cm}^2}\right) = 0.330 \text{ m}^2$$

> **Review Video: Measurement Conversions**
> Visit mometrix.com/academy and enter code: 316703

COMMON UNITS AND EQUIVALENTS

WEIGHT MEASUREMENTS

Unit	Abbreviation	US equivalent	Metric equivalent
Ounce	oz	16 drams	28.35 grams
Pound	lb	16 ounces	453.6 grams
Ton	tn.	2,000 pounds	907.2 kilograms

DISTANCE AND AREA MEASUREMENT

Unit	Abbreviation	US equivalent	Metric equivalent
Inch	in	1 inch	2.54 centimeters
Foot	ft	12 inches	0.305 meters
Yard	yd	3 feet	0.914 meters
Mile	mi	5280 feet	1.609 kilometers
Acre	ac	4840 square yards	0.405 hectares
Square Mile	sq. mi. or mi.^{2}	640 acres	2.590 square kilometers

CAPACITY MEASUREMENTS

Unit	Abbreviation	US equivalent	Metric equivalent
Fluid Ounce	fl oz	8 fluid drams	29.573 milliliters
Cup	c	8 fluid ounces	0.237 liter
Pint	pt.	16 fluid ounces	0.473 liter
Quart	qt.	2 pints	0.946 liter
Gallon	gal.	4 quarts	3.785 liters
Teaspoon	t or tsp.	1 fluid dram	5 milliliters
Tablespoon	T or tbsp.	4 fluid drams	15 or 16 milliliters
Cubic Centimeter	cc or cm^3	0.271 drams	1 milliliter

METRIC EQUIVALENTS

1000 µg (microgram)	1 mg
1000 mg (milligram)	1 g
1000 g (gram)	1 kg
1000 kg (kilogram)	1 metric ton
1000 mL (milliliter)	1 L
1000 µm (micrometer)	1 mm
1000 mm (millimeter)	1 m
100 cm (centimeter)	1 m
1000 m (meter)	1 km

Review Video: Metric System Conversions
Visit mometrix.com/academy and enter code: 163709

VOLUME AND WEIGHT MEASUREMENT CLARIFICATIONS

Always be careful when using ounces and fluid ounces. They are not equivalent.

1 pint = 16 fluid ounces	1 fluid ounce ≠ 1 ounce
1 pound = 16 ounces	1 pint ≠ 1 pound

Having one pint of something does not mean you have one pound of it. In the same way, just because something weighs one pound does not mean that its volume is one pint.

In the United States, the word "ton" by itself refers to a short ton or a net ton. Do not confuse this with a long ton (also called a gross ton) or a metric ton (also spelled *tonne*), which have different measurement equivalents.

1 US ton = 2000 pounds   ≠   1 metric ton = 1000 kilograms

Displaying Information

INDEPENDENT AND DEPENDENT VARIABLES

When displaying information, it is important to know which of the aspects you are presenting are dependent and which are independent. **Independent variables** are those that determine the grouping or the order of your information, like time or category. **Dependent variables** are those that are of interest when compared across the independent variables, like growth or frequency.

> **Review Video and Practice: <u>Identifying Independent and Dependent Variables</u>**
> Visit mometrix.com/academy and enter code: 627181

FREQUENCY TABLES

Frequency tables show how frequently each unique value appears in a set. A **relative frequency table** is one that shows the proportions of each unique value compared to the entire set. Relative frequencies are given as percentages; however, the total percent for a relative frequency table will not necessarily equal 100 percent due to rounding. An example of a frequency table with relative frequencies is below.

Favorite Color	Frequency	Relative Frequency
Blue	4	13%
Red	7	22%
Green	3	9%
Purple	6	19%
Cyan	12	38%

> **Review Video: <u>Data Interpretation of Graphs</u>**
> Visit mometrix.com/academy and enter code: 200439

CIRCLE GRAPHS

Circle graphs, also known as *pie charts*, provide a visual depiction of the relationship of each type of data compared to the whole set of data. The circle graph is divided into sections by drawing radii to create central angles whose percentage of the circle is equal to the individual data's percentage of the whole set. Each 1% of data is equal to 3.6° in the circle graph. Therefore, data represented by a 90° section of the circle graph makes up 25% of the whole. When complete, a circle graph often looks like a pie cut into uneven wedges. The pie chart below shows the data from the frequency table referenced earlier where people were asked their favorite color.

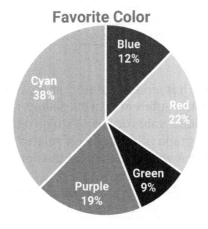

153

PICTOGRAPHS

A pictograph is a graph, generally in the horizontal orientation, that uses pictures or symbols to represent the data. Each pictograph must have a key that defines the picture or symbol and gives the quantity each picture or symbol represents. Pictures or symbols on a pictograph are not always shown as whole elements. In this case, the fraction of the picture or symbol shown represents the same fraction of the quantity a whole picture or symbol stands for. For example, a row with $3\frac{1}{2}$ ears of corn, where each ear of corn represents 100 stalks of corn in a field, would equal $3\frac{1}{2} \times 100 = 350$ stalks of corn in the field.

> **Review Video: Pictographs**
> Visit mometrix.com/academy and enter code: 147860

LINE GRAPHS

Line graphs have one or more lines of varying styles (solid or broken) to show the different values for a set of data. The individual data are represented as ordered pairs, much like on a Cartesian plane. In this case, the x- and y-axes are defined in terms of their units, such as dollars or time. The individual plotted points are joined by line segments to show whether the value of the data is increasing (line sloping upward), decreasing (line sloping downward), or staying the same (horizontal line). Multiple sets of data can be graphed on the same line graph to give an easy visual comparison. An example of this would be graphing achievement test scores for different groups of students over the same time period to see which group had the greatest increase or decrease in performance from year to year (as shown below).

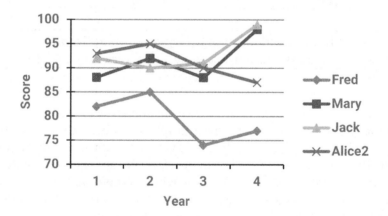

> **Review Video: How to Create a Line Graph**
> Visit mometrix.com/academy and enter code: 480147

LINE PLOTS

A line plot, also known as a *dot plot*, has plotted points that are not connected by line segments. In this graph, the horizontal axis lists the different possible values for the data, and the vertical axis lists the number of times the individual value occurs. A single dot is graphed for each value to show the number of times it occurs. This graph is more closely related to a bar graph than a line graph. Do not connect the dots in a line plot or it will misrepresent the data.

> **Review Video: Line Plot**
> Visit mometrix.com/academy and enter code: 754610

STEM AND LEAF PLOTS

A stem and leaf plot is useful for depicting groups of data that fall into a range of values. Each piece of data is separated into two parts: the first, or left, part is called the **stem**; the second, or right, part is called the **leaf**. Each stem is listed in a column from smallest to largest. Each leaf that has the common stem is listed in that stem's row from smallest to largest. For example, in a set of two-digit numbers, the digit in the tens place is the stem, and the digit in the ones place is the leaf. With a stem and leaf plot, you can easily see which subset of numbers (10s, 20s, 30s, etc.) is the largest. This information is also readily available by looking at a histogram, but a stem and leaf plot also allows you to look closer and see exactly which values fall in that range. Using a sample set of test scores (82, 88, 92, 93, 85, 90, 92, 95, 74, 88, 90, 91, 78, 87, 98, 99), we can assemble a stem and leaf plot like the one below.

Test Scores

7	4	8						
8	2	5	7	8	8			
9	0	0	1	2	2	3	5	8	9

> **Review Video: Stem and Leaf Plots**
> Visit mometrix.com/academy and enter code: 302339

BAR GRAPHS

A bar graph is one of the few graphs that can be drawn correctly in two different configurations – both horizontally and vertically. A bar graph is similar to a line plot in the way the data is organized on the graph. Both axes must have their categories defined for the graph to be useful. Rather than placing a single dot to mark the point of the data's value, a bar, or thick line, is drawn from zero to the exact value of the data, whether it is a number, percentage, or other numerical value. Longer bar lengths correspond to greater data values. To read a bar graph, read the labels for the axes to find the units being reported. Then, look where the bars end in relation to the scale given on the corresponding axis and determine the associated value.

The bar chart below represents the responses from our favorite-color survey.

Favorite Color

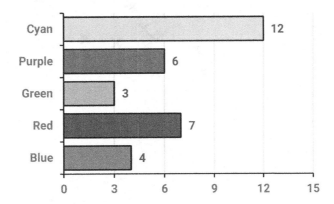

HISTOGRAMS

At first glance, a histogram looks like a vertical bar graph. The difference is that a bar graph has a separate bar for each piece of data and a histogram has one continuous bar for each *range* of data. For example, a histogram may have one bar for the range 0–9, one bar for 10–19, etc. While a bar graph has numerical values on one axis, a histogram has numerical values on both axes. Each range is of equal size, and they are ordered left to right from lowest to highest. The height of each column on a histogram represents the number of data values within that range. Like a stem and leaf plot, a histogram makes it easy to glance at the graph and quickly determine which range has the greatest quantity of values. A simple example of a histogram is below.

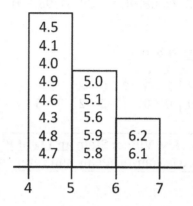

BIVARIATE DATA

Bivariate data is simply data from two different variables. (The prefix *bi-* means *two*.) In a *scatter plot*, each value in the set of data is plotted on a grid similar to a Cartesian plane, where each axis represents one of the two variables. By looking at the pattern formed by the points on the grid, you can often determine whether or not there is a relationship between the two variables, and what that relationship is, if it exists. The variables may be directly proportionate, inversely proportionate, or show no proportion at all. It may also be possible to determine if the data is linear, and if so, to find an equation to relate the two variables. The following scatter plot shows the relationship between preference for brand "A" and the age of the consumers surveyed.

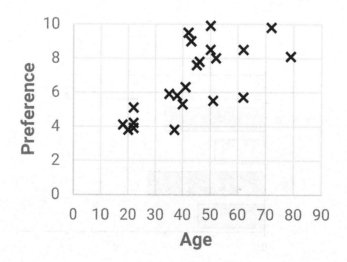

SCATTER PLOTS

Scatter plots are also useful in determining the type of function represented by the data and finding the simple regression. Linear scatter plots may be positive or negative. Nonlinear scatter plots are generally exponential or quadratic. Below are some common types of scatter plots:

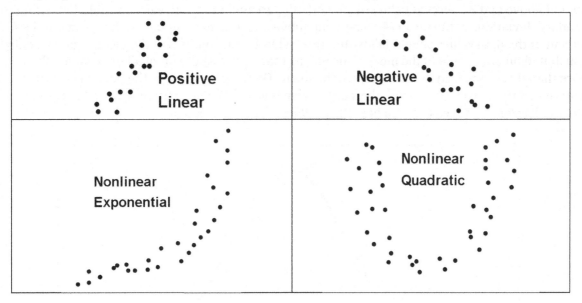

5-NUMBER SUMMARY

The 5-number summary of a set of data gives a very informative picture of the set. The five numbers in the summary include the minimum value, maximum value, and the three quartiles. This information gives the reader the range and median of the set, as well as an indication of how the data is spread about the median.

BOX AND WHISKER PLOTS

A box-and-whiskers plot is a graphical representation of the 5-number summary. To draw a box-and-whiskers plot, plot the points of the 5-number summary on a number line. Draw a box whose ends are through the points for the first and third quartiles. Draw a vertical line in the box through the median to divide the box in half. Draw a line segment from the first quartile point to the minimum value, and from the third quartile point to the maximum value.

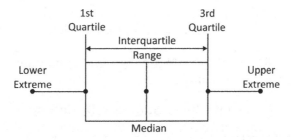

68-95-99.7 RULE

The 68–95–99.7 rule describes how a normal distribution of data should appear when compared to the mean. This is also a description of a normal bell curve. According to this rule, 68 percent of the data values in a normally distributed set should fall within one standard deviation of the mean (34 percent above and 34 percent below the mean), 95 percent of the data values should fall within two standard deviations of the mean (47.5 percent above and 47.5 percent below the mean), and 99.7 percent of the data values should fall within three standard deviations of the mean, again, equally distributed on either side of the mean. This means that only 0.3 percent of all data values should fall more than three standard deviations from the mean. On the graph below, the normal curve is centered on the y-axis. The x-axis labels are how many standard deviations away from the center you are. Therefore, it is easy to see how the 68-95-99.7 rule can apply.

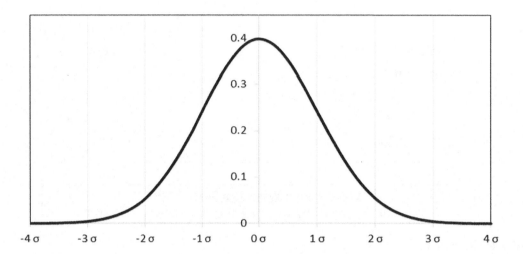

STATISTICAL TERMINOLOGY

- **Mean** - The average, found by taking the sum of a set of numbers and dividing by the number of numbers in the set.
- **Median** - The middle number in a set of numbers sorted from least to greatest. If the set has an even number of entries, the median is the average of the two in the middle.
- **Mode** - The value that appears most frequently in a data set. There may be more than one mode. If no value appears more than once, there is no mode.
- **Range** - The difference between the highest and lowest numbers in a data set.
- **Standard deviation** - Measures the dispersion of a data set or how far from the mean a single data point is likely to be.
- **Regression analysis** - A method of analyzing sets of data and sets of variables that involves studying how the typical value of the dependent variable changes when any one of the independent variables is varied and the other independent variables remain fixed.

> **Review Video: Mean, Median, and Mode**
> Visit mometrix.com/academy and enter code: 286207
>
> **Review Video: Standard Deviation**
> Visit mometrix.com/academy and enter code: 419469

ACS General Chemistry Practice Questions

TABLE OF CONTENTS

ACS General Chemistry Practice Test #1

Want to take this practice test in an online interactive format?
Check out the bonus page, which includes interactive practice questions and much more: **mometrix.com/bonus948/acsgenchem**

SCAN HERE

1. Which of the following processes absorbs heat?

a. Dry ice sublimates at room temperature to form CO_2 gas.
b. NH_3 gas condenses under a cold bath of –35 °C to the liquid form.
c. Liquid glacial acetic acid freezes in an ice-water bath.
d. Iodine vapor captured in a jar forms crystalline iodine when it contacts the cooler lid.

2. A reaction is experimentally determined to have a change of enthalpy (ΔH) of -327.1 kJ at -15.0 °C. Calculate the entropy change brought by this reaction to the surroundings at the given temperature.

a. 1.27 kJ/K
b. −1.27 kJ/K
c. 21.8 kJ/°C
d. −21.8 kJ/°C

3. How many resonance structures does an SO_3 molecule have?

a. 0
b. 1
c. 2
d. 3

4. Select the statement that is NOT true regarding the trend in the properties of elements in group 7A.

a. The melting point decreases in group 7A when going down the column.
b. The atomic radii increase in group 7A when going down the column.
c. The first ionization energy decreases in group 7A when going down the column.
d. The electronegativity decreases in group 7A when going down the column.

5. Which of the following equations does not count as an oxidation-reduction reaction?

a. $2\,SO_2(g) + O_2(g) \rightarrow 2\,SO_3(g)$
b. $2\,Na(s) + Cl_2(g) \rightarrow 2\,NaCl(s)$
c. $4\,Al(s) + 3\,O_2(g) \rightarrow 2\,Al_2O_3(s)$
d. $CO_2(g) + H_2O(l) \rightarrow H_2CO_3(aq)$

6. An alkaline battery has one electrode that is made with Zn and KOH, the other electrode made with MnO_2 and graphite. Its half-cell reactions are:

$$MnO_2(s) + H_2O(l) + e^- \rightarrow MnO(OH)(s) + OH^-(aq), E_{red}^{\circ} = +0.27 \text{ V}$$
$$Zn(OH)_2(s) + 2 e^- \rightarrow Zn(s) + 2 OH^-(aq), E_{red}^{\circ} = -1.28 \text{ V}$$

Based on the standard reduction potentials, identify the anode, the cathode, and the emf of this battery.

    a. (Zn + KOH) is the anode, (MnO_2 + graphite) is the cathode, $E_{cell}^{\circ} = +1.01$ V
    b. (Zn + KOH) is the anode, (MnO_2 + graphite) is the cathode, $E_{cell}^{\circ} = +1.55$ V
    c. (MnO_2 + graphite) is the anode, (Zn + KOH) is the cathode, $E_{cell}^{\circ} = +1.01$ V
    d. (MnO_2 + graphite) is the anode, (Zn + KOH) is the cathode, $E_{cell}^{\circ} = +1.55$ V

7. The solubility product (K_{sp}) of barium fluoride (BaF_2) at 25 °C is 1.7×10^{-6}. What is the solubility of BaF_2 in grams per liter?

    a. 0.0075
    b. 0.023
    c. 2.1
    d. 1.3

8. Select the correct statement about the following combustion reaction of methane in open air:

$$CH_4(g) + 2 O_2(g) \rightarrow CO_2(g) + 2 H_2O(g)$$

    a. This equation is unbalanced.
    b. This equation represents an incomplete combustion of CH_4.
    c. The combustion reaction occurs rapidly at high temperatures.
    d. This combustion reaction involves no oxidation state changes between products and reactants.

9. Given an open tank of water that is in an environment with 1 atm in total pressure, what could be done to increase the solubility of oxygen in the water?

    a. Nothing, the oxygen solubility cannot be changed.
    b. Increase the temperature in the tank.
    c. Increase the amount of water in the tank.
    d. Increase the partial pressure of oxygen above the tank.

10. A solution with a pH of 9.00 also has a Mg^{2+} concentration of 0.235 M. Given that the solubility product $\left(K_{sp}\right)$ of $Mg(OH)_2$ is 1.8×10^{-11}, is any $Mg(OH)_2$ going to precipitate from this solution?

    a. Yes.
    b. No, because the solution is not saturated yet.
    c. No, because it is at saturation.
    d. The result cannot be determined from the information given.

11. Which one of the following molecules have a net dipole moment?

    a. CO_2
    b. SO_2
    c. BF_3
    d. CH_4

12. What are the products from the reaction between dilute solutions of carbonic acid (H_2CO_3) and calcium hydroxide ($Ca(OH)_2$)?

    a. $CaO(s)$ and $H_2O(l)$
    b. $CaCO_3(s)$ and $H_2O(l)$
    c. $Ca(OH)_2(s)$ and $CO_2(g)$
    d. $CaCO_3(s)$ and $CO_2(g)$

13. Which set of quantum numbers below are not allowed?

    a. $n = 3, l = 3, m_l = 0$
    b. $n = 4, l = 3, m_l = -2$
    c. $n = 2, l = 1, m_l = -1$
    d. $n = 3, l = 0, m_l = 0$

14. What is the hybridization on the central atom of $SnCl_3{}^-$ ion?

    a. sp
    b. sp^2
    c. sp^3
    d. sp^3d

15. The following is the unbalanced chemical equation for the reaction between sodium metal and water:

$$Na(s) + H_2O(l) \rightarrow NaOH(aq) + H_2(g)$$

After balancing the reaction, how many moles of hydrogen gas are produced if one mole of water takes part in the reaction?

    a. 0.5
    b. 1
    c. 2
    d. 4

16. Which of the following molecules is NOT polar?

a. Chlorobenzene

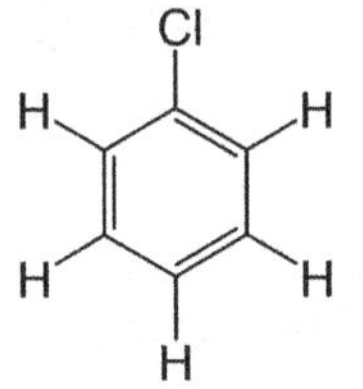

b. *Para*-dichlorobenzene

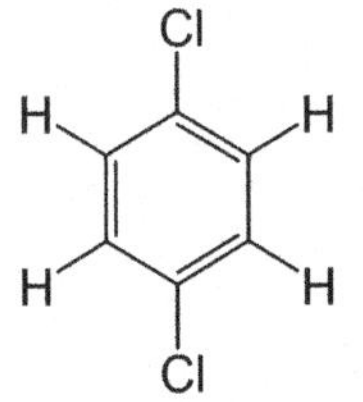

c. Chloromethane

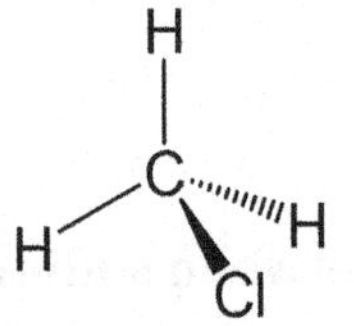

d. Dichloromethane

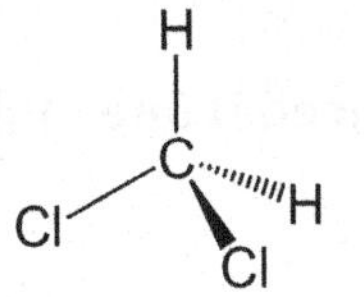

17. The standard free-energy change ($\Delta G°$) at 298 K for the reaction between SO_2 and O_2 is -120.8 kJ/mol:

$$2\,SO_2(g) + O_2(g) \rightarrow 2\,SO_3\,(g)$$

Calculate the free-energy change for this reaction at 330 K, if the reaction occurs in a vessel that contains 0.35 atm of SO_2, 0.22 atm of O_2, and 0.17 atm of SO_3.

a. -121 kJ
b. -127 kJ
c. $+2,810$ kJ
d. $+5,420$ kJ

18. The reaction between ozone (O_3) and NO_2 is proposed to occur in two steps:

Step 1: $O_3(g) + NO_2(g) \xrightarrow{k_1} NO_3(g) + O_2(g)$

Step 2: $NO_3(g) + NO_2(g) \xrightarrow{k_2} N_2O_5(g)$

Overall: $O_3(g) + 2\,NO_2(g) \xrightarrow{k} N_2O_5(g) + O_2(g)$

What is the rate law of this reaction if Step 1 is rate-determining?

a. $k_1[O_3][NO_2]$
b. $k_2[NO_3][NO_2]$
c. $k_1[O_3]$
d. $k_1[NO_2]$

19. The standard enthalpy change ($\Delta H°$) of $SiCl_4$ reacting with water is -69.4 kJ/mol:

$$SiCl_4(l) + 2\,H_2O(l) \rightarrow SiO_2(s) + 4\,HCl(g)$$

What is the standard enthalpy of formation (ΔH_f°) for $SiCl_4(l)$ if the ΔH_f° for the following compounds are known?

$$\Delta H_f^\circ[SiO_2(s)] = -910.9 \text{ kJ/mol}$$
$$\Delta H_f^\circ[\,HCl(aq)] = -167.2 \text{ kJ/mol}$$
$$\Delta H_f^\circ[\,HCl(g)] = -92.30 \text{ kJ/mol}$$
$$\Delta H_f^\circ[H_2O(l)] = -285.3 \text{ kJ/mol}$$
$$\Delta H_f^\circ[H_2O(g)] = -241.8 \text{ kJ/mol}$$

    a. -692 kJ/mol
    b. -640 kJ/mol
    c. -727 kJ/mol
    d. -940 kJ/mol

20. Assuming that all the reactions below are elementary reactions, which one does NOT have the correct expression for its rate law?

    a. $2\,A \rightarrow P, Rate = k[A]^2$
    b. $A + 2\,B + C \rightarrow P, Rate = k[A][B]^2[C]$
    c. $A + 2\,B \rightarrow P, Rate = k[A][B]$
    d. $2\,A + B + C \rightarrow P, Rate = k[A]^2[B][C]$

21. The combustion of butane (C_4H_{10}) has the balanced chemical equation:

$$2\,C_4H_{10}(g) + 13\,O_2(g) \rightarrow 8\,CO_2(g) + 10\,H_2O(g)$$

Which one of the following expressions does NOT represent the relative reaction rates of the reactants or products?

    a. $-\dfrac{1}{2}\dfrac{\Delta[C_4H_{10}]}{\Delta t} = -\dfrac{1}{13}\dfrac{\Delta[O_2]}{\Delta t}$

    b. $-\dfrac{1}{13}\dfrac{\Delta[O_2]}{\Delta t} = \dfrac{1}{8}\dfrac{\Delta[CO_2]}{\Delta t}$

    c. $-\dfrac{1}{13}\dfrac{\Delta[O_2]}{\Delta t} = \dfrac{1}{10}\dfrac{\Delta[H_2O]}{\Delta t}$

    d. $-\dfrac{1}{2}\dfrac{\Delta[C_4H_{10}]}{\Delta t} = \dfrac{1}{13}\dfrac{\Delta[CO_2]}{\Delta t}$

22. Methane (CH_4) undergoes substitution reaction with chlorine (Cl_2) under UV-light:

$$CH_4(g) + Cl_2(g) \rightarrow CH_3Cl(g) + HCl(g)$$

4.02 grams of methane and 17.8 grams of chlorine are placed in a reaction vessel and produce 5.65 grams of chloromethane (CH_3Cl). What is the percent yield of this reaction?

    a. 71.1%
    b. 61.8%
    c. 45.5%
    d. 31.7%

23. The hydrogen peroxide (H_2O_2) decomposes into water and oxygen under light:

$$H_2O_2(g) \rightarrow H_2O(l) + \frac{1}{2}O_2(g)$$

The enthalpy change (ΔH) for one mole of H_2O_2 is -196 kJ. Is this reaction endothermic or exothermic, and what is the amount of heat being transferred to the surroundings if 1.33 g H_2O_2 decomposes under constant pressure?

    a. Endothermic, 0.231 kJ
    b. Exothermic, 0.231 kJ
    c. Endothermic, 7.67 kJ
    d. Exothermic, 7.67 kJ

24. Which one of the following represents the balanced chemical equation of sodium azide (NaN_3) decomposing to sodium element and nitrogen gas?

    a. $NaN_3(s) \rightarrow Na(s) + N_2(g)$
    b. $2\,NaN_3(s) \rightarrow 2\,Na(s) + 3\,N_2(g)$
    c. $NaN_3(s) \rightarrow Na(s) + N_3(g)$
    d. $2\,NaN_3(s) \rightarrow 3\,Na(s) + 3\,N_2(g)$

25. Select the correct statements about the catalyst of a reaction from the following:

    a. The catalyst does not change the speed of a chemical reaction.
    b. The catalyst is produced during the reaction.
    c. The catalyst lowers the energy barrier of a reaction.
    d. The catalyst changes the final energy level of the reaction.

26. A combustion test of 2.00 g naphthalene ($C_{10}H_8$) is carried out in a bomb calorimeter. If the heat capacity of the calorimeter is 5.54 kJ/°C, and the temperature of the bomb calorimeter is raised by 17.9 °C, calculate the amount of heat that would be released during the combustion of 1.00 mole of naphthalene.

    a. 1.55 kJ
    b. 99.2 kJ
    c. 198.4 kJ
    d. 6.36×10^3 kJ

27. A first order reaction has a rate constant of 1.99×10^{-5} s^{-1} at 91.7 °C, and its rate constant becomes 2.49×10^{-3} s^{-1} at 140.3 °C. What is the activation energy of this reaction?

    a. $+10.7$ kJ/mol
    b. $+125$ kJ/mol
    c. -10.7 kJ/mol
    d. -125 kJ/mol

28. Using the average bond enthalpies given in kJ/mol below, estimate the enthalpy of the following reaction:

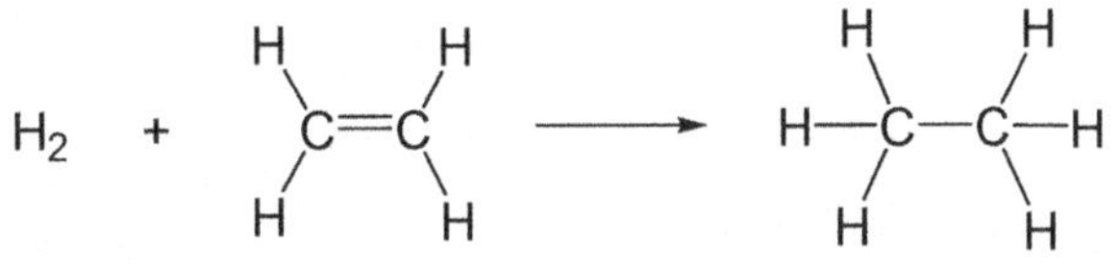

$$D(C - H) = 413, D(C - C) = 348, D(H - H) = 436, D(C = C) = 614$$

  a. -702 kJ/mol
  b. $+702$ kJ/mol
  c. $+124$ kJ/mol
  d. -124 kJ/mol

29. What is the net ionic equation between the reaction of aqueous K_2CO_3 and $Ba(NO_3)_2$ solutions?

  a. $CO_3{}^{2+}(aq) + Ba^{2+}(aq) \rightarrow BaCO_3(s)$
  b. $2 K^+(aq) + CO_3{}^{2+}(aq) \rightarrow K_2CO_3(aq)$
  c. $K^+(aq) + CO_3{}^{2+}(aq) + Ba^{2+}(aq) + NO_3{}^-(aq) \rightarrow BaCO_3(s) + K^+(aq) + NO_3{}^-(aq)$
  d. $2 K^+(aq) + CO_3{}^{2+}(aq) + Ba^{2+}(aq) + 2 NO_3{}^-(aq) \rightarrow BaCO_3(s) + 2 K^+(aq) + 2 NO_3{}^-(aq)$

30. Which of the following is NOT a property of metallic solids?

  a. The hardness of metallic solids can vary from soft to very hard.
  b. The melting points of metallic solids can vary from low to very high.
  c. They have excellent thermal and electrical conductivity.
  d. Metallic solids are held together by electrostatic attractions.

31. A galvanic cell is constructed using Ni and Ag metal stripes as electrodes:

$$Ni(s) + 2 Ag^+(aq) \rightarrow Ni^{2+}(aq) + 2 Ag(s)$$

The cell has a standard emf of $+1.08$ V. Calculate the standard free energy change, $\Delta G°$, and the equilibrium constant, K_{eq}, for this cell at 298 K. (Use $F = 96,485$ J/(V $\cdot$ mol) and $R = 8.314$ J/(mol $\cdot$ K))

  a. $\Delta G° = -104$ kJ/mol, $K_{eq} = 1.70 \times 10^{18}$
  b. $\Delta G° = -104$ kJ/mol, $K_{eq} = 1.04$
  c. $\Delta G° = -208$ kJ/mol, $K_{eq} = 3.02 \times 10^{36}$
  d. $\Delta G° = -208$ kJ/mol, $K_{eq} = 1.08$

32. The solubility of ammonium chloride (NH_4Cl) is 55.3 g per 100 mL of water at 60 °C. What are the molality and molarity of a saturated NH_4Cl solution at this temperature? (The density of water is 0.98338 g/mL at 60 °C)

  a. 1.03 m, 1.05 M
  b. 0.550 m, 0.133 M
  c. 10.5 m, 10.3 M
  d. 5.50 m, 5.30 M

33. How much of a 6.00 M HNO$_3$ stock solution is needed to prepare 400 mL of 0.0250 M HNO$_3$ solution?

    a. 24.0 mL

    b. 16.7 mL

    c. 1.67 mL

    d. 2.40 mL

34. Which one of the following radioactive decay processes represents a beta (β) emission?

    a. $^{11}_{6}C \rightarrow \,^{11}_{5}B + \,^{0}_{1}e$

    b. $^{81}_{37}Rb + \,^{0}_{-1}e \rightarrow \,^{81}_{36}Kr$

    c. $^{201}_{80}Hg + \,^{0}_{-1}e \rightarrow \,^{201}_{79}Au$

    d. $^{131}_{53}I \rightarrow \,^{131}_{54}Xe + \,^{0}_{-1}e$

35. Copper metal reacts with concentrated nitric acid. Here is the unbalanced equation for this reaction:

$$Cu(s) + HNO_3(aq) \rightarrow Cu(NO_3)_2(aq) + H_2O(l) + NO_2(g)$$

What should the coefficients be for the reactants and products (in the exact given order) after the equation is balanced?

    a. 2, 4, 1, 2, 2

    b. 1, 2, 1, 1, 1

    c. 1, 4, 1, 2, 2

    d. 1, 3, 1, 2, 1

36. Which of the following molecules has the highest boiling point?

    a. Propane

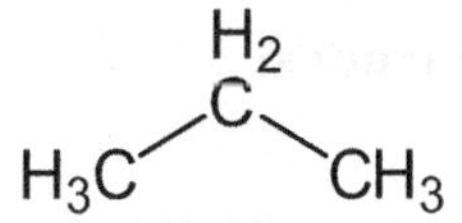

    b. Isobutane

    c. Propyl alcohol

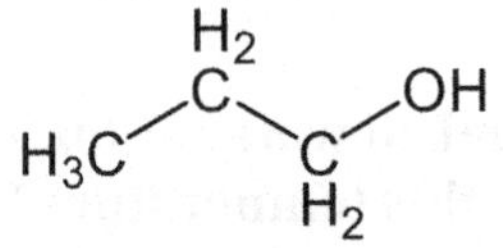

    d. Isopropyl alcohol

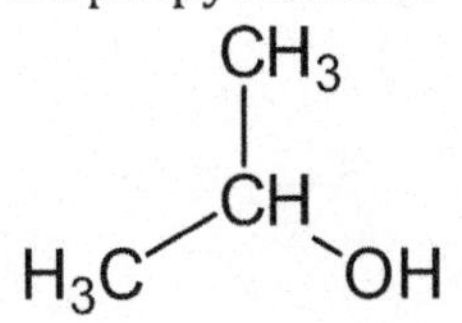

37. What is and the mass percentage of nitrogen, and how many moles of nitrogen atoms are in 1.45 g of Mg(NO$_3$)$_2$?

    a. 9.45%, 0.0196 mol
    b. 9.45%, 9.78×10^{-3} mol
    c. 18.9%, 0.0196 mol
    d. 18.9%, 9.78×10^{-3} mol

38. The values of the heat of reaction are known for the two reactions below:

$$A_2(g) + B_2(g) \rightarrow 2\,AB(g),\ \Delta H = 179.8\ kJ$$
$$2\,AB_2(g) \rightarrow 2\,AB(g) + B_2(g),\ \Delta H = -30.67\ kJ$$

What is the heat of reaction for the following reaction?

$$A_2(g) + 2\,B_2(g) \rightarrow 2\,AB_2(g)$$

    a. 210.5 kJ
    b. 149.1 kJ
    c. −210.5 kJ
    d. −149.1 kJ

39. The magnesium metal can combust in gaseous CO$_2$:

$$2\,Mg(s) + CO_2(g) \xrightarrow{\Delta} 2\,MgO(s) + C(s)$$

How many grams of MgO is produced if an 18.4-gram piece of metallic Mg is ignited in a container that has 12.3 grams of CO$_2$ in it?

    a. 30.5 g
    b. 15.3 g
    c. 11.3 g
    d. 22.6 g

40. Which one of the following is predicted to have the greatest solubility in methanol?

    a. Ethanol
    b. Cyclohexane
    c. Potassium bromide
    d. Pentane

41. Rank the bond length of the following in increasing order:

    (1) Br − Br
    (2) N ≡ N
    (3) C = C
    (4) F − F

    a. (2) < (3) < (4) < (1)
    b. (3) < (2) < (1) < (4)
    c. (2) < (3) < (1) < (4)
    d. (3) < (2) < (4) < (1)

42. 5.00 grams of iron is added to a solution that has 2.75 grams of $Cu(NO_3)_2$ to displace the copper from the solution:

$$Fe(s) + Cu(NO_3)_2(aq) \rightarrow Cu(s) + Fe(NO_3)_2(aq)$$

What is the limiting reactant, and how many grams of copper is produced in this reaction?

    a. Fe, 0.934 g
    b. $Cu(NO_3)_2$, 0.934 g
    c. Fe, 5.69 g
    d. $Cu(NO_3)_2$, 5.69 g

43. When OH^- is added to Cr^{3+} in solution phase, complex ion $Cr(OH)_4^-$ forms:

$$Cr^{3+}(aq) + 4\,OH^-(aq) \rightleftharpoons Cr(OH)_4^-(aq)$$

The formation constant, K_f, for the above reaction is 8×10^{29}. If 0.010 moles of $Cr(NO_3)_3$ is dissolved in 1.00 L of buffer solution that is kept at a pH of 9.00, what is the concentration of Cr^{3+} that is in equilibrium of $Cr(OH)_4^-$ in this solution?

    a. 1×10^{23} M
    b. 1×10^6 M
    c. 1×10^{-12} M
    d. 1×10^{-23} M

44. **Which one of the following equations is properly balanced?**

    a. $NO(g) + O_2(g) \rightarrow NO_2(g)$
    b. $Li(s) + F_2(g) \rightarrow LiF(s)$
    c. $H_2(g) + O_2(g) \rightarrow H_2O(g)$
    d. $CaO(s) + H_2O(l) \rightarrow Ca(OH)_2(s)$

45. **To determine the calcium content in a dietary support calcium tablet that weighs 1.05 g, the tablet is crushed and dissolved in 15.0 mL of 1.0 M HCl. The solution is filtered to remove insoluble impurities, then an access amount of 1.0 M Na_2CO_3 solution is added until the precipitation is complete. In the end, 245 mg precipitation is recovered. What is the percent by mass of calcium in this tablet?**

    a. 1.45%
    b. 9.35%
    c. 23.3%
    d. 40.1%

46. **An excess amount of Na_2SO_4 is added to a 20.0 mL portion of an aqueous $BaCl_2$ solution. After the reaction is complete, 0.179 g of precipitate is collected. What is the molar concentration of Ba^{2+} in the $BaCl_2$ solution?**

    a. 0.0192 M
    b. 0.0383 M
    c. 0.0455M
    d. 0.0652 M

Mometrix

47. Is any reaction going to occur when mixing iron(III) sulfate and sodium hydroxide solutions? If a reaction occurs, what are the products?

    a. No, there is no reaction between them.
    b. Yes, the products are $Fe_2(SO_4)_3(s)$ and $Na_2SO_4(aq)$
    c. Yes, the products are $Fe(OH)_3(s)$ and $Na_2SO_4(aq)$
    d. Yes, the products are $Fe(OH)_3(s)$ and $NaOH(aq)$

48. In a neutralization reaction, 75.0 mL of 0.150 M HCl is mixed with 75.0 mL of 0.150 M NaOH. As a result, the temperature of the mixture changes from 19.8 °C to 31.2 °C. Assuming that the specific heat of the solution mixture is 4.18 $J/(g \cdot K)$, and its density is 1.00 g/mL, how much heat is gained by the solution?

    a. 3.58 kJ
    b. 7.15 kJ
    c. 1.07 kJ
    d. 0.54 kJ

49. A 1.00 L flask contains 0.200 moles of N_2O which undergo decomposition:

$$2 N_2O(g) \rightarrow 2 N_2(g) + O_2(g)$$

The measured amount of N_2O against time is tabulated below:

Time (s)	0	30	60	90	120
[N₂O] (mol)	0.200	0.139	0.905	0.058	0.037

What are the average rates of disappearance of N_2O between 0 and 30 s, as well as between 60 and 120 s?

    a. 2.30×10^{-2} and 1.45×10^{-2} $M \cdot s^{-1}$
    b. 2.03×10^{-3} and 1.45×10^{-2} $M \cdot s^{-1}$
    c. 2.03×10^{-3} and 2.82×10^{-2} $M \cdot s^{-1}$
    d. 2.30×10^{-2} and 2.82×10^{-2} $M \cdot s^{-1}$

50. A reaction that is held constant at a pressure and at 303 K has an enthalpy change (ΔH) of 15.9 kJ and entropy change (ΔS) of -1.87 J/K. Determine the change in free energy (ΔG) of this reaction and whether it is spontaneous at this specific temperature.

    a. −16.5 kJ, spontaneous
    b. −583 kJ, spontaneous
    c. 16.5 kJ, nonspontaneous
    d. 583 kJ, nonspontaneous

51. What is the geometry of a BrF_3 molecule and the hybridization on its central atom?

    a. Trigonal pyramidal, sp^3
    b. T-shaped, sp^3d
    c. Trigonal planar, sp^2
    d. Seesaw, sp^3d

52. Which of the following statements is true regarding state functions?

    a. A state function's value is only dependent on the current state of the system.
    b. A state function's value is only dependent on the path that led to its current state.
    c. A state function's value is only dependent on the order of steps that led to its current state.
    d. A state function's value is dependent on both the path and the order of steps that led to its current state.

171

53. A combustion analysis is performed on 2.11 g of an organic compound that is composed of carbon, hydrogen, and oxygen. After combustion, 4.80 g of CO_2 and 1.96 g of H_2O are collected. What is the empirical formula of this organic compound?

    a. C_3H_6O
    b. C_2H_4O
    c. C_2H_3O
    d. $C_3H_6O_2$

54. To decrease the freezing point of 100 g water by 0.500 °C, how much NaCl should be added to this amount of water? ($K_f = 1.86\,°C/m$ for water)

    a. 1.57 g
    b. 1.86 g
    c. 2.69 g
    d. 15.7 g

55. Which of the following statements about atoms are true?

(1) An atom has the same number of protons and electrons.
(2) The protons and neutrons in an atom's nucleus are held together by strong nuclear force.
(3) Isotopes of an element all have the same number of neutrons.

    a. (1) and (3)
    b. (2) and (3)
    c. (1) and (2)
    d. (1), (2), and (3)

56. In the titration experiment, a 0.100 M NaOH solution is added to 20.0 mL of 0.100 M CH_3COOH solution. What is the pH of the titration solution when 15.0 mL NaOH solution is added? (K_a for CH_3COOH is 1.8×10^{-5}.)

    a. 4.26
    b. 5.22
    c. 5.34
    d. 4.74

57. Which of the following will shift the equilibrium to the product side for the reaction below?

$$2\ POCl_3(g) \rightleftharpoons 2\ PCl_3(g) + O_2(g),\ \Delta H > 0$$

    a. Increasing the concentration of PCl_3
    b. Increasing the reaction temperature
    c. Decreasing the volume of the reaction system
    d. Decreasing the concentration of $POCl_3$

58. Of an initial 1.00 g of a radioactive isotope, 0.712 g remains after 3.00 years. What is the half-life of this isotope?

    a. 6.12 years
    b. 3.06 years
    c. 1.54 years
    d. 12.3 years

59. **Which statement about the bonds in ethylene is NOT true?**

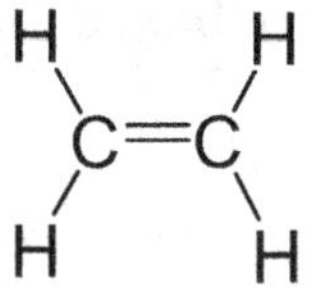

a. All bond angles are approximately 120°.
b. The $C = C$ double bond consists of one σ bond and one π bond.
c. The $C - H$ bonds are formed by overlapping the $1s$ orbital on H and one $2p$ orbital on C.
d. The π bond within the $C = C$ double bond results from two overlapping $2p$ orbitals (in parallel) on the two C atoms.

60. **Which of the following reactions will yield precipitations?**

a. $HCl(aq) + Na_2CO_3(aq)$
b. $HCl(aq) + Ca(OH)_2(aq)$
c. $Na_2S(aq) + HCl(aq)$
d. $CuSO_4(aq) + Na_2CO_3(aq)$

61. **Antimony (Sb) has the atomic number 51 and two naturally occurring isotopes, antimony-121 (120.903818 amu, abundance 57.21%), and antimony-123 (122.904216 amu, abundance 42.79%). What is the atomic weight of antimony, and which are the correct symbols of these two isotopes?**

a. 122.1 amu, $^{121}_{51}Sb$, $^{123}_{51}Sb$
b. 121.8 amu, $^{121}_{51}Sb$, $^{123}_{51}Sb$
c. 122.1 amu, $^{70}_{51}Sb$, $^{72}_{51}Sb$
d. 121.8 amu, $^{70}_{51}Sb$, $^{72}_{51}Sb$

62. **Which of the following molecules and ions obeys the octet rule at the central atom?**

a. NO_3^-
b. SF_4
c. XeF_2
d. PCl_5

63. **Which one of the following observations describes a chemical change?**

a. A mothball (naphthalene) disappears when left in the closet for a long time.
b. Dew drops form on the grass on a chilly autumn morning.
c. Wax pillar candles soften during shipping in a hot summer day.
d. A copper penny dissolves in nitric acid, turns the solution blue-green in color, and produces a reddish-brown gas.

64. Below is the phase diagram of a hypothetical substance A. Select the statement that is false about the properties of this substance based on its phase diagram.

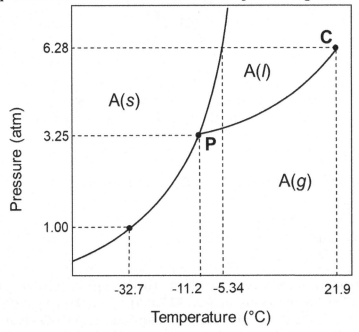

a. The triple point of substance A occurs at 3.25 atm and –11.2 °C.
b. The substance has a normal melting point of –32.7 °C.
c. Beyond point C (6.28 atm and 21.9 °C), substance A becomes a supercritical fluid.
d. At 6.28 atm, substance A has a melting point of –5.34 °C.

65. An atom needs to absorb a photon with a minimum energy of 4.67×10^{-19} J to emit an electron. Which of the following wavelengths may be used as the light source shining on the atom for it to emit electrons?

a. 658 nm
b. 592 nm
c. 447 nm
d. 315 nm

66. Predict the effect of the following operations on the solubility of $Ca(OH)_2$:

  (1) Adding HCl solution to it
  (2) Adding $CaCl_2$ solution to it

a. (1) increases solubility, (2) decreases solubility
b. (1) increases solubility, (2) increases solubility
c. (1) decreases solubility, (2) increases solubility
d. (1) decreases solubility, (2) decreases solubility

67. The density of solid iron is 7.87 g/cm^3. What is the mass (in grams) of an iron cube that is 1.00 cubic inch in volume? (1 in = 2.54 cm)

a. 20.0
b. 50.8
c. 129
d. 328

68. Using the molecular interpretation for entropy change, which one of the following reactions has a net decrease in total entropy after the reaction?

    a. $2\,CH_3OH(g) + H_2(g) \rightarrow C_2H_6(g) + 2\,H_2O(g)$
    b. $FeCl_2(s) + H_2(g) \rightarrow Fe(s) + 2\,HCl(g)$
    c. $C_2H_4(g) + H_2(g) \rightarrow C_2H_6(g)$
    d. $Be(OH)_2(s) \rightarrow BeO(s) + H_2O(g)$

69. A buffer solution is prepared by dissolving 0.250 moles of HCOOH (formic acid) and 0.250 moles of HCOONa (sodium formate) in 1.50 L of water. What is the pH of this solution if 50.0 mL of a 0.100 M HCl solution is added to it? (K_a of HCOOH is 1.80×10^{-4})

    a. 3.73
    b. 3.76
    c. 3.79
    d. 3.82

70. Which solid below is expected to have the lowest melting point?

    a. Boron nitride (BN)
    b. Calcium oxide (CaO)
    c. Phenol (C_6H_5OH)
    d. Cesium fluoride (CsF)

Answer Key and Explanations for Test #1

1. A: The energy levels represented by physical states are determined by the degrees of freedom of movement and the extent of energetic motions. For the processes of a substance changing from solid to liquid (melting), solid to gas (sublimation), or liquid to gas (vaporization), the final states of these processes contain more degrees of freedom and increase the extent of energetic motions, so heat is absorbed to complete these processes. The opposite of those processes (i.e., freezing, deposition, and condensation, respectively) release heat. So in this question, the sublimation of CO_2 is the only process among the four that absorbs heat. The condensation of NH_3, the freezing of acetic acid, and the deposition of I_2 all release heat.

2. A: The entropy change of the surroundings that is caused by the reaction has the opposite sign than its enthalpy change:

$$\Delta S_{surr} = \frac{-\Delta H_{sys}}{T} = \frac{-\Delta H_{rxn}}{T}$$

The temperature in this equation should be the absolute temperature in Kelvin. Substituting the values of ΔH and T into the equation above:

$$\Delta S_{surr} = \frac{-\Delta H_{rxn}}{T} = -\frac{(-327.1 \text{ kJ})}{(-15.0 + 273.15) \text{ K}} = 1.27 \text{ kJ/K}$$

A positive sign in ΔS_{surr} means that there is a net increase for the entropy in the surroundings.

3. D: The SO_3 molecule has 24 valence electrons in total. When constructing a Lewis structure for it, one $S = O$ double bond and two $S - O$ single bonds are needed around the central S atom to fulfill the total electron count. However, there are three ways to place the double bond, and all of them correct. These three structures are therefore the resonance structures for the SO_3 molecule:

4. A: Atomic mass increases when going down a column in any group of elements in the periodic table. All the elements in group 7A (F_2, Cl_2, Br_2, and I_2) make diatomic molecules, which are non-polar, and intermolecular interactions are dominated by dispersion forces. With the increasing mass down the column, the strength of intermolecular dispersion force increases; therefore, the melting points of the elements should increase when going down the group. Therefore, choice A is a false statement.

Atomic radii increase going down a group, as there are more shells of electrons in heavier elements. Increased radii with the same effective charge within the group makes the attraction between the valence electrons and the nucleus weaker. So, the electronegativity decreases when going down the group, and it becomes easier to lose the valence electrons as well, meaning that the first ionization energies decrease.

5. D: The reaction in choice A oxidizes the S atom from a +4 state in SO_2 to a +6 state in SO_3; meanwhile, the O atom in O_2 (oxidation state of 0) gets reduced to –2 in SO_3, making it a redox reaction. Choice B has sodium metal (oxidation state of 0) oxidized to +1, and Cl_2 (oxidation state of 0) reduced to –1 in the final product, NaCl. Choice C has Al metal (oxidation state of 0) oxidized to +3, and O_2 (oxidation state of 0) reduced to –2 in Al_2O_3. So, options B and C are also redox reactions. The reaction in choice D has C in a +4 state, O in a –2 state, and H in a +1 state before and after the reaction; therefore, it does not involve any redox process.

6. B: The standard reduction potential of an electrode indicates how readily the electrode can be reduced. A positive value in the E_{red}° suggests that the electrode prefers to be reduced, while a negative value of E_{red}° means that the reduction is not preferred by the electrode—it tends toward oxidization instead. Therefore, the (Zn + KOH) electrode is going to be oxidized, which makes it the anode in the battery. The (MnO_2 + graphite) electrode is the one that gets reduced, so it is the cathode in the battery. The graphite does not directly participate in the cell redox reaction; it helps to increase the conductivity for the electrode. The standard cell potential (or emf) of this battery is:

$$E_{cell}^\circ = E_{red}^\circ(\text{cathode}) - E_{red}^\circ(\text{anode}) = +1.55 \text{ V}$$

7. D: To convert the solubility to grams per liter from the solubility product, use an ICE table to calculate the equilibrium concentration of Ba^{2+} in the saturated solution:

	$BaF_2(s) \rightleftharpoons$	$Ba^{2+}(aq) +$	$2 F^-(aq)$
Initial	—	0	0
Change	—	+x M	+2x M
Equilibrium	—	x M	2x M

Then use the solubility product to solve for x:

$$K_{sp} = [Ba^{2+}][F^-]^2$$
$$1.7 \times 10^{-6} = (x)(2x)^2$$
$$1.7 \times 10^{-6} = 4x^3$$

$$x = \sqrt[3]{\frac{1.7 \times 10^{-6}}{4}} \approx 7.5 \times 10^{-3}$$

The equilibrium concentration of Ba^{2+}, which is equal to the concentration of BaF_2 in solution by its stoichiometry, is 7.5×10^{-3} M = 7.5×10^{-3} mol/L. The solubility in grams per liter is then obtained by multiplying this concentration by the molar mass of BaF_2:

$$\left(\frac{175.32 \text{ g}}{1.0 \text{ mol}}\right)\left(\frac{7.5 \times 10^{-3} \text{ mol}}{1.0 \text{ L}}\right) = 1.3 \text{ g/L}$$

8. C: Combustion reactions are rapid reactions that occur at a high temperature. If the substance being combusted is a hydrocarbon like methane, the carbon element in the hydrocarbon molecule gets oxidized, while the oxygen gets reduced. So, the combustion reaction also involves the oxidation state changes between the products and reactants. If the hydrocarbon is completely combusted with sufficient oxygen, the carbon gets oxidized to CO_2, and the hydrogen forms H_2O. If the hydrocarbon is combusted under limited oxygen supply, such as in a confined space, the carbon gets oxidized to CO instead. The given equation is balanced for all species, and the formation of CO_2 (and combusted in open air) suggests it is combusted completely. Therefore, only choice C has the correct statement.

9. D: The solubility of gases in liquid solvents depends on both temperature and pressure. Merely increasing the amount of liquid solvent cannot change the solubility of the gas. The solubility of gas increases as the partial pressure increases above the solvent (note that it needs to be the partial pressure of the solute gas; if the total pressure increases but the partial pressure for the gas is unchanged, the solubility of the gas will not be changed), or when the temperature decreases. Therefore, increasing the partial pressure of oxygen or decreasing the temperature can both increase the solubility of oxygen in the water tank.

10. A: To find whether the $Mg(OH)_2$ is going to stay dissolved or start to precipitate from the solution, calculate the value of reaction quotient Q at this point and compare its value to K_{sp}. The solubility product of $Mg(OH)_2$ is expressed as:

$$Mg(OH)_2(s) \rightleftharpoons Mg^{2+}(aq) + 2\,OH^-(aq)$$

$$K_{sp} = [Mg^{2+}][OH^-]^2 = 1.8 \times 10^{-11}$$

The reaction quotient for this dissolution process is:

$$Q = [Mg^{2+}][OH^-]^2$$

Since the pH of the solution is 9.00, the pOH of this solution is 5.00. The concentration of OH^- is then:

$$[OH^-] = 10^{-pOH} = 1.0 \times 10^{-5}\ M$$

Plugging in the concentration of Mg^{2+} and OH^- in the expression of reaction quotient:

$$Q = [Mg^{2+}][OH^-]^2 = (0.235)(1.0 \times 10^{-5})^2 = 2.35 \times 10^{-11} > K_{sp}$$

Since the reaction quotient Q is greater than that of K_{sp}, the Mg^{2+} and OH^- are in excess. The reaction favors the reactant side, therefore $Mg(OH)_2$ is going to precipitate from the solution in this case.

11. B: Both bond polarity and molecule geometry affect whether a molecule displays a net dipole moment or not. All the listed molecules are made up of polar covalent bonds, so their geometry determines whether the polarity of the bonds is canceled out or not. The CO_2 molecule is linear, so the polarity in each $C = O$ double bond gets canceled; the molecule is non-polar and does not display any net dipole moment.

The SO_2 molecule has a lone electron pair on the S atom, so the molecule adopts a bent geometry as the result of the repulsion by the lone pair. The polarity brought by the $S = O$ bonds then do not cancel each other. Since O is more electronegative than the S atom, it is partially positive towards the S end and partially negative towards the O ends.

The BF_3 and CH_4 molecules are symmetrical. The geometry of BF_3 is trigonal planar, meaning that all the $B - F$ bonds are 120° away from each other and their polarity gets cancelled out. The CH_4 is tetrahedral, and the $C - H$ bonds are 109.5° away from each other. The polarity from each of the $C - H$ bonds also gets cancelled out, so neither of these two molecules has a net dipole moment.

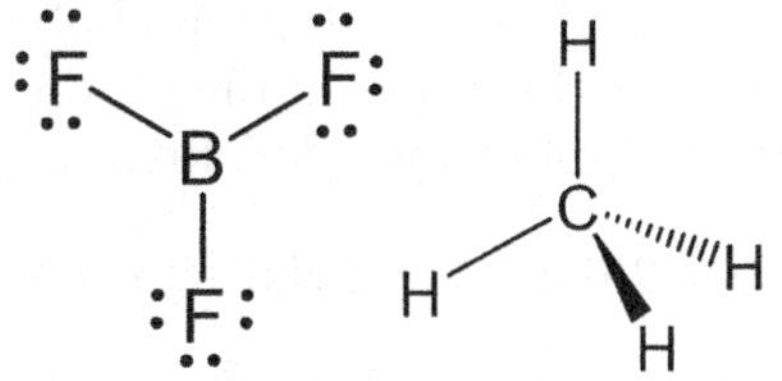

12. B: The reactions between acids and bases are a special type of double exchange reaction. The proton from the acid combines with the hydroxide anion in the base to yield water, and the remaining ions combine as a salt. If the resulting salt is water soluble, the ions in the salt do not directly take part in the neutralization process of H^+ and OH^-. If the product salt is insoluble in water, it will precipitate out from the solution. Therefore, by exchanging the ionic species for $Ca(OH)_2$ and H_2CO_3, the reaction between them should be:

$$Ca(OH)_2(aq) + H_2CO_3(aq) \rightarrow CaCO_3(s) + 2\,H_2O(l)$$

The products are then $CaCO_3$ as a precipitate and H_2O.

13. A: The principal quantum number n can be any positive integer ($n = 1, 2, 3, ...$). The angular momentum quantum number l may have any integer value from 0 up to $(n - 1)$: $l = 0, 1, 2, ..., (n - 1)$. The magnetic quantum number can possess any integer value between $-l$ and l, including 0. Therefore, in choice (A), the angular momentum quantum number l may not have the equal value to the principal quantum number n; for $n = 3$, l can be 0, 1, or 2. All the other sets of quantum numbers are within the values allowed by the rules of quantum mechanics.

14. C: First, draw out the Lewis structure for the $SnCl_3^-$ ion:

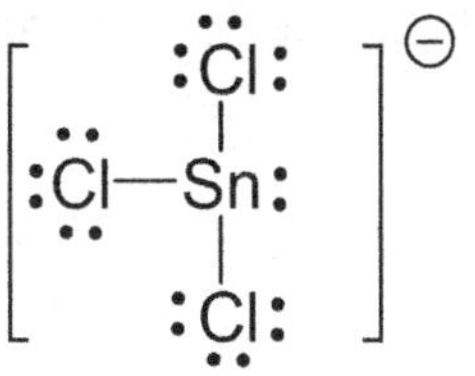

There are 4 electron domains around the central atom Sn in tetrahedral shape, including one lone electron pair. The hybridization that has electron domains arranged in tetrahedral shape is sp^3. Since the lone electron pair is invisible in the tetrahedral domain, the ion displays a trigonal pyramidal shape:

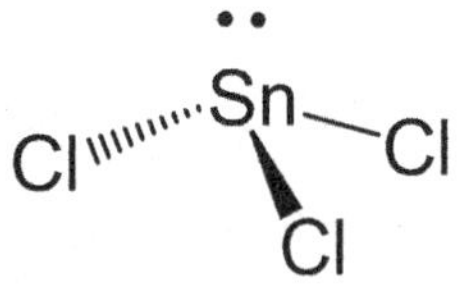

15. A: The number of H atoms in the reactants is even, but the number of H atoms in the products is odd. One way to start the balancing process is to multiply the number of NaOH molecules by 2. Then the product side has 4 H atoms in total: 2 from the NaOH, and 2 from the H_2. The reactant side only has 2 H atoms to start with, so the number of water molecules also needs to be multiplied by 2, to make the number of H atoms on the reactant side equal to 4:

$$Na(s) + 2\,H_2O(l) \rightarrow 2\,NaOH(aq) + H_2(g)$$

Balancing the H atoms also leaves the number of O atoms on both sides equal to 2. The last atom species to balance is Na. Since there are 2 Na atoms on the product side in NaOH, the number of Na atoms in the reactant should also be multiplied by 2. The final balanced result is then:

$$2\,Na(s) + 2\,H_2O(l) \rightarrow 2\,NaOH(aq) + H_2(g)$$

Therefore, the molar ratio between water and H_2 gas is 2 : 1. When one mole of water takes part in the reaction, half of a mole of H_2 gas is generated.

16. B: The Cl atom is more electronegative than the H atom, so the $C - Cl$ bond in chlorobenzene should have a larger dipole moment than the other 5 $C - H$ bonds, which makes the molecule polar. In *para*-dichlorobenzene, however, the two $C - Cl$ are exactly opposite each other on the benzene ring. Due to this symmetry, the dipole moments of these two bonds cancel out, and the molecule is non-polar. In both chloromethane and dichloromethane, the dipole moment brought by the $C - Cl$ bonds cannot be cancelled out around the central C atom, so they are both polar molecules.

17. A: The relationship between the standard free-energy change, $\Delta G°$, and the free-energy change under non-standard conditions, ΔG, are:

$$\Delta G = \Delta G° + RT \ln Q$$

The Q is the reaction quotient, which can be expressed in terms of partial pressure in this case:

$$Q = \frac{\left(P_{SO_3}\right)^2}{P_{O_2} \times \left(P_{SO_2}\right)^2} = \frac{(0.17)^2}{(0.22)(0.35)^2} = 1.07$$

Substituting the values of $\Delta G°$, constant R, and temperature T, the free-energy change for this condition is:

$$\Delta G = (-120.8)\text{ kJ/mol} + (8.314\text{ J/(mol}\cdot\text{K}))(330\text{ K})\left(\frac{1\text{ kJ}}{1000\text{ J}}\right)\ln(1.07) = -121\text{ kJ}$$

18. A: For multi-step reactions, the rate law is dependent on the slow (rate-determining) step. In this reaction, the initial step is rate-determining and elementary, therefore the rate law is only dependent on this initial step and is written based on its molecularity: one molecule of O_3 and one molecule of NO_2:

$$\text{Rate} = k_1[O_3][NO_2]$$

The reaction is then first order in both O_3 and NO_2; it is second order overall.

19. B: The $\Delta H°$ of the reaction can by obtained by summing the $\Delta H_f°$ values of the products, then subtracting the sum of the $\Delta H_f°$ values of the reactants. Since the value of $\Delta H_f°$ is dependent on the physical state of the substance, it is important to use the ΔH_f° value that is represented by the state of each reactant and product exactly as specified in the reaction:

$$\Delta H^\circ = \left(\Delta H_f^\circ[\mathrm{SiO_2(s)}] + 4 \times \Delta H_f^\circ[\,\mathrm{HCl(g)}]\right) - \left(\Delta H_f^\circ[\mathrm{SiCl_4(l)}] + 2 \times \Delta H_f^\circ[\mathrm{H_2O(l)}]\right)$$

$$-69.4 \text{ kJ/mol} = \left(\left((-910.9) + 4 \times (-92.30)\right) - \left(\Delta H_f^\circ[\mathrm{SiCl_4(l)}] + 2 \times (-285.3)\right)\right) \text{ kJ/mol}$$

$$-640 \text{ kJ/mol} = \Delta H_f^\circ[\mathrm{SiCl_4(l)}]$$

20. C: For elementary reactions, rate laws are written by their molecularity. Choice A is a bimolecular reaction; it should have the second order, which matches with the expression in the choice. Choice B is a termolecular reaction, and it also has the correct molecularity based on the expression. Choice C is a trimolecular reaction; however, the rate law expression is in the second order, which is incorrect. The correct form for its rate law should be $k[A][B]^2$. Choice D is also a termolecular reaction, and it has the correct molecularity in its rate law expression.

21. D: For a generic reaction, like $a\,A + b\,B \rightarrow c\,C + d\,D$, the reaction rates for the disappearance of reactants and appearance of products are related by their coefficients in the balanced equation:

$$Rate = -\frac{1}{a}\frac{\Delta[A]}{\Delta t} = -\frac{1}{b}\frac{\Delta[B]}{\Delta t} = \frac{1}{c}\frac{\Delta[C]}{\Delta t} = \frac{1}{d}\frac{\Delta[D]}{\Delta t}$$

Substituting the coefficients for the given reaction into the expression above:

$$-\frac{1}{2}\frac{\Delta[\mathrm{C_4H_{10}}]}{\Delta t} = -\frac{1}{13}\frac{\Delta[\mathrm{O_2}]}{\Delta t} = \frac{1}{8}\frac{\Delta[\mathrm{CO_2}]}{\Delta t} = \frac{1}{10}\frac{\Delta[\mathrm{H_2O}]}{\Delta t}$$

Therefore, after comparing the choices, choice D has the incorrect coefficients for CO_2. The correct form should be:

$$-\frac{1}{2}\frac{\Delta[\mathrm{C_4H_{10}}]}{\Delta t} = \frac{1}{8}\frac{\Delta[\mathrm{CO_2}]}{\Delta t}$$

22. C: The theoretical yield is needed to calculate the percent yield. The number of moles of the reactants based on the masses given is:

$$moles \; of \; \mathrm{CH_4} = \frac{4.02 \text{ g}}{16.0 \text{ g/mol}} = 0.251 \text{ mol}$$

$$moles \; of \; \mathrm{Cl_2} = \frac{17.8 \text{ g}}{70.9 \text{ g/mol}} = 0.251 \text{ mol}$$

The molar ratio of the reactants matches the coefficients in the balanced equation; thus, in theory, neither reactant would be left over. The theoretical yield of CH_3Cl is:

$$(0.251 \text{ mol}) \times (49.5 \text{ g/mol}) = 12.4 \text{ g}$$

The percent yield is:

$$\frac{5.65 \text{ g}}{12.4 \text{ g}} \times 100\% = 45.5\%$$

23. D: First, notice that the ΔH of this reaction is negative, which means that the final products possess less heat than the reactant. The reaction releases heat to the surroundings, so it is an exothermic reaction. The amount of heat that is being transferred to the surroundings is equal to the absolute value of the enthalpy change. To convert the molar enthalpy to a value in terms of the given amount of reactant, the mass of the product is divided by its molar mass (or multiplied by the reciprocal), then multiplied by the molar enthalpy. The units of the quantities during the calculations should be canceled out nicely to obtain the final answer in kJ:

$$(1.33 \text{ g}) \left(\frac{1 \text{ mol}}{34.01 \text{ g}}\right)\left(\frac{|-196 \text{ kJ}|}{1 \text{ mol}}\right) = 7.67 \text{ kJ}$$

24. B: Based on the information given, the products with correct chemical formulae should be Na and N_2. The unbalanced reaction equation is:

$$NaN_3(s) \rightarrow Na(s) + N_2(g)$$

A good start for balancing the equation is to balance the number of nitrogen atoms. Multiply the number of NaN_3 molecules by 2 and N_2 molecules by 3 so that both sides have a total of 6 N atoms:

$$2 \text{ NaN}_3(s) \rightarrow Na(s) + 3 \text{ N}_2(g)$$

Then multiply the elemental sodium atoms in the product by 2, and the reaction is balanced.

$$2 \text{ NaN}_3(s) \rightarrow 2 \text{ Na}(s) + 3 \text{ N}_2(g)$$

25. C: A catalyst is added to a reaction to lower the activation energy (i.e., the energy barrier) and make it easier for the reaction to occur. Because of the lowered energy barrier, the speed of the reaction is also changed. (In most lab demonstrations, the added catalysts speed up the desired reactions; however, negative catalysts that slow down reactions do exist.) Even though catalysts lower the activation energy, they do not affect the starting energy level for reactants, nor the final energy level represented by the products. Catalysts are added and present in a reaction from the start; they participate in the reaction but are regenerated at the end of a catalytic cycle. In contrast, intermediates are only generated during a reaction and are consumed.

26. D: The total amount of heat released by the 2.00 g sample of naphthalene is given by:

$$q = C_{cal} \times \Delta T$$

The C_{cal} is the heat capacity of the calorimeter, while ΔT is the temperature change for the calorimeter. The reaction is exothermic, so the sign of the q_{rxn} should be negative. However, as only the amount of heat is being calculated, which is the absolute value of q_{rxn}, its sign can be ignored. Therefore, the amount of heat being released is:

$$q = C_{cal} \times \Delta T = (5.54 \text{ kJ/°C})(17.9 \text{ °C}) = 99.2 \text{ kJ}$$

Now, convert the value above to the amount of heat that is released by one mole of naphthalene:

$$\left(\frac{99.2 \text{ kJ}}{2.00 \text{ g C}_{10}\text{H}_8}\right)\left(\frac{128.2 \text{ g C}_{10}\text{H}_8}{1.00 \text{ mol}}\right) = 6.36 \times 10^3 \text{ kJ}$$

27. B: The activation energy for a reaction can be calculated if its rate constants (k_1 and k_2) at two different temperatures (T_1 and T_2) are known:

$$\ln\frac{k_1}{k_2} = \frac{E_a}{R}\left(\frac{1}{T_2} - \frac{1}{T_1}\right)$$

Substitute the given sets of temperature and rate constant data into this equation, and solve for E_a:

$$\ln\frac{1.99 \times 10^{-5}}{2.49 \times 10^{-3}} = \frac{E_a}{8.314 \text{ J/(mol} \cdot \text{K)}}\left(\frac{1}{(140.3 + 273.15) \text{ K}} - \frac{1}{(91.7 + 273.15) \text{ K}}\right)$$

$$-4.83 = \frac{E_a}{8.314 \text{ J/(mol} \cdot \text{K)}}(-3.20 \times 10^{-4} \text{ K}^{-1})$$

$$E_a = \frac{(-4.83)(8.314 \text{ J/(mol} \cdot \text{K)})}{(-3.20 \times 10^{-4} \text{ K}^{-1})} \times \left(\frac{1 \text{ kJ}}{1000 \text{ J}}\right) = 125 \text{ kJ/mol}$$

28. D: A reaction involves the breaking of bonds in the reactants (absorbing energy) and the formation of bonds in the products (releasing energy). The reaction enthalpy (ΔH_{rxn}) can be then estimated by the sum of bond enthalpy in the reactants minus the sum of bond enthalpy in the products. So for this reaction, ΔH_{rxn} is:

$$\Delta H_{rxn} = \left(D(\text{H} - \text{H}) + 4D(\text{C} - \text{H}) + D(\text{C} = \text{C})\right) - \left(6D(\text{C} - \text{H}) + D(\text{C} - \text{C})\right)$$
$$= (436 + 4 \times 413 + 614) - (6 \times 413 + 348) \text{ kJ/mol}$$
$$= -124 \text{ kJ/mol}$$

The bond formation in the products releases more energy than breaking the bonds in the reactants. Therefore, this reaction is exothermic.

29. A: The balanced chemical reaction of this reaction is:

$$\text{K}_2\text{CO}_3(\text{aq}) + \text{Ba(NO}_3)_2(\text{aq}) \rightarrow \text{BaCO}_3(\text{s}) + 2\text{ KNO}_3(\text{aq})$$

Next, write the complete ionic equation for the above reaction:

$$2\text{ K}^+(\text{aq}) + \text{CO}_3{}^{2+}(\text{aq}) + \text{Ba}^{2+}(\text{aq}) + 2\text{ NO}_3{}^-(\text{aq}) \rightarrow \text{BaCO}_3(\text{s}) + 2\text{ K}^+(\text{aq}) + 2\text{ NO}_3{}^-(\text{aq})$$

Note that the product BaCO_3 is insoluble, while KNO_3 is soluble. Eliminating the spectator ions on both sides of the equation yields the net ionic equation:

$$\text{CO}_3{}^{2+}(\text{aq}) + \text{Ba}^{2+}(\text{aq}) \rightarrow \text{BaCO}_3(\text{s})$$

30. D: The bonding in the metals is called metallic bonding, which can be pictured as an ordered, packed array of cations surrounded by delocalized electrons from the metal atom's valance shell. This type of bonding is different from the ionic bonds and electrostatic attractions in the ionic solids. The electrostatic attractions in ionic bonds come from the attraction between the opposite charges in cations and anions, not the electrons. So option D is not a property of metallic solids. Because of the delocalized electrons in metals, they display excellent thermal and electrical conductivity. The strength of metallic bonding in different metals can vary a lot, therefore properties such as hardness and melting point also vary by metal.

31. C: $\Delta G°$ of the cell can be calculated from the standard cell emf:

$$\Delta G° = -nFE°_{cell}$$

The next step is to determine the value of n, which is the number of electrons involved in the cell redox reaction. The half-cell reactions are:

- Anode: $\text{Ni}(\text{s}) \rightarrow \text{Ni}^{2+}(\text{aq}) + 2\text{ e}^-$
- Cathode: $2\text{ Ag}^+(\text{aq}) + 2\text{ e}^- \rightarrow 2\text{ Ag}(\text{s})$

Two electrons are needed to complete a full cell reaction, so $n = 2$ for this cell. The $\Delta G°$ of this cell is:

$$\Delta G° = -nFE°_{cell} = -2 \times (96{,}485 \text{ J}/(\text{V} \cdot \text{mol})) \times (+1.08 \text{ V}) \times \frac{1 \text{ kJ}}{1{,}000 \text{ J}} = -208 \text{ kJ}/\text{mol}$$

The $\Delta G°$ is also related to the equilibrium constant K_{eq}:

$$\Delta G° = -RT \ln K_{eq}$$

Substituting the given values of $\Delta G°$, R, and T into the equation above:

$$-208 \text{ kJ}/\text{mol} \times \frac{1000 \text{ J}}{1 \text{ kJ}} = -(8.314 \text{ J}/(\text{mol} \cdot \text{K}))(298 \text{ K}) \ln K_{eq}$$

$$\ln K_{eq} = 84.0$$

$$K_{eq} = e^{84.0} = 3.02 \times 10^{36}$$

32. C: The molality (m) is defined as the number of moles of solute divided by the mass of solvent in kilograms, while the molarity (M) is the number of moles of solute divided by the volume of solvent in liters. The number of moles of solute NH_4Cl is:

$$\frac{55.3 \text{ g}}{53.49 \text{ g}/\text{mol}} = 1.03 \text{ mol}$$

The mass of solvent water at this temperature is:

$$(100 \text{ mL})(0.98338 \text{ g}/\text{mL})\left(\frac{1 \text{ kg}}{1000 \text{ g}}\right) = 0.0983 \text{ kg}$$

Therefore, the molality of the solution is:

$$\frac{1.03 \text{ mol}}{0.0983 \text{ kg}} = 10.5 \text{ m}$$

The molarity of this solution is:

$$\left(\frac{1.03 \text{ mol}}{100 \text{ mL}}\right)\left(\frac{1000 \text{ mL}}{1 \text{ L}}\right) = 10.3 \text{ M}$$

33. C: The number of moles of the solute remains the same in any dilution process. If the concentration and volume before the dilution are M_1 and V_1, and the concentration and volume after the dilution are M_2 and V_2, then $M_1V_1 = M_2V_2$.

Using this correlation and the quantities given, calculate the volume of the stock solution, and solve for V_1:

$$(6.00 \text{ M})V_1 = (0.0250 \text{ M})(400 \text{ mL})$$
$$V_1 = 1.67 \text{ mL}$$

34. D: A beta emission generates beta particles, which are high-speed electrons (denoted as $_{-1}^{0}e$ or $_{-1}^{0}\beta$). Choice D is a representation of the beta decay of iodine. Choices B and C represent a different type of nuclear decay which is called electron capture. In this type of decay, electrons are captured and reacted rather than being produced as in the beta emission. Choice A represents a positron emission; although it looks very similar to the beta emission, it produces a positron (^0_1e), which has the same mass as an electron but has a positive charge instead.

35. C: The given reaction is a redox reaction. An easy start for balancing this equation is to look at its number of electrons lost by oxidation and electron gain by reduction through any oxidation state changes of reactants and products. As illustrated below, Cu metal is oxidized and loses two electrons, while the nitrogen in HNO_3 is reduced and forms NO_2, gaining 1 electron in the process. Some of the HNO_3 does not participate in the redox reaction but combines with Cu^{2+} to form $Cu(NO_3)_2$:

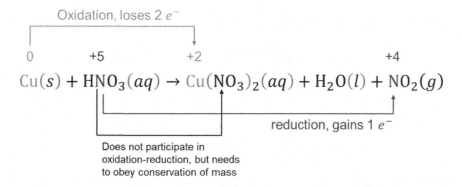

The final numbers of electron gain/loss should be equal, so the factor 2 is multiplied to balance the number of electrons. For the products that are not oxidized or reduced, the conservation of mass still applies. There are two nitrate ions in $Cu(NO_3)_2$, so another factor of two is added to the coefficients in front of HNO_3. The last species to balance is H_2O; its coefficient is obtained by dividing the total number of H atoms in HNO_3 by two, which is the number of H atoms contain in one H_2O molecule.

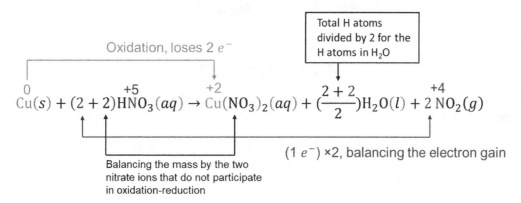

The final balanced equation then becomes:

$$Cu(s) + 4\ HNO_3(aq) \rightarrow Cu(NO_3)_2(aq) + 2\ H_2O(l) + 2\ NO_2(g)$$

36. C: Propane and isobutane are non-polar hydrocarbons that experience London dispersion forces as the source of intermolecular forces. Propyl alcohol and isopropyl alcohol have hydrogen bonding in addition to dispersion forces, which increases their boiling points significantly. Both alcohols have the same molecular weight, but propyl alcohol is longer in shape than isopropyl alcohol, so it experiences more dispersion force than isopropyl alcohol (due to the larger surface area the molecules have more contact with one another). Therefore, propyl alcohol has the highest boiling point of this set.

37. C: The molecule weight of $Mg(NO_3)_2$ can be obtained by adding the atomic weights of all atoms:

$$((14.0 + 16.0 \times 3) \times 2 + 24.3) \text{ g/mol} = 148.3 \text{ g/mol}$$

The mass percentage of nitrogen is equal to:

$$\frac{sum \ of \ atomic \ weight \ of \ N}{molecular \ weight \ of \ Mg(NO_3)_2} \times 100\% = \frac{14.0 \times 2}{148.3} \times 100\% = 18.9 \ \%$$

The number of moles of $Mg(NO_3)_2$ in 1.45 g is:

$$(1.45 \text{ g}) \times \left(\frac{1.00 \text{ mol}}{148.3 \text{ g}}\right) = 9.78 \times 10^{-3} \text{ mol}$$

Since there are two nitrogen atoms in each $Mg(NO_3)_2$ molecule, the number of moles of N atoms are twice of the moles $Mg(NO_3)_2$:

$$((9.78 \times 10^{-3}) \times 2) \text{ mol} = 0.0196 \text{ mol}$$

38. A: The last reaction $A_2(g) + 2 B_2(g) \rightarrow 2 AB_2(g)$ can be obtained by manipulating the first two reactions. Since the final product contains the species AB_2 and AB_2 is contained in the second reaction (but on the reactant side), the second reaction must be reversed and then add to the first reaction. Note that when the reaction is reversed, the sign of reaction enthalpy must also be reversed:

$$A_2(g) + B_2(g) \rightarrow 2 AB(g), \Delta H = 179.8 \text{ kJ}$$

$$2 AB(g) + B_2(g) \rightarrow 2 AB_2(g), \Delta H = 30.67 \text{ kJ}$$

Total reaction:

$$A_2(g) + 2 B_2(g) \rightarrow 2 AB_2(g)$$

The overall reaction enthalpy/heat of reaction is the sum of the two reactions after manipulation, based on Hess' Law:

$$\Delta H = 179.8 \text{ kJ} + 30.67 \text{ kJ} = +210.5 \text{ kJ}$$

39. D: To calculate the amount of product being produced, first convert the mass of reactants into moles:

$$\text{moles of Mg} = \frac{18.4 \text{ g}}{24.3 \text{ g/mol}} = 0.757 \text{ mol}$$

$$\text{moles of CO}_2 = \frac{12.3 \text{ g}}{44.0 \text{ g/mol}} = 0.280 \text{ mol}$$

Based on the stoichiometry of the reaction, for every mole of CO_2, two moles of Mg are consumed. The 0.280 moles of CO_2 given are only capable of consuming 0.560 moles Mg metal, so the Mg is in excess and CO_2 is the limiting reagent. The amount of MgO being produced is dependent on the amount of CO_2:

$$\frac{2 \text{ mol MgO}}{1 \text{ mol } CO_2} \times (0.280 \text{ mol}) \times (40.3 \text{ g/mol}) = 22.6 \text{ g}$$

40. A: Methanol is a polar compound, so it tends to dissolve compounds that are also polar. Two of the substances, cyclohexane and pentane, are hydrocarbon compounds which are non-polar, so they are not soluble in the polar solvent methanol. The KBr is an ionic compound that is highly polar, so methanol is capable of dissolving KBr through ion-dipole interactions. However, methanol is a covalent compound; the organic methyl group has less polarity than water (which is a great solvent for KBr). As the result, KBr is only somewhat soluble in methanol. Ethanol, on the other hand, has very similar polarity to methanol and is also a polar covalent compound. Its similarity to methanol makes it the most soluble of the options.

41. A: Bond length is related to bond order. When bond order increases, the bond becomes stronger, thus shorter. As a result, triple bonds are shorter than double bonds, and double bonds are shorter than single bonds. So, the bond length of $N \equiv N$ is shorter than that of $C = C$. When the bond orders are the same, the atomic radius plays an important role in affecting the bond length. As the atomic radii increases when going down a group in the periodic table, the $Br - Br$ thus has a longer bond length than $F - F$. The overall order of bond length is therefore:

$$N \equiv N < C = C < Br - Br < F - F$$

42. B: The number of moles of Fe in this given reaction is equal to:

$$(5.00 \text{ g}) \left(\frac{1 \text{ mol}}{55.8 \text{ g}}\right) = 0.0896 \text{ mol}$$

While the number of moles of $Cu(NO_3)_2$ in this given reaction is equal to:

$$(2.75 \text{ g}) \left(\frac{1 \text{ mol}}{187.56 \text{ g}}\right) = 0.0147 \text{ mol}$$

From the stoichiometry of this reaction, 1 part of Fe reacts with 1 part of $Cu(NO_3)_2$, and the amount of Fe significantly exceeds the amount of $Cu(NO_3)_2$ given here. Therefore, the $Cu(NO_3)_2$ is the limiting reagent, and the amount of Cu produced is dependent on the amount of $Cu(NO_3)_2$:

$$(0.0147 \text{ mol}) \left(\frac{1 \text{ mol Cu}}{1 \text{ mol } Cu(NO_3)_2}\right) \left(\frac{63.55 \text{ g Cu}}{1 \text{ mol Cu}}\right) = 0.934 \text{ g}$$

43. C: The formation constant of the $Cr(OH)_4^-$ is very large, which means that the formation of this complex in basic solutions is greatly favored. Given the information that the complex is prepared by dissolving a small amount of $Cr(NO_3)_3$ in a constant basic buffer solution (i.e., it has a reservoir of OH^-), it can be assumed that the added Cr^{3+} ions predominately form the complex in this solution.

However, a very small amount of the complex species still dissociates into Cr^{3+} and OH^- as below, and note that the equilibrium constant for this process is the inverse of the given K_f:

$$Cr(OH)_4^-(aq) \rightleftharpoons Cr^{3+}(aq) + 4\,OH^-(aq)$$

	$Cr(OH)_4^-(aq)$	$Cr^{3+}(aq)$	$4\,OH^-(aq)$
Initial	0.010 M	0	0
Change	$-x$ M	$+x$ M	$+4x$ M
Equilibrium	$(0.010 - x)$ M	x M	1.0×10^{-5} M

From this, use the formation constant to solve for x:

$$\frac{1}{K_f} = \frac{1}{8 \times 10^{29}} = \frac{[Cr^{3+}][OH^-]^4}{[Cr(OH)_4^-]} = \frac{x(1.0 \times 10^{-5})^4}{(0.010 - x)}$$

$$(8 \times 10^{29})(1.0 \times 10^{-20})x = (0.010 - x)$$
$$(8 \times 10^9)x + x = 0.01$$
$$(8 \times 10^9 + 1)x = 0.01$$
$$x = 1 \times 10^{-12}$$

Therefore, the amount of dissociated complex is very small; the vast majority of them exist in the $Cr(OH)_4^-$ form.

44. D: In choice A, the reaction $NO(g) + O_2(g) \rightarrow NO_2(g)$ has 3 O atoms (1 in NO and 2 in O_2) on the left but only 2 N atoms (NO_2) on the right, so it is still in the unbalanced form. In choice B, there are 2 F atoms in F_2 on the left but only 1 F atom in LiF on the right. Therefore, it is also in the unbalanced form. In choice C, there are 2 O atoms in O_2 on the left but only 1 O atom in water molecule on the right, revealing that it is still unbalanced. The reaction in choice D has 1 Ca atom on both sides, as well as 2 O atoms and 2 H atoms on both sides. The atom counts on both sides are equal for all species, so it is balanced.

45. B: It can be assumed that the calcium tablet is composed of CaX_2, where X is an assumed anion with -1 charge. Dissolving the tablet in the HCl yields a solution that contains $CaCl_2$, which is soluble in water:

$$CaX_2(s) + 2\,HCl(aq) \rightarrow CaCl_2(aq) + 2\,HX\,(aq)$$

Adding excess Na_2CO_3 re-precipitates the dissolved Ca^{2+} from the solution:

$$CaCl_2(aq) + Na_2CO_3(aq) \rightarrow CaCO_3(s) + 2\,NaCl(aq)$$

The collected 245 mg precipitation at the end is pure $CaCO_3$. The calcium content by mass is:

$$\left(\frac{40.1 \text{ g/mol Ca}}{100.1 \text{ g/mol CaCO}_3}\right)(245 \text{ mg})\left(\frac{1 \text{ g}}{1000 \text{ mg}}\right) = 0.0981 \text{ g}$$

The percent by mass of calcium is then:

$$\frac{0.0981 \text{ g}}{1.05 \text{ g}} \times 100\% = 9.35\%$$

46. B: Adding Na_2SO_4 solution to a $BaCl_2$ solution produces $BaSO_4$ as a precipitate:

$$BaCl_2(aq) + Na_2SO_4(aq) \rightarrow BaSO_4(s) + 2\,NaCl(aq)$$

The number of moles of the precipitate is equal to:

$$\frac{0.179 \text{ g}}{233.4 \text{ g/mol}} = 7.67 \times 10^{-4} \text{ mol}$$

This is then equivalent to the number of moles of Ba^{2+} in the original solution. So, the concentration of Ba^{2+} in the original solution is then:

$$[Ba^{2+}] = \left(\frac{7.67 \times 10^{-4} \text{ mol}}{20.0 \text{ mL}}\right)\left(\frac{1000 \text{ mL}}{1 \text{ L}}\right) = 0.0383 \text{ M}$$

47. C: The molecular formulas for iron(III) sulfate and sodium hydroxide are $Fe_2(SO_4)_3$ and NaOH, respectively. Both are water soluble and dissociate completely into ionic form, so they may undergo an ionic metathesis (or double displacement) reaction. The $Fe(OH)_3$ is a precipitate, so there is indeed a reaction between these two. Thus, a draft unbalanced reaction would be:

$$NaOH(aq) + Fe_2(SO_4)_3(aq) \rightarrow Fe(OH)_3(s) + Na_2SO_4(aq)$$

After the reaction is balanced, the molecular equation should be:

$$6 \text{ NaOH}(aq) + Fe_2(SO_4)_3(aq) \rightarrow 2 \text{ Fe}(OH)_3(s) + 3 \text{ Na}_2SO_4(aq)$$

Na_2SO_4 is the other product in this reaction. Although it counts towards a product, it does not directly participate in the reaction. The Na^+ and SO_4^{2-} dissociated from Na_2SO_4 are spectator ions.

48. B: The heat of the reaction can be calculated using the equation $q = C_s \times m \times \Delta T$, where C_s is specific heat of the solution, m is the mass of the solution, and ΔT is the temperature change during the reaction. Using this equation, find the values of mass and temperature change:

$$mass = density \times volume = (1.00 \text{ g/mL})(75.0 \text{ mL} + 75.0 \text{ mL}) = 150 \text{ g}$$

$$\Delta T = T_{final} - T_{initial} = 31.2 \text{ °C} - 19.8 \text{ °C} = 11.4 \text{ °C} = 11.4 \text{ K}$$

Since the temperature of the solution rises, it gains the heat that is released from the reaction. The sign of the heat gain is positive, and the total amount of heat is then:

$$(4.18 \text{ J/(g} \cdot \text{K)})(150 \text{ g})(11.4 \text{ K}) = (7{,}148 \text{ J})\left(\frac{1 \text{ kJ}}{1{,}000 \text{ J}}\right) = 7.15 \text{ kJ}$$

49. B: The average rate in each time interval is calculated by the change in the concentration during the time interval over the change in time. Therefore, the average rate of N_2O disappearance between 0 and 30 s is:

$$Rate = -\frac{\Delta[N_2O]}{\Delta t} = -\frac{(0.139 - 0.200) \text{ mol} \times \left(\frac{1}{1.00 \text{ L}}\right)}{(30 - 0) \text{ s}} = 2.03 \times 10^{-3} \text{ M} \cdot \text{s}^{-1}$$

The average rate of N_2O disappearance between 60 and 120 s is then:

$$-\frac{(0.037 - 0.905) \text{ mol} \times \left(\frac{1}{1.00 \text{ L}}\right)}{(120 - 60) \text{ s}} = 1.45 \times 10^{-2} \text{ M} \cdot \text{s}^{-1}$$

50. C: The value of ΔG can be calculated from ΔH, ΔS, and temperature in Kelvin using the equation $\Delta G = \Delta H - T\Delta S$. (Note that ΔS is given in J/K, but ΔH is in kJ, so unit conversion from J/K to kJ/K is needed for ΔS.)

$$\Delta G = \Delta H - T\Delta S = (15.9 \text{ kJ}) - (303 \text{ K})(-1.87 \text{ J/K})\left(\frac{1 \text{ kJ}}{1,000 \text{ J}}\right) = 16.5 \text{ kJ}$$

The calculated value of ΔG is positive in sign. Recall that when ΔG is positive, a reaction held at constant temperature (T) and pressure (P) is nonspontaneous. For a reaction with constant T and P to occur spontaneously, its ΔG needs to be negative.

51. B: The Lewis structure for BrF_3 is:

There are five electron domains around the central atom Br in the trigonal bipyramidal shape. It is an exception to the octet rule; to achieve the five electron domains, one unfilled d orbital participates in the hybridization along with one s and three p orbitals. The hybridization is then sp^3d. The five electron domains have three equatorial positions which are 120° away from each other, and two axial positions which are 90° from each other. If the two lone pairs both occupy the axial positions, each of them will interact with all three electron domains at 90°, making up a total of six sets of interactions at 90°, which contains a lot of repulsive force. If one lone pair occupies the equatorial position and the other occupies the axial position, then the two lone pairs will interact with each other at 90° (which is not favorable), and there are another three sets of 90° repulsion with the electron domains. Therefore, to minimize the overall repulsive force, the two non-bonding lone pairs occupy two of the equatorial positions which are further apart from each other at 120°. Although there are still four sets of interactions between the lone pairs and electron domains, it has the smallest magnitude of overall repulsive force (as it avoided the largest repulsion of two lone pairs at 90°). Since the two lone pairs of electrons are not visible in the trigonal bipyramidal shaped electron domains, the molecule appears T-shaped in geometry.

52. A: By its definition, the value of a state function is determined by the condition of the system at a given moment. The condition of the system can be detailed using a combination of parameters like pressure, temperature, volume, etc. The path that it takes to arrive at that combination of parameters does not affect the final value of the state function. For example, one path is a one-step process, the second path consists of step A then step B, and the third path consists of the reverse (step B followed by step A). If these paths all lead to the same final condition, the resulting values for the state functions at this condition by all the three paths should be the same. Therefore, only the statement in choice A is correct.

53. A: In the combustion analysis, the CO_2 is the product from the carbon in the sample, while the H_2O results from the hydrogen in the sample. From the masses of CO_2 and H_2O, it can be determined that:

$$Amount_C = (4.80 \text{ g } CO_2)\left(\frac{1 \text{ mol } CO_2}{44.0 \text{ g } CO_2}\right)\left(\frac{1 \text{ mol } C}{1 \text{ mol } CO_2}\right) = 0.109 \text{ mol}$$

$$Mass_C = (0.109 \text{ mol})\left(\frac{12.0 \text{ g}}{1 \text{ mol}}\right) = 1.308 \text{ g}$$

$$Amount_H = (1.96 \text{ g } H_2O)\left(\frac{1 \text{ mol } H_2O}{18.0 \text{ g } H_2O}\right)\left(\frac{2 \text{ mol } H}{1 \text{ mol } H_2O}\right) = 0.216 \text{ mol}$$

$$Mass_H = (0.216 \text{ mol})\left(\frac{1.00 \text{ g}}{1 \text{ mol}}\right) = 0.216 \text{ g}$$

The total mass by C and H is: $1.308 \text{ g} + 0.216 \text{ g} = 1.524 \text{ g}$; the remaining mass is $(2.11 - 1.524)\text{g} = 0.586 \text{ g}$, which is the mass of remaining oxygen. Therefore, the amount of O:

$$(0.586 \text{ g})\left(\frac{1 \text{ mol}}{16.0 \text{ g}}\right) = 0.0366 \text{ mol}$$

The molar ratio among C : H : O in the empirical formula is the closest ratio in whole numbers from the above quantities:

$$0.109 \text{ mol} : 0.216 \text{ mol} : 0.0366 \text{ mol} \approx 3 : 6 : 1$$

The final empirical formula is then C_3H_6O

54. A: The decrease in the freezing point (ΔT_f) by adding a solute to a pure solvent is given by the equation $\Delta T_f = K_f \times m$, where K_f is the molal freezing-point-depression constant and m is the molality of the solution. Since the amount of freezing point decrease is known, the desired concentration of salt solution can be determined:

$$0.500 = (1.86) \cdot m$$
$$m = 0.269$$

Knowing the molality of the solution and the mass of the solvent, the moles of solute can be determined:

$$0.269 = \frac{\text{moles of NaCl}}{\text{kg of water}} = \frac{\text{moles of NaCl}}{0.100 \text{ kg}}$$

$$\text{moles of NaCl} = 0.0269$$

So the mass of NaCl needed is:

$$(0.0269 \text{ mol})(58.4 \text{ g/mol}) = 1.57 \text{ g}$$

55. C: An atom is composed of these subatomic particles: protons (positively charged), neutrons (uncharged), and electrons (negatively charged). The number of protons is equal to the number of electrons in an atom, so that the electrical charges are balanced out. Since the protons all have the positive charges, a very strong attractive force is needed to overcome the repulsion among the positive charges and keep all the protons (as well as the neutrons) intact within the nucleus. This attractive force is referred to as the strong nuclear force (or strong interactions). The number of protons determines the identity of an element. Isotopes of an element all have the same number of protons but may have different numbers of neutrons and mass numbers, so statement (3) is incorrect.

56. B: Adding OH^- to CH_3COOH produces water and CH_3COO^-:

$$CH_3COOH(aq) + OH^-(aq) \rightarrow CH_3COO^-(aq) + H_2O(l)$$

Before the equivalence point in the titration, the solution is a buffer composed of CH_3COOH and CH_3COO^-. Find the concentration of CH_3COOH and CH_3COO^- in the solution to apply the Henderson-Hasselbalch equation and calculate the pH of the solution. At this point of titration, the number of moles of CH_3COOH in the stock solution is:

$$\left(\frac{0.100 \text{ mol}}{L}\right)(20.0 \text{ mL})\left(\frac{1 \text{ L}}{1000 \text{ mL}}\right) = 2.00 \times 10^{-3} \text{ mol}$$

The number of moles of NaOH added is:

$$\left(\frac{0.100 \text{ mol}}{L}\right)(15.0 \text{ mL})\left(\frac{1 \text{ L}}{1000 \text{ mL}}\right) = 1.50 \times 10^{-3} \text{ mol}$$

The 1.50×10^{-3} mol added NaOH consumes 1.50×10^{-3} mol of CH_3COOH and produces 1.50×10^{-3} mol of CH_3COO^-. The remaining amount of CH_3COOH is: 2.00×10^{-3} mol $- 1.50 \times 10^{-3}$ mol $= 5.00 \times 10^{-4}$ mol.

The total volume of the solution is: $(15.0 \text{ mL} + 20.0 \text{ mL})\left(\frac{1 \text{ L}}{1000 \text{ mL}}\right) = 0.0350$ L. Therefore, the concentrations of CH_3COO^- and CH_3COOH are:

$$[CH_3COO^-] = \frac{1.50 \times 10^{-3} \text{ mol}}{0.035 \text{ L}} = 0.0428 \text{ M}$$

$$[CH_3COOH] = \frac{5.00 \times 10^{-4} \text{ mol}}{0.035 \text{ L}} = 0.0143 \text{ M}$$

The pH of the solution at this point is then:

$$pH = pK_a + \log\frac{[CH_3COO^-]}{[CH_3COOH]} = -\log(1.8 \times 10^{-5}) + \log\frac{0.0428}{0.0143} = 5.22$$

57. B: When the concentration of products/reactants changes and disturbs the equilibrium, the reaction is going to shift to the direction that can absorb the change in the concentration and return to an equilibrium state. If the concentration of PCl_3, a product, is increased, the reaction is going to shift to the left (the reactant side) to consume the excess PCl_3. When the concentration of $POCl_3$, the reactant, is decreased, the reaction is also going to shift to the reactant side to make up for the loss in $POCl_3$. The given reaction is endothermic, so when the reaction temperature is increased, the forward reaction is promoted to consume the excess heat input. Therefore, the reaction shifts to the right (product side) under increased temperature. The total coefficient number increases in the products. When the volume of the reaction system is decreased, it is going to shift to the direction with fewer number of gas molecules. As a result, decreasing the volume of the system shifts the equilibrium towards the reactant side.

58. A: To calculate the half-life of this isotope, first find the decay constant k:

$$k = -\frac{1}{t}\ln\frac{N_t}{N_0} = -\frac{1}{3.00 \text{ yr}}\ln\frac{0.712 \text{ g}}{1.00 \text{ g}} = 0.113 \text{ yr}^{-1}$$

The half-life $t_{1/2}$ is solved using the relationship between k and $t_{1/2}$:

$$t_{1/2} = \frac{0.693}{k} = \frac{0.693}{0.113 \text{ yr}^{-1}} = 6.12 \text{ yr}$$

59. C: The carbon atoms are sp^2 hybridized in ethylene. The geometric construction of ethylene molecule is shown below:

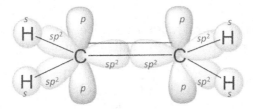

The geometry around both central C atoms is trigonal planar; therefore, the bond angles are around 120°. The three sp^2 hybridized orbitals on each carbon atom form three σ bonds: one with another sp^2 orbital on the other C atom, the other two with the $1s$ orbitals on the H atoms. So, the statement in choice C is incorrect; the C − H bonds are formed by overlapping the $1s$ orbital on H and sp^2 orbital on C, not the unhybridized $2p$ orbital. There is indeed one unhybridized $2p$ orbital on each C atom, but they overlap in a side-by-side way and form the π bond of the C = C double bond. This π bond, together with the σ bond formed by overlapping the two sp^2 orbitals on the two C atoms, make up for the C = C double bond.

60. D: All these mixtures undergo potential double displacement reactions. The first reaction produces CO_2 gas and water, but not any precipitations:

$$2 \text{ HCl(aq)} + \text{Na}_2\text{CO}_3(\text{aq}) \rightarrow 2 \text{ NaCl(aq)} + \text{H}_2\text{O(l)} + \text{CO}_2(\text{g})$$

The second mixture leads to the neutralization of an acid and a base:

$$2 \text{ HCl(aq)} + \text{Ca(OH)}_2(\text{aq}) \rightarrow \text{CaCl}_2(\text{aq}) + 2 \text{ H}_2\text{O(l)}$$

The resulting products are water and another water-soluble salt, $CaCl_2$, so there is no precipitation formation in the first reaction. The third reaction is:

$$\text{Na}_2\text{S(aq)} + 2 \text{ HCl(aq)} \rightarrow \text{H}_2\text{S(g)} + 2 \text{ NaCl(aq)}$$

It does not form any precipitations, but forms a gas, H_2S, and salt NaCl instead. The last reaction is:

$$\text{CuSO}_4(\text{aq}) + \text{Na}_2\text{CO}_3(\text{aq}) \rightarrow \text{CuCO}_3(\text{s}) + \text{Na}_2\text{SO}_4(\text{aq})$$

The precipitation $CuCO_3$ forms in this reaction, and it is the only reaction among the three that produces a precipitation.

61. B: The correct symbol of an isotope should have the atomic mass number in the superscript and atomic number in the subscript. So, the atomic mass numbers 121 and 123 should be present in the superscript, while the atomic number 51 should be in the subscript. The symbols of the two isotopes for antimony are then $^{121}_{51}Sb$ and $^{123}_{51}Sb$. The atomic weight of an element is the weighted average of its isotopes:

$$(120.903818 \text{ amu}) \times 57.21\% + (122.904216 \text{ amu}) \times 42.79\% = 121.8 \text{ amu}$$

62. A: One of the straightforward ways to look at whether the central atom obeys the octet rule or not is to draw out their Lewis structures first. The Lewis structure for NO_3^- is:

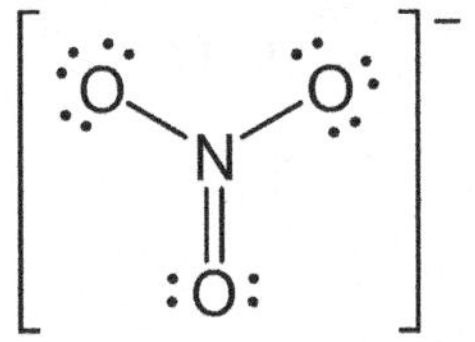

There are 8 electrons around the central N atom, so it does obey the octet rule. Note that there are a total of three resonance structures for NO_3^-, and all of them obey the octet rule:

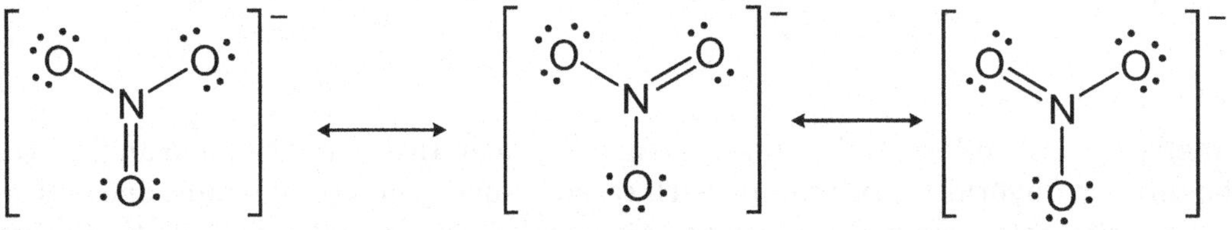

For the SF_4 molecule, the central S atom has 6 valence electrons. After 4 of them form single $S - F$ bonds with F atoms, there are 2 lone electrons left as a pair. Since there are 10 electrons around the central S atom, it violates the octet rule.

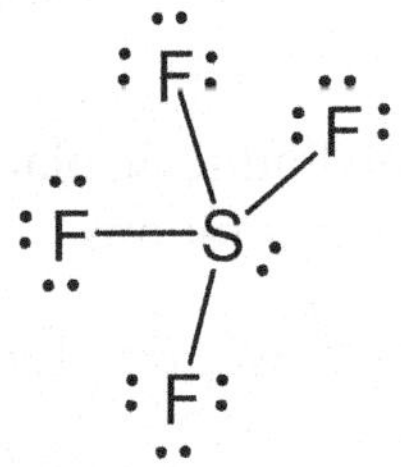

In the XeF_2 molecule, two out of the 8 valence electrons in the central Xe atom form single bonds with the F atoms, leaving 6 non-bonding electrons. The total electron count around the Xe atom is 10, so it does not follow the octet rule.

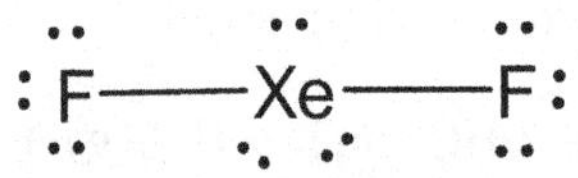

In the PCl_5 molecule, the 5 valence electrons on the central P atom all form single bonds with the Cl atoms, resulting in a total of 10 electrons around the P atom. Therefore, the PCl_5 also violates the octet rule.

63. D: A physical change does not convert the substance into a new one, but rather only involves a change in its physical appearance. The disappearance of a mothball is called the sublimination (from solid to gas), the forming of dew drops describes the condensation process (gas to liquid), and the softening of wax is the result of partial melting (solid to liquid). All these processes are changes in their physical states only, and none are converted to new substances. Therefore, they are physical changes. When copper is added to nitric acid, it reacts with the acid, producing copper nitrate and nitrogen dioxide. Since the copper and nitric acid are being converted into new substances with different chemical properties, it is a chemical change.

64. B: The phase diagram of a substance shows the conditions (temperature and pressure) for different physical states. The triple point is the pressure and temperature where all the gas, liquid, and solid phases are in equilibrium with each other. For this substance, it occurs at 3.25 atm and -11.2 °C (where the curves dividing the three states meet), so the statement in choice A is correct. The melting point can be read along the curve that divides the solid and liquid phase. In choice D, at 6.28 atm, the curve dividing the solid and liquid phase does have a temperature of – 5.34 °C on the horizontal axis, so this statement is also correct. The normal melting point is the melting point of the substance at 1 atm. For this substance, however, it does not have a liquid phase at 1.00 atm. As a result, it does not have a normal melting point: it sublimates at 1.00 atm, forming gas directly from the solid state when temperature increases at this pressure. So, the statement in choice B is incorrect. The liquid phase of this substance only exists at higher pressures and temperatures. But when the pressure and temperature increase to a certain point for some substances, their liquid and gaseous phases become indistinguishable. Known as the critical point of a substance, it is represented by point C on this diagram. Beyond this temperature and pressure the substance becomes supercritical. The statement in choice C is correct.

65. D: The frequency associated with the minimal energy is:

$$f = \frac{E}{h} = \frac{4.67 \times 10^{-19}}{6.626 \times 10^{-34}} \; s^{-1} = 7.05 \times 10^{14} \; s^{-1}$$

The wavelength of the above radiation is:

$$\lambda = \frac{c}{f} = \frac{3.00 \times 10^8 \; m/s}{7.05 \times 10^{14} \; s^{-1}} = (4.26 \times 10^{-7} \; m) \left(\frac{1 \times 10^9 \; nm}{1 \; m} \right) = 426 \; nm$$

This calculated value is the maximum value that a light source may have in wavelength. Note that the shorter the wavelength, the higher the energy associated with the wavelength. Therefore, any wavelength that is shorter than 426 nm can be used as the light source. Only choice D is shorter than 426 nm.

66. A: The solubility equilibrium for $Ca(OH)_2$ is shown below:

$$Ca(OH)_2(s) \rightleftharpoons Ca^{2+}(aq) + 2\,OH^-(aq)$$

When HCl is added to the $Ca(OH)_2$ solution, the added H^+ ions react and removes OH^- from the solution. The equilibrium above shifts to the right to make up for the loss OH^-, thus the solubility of $Ca(OH)_2$ is increased. On the other hand, when a $CaCl_2$ solution is added, it introduces excess Ca^{2+} ions to the solution. To consume the excess Ca^{2+}, the equilibrium above needs to be shifted to the left. The solubility of $Ca(OH)_2$ is then decreased, as the equilibrium favors the reverse of dissolution to form more solids.

67. C: The mass of the iron cube is $mass = density \times volume$. Since the density is given in the units of g/cm^3, the conversion factor from centimeters to inches needs to be included in the calculation for the mass. Also, as the unit of volume is a cubed factor, the unit conversion factor (which is linear) also needs to be cubed:

$$(1.00 \text{ in}^3) \times \left(\frac{7.87 \text{ g}}{1 \text{ cm}^3}\right) \times \left(\frac{2.54 \text{ cm}}{1 \text{ in}}\right)^3 = 129 \text{ g}$$

68. C: The molecular interpretation of entropy change examines the change in the degree of disorder between the products and reactants.

The $2\,CH_3OH(g) + H_2(g) \rightarrow C_2H_6(g) + 2\,H_2O(g)$ reaction has the same number of molecules (calculated by the sum of coefficients in the balanced equation) in its reactants and products, and there is no change in the phases of any reactants or products. The entropy change of this reaction should be very close to zero, since there is no obvious change in the degrees of disorder before and after the reaction.

The $FeCl_2(s) + H_2(g) \rightarrow Fe(s) + 2\,HCl(g)$ reaction has a net increase in one gas molecule after the reaction. The increased number of gas molecules contributes to the increase in degree of disorder, so the overall entropy increases after the reaction.

This same pattern of entropy increase occurs with the $Be(OH)_2(s) \rightarrow BeO(s) + H_2O(g)$ reaction.

However, in the $C_2H_4(g) + H_2(g) \rightarrow C_2H_6(g)$ reaction there is a net decrease in the number of gas molecules after the reaction; therefore it is the only one out of the four that has a net decrease in entropy.

69. A: The pH of a buffer solution can be calculated with the Henderson-Hasselbalch equation:

$$pH = pK_a + \log\frac{[HCOO^-]}{[HCOOH]}$$

First calculate the new concentration of $HCOO^-$ and $HCOOH$. As the HCl solution is added, its H^+ ions combine with the $HCOO^-$ to produce more conjugate acid $HCOOH$:

$$H^+(aq) + HCOO^-(aq) \rightarrow HCOOH(aq)$$

The amount of HCOOH being produced is:

$$(0.100 \text{ M})(50.0 \text{ mL})\left(\frac{1 \text{ L}}{1000 \text{ mL}}\right) = 5.00 \times 10^{-3} \text{ mol}$$

The new volume of the solution is:

$$1.50 \text{ L} + (50.0 \text{ mL})\left(\frac{1 \text{ L}}{1000 \text{ mL}}\right) = 1.55 \text{ L}$$

As HCOOH is produced and $HCOO^-$ is consumed, their new concentrations become:

$$[HCOOH] = \frac{(0.250 + 5.00 \times 10^{-3}) \text{ mol}}{1.55 \text{ L}} = 0.165 \text{ M}$$

$$[HCOO^-] = \frac{(0.250 - 5.00 \times 10^{-3}) \text{ mol}}{1.55 \text{ L}} = 0.158 \text{ M}$$

Substituting the K_a value and the new concentrations into the equation yields:

$$pH = pK_a + \log\frac{[HCOO^-]}{[HCOOH]} = -\log(1.80 \times 10^{-4}) + \log\frac{0.158}{0.165} = 3.73$$

70. C: The melting point of a solid depends on the constituent elements and molecules, and the interactions of the constituents with each other. The BN is a covalent-network solid, meaning that all the B and N atoms are held together by the strong covalent bonds. Because of the strong bonding type, the resulting solid has a very high melting point of 2,973 °C. As they are ionic solids, CaO and CsF are held together by ionic bonds. While the attractive forces between charges in ionic bonds may vary, they are still much stronger interactions than the intermolecular forces and will result in relatively high melting points (2,572 °C for CaO and 682 °C for CsF). Phenol is an example of molecular solid held together by intermolar forces (dipole-dipole interactions and hydrogen bonds in this case). These interactions are much weaker, so the resulting solids have much lower melting points (typically lower than 200 °C) when compared to the other two types of solids. In fact, the melting point of phenol is only 41 °C.

ACS General Chemistry Practice Test #2

1. Which of the following equations represents the balanced chemical reaction between Mg_3N_2 and H_2O?

    a. $Mg_3N_2(s) + 6\,H_2O(l) \rightarrow 3\,Mg(OH)_2(s) + 2\,NH_3(g)$
    b. $Mg_3N_2(s) + 3\,H_2O(l) \rightarrow 3\,Mg(OH)_2(s) + 2\,NH_3(g)$
    c. $2\,Mg_3N_2(s) + 3\,H_2O(l) \rightarrow 6\,Mg(OH)_2(s) + 2\,NH_3(g)$
    d. $Mg_3N_2(s) + H_2O(l) \rightarrow 3\,Mg(OH)_2(s) + 2\,NH_3(g)$

2. An object with a mass of 3.70 g is heated to 85.0 °C in an oven. It is then removed from the oven and placed in a container with exactly 200.0 g of water at 19.0 °C. The object increased the water temperature by 0.810 °C. What is the specific heat capacity of this object? (The specific heat capacity for water is $4.18\ J/(g \cdot K)$.)

    a. $9.24\ J/(g \cdot K)$
    b. $225\ J/(g \cdot K)$
    c. $2.75\ J/(g \cdot K)$
    d. $2.80\ J/(g \cdot K)$

3. Consider the following two-step reaction mechanism:

$$\text{Step 1: NO(g)} + Cl_2(g) \underset{k_{-1}}{\overset{k_1}{\longleftrightarrow}} NOCl_2(g)$$

$$\text{Step 2: } NOCl_2(g) + NO(g) \overset{k_2}{\longrightarrow} 2\,NOCl(g)$$
$$\text{Overall: } 2\,NO(g) + Cl_2(g) \longrightarrow 2\,NOCl(g)$$

If Step 1 is fast and has a rate constant of k_1 in the forward reaction (the rate constant of the reverse reaction is k_{-1}), while Step 2 is slow and has a rate constant of k_2, what is the rate law of the overall reaction?

    a. $\dfrac{k_1}{k_2 k_{-1}}[NO][Cl_2]$
    b. $\dfrac{k_1}{k_2 k_{-1}}[NO]^2[Cl_2]$
    c. $\dfrac{k_1 k_2}{k_{-1}}[NO][Cl_2]$
    d. $\dfrac{k_1 k_2}{k_{-1}}[NO]^2[Cl_2]$

4. Iron(III) oxide (Fe_2O_3) dissolves in dilute HCl solution:

$$Fe_2O_3(s) + 6\,HCl(aq) \rightarrow 2\,FeCl_3(aq) + 3\,H_2O(l)$$

75.0 mL HCl solution of 0.325 M is added to 0.432 g Fe_2O_3. Which one is the limiting reactant in this case, and how much more of the limiting reactant is needed to fully react with the excess reactant?

    a. Fe_2O_3, 0.0135 g
    b. Fe_2O_3, 0.217 g
    c. HCl, 5.00 mL
    d. HCl, 25.00 mL

5. Which of the following pairs of isotopes belong to the same element?
   a. $^{78}_{34}X$ and $^{82}_{34}X$
   b. $^{82}_{34}X$ and $^{82}_{36}X$
   c. $^{78}_{34}X$ and $^{78}_{36}X$
   d. $^{78}_{34}X$ and $^{76}_{32}X$

6. Methoxyethane and propyl alcohol both have the chemical formula of C_3H_8O. Methoxyethane has a boiling point of 7.4 °C, but propyl alcohol has a boiling point of 97.2 °C. What intermolecular forces contribute to such a difference in their boiling points?

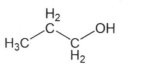

Propyl alcohol 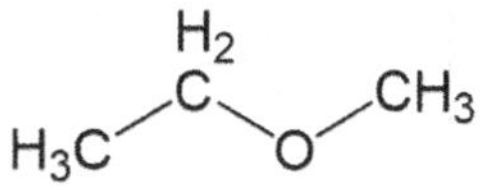   Methoxyethane

   a. Hydrogen bonding
   b. Dipole-dipole interactions
   c. London dispersion forces
   d. Ion-dipole interactions

7. Consider again the reaction of oxidizing NO with O_2:
$$2\,NO(g) + O_2(g) \rightarrow 2\,NO_2(g)$$
Both the NO and O_2 are colorless, while the NO_2 is reddish-brown in color. If the pressure of the reaction is increased by reducing the volume of the reaction flask, in which direction is the equilibrium going to shift and is the reaction mixture going to become lighter or darker in color?
   a. Equilibrium shifts to the right, and the mixture becomes darker.
   b. Equilibrium shifts to the right, and the mixture becomes lighter.
   c. Equilibrium shifts to the left, and the mixture becomes darker.
   d. Equilibrium shifts to the left, and the mixture becomes lighter.

8. A saturated solution of calcium sulfate ($CaSO_4$) contains 0.525 g $CaSO_4$ in 2.50 L water. What is the solubility product (K_{sp}) of $CaSO_4$?
   a. 3.65×10^{-9}
   b. 2.38×10^{-6}
   c. 1.49×10^{-5}
   d. 1.54×10^{-3}

9. A compound that is composed of elements A and B adopts the following unit cell structure in its crystals:

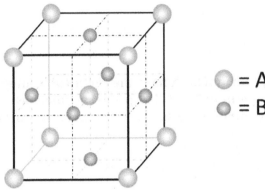

How many A and B atoms are there in each unit cell?

a. 9 and 6
b. 5 and 3
c. 3 and 2
d. 2 and 3

10. In the $n = 4$ electron shell of an atom, how many subshells and orbitals are present?

a. 4 subshells, 9 orbitals
b. 4 subshells, 16 orbitals
c. 3 subshells, 9 orbitals
d. 3 subshells, 16 orbitals

11. Rank the melting points of the following substances from high to low:

(1) Ethylene glycol ($HOCH_2CH_2OH$)
(2) Magnesium oxide (MgO)
(3) Ethanol (CH_3CH_2OH)
(4) Cesium fluoride (CsF)

a. $(2) > (4) > (1) > (3)$
b. $(4) > (2) > (3) > (1)$
c. $(1) > (3) > (2) > (4)$
d. $(3) > (1) > (4) > (2)$

12. How many moles of nitrogen atoms are contained in 4.50 g of ammonium nitrate (NH_4NO_3), and what is the percent by mass of nitrogen?

a. 0.0562 mol, 17.5%
b. 0.0562 mol, 35.0%
c. 0.112 mol, 17.5%
d. 0.112 mol, 35.0%

13. For the elements in the third period on the periodic table, which statement below is FALSE?

a. When going across the period from left to right, electronegativity increases.
b. When going across the period from left to right, the first ionization energy increases.
c. When going across the period from left to right, atomic radii increase.
d. When going across the period from left to right, the nonmetallic character of elements increases.

14. Below is a Lewis structure of the cyanate ion:

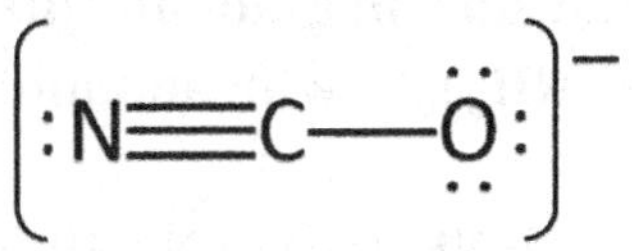

$$\left[:N\equiv C-\ddot{O}: \right]^{-}$$

What are the formal charges on the N, C, and O atoms, respectively?
   a. $-1, 0, 0$
   b. $+1, 0, -1$
   c. $+1, 0, -2$
   d. $0, 0, -1$

15. Which one of the following has the shortest bond length?
   a. $O_2{}^{+}$
   b. $O_2{}^{2+}$
   c. $O_2{}^{-}$
   d. $O_2{}^{2-}$

16. The $\Delta G°$ is -156.7 kJ/mol for the following reaction:

$$SO_2(g) + 2\,H_2(g) \rightarrow S(s) + 2\,H_2O(g)$$

What is the equilibrium constant K for this reaction at 298 K, and if the concentration of H_2 is increased at this temperature, how will the ΔG for this reaction change?
   a. 1.06, less negative
   b. 1.06, more negative
   c. 2.94×10^{27}, less negative
   d. 2.94×10^{27}, more negative

17. Which pair of substances below does NOT involve intermolecular forces caused by a dipole?
   a. Ethylene glycol ($HOCH_2CH_2OH$) and acetone (C_3H_6O)
   b. Neopentane ($C(CH_3)_4$) and iodine (I_2).
   c. Dichloromethane (CH_2Cl_2) and n-pentane ($CH_3CH_2CH_2CH_2CH_3$)
   d. Acetonitrile (CH_3CN) and benzene (C_6H_6)

18. The enthalpy change (ΔH) for combustion of methanol is -726 kJ/mol:

$$CH_3OH(l) + \frac{3}{2}O_2(g) \rightarrow CO_2(g) + 2\,H_2O(l)$$

What are the values of ΔH for (1) the combustion of 4.30 grams of CH_3OH, and (2) the formation of 33.1 grams of CO_2?
   a. -97.4 kJ, -546 kJ
   b. -146.1 kJ, -1090 kJ
   c. -194 kJ, -546 kJ
   d. -194 kJ, -273 kJ

19. The K_{sp} of $NiCO_3$ is 1.30×10^{-7}. Although $NiCO_3$ is a sparingly soluble salt in water, adding a concentrated ammonia solution will gradually dissolve the $NiCO_3$ because the Ni^{2+} ion can form the soluble complex $Ni(NH_3)_6{}^{2+}$ with ammonia (which pushes the dissolution equilibrium of $NiCO_3$ to the right):

$$Ni^{2+}(aq) + 6\,NH_3(aq) \rightleftharpoons Ni(NH_3)_6{}^{2+}(aq)$$

If the formation constant (K_f) for the above constant is 1.20×10^9, what is the equilibrium constant K of $NiCO_3$ dissolving by adding ammonia?

$$NiCO_3(s) + 6\,NH_3(aq) \rightleftharpoons Ni(NH_3)_6{}^{2+}(aq) + CO_3{}^{2-}(aq)$$

    a. 1.08×10^{-16}
    b. 9.23×10^{15}
    c. 1.20×10^9
    d. 156

20. Plutonium-242 $\left({}^{242}_{94}Pu\right)$ is radioactive and can undergo α-decay. What is the nuclear equation of this decaying process?

    a. ${}^{242}_{94}Pu + {}^{4}_{2}He \rightarrow {}^{246}_{96}Cm$
    b. ${}^{242}_{94}Pu + {}^{4}_{2}He \rightarrow {}^{238}_{92}U$
    c. ${}^{242}_{94}Pu \rightarrow {}^{4}_{2}He + {}^{238}_{92}U$
    d. ${}^{242}_{94}Pu \rightarrow {}^{4}_{2}He + {}^{246}_{96}Cm$

21. Bromide ion (Br^-) can be oxidized by hydrogen peroxide (H_2O_2) under acidic conditions:

$$2\,Br^-(aq) + H_2O_2(aq) + 2\,H^+(aq) \rightarrow Br_2(aq) + 2\,H_2O(l)$$

If the rate of consumption of Br^- is 0.034 M/s, what are the disappearance rate of H^+ and formation rate of Br_2, respectively?

    a. 0.017 M/s and 0.017 M/s
    b. 0.017 M/s and 0.068 M/s
    c. 0.068 M/s and 0.034 M/s
    d. 0.034 M/s and 0.017 M/s

22. In one experiment, stock $CuSO_4$ solutions at two different concentrations are prepared. Solution A is prepared by dissolving 2.00 g anhydrous $CuSO_4$ solid in exactly 150.0 mL of distilled water. Solution B is prepared by taking 10.00 mL of solution A and diluting it to a total volume of 150.0 mL with distilled water. What are the concentrations of solutions A and B, respectively?

    a. 1.25 M, 5.57×10^{-3} M
    b. 1.25 M, 0.0835 M
    c. 0.0835 M, 5.57×10^{-3} M
    d. 0.0835 M, 1.25 M

23. A voltaic cell is constructed using Ag and Cu as electrodes:

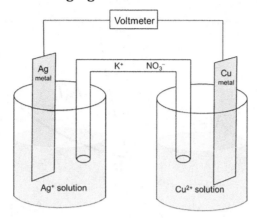

Given the standard reduction potential:

$$Ag^+(aq) + e^- \rightarrow Ag(s), E^\circ_{red} = +0.80\ V$$
$$Cu^{2+}(aq) + 2\ e^- \rightarrow Cu(s), E^\circ_{red} = +0.34\ V$$

What is the standard cell potential of this voltaic cell? If the concentration for Ag$^+$ solution is 1.25 M and the concentration for Cu^{2+} solution is 0.75 M, what does the cell potential become when it is at 45.0 °C?

   a. 0.46 V, 0.45 V
   b. 0.46 V, 0.47 V
   c. 1.14 V, 1.13 V
   d. 1.14 V, 1.15 V

24. A compound contains 37.7% of Na, 22.9% of Si, and 39.3% of O by mass. What is its empirical formula?

   a. Na_2SiO_3
   b. $NaSiO_3$
   c. Na_2SiO_2
   d. Na_2SiO_4

25. The decomposition of N_2O can be catalyzed by NO in two steps:

$$\text{Step 1: } NO(g) + N_2O(g) \rightarrow N_2(g) + NO_2(g)$$
$$\text{Step 2: } 2\ NO_2(g) \rightarrow 2\ NO(g) + O_2(g)$$

What is the balanced equation for the overall reaction, based on this mechanism?

   a. $2\ N_2O \rightarrow 2\ N_2(g) + O_2(g)$
   b. $2\ N_2O + 2\ NO_2(g) \rightarrow 3\ N_2(g) + 3\ O_2(g)$
   c. $2\ N_2O + O_2(g) \rightarrow N_2(g) + 2\ NO_2(g)$
   d. $2\ N_2O + 2\ NO\ (g) \rightarrow 2\ N_2(g) + 2\ O_2(g)$

26. Name the phase change processes of the substance A indicated by the two arrows on the following phase diagram:

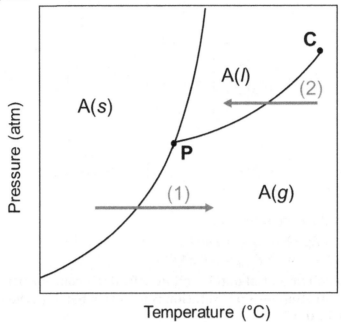

a.   Arrow 1 is vaporization, and arrow 2 freezing.
b.   Arrow 1 is melting, and arrow 2 condensation.
c.   Arrow 1 is sublimation, and arrow 2 freezing.
d.   Arrow 1 is sublimation, and arrow 2 condensation.

27. Predict the approximate bond angles labeled 1 and 2:

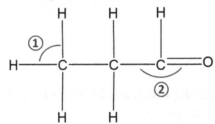

a.   120°, 109.5°
b.   109.5°, 120°
c.   90°, 109.5°
d.   90°, 120°

28. Aluminum metal can be used to reduce the Zn^{2+} in $Zn(NO_3)_2$ solution to zinc metal. What is the net ionic equation for this chemical process?

a. $2\,Al(s) + 3\,Zn^{2+}(aq) \rightarrow 2\,Al^{3+}(aq) + 3\,Zn(s)$
b. $3\,Al(s) + 2\,Zn^{2+}(aq) \rightarrow 3\,Al^{3+}(aq) + 2\,Zn(s)$
c. $Al(s) + 3\,NO_3^{-}(aq) \rightarrow Al(NO_3)_3(aq)$
d. $Al(s) + Zn^{2+}(aq) + {+}3\,NO_3^{-}(aq) \rightarrow Al(NO_3)_3(aq) + 2\,Zn(s)$

29. The mineral fluorite is chemically composed of calcium fluoride. When it is heated with concentrated sulfuric acid, it releases hydrogen fluoride gas and forms calcium sulfate in solid form. Which one of the following equations represents the balanced chemical process?

a. $CaF_2(s) + H_2SO_4(l) \xrightarrow{\Delta} HF(g) + CaSO_4(s)$

b. $CaF_2(s) + H_2SO_4(l) \xrightarrow{\Delta} 2\,HF(g) + CaSO_4(s)$

c. $2\,CaF(s) + H_2SO_4(l) \xrightarrow{\Delta} HF_2(g) + 2\,CaSO_4(s)$

d. $CaF_2(s) + HSO_4(l) \xrightarrow{\Delta} HF_2(g) + CaSO_4(s)$

30. For the reaction between lead acetate $(Pb(C_2H_3O_2)_2)$ and sodium bromide (NaBr) solutions, which ions are spectator ions?

a. $C_2H_3O_2{}^-$ and Na^+

b. Br^- and Na^+

c. $C_2H_3O_2{}^-$ and Pb^{2+}

d. Br^- and Pb^{2+}

31. Predict the shape of the SF_6 molecule. What is the hybridization on the central atom?

a. Trigonal bipyramidal, sp^3

b. Trigonal bipyramidal, sp^3d^2

c. Octahedral, sp^3d^2

d. Octahedral, sp^3

32. Acetone is a common household chemical that has a normal boiling point of 56.0 °C The heat of vaporization (ΔH_{vap}) for acetone is 31.3 kJ/mol. What is the entropy change (ΔS_{vap}) of acetone evaporating at its normal boiling point?

a. -559 J/(mol · K)

b. 559 J/(mol · K)

c. 95.1 J/(mol · K)

d. -95.1 J/(mol · K)

33. To make a stock aqueous solution of 3.000 L KOH with a concentration of 0.4500 M, how many grams of KOH are needed?

a. 1.350 g

b. 25.25 g

c. 75.75 g

d. 151.5 g

34. The radius of a rubidium (Rb) atom is 2.48 Å. What is its atomic radius in picometers (pm), and how many Rb atoms can be fit within a length of 1.50 micrometers (μm), if the atoms are arranged side by side?

a. 0.248 pm, 3.02×10^6

b. 0.248 pm, 6.04×10^6

c. 248 pm, 3.02×10^3

d. 248 pm, 6.04×10^3

35. What is the bond order of O_2^+? Is it paramagnetic or diamagnetic?

    a. $\frac{5}{2}$, diamagnetic

    b. $\frac{3}{2}$, diamagnetic

    c. $\frac{5}{2}$, paramagnetic

    d. $\frac{3}{2}$, paramagnetic

36. To determine the Pb^{2+} ion content in a $Pb(NO_3)_2$ solution with unknown concentration, an excess amount of Na_2SO_4 solution is added to a 10.00 mL portion of the $Pb(NO_3)_2$ solution. After the reaction is complete, the precipitation is collected, thoroughly washed, and dried. The final yield of the precipitation is 0.487 g. What is the concentration of this $Pb(NO_3)_2$ solution?

    a. 0.161 M
    b. 0.321 M
    c. 3.21×10^{-3} M
    d. 1.61×10^{-3} M

37. To measure the density of a metal block, it is first weighed on a balance. The weighing dish is 90.459 g, and the weighing dish with the metal block is 105.437 g. The metal block's volume is measured by completely submerging the metal cube under water and reading the total volume of water displaced, which is 5.35 mL. What is the density of this metal?

    a. 2.7996 g/cm^3
    b. 2.800 g/cm^3
    c. 2.80 g/cm^3
    d. 2.8 g/cm^3

38. If the average velocity of nitrogen molecules at room temperature is 1,073 miles per hour, what is the average velocity of N_2 molecules in SI units, m/s?

(1 hour $= 3,600$ s, 1 m $= 6.21 \times 10^{-4}$ miles)

    a. 480 m/s
    b. 1.85×10^{-4} m/s
    c. 62.2 m/s
    d. 2,400 m/s

39. A confined gas system that is kept at constant pressure absorbs 17.2 kJ of heat and does 1.19 kJ of work on the surroundings. What is the ΔH and ΔE of this system?

    a. $\Delta H = -17.2$ kJ, $\Delta E = -16.0$ kJ
    b. $\Delta H = -17.2$ kJ, $\Delta E = -18.4$ kJ
    c. $\Delta H = 17.2$ kJ, $\Delta E = 16.0$ kJ
    d. $\Delta H = 17.2$ kJ, $\Delta E = 18.4$ kJ

40. Which one of the following equations is both balanced and describes the complete combustion of acetylene (C_2H_2) in open air?

    a. $2 C_2H_2(g) + 3 O_2(g) \rightarrow 4 CO(g) + 2 H_2O(g)$
    b. $C_2H_2(g) + 3 O_2(g) \rightarrow 2 CO(g) + H_2O(g)$
    c. $2 C_2H_2(g) + 5 O_2(g) \rightarrow 4 CO_2(g) + 2 H_2O(g)$
    d. $C_2H_2(g) + 3 O_2(g) \rightarrow 2 CO_2(g) + H_2O(g)$

41. Rank the polarity of the following bonds in the increasing order:

    (1) Si − F
    (2) N − F
    (3) C − F
    (4) O − F

  a. $(1) < (3) < (2) < (4)$
  b. $(3) < (2) < (4) < (1)$
  c. $(1) < (4) < (2) < (3)$
  d. $(4) < (2) < (3) < (1)$

42. Which one of the following quantities is not a state function?

  a. Enthalpy (H)
  b. Internal energy (U)
  c. Gibbs free energy (G)
  d. Work (w)

43. A reaction has a standard enthalpy change $(\Delta H°)$ of -68.4 kJ/mol and a standard entropy change $(\Delta S°)$ of -139.0 J/K. Assuming that the changes in ΔH and ΔS are negligible with temperature change, is this reaction spontaneous?

  a. Yes, it is always spontaneous.
  b. It is only spontaneous at low temperatures.
  c. It is only spontaneous at high temperatures.
  d. No, it is always nonspontaneous.

44. The electrolysis of aqueous NaCl solution produces NaOH, hydrogen gas, and chlorine gas:

$$2\,NaCl(aq) + 2\,H_2O(l) \rightarrow 2\,NaOH(aq) + H_2(g) + Cl_2(g)$$

To produce 3.00 kg of H_2 gas, how much NaCl and water must be consumed?

  a. 53.6 kg NaCl, 173 kg H_2O
  b. 26.8 kg NaCl, 86.5 kg H_2O
  c. 26.8 kg NaCl, 173 kg H_2O
  d. 53.6 kg NaCl, 86.5 kg H_2O

45. HCl gas for laboratory use can be prepared by dropping concentrated sulfuric acid onto sodium chloride solid:

$$H_2SO_4(l) + 2\,NaCl(s) \rightarrow 2\,HCl(g) + Na_2SO_4(s)$$

The produced HCl gas is passed through another flask with desiccant to get thoroughly dried. In a trial experiment, 5.00 g of NaCl solid and an excess of concentrated H_2SO_4 are used. After the reaction, 1.50 L of HCl gas is collected at room temperature (25.0 °C) and pressure (1.00 atm). What is the percent yield for this trial of experiment?

  a. 8.43%
  b. 16.9%
  c. 35.8%
  d. 71.6%

46. In the oxidation-reduction titration experiment of permanganate (deep purple color in solution) and oxalate ions under acidic conditions, the permanganate ions are reduced to Mn^{2+} (very pale pink, almost colorless in solution) after the reaction is complete; CO_2 and water are produced as side-products:

$$2\ MnO_4^-(aq) + 5\ C_2O_4^-(aq) + 6\ H^+(aq) \rightarrow 2\ Mn^{2+}(aq) + 10\ CO_2(g) + 8\ H_2O(l)$$

In one trial experiment, a 0.1292 g sample of sodium oxalate $(Na_2C_2O_4)$ is used and it takes 17.85 mL of a $KMnO_4$ solution to reach the end point of the titration. Based on this, what is the concentration of the $KMnO_4$ solution?

    a. 0.1351 M
    b. 0.1080 M
    c. 0.05402 M
    d. 0.02161 M

47. Estimate the enthalpy change of the reaction (ΔH_{rxn}) below using the provided bond enthalpies:

$$CO_2(g) + 4\ F_2(g) \rightarrow CF_4(g) + 2\ OF_2(g)$$

$D(C - F) = 485$ kJ/mol
$D(O - F) = 190$ kJ/mol
$D(F - F) = 155$ kJ/mol
$D(C - O) = 358$ kJ/mol
$D(C = O) = 799$ kJ/mol

    a. −482 kJ/mol
    b. 482 kJ/mol
    c. −1,364 kJ/mol
    d. 1,364 kJ/mol

48. Which one of the below does not have the same electron configuration as the Cl^-?

    a. Ar
    b. Br^-
    c. S^{2-}
    d. Ca^{2+}

49. A reaction vessel is filled with NO_2, O_2, and SO_2 molecules. The following two-step reactions take place in the vessel:

Step 1: $NO_2(g) + SO_2(g) \rightarrow SO_3(g) + NO(g)$
Step 2: $2\ NO(g) + O_2(g) \rightarrow 2\ NO_2(g)$

After the above two steps, the reaction is complete. Which gas molecule species is the catalyst?

    a. NO_2
    b. NO
    c. SO_2
    d. O_2

50. Calculate the $\Delta S°$ for the following reaction using the provided $S°$ values:

$$2\,C_4H_{10}(g) + 13\,O_2(g) \rightarrow 8\,CO_2(g) + 10\,H_2O(g)$$

$S°[C_4H_{10}(g)] = 310.0\ \text{J/(mol}\cdot\text{K)}$
$S°[O_2(g)] = 205.0\ \text{J/(mol}\cdot\text{K)}$
$S°[CO_2(g)] = 213.6\ \text{J/(mol}\cdot\text{K)}$
$S°[H_2O(g)] = 188.83\ \text{J/(mol}\cdot\text{K)}$
$S°[H_2O(l)] = 69.91\ \text{J/(mol}\cdot\text{K)}$

 a. 312.1 J/(mol · K)
 b. −312.1 J/(mol · K)
 c. 877.1 J/(mol · K)
 d. −877.1 J/(mol · K)

51. Sodium metal can be produced by electrolysis of molten NaCl:

$$2\,NaCl(l) \rightarrow 2\,Na(l) + Cl_2(g)$$

If the applied external voltage is 10.0 V, what is the electric energy (in kWh) needed to produce 2.00 kg of sodium metal?

 a. 2.33 kWh
 b. 4.66 kWh
 c. 11.6 kWh
 d. 23.3 kWh

52. Acetone (C_3H_6O) has a normal boiling point of 56.0 °C. Its liquid phase specific heat is 2.17 J/(g · K), and enthalpy of vaporization is 31.27 kJ/mol. How much heat is needed when 30.0 g of acetone at 21.0 °C is heated to vapor phase at 56.0 °C?

 a. 2296 kJ
 b. 18.5 kJ
 c. 2.30 kJ
 d. 1850 kJ

53. For the decomposition reaction of SO_2Cl_2, it has a K_c of 0.078 at 373 K:

$$SO_2Cl_2(g) \rightleftharpoons SO_2(g) + Cl_2(g)$$

What is the K_p of this reaction? If a gas mixture in a reaction vessel contains 0.289 atm of SO_2Cl_2, 0.143 atm of SO_2, and 0.0756 atm of Cl_2 at 373 K, which direction will this equilibrium be shifted to?

 a. 242, to the left
 b. 242, to the right
 c. 2.39, to the left
 d. 2.39, to the right

54. A reaction's rate constants at various temperatures are determined experimentally. The plot of ln k vs. $\frac{1}{T}$ is generated, and its best-fit line is obtained as:

$$y = -15{,}274x + 120.21$$

What is the activation energy of this reaction?

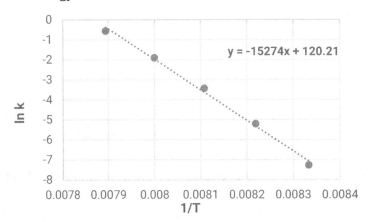

a. 1,250 kJ/mol
b. 999 kJ/mol
c. 127 kJ/mol
d. 9.87 kJ/mol

55. Aluminum metal has the specific heat capacity of 0.900 J/(g · K). If an aluminum block of 65.0 g at 21.0 °C is heated and absorbed 1.43 kJ of energy, what is the final temperature of the aluminum block after the heating process?

a. 40.8 °C
b. 45.4 °C
c. 104.6 °C
d. 38.8 °C

56. In a trial of combustion analysis of an organic compound (0.2308 g sample size), it produces 0.3172 g CO_2 and 0.2605 g water. If the compound only contains C, H, and O, what is its empirical formula?

a. C_3HO
b. CH_4O_3
c. CH_3O
d. CH_4O

57. In addition to hydrogen bonding, what is the major type of intermolecular force in the aqueous solution of KCl? The solubility of KCl at 50 °C is 42 g per 100 g of water. If a KCl solution at 50 °C has a concentration of 3.70 M, is this solution undersaturated, saturated, or supersaturated?

a. Dipole-dipole forces, oversaturated
b. Dipole-dipole forces, undersaturated
c. Ion-dipole forces, undersaturated
d. Ion-dipole forces, saturated

58. Which pair of liquid substances below (at room temperature and standard atmospheric pressure) is predicted to be miscible?

a. Benzene (C_6H_6) and water
b. Methanol (CH_3OH) and cyclohexane (C_6H_{12})
c. Pentane ($CH_3CH_2CH_2CH_2CH_3$) and hexane ($CH_3CH_2CH_2CH_2CH_2CH_3$)
d. Carbon tetrachloride (CCl_4) and water

59. What is the balanced form of the following reaction?
$$C_7H_8O_2(l) + O_2(g) \rightarrow CO_2(g) + H_2O(g)$$

a. $C_7H_8O_2(l) + 10\ O_2(g) \rightarrow 7\ CO_2(g) + 8\ H_2O(g)$
b. $C_7H_8O_2(l) + 16\ O_2(g) \rightarrow 7\ CO_2(g) + 8\ H_2O(g)$
c. $C_7H_8O_2(l) + 14\ O_2(g) \rightarrow 7\ CO_2(g) + 4\ H_2O(g)$
d. $C_7H_8O_2(l) + 8\ O_2(g) \rightarrow 7\ CO_2(g) + 4\ H_2O(g)$

60. What is the energy change for the fission of 1.000 moles of $^{235}_{92}U$ based on the following nuclear equation:
$$^{235}_{92}U + ^{1}_{0}n \rightarrow ^{141}_{56}Ba + ^{92}_{36}Kr + 3\ ^{1}_{0}n$$

Nuclear mass values:

$^{235}_{92}U = 234.9935$ amu
$^{141}_{56}Ba = 140.8833$ amu
$^{92}_{36}Kr = 91.9021$ amu
$^{1}_{0}n = 1.00866$ amu

a. -1.715×10^{16} J
b. -1.715×10^{13} J
c. -1.715×10^{-16} J
d. -1.715×10^{-13} J

61. The oxidation of NO is second order in NO and first order in O_2:
$$2\ NO(g) + O_2(g) \rightarrow 2\ NO_2(g)$$

The rate constant at a specific temperature is measured to be $6.19 \times 10^3\ M^{-2} \cdot s^{-1}$. If the concentration of NO is 0.0331 M and the concentration of O_2 is 0.0149 M, what are the rate of disappearance of O_2 and the rate of appearance of NO_2, respectively?

a. 0.101 M/s and 0.101 M/s
b. 0.101 M/s and 0.202 M/s
c. 0.404 M/s and 0.101 M/s
d. 0.202 M/s and 0.404 M/s

62. Calculate the $\Delta H°$ for the following reaction using the provided $\Delta H_f°$ values:

$$2\,C_4H_{10}(g) + 13\,O_2(g) \rightarrow 8\,CO_2(g) + 10\,H_2O(g)$$

$\Delta H_f°[C_4H_{10}(g)] = -124.73$ kJ/mol

$\Delta H_f°[O_2(g)] = 0.0$ kJ/mol

$\Delta H_f°[CO_2(g)] = -393.5$ kJ/mol

$\Delta H_f°[H_2O(l)] = -285.3$ kJ/mol

$\Delta H_f°[H_2O(g)] = -241.8$ kJ/mol

   a. $-5{,}752$ kJ/mol
   b. $5{,}752$ kJ/mol
   c. $-5{,}317$ kJ/mol
   d. $5{,}317$ kJ/mol

63. What are the coefficients for each of the reactants and products after the following reaction is balanced? (In the order w, x, y, z.)

$$w\,Fe_3O_4(s) + x\,CO(g) \rightarrow y\,Fe(s) + z\,CO_2(g)$$

   a. 2, 3, 6, 3
   b. 1, 2, 3, 2
   c. 1, 3, 3, 3
   d. 1, 4, 3, 4

64. Which one of the reactions below is NOT an acid-base neutralization reaction?

   a. $2\,HBr(aq) + Ca(OH)_2(aq) \rightarrow CaBr_2(aq) + 2\,H_2O(l)$
   b. $Fe(OH)_3(s) + 3\,HNO_3(aq) \rightarrow Fe(NO_3)_3(aq) + 3\,H_2O(l)$
   c. $KOH\,(aq) + HClO_4(aq) \rightarrow KClO_4(aq) + H_2O(l)$
   d. $Fe(NO_3)_3(aq) + 3\,KOH(aq) \rightarrow Fe(OH)_3(s) + 3\,KNO_3(aq)$

65. Which one of the following molecules does NOT have sp hybridization on the central atom(s)?

   a. XeF_2
   b. BeF_2
   c. $HgCl_2$
   d. C_2H_2

66. The K_{sp} of AgCl is 1.80×10^{-10} at 25 °C. What does the solubility of AgCl (in mol/L) become in a 0.020 M NaCl solution?

   a. 1.34×10^{-9}
   b. 9.00×10^{-9}
   c. 1.34×10^{-5}
   d. 9.00×10^{-5}

67. Which mixture below will not result into a precipitation reaction?

   a. $K_2CO_3(aq) + HBr(aq)$
   b. $Na_2S(aq) + ZnCl_2(aq)$
   c. $Cu(NO_3)_2(aq) + NaOH(aq)$
   d. $AgNO_3(aq) + HCl(aq)$

68. Which one of the following is NOT considered to be a solution?

    a. Sodium amalgam (alloy of sodium and mercury)
    b. Milk
    c. Air
    d. Brine

69. You are making a pH = 3.8 buffer solution by dissolving benzoic acid (C_6H_5COOH, 122.123 amu, $K_a = 6.3 \times 10^{-5}$) and sodium benzoate (C_6H_5COONa, 144.105 amu) solids in 100 mL distilled water. If 0.600 g of benzoic acid is used, how many grams of sodium benzoate will you need?

    a. 0.151 g
    b. 0.239 g
    c. 1.51 g
    d. 2.39 g

70. In the redox reaction below:

$$2\,ZnS(s) + 3\,O_2(g) \rightarrow 2\,ZnO(s) + 2\,SO_2(g)$$

Which element is reduced, and which one is oxidized after the reaction?

    a. O is oxidized, S is reduced
    b. S is oxidized, O is reduced
    c. Zn is oxidized, O is reduced
    d. Zn is oxidized, S is reduced

Answer Key and Explanations for Test #2

1. A: The unbalanced form for this chemical equation is:

$$Mg_3N_2(s) + H_2O(l) \rightarrow Mg(OH)_2(s) + NH_3(g)$$

There are 3 Mg atoms and 2 N atoms on the reactant side, so the number of $Mg(OH)_2$ molecules needs to be multiplied by 3 and number of NH_3 molecules needs to be multiplied by 2:

$$Mg_3N_2(s) + H_2O(l) \rightarrow 3\,Mg(OH)_2(s) + 2\,NH_3(g)$$

Next, balance the number of H atoms. There are $3 \times 2 + 2 \times 3 = 12$ H atoms on the product side, so multiply the number of water molecules on the reactant side by 6:

$$Mg_3N_2(s) + 6\,H_2O(l) \rightarrow 3\,Mg(OH)_2(s) + 2\,NH_3(g)$$

Lastly, check the number of O atoms. There are 6 O atoms on the reactant side, and $3 \times (1 \times 2) = 6$ O atoms on the product side, which means that the number of O atoms is balanced. The reaction is balanced.

2. D: The object absorbed heat in the oven then released heat to the water in the container. Using the equation below, calculate the amount of heat being released to the water, as the mass, specific heat capacity, and change in temperature of the water in the container are known. (Since the increments of kelvin and degrees Celsius are equivalent, they can be used interchangeably for the units of change in temperature: $\Delta T = 0.810\ °C = 0.810\ K$.)

$$q = C_s \times m \times \Delta T$$

$$q = (4.18\ J/(g \cdot K))(200.0\ g)(0.810\ K) = 677.16\ J$$

The amount of heat that the water absorbed is equal to the amount of heat released by the object. The final temperature for the water and the object should be the same. The final temperature for the water is $0.810\ °C + 19.0\ °C = 19.81\ °C$. This means the absolute value of the temperature change for the object is $(85.0 - 19.81)\ °C = 65.19\ °C$.

Apply the specific heat equation for the object and solve for C_s:

$$677.16\ J = C_s \times (3.70\ g) \times 65.19\ K$$

$$C_s = 2.80\ J/(g \cdot K)$$

3. D: Since Step 2 is the rate-determining step, the rate law of the reaction is dependent on this step. The rate law should be written as:

$$Rate = k_2[NOCl_2][NO]$$

However, $NOCl_2$ is an intermediate that is produced in step 1 and soon consumed in Step 2. Its concentration is difficult to measure, so it is the best to write the rate law in terms of the species whose concentrations can be measured easily. The Step 1 is fast and at equilibrium, which means its rates for the forward and reverse reaction are the same:

$$Rate = k_1[NO][Cl_2] = k_{-1}[NOCl_2]$$

Rearrange the rate law above and write the concentration of $NOCl_2$ in terms of the concentration of NO and Cl_2. Both NO and Cl_2 are reactants, so their concentrations are easy to measure:

$$[NOCl_2] = \frac{k_1}{k_{-1}}[NO][Cl_2]$$

Substitute the above expression into the rate law for Step 2 to get the rate law as:

$$Rate = k_2[NOCl_2][NO] = k_2\left(\frac{k_1}{k_{-1}}[NO][Cl_2]\right)[NO] = \frac{k_1 k_2}{k_{-1}}[NO]^2[Cl_2]$$

4. B: To determine which reactant is the limiting reactant, convert their amounts to number of moles, then compare the numbers with the molar ratio that is indicated by the stoichiometric coefficients in the equation. The amount of HCl is:

$$M \times V = (0.325 \text{ M})(75.0 \text{ mL}) = \left(0.325 \frac{\text{mol}}{\text{L}}\right)(75.0 \text{ mL})\left(\frac{1 \text{ L}}{1000 \text{ mL}}\right) = 0.0244 \text{ mol}$$

The amount of Fe_2O_3 is:

$$(0.432 \text{ g})\left(\frac{1 \text{ mol}}{159.7 \text{ g}}\right) = 2.71 \times 10^{-3} \text{ mol}$$

In the balanced chemical equation, the molar ratio between Fe_2O_3 and HCl is 1:6. The molar ratio of the actual amount of Fe_2O_3 to HCl is:

$$(2.71 \times 10^{-3}) : (0.0244) = 1 : 8.99$$

So HCl is in excess. Therefore, Fe_2O_3 is the limiting reactant. To fully consume the excess HCl, the amount of Fe_2O_3 needed is:

$$\frac{0.0244 \text{ mol}}{6} = 4.06 \times 10^{-3} \text{ mol}$$

The amount of additional Fe_2O_3 needed to add into the reaction is:

$$(4.06 \times 10^{-3} - 2.71 \times 10^{-3}) \text{ mol} = 1.35 \times 10^{-3} \text{ mol}$$

The mass of this portion of Fe_2O_3 is:

$$(1.35 \times 10^{-3} \text{ mol})(159.7 \text{ g/mol}) = 0.217 \text{ g}$$

5. A: The isotopes of the same element all have the same atomic number (the same number of protons). They can vary in their number of neutrons and atomic mass. The only pair of isotopes that match this criteria are the ones in choice A. Other pairs may have the same atomic mass or number of neutrons, but not the same atomic number, which means that they are different elements.

6. A: Since the chemical formulae of both compounds are the same, their molecular weights are also the same. They both experience dipole-dipole interactions and London dispersion forces, but there is no ionic species involved in neither of them, so the ion-dipole interactions do not apply. London dispersion forces largely depend on the polarizability the molecules, which is mainly affected by molecular weight. As they have the same molecular weight, the differences in the dispersion forces they experience are not likely to affect their boiling points. Propyl alcohol is more polar than methoxyethane and has a hydroxy functional group ($-OH$) which is subject to hydrogen bonding. The propyl alcohol experiences greater dipole-dipole interactions than the methoxyethane, but the magnitude of hydrogen bonding is typically much greater than that of the dipole-dipole interactions. As a result, the extra sets of hydrogen bonding in propyl alcohol raise its boiling point.

7. A: The given reaction has a larger total number of gas molecules on the reactant side than the product side. If the pressure of the reaction is increased by decreasing the volume, the equilibrium is going to shift to the direction with a smaller number of gas molecules, which is the product side (to the right). Since the equilibrium is shifted to the product side, there are more NO_2 molecules than before. Therefore, the reaction mixture is going to appear darker in color.

8. B: The solubility of $CaSO_4$ in mol/L (in other words, M) is:

$$[Ca^{2+}] = [SO_4^{2-}] = \left(\frac{0.525 \text{ g}}{2.50 \text{ L}}\right)\left(\frac{1.00 \text{ mol}}{136.14 \text{ g}}\right) = 1.54 \times 10^{-3} \text{ mol/L}$$

The dissociation process for $CaSO_4$ in water is:

$$CaSO_4(s) \rightleftharpoons Ca^{2+}(aq) + SO_4^{2-}(aq)$$

The K_{sp} for $CaSO_4$ is written as:

$$K_{sp} = [Ca^{2+}][SO_4^{2-}]$$

Substituting the values of Ca^{2+} and SO_4^{2-} concentrations yields:

$$K_{sp} = [Ca^{2+}][SO_4^{2-}] = (1.54 \times 10^{-3})(1.54 \times 10^{-3}) = 2.38 \times 10^{-6}$$

9. D: The unit cell is a combination of face- and body-centered cubic packing. For the A atoms in this unit cell, there are 8 on the corners and 1 in the center of the cell. For the 8 corner atoms, each of them is shared among a total of 8 unit cells (as illustrated for the central atom below), so the atom count of the corner atoms is: $8 \times \frac{1}{8} = 1$. The atom in the center of the cubic cell is not shared with any other unit cells. Therefore, the atom count for A is: $1 + 8 \times \frac{1}{8} = 2$.

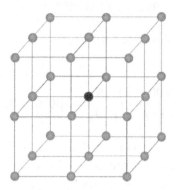

As for the B atoms, there are 6 on the center of each face in the unit cell. Each of these atoms is shared between 2 unit cells, so the atom count for B is: $6 \times \frac{1}{2} = 3$.

10. B: When $n = 4$ for a shell of electrons, there are 4 possible values for the angular momentum quantum number l: 0, 1, 2, and 3. Each value corresponds to a subshell of electrons, so there are 4 subshells with this value of principle quantum number. The number of orbitals for each subshell can be summarized in the table below:

Values of l	Subshell Designation	Values of m_l	Number of Orbitals
0	$4s$	0	1
1	$4p$	$-1, 0, 1$	3
2	$4d$	$-2, -1, 0, 1, 2$	5
3	$4f$	$-3, -2, -1, 0, 1, 2, 3$	7

By adding the number of orbitals in each subshell, the total number of orbitals in this shell of electrons is 16.

11. A: Ethylene glycol and ethanol are molecular compounds, while magnesium oxide and cesium fluoride are ionic compounds. Since the attractional forces of the ionic bonding are very strong (much stronger than the intermolecular forces in the molecular compounds), the ionic compounds usually have very high melting points. The strength of the ionic bonding depends on the charges and sizes of the ionic species; the ones that have more charges and are smaller in size lead to stronger ionic bonds. The Mg^{2+} and O^{2-} ions have more charge than Cs^+ and F^- ions, and Mg^{2+} is much smaller than Cs^+., Therefore, the ionic bonds in MgO are stronger than in CsF, so MgO has a higher melting point than CsF. Ethylene glycol has twice as many hydroxyl groups as ethanol, thus it has stronger intermolecular forces caused by hydrogen bonding. The melting point of ethylene glycol is higher than that of ethanol. The overall ranking of the melting points is then:

$$(MgO) > (CsF) > (HOCH_2CH_2OH) > (CH_3CH_2OH)$$

12. D: The number of moles in 4.50 g of NH_4NO_3 is:

$$(4.50 \text{ g}) \left(\frac{1 \text{ mol}}{80.043 \text{ g } NH_4NO_3} \right) = 0.0562 \text{ mol}$$

In 1 mole of NH_4NO_3, there are 2 moles of N. So, the number of moles of N is 0.112 mol. The mass percentage of N is:

$$\frac{(14.00 \times 2) \text{ g N}}{80.043 \text{ g } NH_4NO_3} \times 100\% = 35.0\%$$

13. C: When going left to right across a period of elements on the periodic table, the effective nuclear charges (Z_{eff}) increase. Because of the increasing effective nuclear charges, the electrons are more attracted to the nucleus, causing contraction in the electron clouds and making the atom sizes smaller. Therefore, choice C is a false statement. The tighter attraction of the electrons due to increasing effective nuclear charges across the period makes it harder for the atoms to lose electrons, so the ionization energy becomes higher when going across the period. As it becomes harder to lose electrons and easier to gain electrons towards the right-hand side of the period, the elements possess less metallic character and more nonmetallic character. Electronegativity measures the ability of an atom to attract electrons. As it becomes easier for the elements to gain electrons, electronegativity also increases when going across the period

14. D: The formal charge of the atoms on the Lewis structure is equal to:

$$\text{Formal Charge} = [\# \text{ valence } e^- \text{ on the atom}] - [\# \text{ of } e^- \text{ assigned to the atom}]$$

The nitrogen atom has 5 valence electrons. There are 2 electrons in the lone pair and 3 electrons from the shared electron pairs in the triple bond. Its formal charge is:

$$5 - (2 + 3) = 0$$

The carbon atom has 4 valence electrons and 4 electrons from the shared electron pairs in the 4 bonds around it. So its formal charge is:

$$4 - 4 = 0$$

Lastly, the oxygen atom has 6 valence electrons: 6 electrons in the 3 lone pairs, and 1 electron from the shared electron pairs in the single bond with the carbon atom. Its formal charge is then:

$$6 - (6 + 1) = -1$$

15. B: Bond strength and length can be determined using bond orders. Below is the MO diagram for O_2 molecule:

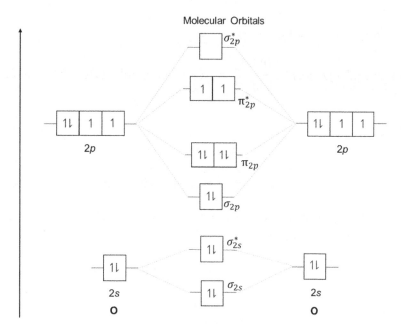

The bond order of O_2 is:

$$\frac{1}{2}(8 - 4) = 2$$

For the positively charged species, the $O_2{}^+$ has one electron removed from the antibonding orbital π_{2p}^*, and the $O_2{}^{2+}$ has two electrons removed from the antibonding orbital π_{2p}^*. So the bond orders are:

$$\text{Bond order of } O_2{}^+ = \frac{1}{2}(8 - 3) = \frac{5}{2}$$

$$\text{Bond order of } O_2{}^{2+} = \frac{1}{2}(8 - 2) = 3$$

For the negatively charged species, the $O_2{}^-$ fills in one additional electron into the antibonding orbital π_{2p}^*, and the $O_2{}^{2-}$ has two one additional electron into the antibonding orbital π_{2p}^*. Their bond orders are:

$$\text{Bond order of } O_2{}^- = \frac{1}{2}(8 - 5) = \frac{3}{2}$$

$$\text{Bond order of } O_2{}^{2-} = \frac{1}{2}(8 - 6) = 1$$

As the bond order increase, the bond strength increases and bond length decreases. The shortest bond is the one with the greatest bond order, so the $O_2{}^{2+}$ should have the shortest bond length.

16. D: The equilibrium constant K and the standard free-energy change $\Delta G°$ are related by:

$$\Delta G° = -RT \ln K$$

Substituting the values of $\Delta G°$, T, and R yields:

$$(-156.7 \text{ kJ/mol})\left(\frac{1{,}000 \text{ J}}{1 \text{ kJ}}\right) = -(8.314 \text{ J/(mol} \cdot \text{K)})(298 \text{ K})(\ln K)$$

Solving for K:

$$\ln K = 63.2$$

$$K = e^{63.2} = 2.94 \times 10^{27}$$

If the concentration of H_2 is increased, the equilibrium at this temperature will be disturbed. The ΔG is affected by its reaction quotient Q:

$$\Delta G = \Delta G° + RT \ln Q$$

$$Q = \frac{[H_2O]^2}{[SO_2][H_2]^2}$$

When the concentration of H_2 is increased, Q is decreased. Therefore, the term $RT \ln Q$ becomes smaller, and ΔG becomes more negative as a result.

17. B: To determine whether the intermolecular forces are caused by a dipole or not, identify which compounds have a net dipole moment. The structures of the compounds are drawn below:

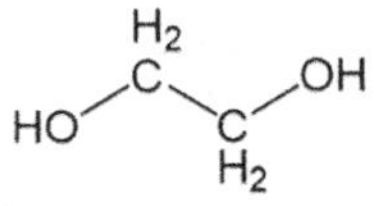

Ethylene glycol 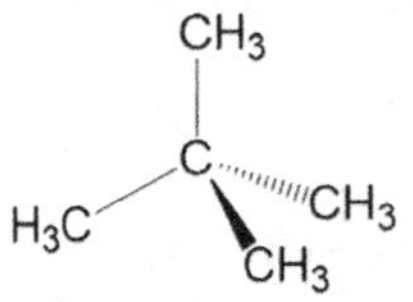   Neopentane 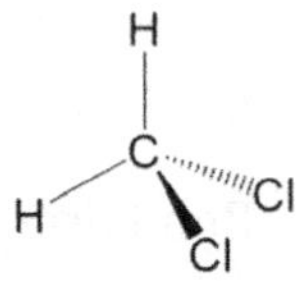   Dichloromethane 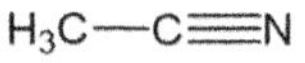   Acetonitrile

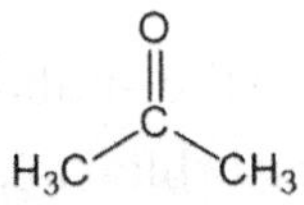

Acetone    Iodine 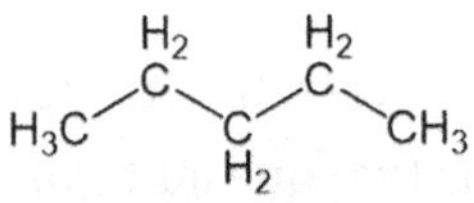   n-pentane    Benzene

Based on the polarity of bonds and molecular shapes, the ethylene glycol, acetone, dichloromethane, and acetonitrile are polar molecules and have net dipole moments, while the neopentane, iodine, n-pentane, and benzene are non-polar. Therefore, the pair of neopentane and iodine has both non-polar molecules and does not experience intermolecular forces from a dipole.

18. A: The molar enthalpy value that is given is for consuming 1 mole of CH_3OH or producing 1 mole of CO_2. The mass of the CH_3OH and CO_2 must be converted to number of moles, then multiply the number of moles by molar enthalpy change to obtain the target ΔH values. For 4.30 grams of CH_3OH:

$$\Delta H_{CH_3OH} = (4.30 \text{ g})\left(\frac{1 \text{ mol}}{32.04 \text{ g}}\right)\left(\frac{-726 \text{ kJ}}{1 \text{ mol}}\right) = -97.4 \text{ kJ}$$

For 33.1 grams of CO_2:

$$\Delta H_{CO_2} = (33.1 \text{ g})\left(\frac{1 \text{ mol}}{44.01 \text{ g}}\right)\left(\frac{-726 \text{ kJ}}{1 \text{ mol}}\right) = -546 \text{ kJ}$$

19. D: The dissociation process of $NiCO_3$ and its K_{sp} can be written as:

$$NiCO_3(s) \rightleftharpoons Ni^{2+}(aq) + CO_3^{2-}(aq)$$

$$K_{sp} = [Ni^{2+}][CO_3^{2-}] = 1.30 \times 10^{-7}.$$

The formation of the $Ni(NH_3)_6{}^{2+}$ complex ion and its K_f are written as:

$$Ni^{2+}(aq) + 6\,NH_3(aq) \rightleftharpoons Ni(NH_3)_6^{2+}(aq)$$

$$K_f = \frac{[Ni(NH_3)_6{}^{2+}]}{[Ni^{2+}][NH_3]^6} = 1.20 \times 10^9$$

Add the previous two equations and eliminate the common ion, Ni^{2+}, on both sides:

$$NiCO_3(s) + Ni^{2+}(aq) + 6\,NH_3(aq) \rightleftharpoons Ni(NH_3)_6{}^{2+}(aq) + Ni^{2+}(aq) + CO_3^{2-}(aq)$$

$$NiCO_3(s) + 6\,NH_3(aq) \rightleftharpoons Ni(NH_3)_6{}^{2+}(aq) + CO_3^{2-}(aq)$$

The equilibrium constant for this equation is:

$$K = \frac{[Ni(NH_3)_6{}^{2+}][CO_3^{2-}]}{[NH_3]^6}$$

Because the last equation is obtained by adding the first two equations, its equilibrium constant is equal to the product of the equilibrium constants of the first two equations, which is $K_{sp} \times K_f$:

$$K = K_{sp} \times K_f = \frac{[Ni(NH_3)_6{}^{2+}][CO_3^{2-}]}{[NH_3]^6} = ([Ni^{2+}][CO_3^{2-}]) \times \left(\frac{[Ni(NH_3)_6{}^{2+}]}{[Ni^{2+}][NH_3]^6}\right)$$

Substituting the values of K_{sp} and K_f yields the value of K:

$$K = (1.20 \times 10^9)(1.30 \times 10^{-7}) = 156$$

20. C: In alpha (α) decay, the radioactive atom $\left(^A_Z X\right)$ produces an alpha particle, which is $^4_2$He. Since the alpha particle is generated from the radioactive atom, its atomic mass is reduced by 4 amu, and its atomic number (number of protons) is reduced by 2 amu. The other product after the decay is then $^{A-4}_{Z-2}X$. In this case, $^{238}_{92}$U is produced after decaying. The nuclear equation for this process is then:

$$^{242}_{94}\text{Pu} \rightarrow {}^4_2\text{He} + {}^{238}_{92}\text{U}$$

21. D: Using the coefficients in the balanced reaction, the rate of disappearance of the H^+ and Br^-, and the rate of formation of the Br_2 are related by:

$$\text{Rate} = -\frac{1}{2}\frac{\Delta[\text{Br}^-]}{\Delta t} = -\frac{1}{2}\frac{\Delta[\text{H}^+]}{\Delta t} = \frac{\Delta[\text{Br}_2]}{\Delta t}$$

Solving for the rate of disappearance of H^+ yields:

$$-\frac{1}{2}\frac{\Delta[\text{Br}^-]}{\Delta t} = -\frac{1}{2}\frac{\Delta[\text{H}^+]}{\Delta t}$$

The coefficients on both sides can be cancelled out, so:

$$-\frac{\Delta[\text{Br}^-]}{\Delta t} = -\frac{\Delta[\text{H}^+]}{\Delta t} = 0.034 \text{ M/s}$$

Solving for the rate of the formation of Br_2:

$$\frac{\Delta[\text{Br}_2]}{\Delta t} = -\frac{1}{2}\frac{\Delta[\text{Br}^-]}{\Delta t} = 0.017 \text{ M/s}$$

Note that the negative signs indicate the reactants are disappearing/consumed. Because the change of concentration for disappearing reactants is negative, the negative signs cancel out, and the reaction rate is reported as a positive quantity.

22. C: The concentration of solution A is:

$$\frac{(2.00 \text{ g})\left(\frac{1 \text{ mol}}{159.6 \text{ g}}\right)}{(150.0 \text{ mL})\left(\frac{1 \text{ L}}{1000 \text{ mL}}\right)} = 0.0835 \text{ M}$$

To calculate the concentration of solution B, use the following relation:

$$M_{\text{conc}}V_{\text{conc}} = M_{\text{dilute}}V_{\text{dilute}}$$

Since solution B is more dilute, its concentration is therefore:

$$M_{\text{dilute}} = \frac{M_{\text{conc}}V_{\text{conc}}}{V_{\text{dilute}}} = \frac{(0.0835 \text{ M})(10.00 \text{ mL})\left(\frac{1 \text{ L}}{1000 \text{ mL}}\right)}{(150.0 \text{ mL})\left(\frac{1 \text{ L}}{1000 \text{ mL}}\right)} = 5.57 \times 10^{-3} \text{ M}$$

23. B: The Cu^{2+} has a smaller standard reduction potential than Ag^+, so Ag^+ is more favored in reduction, and it will be the cathode. The Cu electrode is more favored in oxidation, so it will be the anode. The cell reaction is then:

$$Cu(s) + 2\ Ag^+(aq) \rightarrow Cu^{2+}(aq) + 2\ Ag(s)$$

The standard cell potential for this voltaic cell is then:

$$E°_{cell} = E°_{red}(\text{cathode}) - E°_{red}(\text{anode}) = +0.80\ V - (0.34\ V) = 0.46\ V$$

To calculate the cell potential at non-standard conditions, the Nernst equation should be applied:

$$E = E° - \frac{RT}{nF}\ln Q$$

The reaction quotient Q is equal to:

$$Q = \frac{[Cu^{2+}]}{[Ag^+]^2}$$

Plugging into the concentrations, $E°$, and the constants, the cell potential is then:

$$E = 0.46\ V - \frac{(8.314\ \text{J}/(\text{mol} \cdot \text{K}))((273.15 + 45)\text{K})}{2(96{,}485\ \text{J}/(\text{V} \cdot \text{mol}))}\ln\frac{0.75}{1.25^2} = 0.46 - (-0.01)\ V = 0.47\ V$$

24. A: Assume that there are 100 grams of this compound. This would mean there are 37.7 g of Na, 22.9 g of Si, and 39.3 g of O. The number of moles of the above atoms are:

$$\text{\# of moles of Na} = (37.7\ \text{g})\left(\frac{1\ \text{mol}}{22.99\ \text{g}}\right) = 1.64\ \text{mol}$$

$$\text{\# of moles of Si} = (22.9\ \text{g})\left(\frac{1\ \text{mol}}{28.09\ \text{g}}\right) = 0.815\ \text{mol}$$

$$\text{\# of moles of O} = (39.3\ \text{g})\left(\frac{1\ \text{mol}}{16.00\ \text{g}}\right) = 2.46\ \text{mol}$$

The molar ratio (Na : Si : O) of the atoms is:

$$1.64 : 0.815 : 2.46 \approx 2 : 1 : 3$$

So, the empirical formula for this compound is Na_2SiO_3.

25. A: Since NO is the catalyst for the reaction, it should be present at the beginning of the reaction, take part in the reaction, and get regenerated after the reaction is complete. Therefore, the NO species should be cancelled out after adding the two equations. Also note that there are two molecules of NO being produced in Step 2, but there is only one molecule of NO as the reactant in Step 1. So the equation for Step 1 must be multiplied by a factor of 2:

$$2\ NO(g) + 2\ N_2O(g) \rightarrow 2\ N_2(g) + 2\ NO_2(g)$$

Add this to the equation of Step 2:

$$2\,NO(g) + 2\,N_2O(g) + 2\,NO_2(g) \rightarrow 2\,N_2(g) + 2\,NO_2(g) + 2\,NO(g) + O_2(g)$$

Eliminating the common species on both sides yields the overall reaction as:

$$2\,N_2O \rightarrow 2\,N_2(g) + O_2(g)$$

26. D: In the phase transitions on the diagram, arrow 1 refers to sublimation, the phase change from solid to gas directly. Arrow 2 shows the phase change of gas to liquid, which is called condensation.

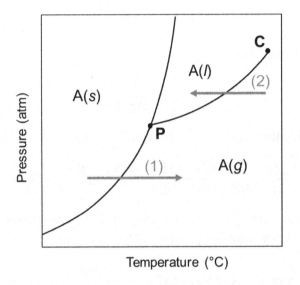

27. B: The central C atom on angle 1 has 4 single bonds, indicating that the $2s$ orbital is hybridized with all the other three $2p$ orbitals. So, it is sp^3 hybridized and adopts tetrahedral geometry. The bond angles in the tetrahedral geometry are around 109.5°; since there are no lone electron pairs repelling with the $C - H$ bonds, the actual bond angle should be very close to this number. The central C on angle 2 forms three bonds, one of which is the double bond with O. It indicates that the C is hybridized with two other $2p$ orbitals, making it sp^2 hybridized. The unhybridized $2p$ orbital on C overlaps side-by-side with another $2p$ orbital on the O to form the π bond in the double bond. The sp^2 hybridization adopts the trigonal planar geometry, with the bond angle between each bond close to 120°.

28. A: The balanced molecular equation for the described reaction is:

$$2\,Al(s) + 3\,Zn(NO_3)_2(aq) \rightarrow 2\,Al(NO_3)_3(aq) + 3\,Zn(s)$$

The complete ionic equation is therefore:

$$2\,Al(s) + 3\,Zn^{2+}(aq) + 6\,NO_3^-(aq) \rightarrow 2\,Al^{3+}(aq) + 6\,NO_3^-(aq) + 3\,Zn(s)$$

Eliminating the common ions (NO_3^-) on both sides yields:

$$2\,Al(s) + 3\,Zn^{2+}(aq) \rightarrow 2\,Al^{3+}(aq) + 3\,Zn(s)$$

29. B: The correct chemical formulae for the substances described in the question are: calcium fluoride (CaF_2), sulfuric acid (H_2SO_4), hydrogen fluoride (HF), and calcium sulfate ($CaSO_4$). The unbalanced chemical equation is then:

$$CaF_2(s) + H_2SO_4(l) \xrightarrow{\Delta} HF(g) + CaSO_4(s)$$

There are 2 F on the reactant side to start with, so the number of HF on the product side needs to be multiplied by 2:

$$CaF_2(s) + H_2SO_4(l) \xrightarrow{\Delta} 2\,HF(g) + CaSO_4(s)$$

After multiplying the number of HF by 2, there are 1 Ca, 2 H, 2 F, 1 S, and 4 O on each side. Since the number of each atom is equal, the reaction is balanced.

30. A: The chemical equation for the described reaction should be:

$$Pb(C_2H_3O_2)_2(aq) + 2\,NaBr(aq) \rightarrow 2\,Na(C_2H_3O_2)(aq) + PbBr_2(s)$$

Next, write out the complete ionic equation for the reaction:

$$Pb^{2+}(aq) + 2\,C_2H_3O_2{}^-(aq) + 2\,Na^+(aq) + 2\,Br^-(aq) \rightarrow 2\,Na^+(aq) + 2\,C_2H_3O_2{}^-(aq) + PbBr_2(s)$$

Cancelling out the common ions on both sides yields:

$$Pb^{2+}(aq) + 2\,Br^-(aq) \rightarrow PbBr_2(s)$$

The $C_2H_3O_2{}^-$ and Na^+ ions are on both sides and did not participate into the reaction. Therefore, they are the spectator ions of this reaction.

31. C: The SF_6 molecule has 6 electron domains, which indicates that it has an expanded valence shell. Its Lewis structure is drawn as:

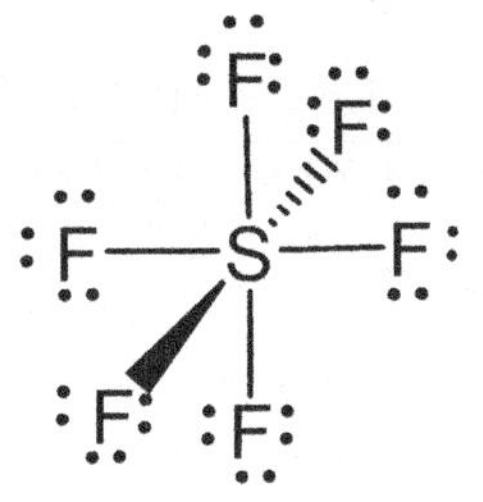

The molecule adopts the octahedral geometry, which is the most stable for 6 electron domains, and all the bonds are 90° away from each other. Since only 4 hybrid orbitals are formed by the sp^3 hybridization, two additional d orbitals need to participate in the hybridization as well to make a total of 6 electron domains. The resulting hybridization is therefore sp^3d^2.

32. C: For the evaporation process at the normal boiling point T, the change in the entropy is equal to:

$$\Delta S_{vap} = \frac{\Delta H_{vap}}{T}$$

Substituting the values for ΔH_{vap} and T yields:

$$\Delta S_{vap} = \frac{31.3 \text{ kJ/mol}}{(273.15 + 56.0) \text{ K}} \times \frac{1000 \text{ J}}{1 \text{ kJ}} = 95.1 \text{ J/(mol} \cdot \text{K)}$$

The evaporation process absorbs heat and has increased amount of randomness, which matches with the positive signs in ΔH_{vap} and ΔS_{vap}.

33. C: Calculate the number of moles of KOH needed:

$$(0.4500 \text{ M})(3.000 \text{ L}) = (0.4500 \text{ mol/L})(3.000 \text{ L}) = 1.350 \text{ mol}$$

The mass of KOH is then calculated by multiplying the number of moles by its molar mass:

$$(56.11 \text{ g/mol})(1.350 \text{ mol}) = 75.75 \text{ g}$$

34. C: The unit of length ångström (Å) is equal to 1×10^{-10} m, while the unit picometer (pm) is equal to 1×10^{-12} m. The unit conversion factor between them is:

$$\frac{1 \text{ Å}}{1 \text{ pm}} = \frac{1 \times 10^{-10} \text{ m}}{1 \times 10^{-12} \text{ m}}$$

$$1 \text{ Å} = 100 \text{ pm}$$

The atomic radius in pm is: $2.48 \times 100 \text{ pm} = 248$ pm. To calculate how many Rb atoms can fit side by side in a span of 1.50 μm, use the diameter of the Rb atom, which is two times its radius. Since $1 \text{ μm} = 1 \times 10^{-6}$ m, the amount of Rb atoms that can be fit into this span is:

$$\frac{1.50 \text{ μm}}{(2.48 \text{ Å}) \times 2} = \frac{1.50 \times 10^{-6} \text{ m}}{4.70 \times 10^{-10} \text{ m}} = 3.02 \times 10^3$$

35. C: To calculate the bond order and determine if the ion is paramagnetic or diamagnetic, construct the molecular orbital (MO) diagram.

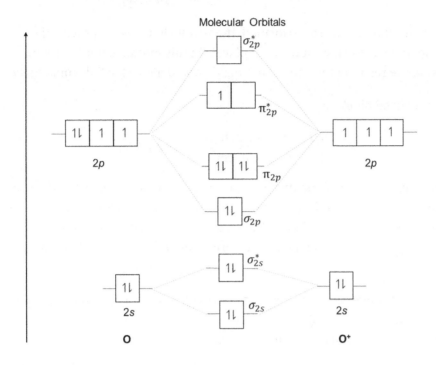

Molecular Orbitals

Paramagnetic substances have unpaired electrons in their MOs, while diamagnetic substances have all electrons paired in MOs. Since there is an unpaired electron in the MO diagram of O_2^+, it is paramagnetic. Its bond order is:

$$\frac{1}{2}\left((\#e^-)_{\text{bonding}} - (\#e^-)_{\text{antibonding}}\right) = \frac{1}{2}(8-3) = \frac{5}{2}$$

36. A: The collected precipitate is $PbSO_4$, which results from the following reaction:

$$Pb(NO_3)_2(aq) + Na_2SO_4(aq) \rightarrow PbSO_4(s) + 2\,NaNO_3(aq)$$

The number of moles of the obtained $PbSO_4$ precipitate is:

$$(0.487\text{ g})\left(\frac{1\text{ mol}}{303.3\text{ g}}\right) = 1.61 \times 10^{-3}\text{ mol}$$

Based on the stoichiometric ratio between $Pb(NO_3)_2$ and $PbSO_4$, there are 1.61×10^{-3} mol of $Pb(NO_3)_2$ in the 10.0 mL portion of solution. So, the concentration of $Pb(NO_3)_2$ is:

$$\left(\frac{1.61 \times 10^{-3}\text{ mol}}{10.00\text{ mL}}\right)\left(\frac{1000\text{ mL}}{1\text{ L}}\right) = 0.161\text{ M}$$

37. C: The mass of the metal is:

$$105.437 \text{ g} - 90.459 \text{ g} = 14.978 \text{ g}$$

When addition and subtraction are performed, the result should be kept with the same decimal places as the one that has the fewest decimal places. In this measurement, both mass values have 3 decimal places, so the result of the subtracted mass should also have 3 decimal places.

The density of the metal block is:

$$\frac{14.978 \text{ g}}{5.35 \text{ mL}} = \frac{14.978 \text{ g}}{5.35 \text{ cm}^3} = 2.7996 \text{ g/cm}^3$$

When performing multiplication and division, the result should be kept with the same number of significant figures as the one that has the fewest significant figures. Since the volume measurement has only 3 significant figures, even though the mass value has 5 significant figures, the density should be kept with 3 significant figures. Therefore, it should be reported as 2.80 g/cm^3 after rounding.

38. A: The key to unit conversions is to make sure that the units in the conversion factors all cancel out to leave the desired units. In this conversion, it is necessary to convert the hour to seconds, and the miles to meters. The overall converting process is:

$$\left(1,073 \; \frac{\text{miles}}{\text{hour}}\right)\left(\frac{1 \text{ m}}{6.21 \times 10^{-4} \text{ miles}}\right)\left(\frac{1 \text{ hour}}{3,600 \text{ s}}\right) = 480 \text{ m/s}$$

Note that the desired unit m/s is kept after the conversion process is complete. The units of miles and hours are cancelled out.

39. C: Recall that for a system at constant pressure, its enthalpy change is equal to the amount of heat gained or lost to the system. When the gas system does work on the surroundings, the surroundings receive the work done by the gas system, so the work done on the surroundings should have a positive sign. The work of the system holds an opposite sign than the work done on the surroundings. In this case, the work done to the system should thus have a negative sign ($-w$). To prove this, start with the relations $\Delta E = q_p + w$ and $-w = P\Delta V$, and substitute these two terms into $\Delta H = \Delta E + P\Delta V$:

$$\Delta H = \Delta E + P\Delta V = (q_p + w) - w = q_p$$

Since the system absorbs heat, the sign of ΔH is positive. Based on the above relation, $\Delta H = 17.2$ kJ. The ΔE of the system is equal to $(q_p + w)$. The ΔE of the system is:

$$\Delta E = q_p + w = (17.2 \text{ kJ}) + (-1.19 \text{ kJ}) = 16.0 \text{ kJ}$$

40. C: The complete combustion reaction of hydrocarbons produces CO_2 and H_2O (while CO is the result of incomplete combustion), so the unbalanced reaction equation should be:

$$C_2H_2(g) + O_2(g) \rightarrow CO_2(g) + H_2O(g)$$

There are 2 O atoms on the reactant side, but $2 + 1 = 3$ O atoms are on the product side. An easy start for balancing this reaction is to multiply the number of water molecules by 2 to make the number of O atoms on the product side even:

$$C_2H_2(g) + O_2(g) \rightarrow CO_2(g) + 2\,H_2O(g)$$

Now there are 4 H atoms on the product side but only 2 on the reactant side, so the number of C_2H_2 molecules should be multiplied by 2. This results in a total of 4 C atoms on the reactant side, so the number of CO_2 molecules on the product side should be multiplied by 4:

$$2\,C_2H_2(g) + O_2(g) \rightarrow 4\,CO_2(g) + 2\,H_2O(g)$$

Lastly, balance the number of O atoms. There are $4 \times 2 + 2 = 10$ O atoms on the product side, meaning that the number of O atoms on the reactant side should be multiplied by 5:

$$2\,C_2H_2(g) + 5\,O_2(g) \rightarrow 4\,CO_2(g) + 2\,H_2O(g)$$

With the amounts of all atom species equal on both sides, the reaction is balanced.

41. D: The polarity of the covalent bonds depends on the differences in the electronegativity between the atoms. Therefore, the greater the electronegativity difference between the other atom and F, the more polar the bond. N, C, O, and F are all in the second row (period), and electronegativity increases when going to the right in a row. Si is in the same group as C, but it has one additional shell of electrons. Going down a group, the electronegativity decreases. So, the electronegativity of the Si, N, C, O atoms are ranked as: $Si < C < N < O$. However, the differences of the electronegativity between them and F is in the reverse order. The polarity of the bonds should be ranked as:

$$(4)O - F < (2)N - F < (3)C - F < (1)Si - F$$

42. D: The value of a state function is independent of the path taken. In other words, knowing only the initial and final states is sufficient to quantify changes to these values. Enthalpy (H), internal energy (U), and Gibbs free energy (G) are all state functions. Work (w) is calculated based on the path that the object or system takes to get to its final state; varying the path will affect the amount of work done. Therefore, work is not a state function.

43. B: The relationship among enthalpy, entropy, and Gibbs free energy is:

$$\Delta G = \Delta H - T\Delta S$$

Recall that when ΔG is negative, the reaction is spontaneous. Since the entropy change is negative, the term $-T\Delta S$ is positive. The entropy change is also negative; when the positive $-T\Delta S$ term is added to it, the obtained ΔG value is temperature dependent. At low temperature, the $-T\Delta S$ term has a small value, so the resulting ΔG value is also negative. The reaction is spontaneous at low temperatures. When the temperature is high, the $-T\Delta S$ term has a large positive value, so the resulting ΔG value becomes positive. The reaction is therefore nonspontaneous at high temperatures.

44. A: The number of moles in 3.00 kg of H_2 is:

$$(3.00 \text{ kg}) \left(\frac{1000 \text{ g}}{1 \text{ kg}}\right) \left(\frac{1 \text{ mol}}{2.016 \text{ g } H_2}\right) = 1488 \text{ mol}$$

To produce 1 mole of H_2, 2 moles of NaCl and 2 moles of water are consumed. So, the masses of the NaCl and water consumed are:

$$\text{mass of NaCl} = 2 \times (1488 \text{ mol}) \left(\frac{58.44 \text{ g}}{1 \text{ mol NaCl}}\right) \left(\frac{1 \text{ kg}}{1000 \text{ g}}\right) = 173 \text{ kg}$$

$$\text{mass of } H_2O = 2 \times (1488 \text{ mol}) \left(\frac{18.02 \text{ g}}{1 \text{ mol } H_2O}\right) \left(\frac{1 \text{ kg}}{1000 \text{ g}}\right) = 53.6 \text{ kg}$$

45. D: The number of moles of HCl gas at a given temperature and pressure can be calculated by:

$$n = \frac{PV}{RT}$$

Substituting the values of R, volume, pressure, and temperature yields:

$$\frac{(1.00 \text{ atm})(1.50 \text{ L})}{\left(0.0821 \frac{\text{L} \cdot \text{atm}}{\text{K} \cdot \text{mol}}\right)(273.15 + 25.0) \text{ K}} = 0.0613 \text{ mol}$$

The number of moles of NaCl solid is:

$$(5.00 \text{ g}) \left(\frac{1 \text{ mol}}{58.44 \text{ g}}\right) = 0.0856 \text{ mol}$$

Based on the molar ratio, when one mole of NaCl is consumed, one mole of HCl should be produced. The theoretical yield of HCl is also 0.0856 mol. Therefore, the percent yield is:

$$\frac{0.0613 \text{ mol}}{0.0856 \text{ mol}} \times 100\% = 71.6\%$$

46. D: The number of moles of the consumed $Na_2C_2O_4$ is:

$$(0.1292 \text{ g}) \left(\frac{1 \text{ mol}}{134.0 \text{ g}}\right) = 9.643 \times 10^{-4} \text{ mol}$$

Based on the stoichiometry of the balanced reaction, the ratio between $KMnO_4$ and $Na_2C_2O_4$ is 2 : 5. Therefore, the number of moles for $KMnO_4$ is:

$$(9.643 \times 10^{-4} \text{ mol}) \left(\frac{2 \text{ mol } KMnO_4}{5 \text{ mol } Na_2C_2O_4}\right) = 3.857 \times 10^{-4} \text{ mol}$$

The concentration of the $KMnO_4$ solution is:

$$\left(\frac{3.857 \times 10^{-4} \text{ mol}}{17.85 \text{ mL}}\right)\left(\frac{1000 \text{ mL}}{1 \text{ L}}\right) = 0.02161 \text{ M}$$

47. A: The ΔH_{rxn} is equal to differences between the sum of the bond enthalpy in the reactants (i.e., enthalpy needed to break bonds) and the sum of the bond enthalpy in the products (i.e., enthalpy needed to form bonds). The correct numbers of bond enthalpy need to be used. Since the CO_2 has two double $C = O$ bonds, the value of $D(C = O)$ should be used, instead of $D(C - O)$:

$$\Delta H_{rxn} = \Big((4 \times D(F - F) + 2 \times D(C = O)) - (2 \times 2 \times D(O - F) + 4 \times D(C - F)\Big)$$
$$= (4 \times 155 + 2 \times 799) - (4 \times 190 + 4 \times 485)\Big) \text{ kJ/mol} = -482 \text{ kJ/mol}$$

48. B: The electron configuration for the Cl atom is: $[Ne]3s^23p^5$. When the Cl atom gains an electron and becomes Cl^-, its electron configuration becomes $[Ne]3s^23p^6$, which is equivalent to the configuration of an Ar atom. The electron configuration of the S atom is $[Ne]3s^23p^4$, when it gains two electrons to become S^{2-}, the configuration becomes $[Ne]3s^23p^6$, also equivalent to the Ar atom configuration. The same is the case for Ca^{2+}: when a Ca atom with electron configuration of $[Ar]4s^2$ loses both of its valence electrons, its electron configuration becomes the same with the Ar atom. The Br^- ion, however, has one extra shell of electrons than the Cl^-. Its electron configuration is $[Ar]3d^{10}4s^24p^6$, which is equivalent to the configuration of a Kr atom, unlike the other three species.

49. A: The catalyst is present in the reaction mixture when the reaction starts, takes part in the reaction, and gets regenerated at the end of the reaction. The NO_2 is the only species that matches with all the above criteria. The species NO is the intermediate, rather than the catalyst, as it is produced during the reaction instead of being present at the beginning. It is later consumed in the second step, so it should not appear on the overall reaction equation. Adding the two equations will yield the overall equation and demonstrate that both the catalyst and intermediate do not show up in the overall reaction. To do this, multiply the equation from Step 1 by a factor of 2:

$$2 \text{ NO}_2(g) + 2 \text{ SO}_2(g) \rightarrow 2 \text{ SO}_3(g) + 2 \text{ NO}(g)$$

Then add the above to the equation from Step 2:

$$2 \text{ NO}_2(g) + 2 \text{ SO}_2(g) + 2 \text{ NO}(g) + O_2(g) \rightarrow 2 \text{ SO}_3(g) + 2 \text{ NO}(g) + 2 \text{ NO}_2(g)$$

Eliminating the common species on both sides, the overall reaction is:

$$2 \text{ SO}_2(g) + O_2(g) \rightarrow 2 \text{ SO}_3(g)$$

As demonstrated above, NO_2 and NO both cancel out after the reaction is complete.

50. A: The $\Delta S°$ value can be calculated by the difference in the sum of $S°$ of the products and the reactants. The physical states of the reactants and products are important, so the value of $S°[H_2O(g)]$ should be used for this reaction:

$$\Delta S° = 8 \times S°[CO_2(g)] + 10 \times S°[H_2O(g)] - (2 \times S°[C_4H_{10}(g)] + 13 \times S°[O_2(g)])$$
$$= \left(8 \times (213.6) + 10 \times (188.83) - \left(2 \times (310.0) + 13 \times (205.0)\right)\right) \text{ J/(mol} \cdot \text{K)}$$
$$= 312.1 \text{ J/(mol} \cdot \text{K)}$$

51. D: The amount of work done on the cell by external potential is calculated by:

$$w = (nF)E_{ext}$$

The term nF is the number of charges (in Coulombs) applied to the cell. Begin by calculating the total charges needed to complete this electrolysis process based on the target mass of the sodium metal:

$$\left(\frac{1 \text{ mol } e^-}{1 \text{ mol Na}}\right)(2.00 \text{ kg Na})\left(\frac{1000 \text{ g}}{1 \text{ kg}}\right)\left(\frac{1 \text{ mol Na}}{23.0 \text{ g Na}}\right)\left(\frac{96{,}485 \text{ C}}{1 \text{ mol } e^-}\right) = 8.39 \times 10^6 \text{ C}$$

The electric work needed on the cell is then:

$$(8.39 \times 10^6 \text{ C})(10.0 \text{ V})\left(\frac{1 \text{ J}}{1 \text{ C} \cdot \text{V}}\right)\left(\frac{1 \text{ kWh}}{3.60 \times 10^6 \text{ J}}\right) = 23.3 \text{ kWh}$$

52. B: The described process involves two steps: 1) heating of the liquid phase acetone from 21.0 to 56.0 °C, and 2) vaporization of the acetone from liquid to gas at 56.0 °C. The amount of heat that is absorbed in heating of the liquid phase acetone is:

$$q = C_s \times m \times \Delta T = (2.17 \text{ J/(g} \cdot \text{K)})(30.0 \text{ g})(56.0 - 21.0 \text{ °C})\left(\frac{1 \text{ K}}{1 \text{ °C}}\right)\left(\frac{1 \text{ kJ}}{1000 \text{ J}}\right) = 2.28 \text{ kJ}$$

The amount of heat that is absorbed during vaporization is:

$$q = (31.27 \text{ kJ/mol})(30.0 \text{ g})\left(\frac{1 \text{ mol}}{58.08 \text{ g}}\right) = 16.2 \text{ kJ}$$

The total amount of heat that is required is then: 16.2 kJ + 2.28 kJ = 18.5 kJ

53. D: The relationship between K_p and K_c is:

$$K_p = K_c(RT)^{\Delta n}$$

Δn is the difference in the number of gas molecules between the products and reactants. The value of Δn is equal to $(2 - 1) = 1$ because there are two molecules of gases on the product side and one molecule of gas on the reactant side. Then substituting the values of K_c, R, and T yields:

$$K_p = (0.078)(0.0821 \times 373)^1 = 2.39$$

The direction of the reaction can be determined by the reaction quotient (Q_P):

$$Q_P = \frac{P_{SO_2} \times P_{Cl_2}}{P_{SO_2Cl_2}}$$

Substituting the values of gas partial pressures, the reaction quotient is:

$$Q_P = \frac{(0.143)(0.0756)}{(0.289)} = 0.0374 < K_p$$

Since $Q_P < K_p$, the reactant is in excess. The equilibrium is going to proceed to the right to form more products.

54. C: The Arrhenius equation relates the rate constant and temperature values. The logarithmic form of the Arrhenius equation below shows that there is a linear correlation between $\ln k$ (the y-values) and $\frac{1}{T}$ (the x-values):

$$\ln k = -\frac{E_a}{R}\left(\frac{1}{T}\right) + \ln A$$

The slope of the best-fit line is equal to $-\frac{E_a}{R}$. From the slope of the best-fit line, solve for the activation energy E_a of this reaction:

$$slope = -\frac{E_a}{R}$$

$$E_a = -slope \times R = -(-15{,}274 \text{ K})(8.314 \text{ J/(mol} \cdot \text{K)}) = \left(126{,}988 \ \frac{\text{J}}{\text{mol}}\right)\left(\frac{1 \text{ kJ}}{1{,}000 \text{ J}}\right) = 127 \text{ kJ/mol}$$

55. B: From the amount of heat being absorbed, the mass, and the specific heat of the aluminum block, calculate the magnitude of the temperature change using the equation below:

$$q = C_s \times m \times \Delta T$$

$$(1.43 \text{ kJ})\left(\frac{1000 \text{ J}}{1 \text{ kJ}}\right) = (0.900 \text{ J/(g} \cdot \text{K)}) \times (65.0 \text{ g}) \times \Delta T$$

$$\frac{1{,}430 \text{ J}}{(0.900 \text{ J/(g} \cdot \text{K)}) \times (65.0 \text{ g})} = \Delta T$$

$$24.4 \text{ K} = \Delta T = 24.4 \ ^\circ\text{C}$$

Since the aluminum block absorbs heat, it should increase in the temperature. Therefore, the final temperature should be:

$$24.4 \ ^\circ\text{C} + 21.0 \ ^\circ\text{C} = 45.4 \ ^\circ\text{C}$$

56. D: In the combustion analysis, the product CO_2 results from the carbon in the sample, while the product water results from the hydrogen element. Therefore, the mass and number of moles of the H and C element in the sample are:

$$\text{\# moles of H} = (0.2605 \text{ g H}_2\text{O})\left(\frac{1 \text{ mol H}_2\text{O}}{18.02 \text{ g H}_2\text{O}}\right)\left(\frac{2 \text{ mol H}}{1 \text{ mol H}_2\text{O}}\right) = 0.02891 \text{ mol}$$

$$\text{mass of H} = (0.02891 \text{ mol H})\left(\frac{1.008 \text{ g H}}{1 \text{ mol H}}\right) = 0.02914 \text{ g}$$

$$\text{\# moles of C} = (0.3172 \text{ g CO}_2)\left(\frac{1 \text{ mol CO}_2}{44.01 \text{ g CO}_2}\right) = 7.207 \times 10^{-3} \text{ mol}$$

$$\text{mass of C} = (7.207 \times 10^{-3} \text{ mol C})\left(\frac{12.01 \text{ g C}}{1 \text{ mol C}}\right) = 0.0865 \text{ g}$$

After the combustion reaction, all the H in the sample is converted to water, and all the C in the sample is converted to CO_2. Since the only other element is oxygen, the mass of the oxygen element in the sample is equal to the original mass of the sample minus the sum of the mass of C and H analyzed from the above:

$$0.2308 \text{ g} - (0.02914 \text{ g} + 0.0865 \text{ g}) = 0.1152 \text{ g}$$

The number of moles of O is then:

$$(0.1152 \text{ g})\left(\frac{1 \text{ mol}}{16.00 \text{ g}}\right) = 7.200 \times 10^{-3} \text{ mol}$$

The empirical formula of this compound is the nearest integer in the ratio of the number of moles in C : H : O:

$$(7.207 \times 10^{-3}) : (0.02891) : (7.200 \times 10^{-3}) \approx 1 : 4 : 1$$

Therefore, the empirical formula of this compound is CH_4O

57. C: The KCl salt completely dissociates into K^+ and Cl^- ions in water (a dipole), so the major type of intermolecular force besides hydrogen bonding is the ion-dipole forces. For the 3.70 M KCl solution, the amount of KCl in 100 g of water is:

$$\left(\frac{74.55 \text{ g}}{1 \text{ mol}}\right)\left(\frac{3.70 \text{ mol}}{1 \text{ L}}\right)(100 \text{ g})\left(\frac{1 \text{ mL}}{1.00 \text{ g}}\right)\left(\frac{1 \text{ L}}{1000 \text{ mL}}\right) = 27.6 \text{ g}$$

Since the maximum amount of KCl that can be dissolved in 100 g of water has not been reached at this concentration and temperature, the solution is undersaturated.

58. C: In the first pair, benzene is a non-polar molecule, but the water molecule is very polar. The same polarity differences exist between methanol (polar) and cyclohexane (non-polar), and between carbon tetrachloride (non-polar) and water (polar). Because of the differences in polarity and the types of intermolecular forces they experience, the above pairs are not miscible with (i.e., soluble in) each other. The pair of pentane and hexane are both non-polar, thus they experience very similar types of intermolecular forces (dispersion) and are miscible with each other.

59. D: To start the balancing process for this equation, multiply the number of CO_2 by 7 and H_2O by 4, since there are 7 C and 8 H on the left:

$$C_7H_8O_2(l) + O_2(g) \rightarrow 7\ CO_2(g) + 4\ H_2O(g)$$

Now there are $7 \times 2 + 4 = 18$ O on the right. To balance out the number of O, a factor must be multiplied by O_2 on the left. Since there are already 2 O in $C_7H_8O_2$, the number of remaining O should be $18 - 2 = 16$. So, the coefficient for O_2 is: $\frac{16}{2} = 8$:

$$C_7H_8O_2(l) + 8\ O_2(g) \rightarrow 7\ CO_2(g) + 4\ H_2O(g)$$

Checking the atom counts for the equation above, there are 7 C, 8 H, and 16 O on both sides. The equation is then balanced.

60. B: The energy change is proportional to the change in the mass during the nuclear reaction (sum of the mass of the products minus the sum of the mass of reactants). The mass change for the fission of 1.000 moles of $^{235}_{92}U$ in this equation is:

$$\Delta m = \big((140.8833 + 91.9021 + 3 \times 1.00866) - (234.9935 + 1.00866)\big)\ g = -0.1908\ g$$

Apply Einstein's equation to calculate the energy change. Note that the mass in Einstein's equation needs to be converted to kg in order to get the energy in J, which is the SI unit for energy:

$$\begin{aligned}
\Delta E &= (\Delta m)c^2 \\
&= (-0.1908\ g)\left(\frac{1\ kg}{1000\ g}\right)(2.9979 \times 10^8\ m/s)^2 \\
&= -1.715 \times 10^{13}\ \frac{kg \cdot m^2}{s^2} \\
&= -1.715 \times 10^{13}\ J
\end{aligned}$$

The negative sign means that energy (an enormous amount) is released in this process.

61. B: The rate law for this reaction is written as:

$$Rate = k[NO]^2[O_2]$$

Plugging in the rate constant and concentration values of the reactants yields:

$$Rate = k[NO]^2[O_2] = (6.19 \times 10^3\ M^{-2} \cdot s^{-1})(0.0331\ M)^2(0.0149\ M) = 0.101\ M/s$$

The rate of disappearance of O_2 and the rate of appearance of NO_2 are related by:

$$-\frac{\Delta[O_2]}{\Delta t} = \frac{1}{2}\frac{\Delta[NO_2]}{\Delta t}$$

So the rate of disappearance of O_2 is:

$$-\frac{\Delta[O_2]}{\Delta t} = 0.101 \text{ M/s}$$

The rate of appearance of NO_2 is:

$$\frac{\Delta[NO_2]}{\Delta t} = -2\frac{\Delta[O_2]}{\Delta t} = 0.202 \text{ M/s}$$

62. C: The $\Delta H°$ value can be calculated by the difference in the sum of $\Delta H_f°$ of the products and the reactants. The physical states of the reactants and products determines the value of $\Delta H°$, so it is important to use the value of $\Delta H_f°[H_2O(g)]$ rather than $\Delta H_f°[H_2O(l)]$ for this reaction:

$$\Delta H° = 8 \times \Delta H_f°[CO_2(g)] + 10 \times \Delta H_f°[H_2O(g)] - (2 \times \Delta H_f°[C_4H_{10}(g)] + 13 \times \Delta H_f°[O_2(g)])$$
$$= \left(8 \times (-393.5) + 10 \times (-241.8) - \left(2 \times (-124.73) + 13 \times (0.0)\right)\right) \text{ kJ/mol}$$
$$= -5{,}317 \text{ kJ/mol}$$

63. D: To balance this reaction:

$$Fe_3O_4(s) + CO(g) \rightarrow Fe(s) + CO_2(g)$$

There are 3 Fe atoms on the left, meaning that the Fe atom on the product side needs to be multiplied by 3:

$$Fe_3O_4(s) + CO(g) \rightarrow 3\ Fe(s) + CO_2(g)$$

Next, balance the number of C and O atoms. Observe that there is an odd number of 5 O atoms on the left, while there is an even number of 2 O atoms on the right to start. Multiplying an even factor of 2 for both CO and CO_2 first yields:

$$Fe_3O_4(s) + 2\ CO(g) \rightarrow 3\ Fe(s) + 2\ CO_2(g)$$

Now there are 6 O atoms on the left, but only 4 O atoms on the right. So, try out the factor of 4 for both CO and CO_2:

$$Fe_3O_4(s) + 4\ CO(g) \rightarrow 3\ Fe(s) + 4\ CO_2(g)$$

After multiplying the factor of 4, there are 8 O and 4 C atoms on the left, while the product side has 8 O and 4 C atoms as well. Therefore, the reaction is balanced.

64. D: The reaction in choice A involves an acid HBr and a base $Ca(OH)_2$, so it belongs to the acid-base reaction category. The same is true for options B and C: each has an acid (HNO_3 and $HClO_4$, respectively) and a base ($Fe(OH)_3$ and KOH, respectively). The last reaction does not contain an acid: KOH is a base, while $Fe(NO_3)_3$ is a salt, not an acid. Therefore, the last reaction is a regular double displacement reaction that also produces a precipitate ($Fe(OH)_3$).

65. A: The Be atom (electron configuration $[He]2s^2$) in BeF_2 and Hg atom (electron configuration $[Xe]4f^{14}5d^{10}6s^2$) $HgCl_2$ both have only two electrons in the valence shell (the $4f$ and $5d$ shells in

Hg are both filled; although they are lowered in energy level, the effective valence electrons for it are those two in the outer $6s$ shell). One of the electrons in their filled s orbitals may be promoted to the p orbital in the nearest energy level and form two sp hybridized orbitals as a result. Therefore, both of them have sp hybridization on the central atoms. The XeF_2 may look similar to them in the chemical formula and does adopt a linear geometry, but in fact, it has the expanded valence shell. Its Lewis structure is:

$$:\ddot{F}\text{---}\ddot{Xe}\text{---}\ddot{F}:$$

There are 5 electron domains on the Xe atom, counting the lone electron pairs that are not forming bonds. Since the s orbital can hybridize with three p orbitals, there can be 4 hybrid orbitals resulting from them. To make up for the additional bonding domain, one d orbital participates in the hybridization as well, so the Xe atom has sp^3d hybridization. In the C_2H_2 molecule, the C atoms form a triple bond (1 σ bond and 2 π bonds) between them. The π bonds result from the "side-by-side" overlapping of two $2p$ orbitals which do not participate in the hybridization. Therefore, there is only one $2p$ orbital being hybridized with the $2s$ orbital on the central carbon resulting in sp hybridization.

66. B: The dissolution process of AgCl in this case is affect by the common ion Cl^- from the NaCl solution. To solve for the equilibrium concentrations of Ag^+ and Cl^-, begin by constructing an ICE table:

$AgCl(s) \rightleftharpoons Ag^+(aq) + Cl^-(aq)$		
Initial	—	0	0.020
Change	—	$+x$ M	$+x$ M
Equilibrium	—	x M	$(0.020 + x)$ M

$$K_{sp} = [Ag^+][Cl^-] = (x)(0.020 + x) = 1.80 \times 10^{-10}$$

Although it is possible to simplify the above equation and solve it using the quadratic formula, notice that the value of x is much smaller than 0.020 (since AgCl is sparingly soluble). This means that $x \ll 0.020$, and the term $0.020 + x \approx 0.020$. Substituting this into the equation:

$$(x)(0.020) = 1.80 \times 10^{-10}$$

$$x = 9.00 \times 10^{-9}$$

Therefore, the solubility of AgCl is 9.00×10^{-9} mol/L when dissolved in the 0.020 M NaCl solution.

67. A: All the mixtures can potentially undergo double displacement reactions. The proposed reactions are listed below. For mixture in option A:

$$K_2CO_3(aq) + 2\ HBr(aq) \rightarrow 2\ KBr(aq) + H_2O(l) + CO_2(g)$$

CO_2 gas and water are produced in this reaction; there is no precipitation formed.

The others yield precipitations after the reaction:

$$Na_2S(aq) + ZnCl_2(aq) \rightarrow ZnS(s) + 2\ NaCl(aq)$$

$$Cu(NO_3)_2(aq) + 2\ NaOH(aq) \rightarrow Cu(OH)_2(s) + 2\ NaNO_3(aq)$$

$$AgNO_3(aq) + HCl(aq) \rightarrow AgCl(s) + HNO_3(aq)$$

The products in the solid state are precipitates that result from double displacement reactions.

68. B: Solutions are homogeneous mixtures of the solute(s) and solvent(s). Both the solute and solvent must be in the same phase, whether gas, liquid, or solid. If the mixture is heterogeneous, it cannot be considered a solution. Sodium amalgam is a solution that has both the solute and solvent in solid phase. Air is a mixture of many gases and can be considered a solution with gaseous solutes and solvents. Brine is a concentrated solution of salts dissolved in water. Milk is composed of a suspension of protein, sugar, and fat. Since the protein and fat remain as small particles in the water, it is not a homogeneous mixture and not considered a solution.

69. B: The pH of the buffer solution can be calculated using the Henderson–Hasselbalch equation:

$$pH = pK_a + \log\frac{[C_6H_5CONa]}{[C_6H_5COOH]}$$

Since the desired pH and the K_a values of the benzoic acid are known, the ratio of sodium benzoate to benzoic acid can be calculated:

$$3.800 = -\log(6.3 \times 10^{-5}) + \log\frac{[C_6H_5COONa]}{[C_6H_5COOH]} = 4.201 + \log\frac{[C_6H_5COONa]}{[C_6H_5COOH]}$$

$$\log\frac{[C_6H_5COONa]}{[C_6H_5COOH]} = -0.401$$

$$\frac{[C_6H_5COONa]}{[C_6H_5COOH]} = 10^{-0.401} = 0.398$$

Since the concentrations of both solids are equal to the mass divided by the volume of the solution, and the total volume for both solutions are the same, the volume factor is cancelled out:

$$\frac{[C_6H_5COONa]}{[C_6H_5COOH]} = \frac{\dfrac{\text{mass of } C_6H_5COONa}{100\text{ mL}}}{\dfrac{\text{mass of } C_6H_5COOH}{100\text{ mL}}} = \frac{\text{mass of } C_6H_5COONa}{0.600\text{ g}} = 0.398$$

$$\text{mass of } C_6H_5COONa = 0.398 \times 0.600\text{ g} = 0.239\text{ g}$$

70. B: The oxidation states of all elements of the reactants and products in this reaction are marked below:

$$2\ \overset{+2\ -2}{ZnS}\text{ (s)} + 3\ \overset{0}{O_2}\text{ (g)} \rightarrow 2\ \overset{+2\ -2}{ZnO}\text{ (s)} + 2\ \overset{+4\ -2}{SO_2}\text{ (g)}$$

The oxidation state of Zn has no change, so it is neither oxidized nor reduced. The oxidation state of S is increased from −2 to +4, so it is oxidized after the reaction. The oxidation state of O is decreased from 0 to −2, so it is reduced after the reaction.

ACS General Chemistry Practice Test #3

To take these additional ACS General Chemistry practice tests, visit our bonus page: **mometrix.com/bonus948/acsgenchem**

How to Overcome Test Anxiety

Just the thought of taking a test is enough to make most people a little nervous. A test is an important event that can have a long-term impact on your future, so it's important to take it seriously and it's natural to feel anxious about performing well. But just because anxiety is normal, that doesn't mean that it's helpful in test taking, or that you should simply accept it as part of your life. Anxiety can have a variety of effects. These effects can be mild, like making you feel slightly nervous, or severe, like blocking your ability to focus or remember even a simple detail.

If you experience test anxiety—whether severe or mild—it's important to know how to beat it. To discover this, first you need to understand what causes test anxiety.

Causes of Test Anxiety

While we often think of anxiety as an uncontrollable emotional state, it can actually be caused by simple, practical things. One of the most common causes of test anxiety is that a person does not feel adequately prepared for their test. This feeling can be the result of many different issues such as poor study habits or lack of organization, but the most common culprit is time management. Starting to study too late, failing to organize your study time to cover all of the material, or being distracted while you study will mean that you're not well prepared for the test. This may lead to cramming the night before, which will cause you to be physically and mentally exhausted for the test. Poor time management also contributes to feelings of stress, fear, and hopelessness as you realize you are not well prepared but don't know what to do about it.

Other times, test anxiety is not related to your preparation for the test but comes from unresolved fear. This may be a past failure on a test, or poor performance on tests in general. It may come from comparing yourself to others who seem to be performing better or from the stress of living up to expectations. Anxiety may be driven by fears of the future—how failure on this test would affect your educational and career goals. These fears are often completely irrational, but they can still negatively impact your test performance.

Elements of Test Anxiety

As mentioned earlier, test anxiety is considered to be an emotional state, but it has physical and mental components as well. Sometimes you may not even realize that you are suffering from test anxiety until you notice the physical symptoms. These can include trembling hands, rapid heartbeat, sweating, nausea, and tense muscles. Extreme anxiety may lead to fainting or vomiting. Obviously, any of these symptoms can have a negative impact on testing. It is important to recognize them as soon as they begin to occur so that you can address the problem before it damages your performance.

The mental components of test anxiety include trouble focusing and inability to remember learned information. During a test, your mind is on high alert, which can help you recall information and stay focused for an extended period of time. However, anxiety interferes with your mind's natural processes, causing you to blank out, even on the questions you know well. The strain of testing during anxiety makes it difficult to stay focused, especially on a test that may take several hours. Extreme anxiety can take a huge mental toll, making it difficult not only to recall test information but even to understand the test questions or pull your thoughts together.

Effects of Test Anxiety

Test anxiety is like a disease—if left untreated, it will get progressively worse. Anxiety leads to poor performance, and this reinforces the feelings of fear and failure, which in turn lead to poor performances on subsequent tests. It can grow from a mild nervousness to a crippling condition. If allowed to progress, test anxiety can have a big impact on your schooling, and consequently on your future.

Test anxiety can spread to other parts of your life. Anxiety on tests can become anxiety in any stressful situation, and blanking on a test can turn into panicking in a job situation. But fortunately, you don't have to let anxiety rule your testing and determine your grades. There are a number of relatively simple steps you can take to move past anxiety and function normally on a test and in the rest of life.

Physical Steps for Beating Test Anxiety

While test anxiety is a serious problem, the good news is that it can be overcome. It doesn't have to control your ability to think and remember information. While it may take time, you can begin taking steps today to beat anxiety.

Just as your first hint that you may be struggling with anxiety comes from the physical symptoms, the first step to treating it is also physical. Rest is crucial for having a clear, strong mind. If you are tired, it is much easier to give in to anxiety. But if you establish good sleep habits, your body and mind will be ready to perform optimally, without the strain of exhaustion. Additionally, sleeping well helps you to retain information better, so you're more likely to recall the answers when you see the test questions.

Getting good sleep means more than going to bed on time. It's important to allow your brain time to relax. Take study breaks from time to time so it doesn't get overworked, and don't study right before bed. Take time to rest your mind before trying to rest your body, or you may find it difficult to fall asleep.

Along with sleep, other aspects of physical health are important in preparing for a test. Good nutrition is vital for good brain function. Sugary foods and drinks may give a burst of energy but this burst is followed by a crash, both physically and emotionally. Instead, fuel your body with protein and vitamin-rich foods.

Also, drink plenty of water. Dehydration can lead to headaches and exhaustion, especially if your brain is already under stress from the rigors of the test. Particularly if your test is a long one, drink water during the breaks. And if possible, take an energy-boosting snack to eat between sections.

Along with sleep and diet, a third important part of physical health is exercise. Maintaining a steady workout schedule is helpful, but even taking 5-minute study breaks to walk can help get your blood pumping faster and clear your head. Exercise also releases endorphins, which contribute to a positive feeling and can help combat test anxiety.

When you nurture your physical health, you are also contributing to your mental health. If your body is healthy, your mind is much more likely to be healthy as well. So take time to rest, nourish your body with healthy food and water, and get moving as much as possible. Taking these physical steps will make you stronger and more able to take the mental steps necessary to overcome test anxiety.

Mental Steps for Beating Test Anxiety

Working on the mental side of test anxiety can be more challenging, but as with the physical side, there are clear steps you can take to overcome it. As mentioned earlier, test anxiety often stems from lack of preparation, so the obvious solution is to prepare for the test. Effective studying may be the most important weapon you have for beating test anxiety, but you can and should employ several other mental tools to combat fear.

First, boost your confidence by reminding yourself of past success—tests or projects that you aced. If you're putting as much effort into preparing for this test as you did for those, there's no reason you should expect to fail here. Work hard to prepare; then trust your preparation.

Second, surround yourself with encouraging people. It can be helpful to find a study group, but be sure that the people you're around will encourage a positive attitude. If you spend time with others who are anxious or cynical, this will only contribute to your own anxiety. Look for others who are motivated to study hard from a desire to succeed, not from a fear of failure.

Third, reward yourself. A test is physically and mentally tiring, even without anxiety, and it can be helpful to have something to look forward to. Plan an activity following the test, regardless of the outcome, such as going to a movie or getting ice cream.

When you are taking the test, if you find yourself beginning to feel anxious, remind yourself that you know the material. Visualize successfully completing the test. Then take a few deep, relaxing breaths and return to it. Work through the questions carefully but with confidence, knowing that you are capable of succeeding.

Developing a healthy mental approach to test taking will also aid in other areas of life. Test anxiety affects more than just the actual test—it can be damaging to your mental health and even contribute to depression. It's important to beat test anxiety before it becomes a problem for more than testing.

Study Strategy

Being prepared for the test is necessary to combat anxiety, but what does being prepared look like? You may study for hours on end and still not feel prepared. What you need is a strategy for test prep. The next few pages outline our recommended steps to help you plan out and conquer the challenge of preparation.

STEP 1: SCOPE OUT THE TEST

Learn everything you can about the format (multiple choice, essay, etc.) and what will be on the test. Gather any study materials, course outlines, or sample exams that may be available. Not only will this help you to prepare, but knowing what to expect can help to alleviate test anxiety.

STEP 2: MAP OUT THE MATERIAL

Look through the textbook or study guide and make note of how many chapters or sections it has. Then divide these over the time you have. For example, if a book has 15 chapters and you have five days to study, you need to cover three chapters each day. Even better, if you have the time, leave an extra day at the end for overall review after you have gone through the material in depth.

If time is limited, you may need to prioritize the material. Look through it and make note of which sections you think you already have a good grasp on, and which need review. While you are studying, skim quickly through the familiar sections and take more time on the challenging parts. Write out your plan so you don't get lost as you go. Having a written plan also helps you feel more in control of the study, so anxiety is less likely to arise from feeling overwhelmed at the amount to cover.

STEP 3: GATHER YOUR TOOLS

Decide what study method works best for you. Do you prefer to highlight in the book as you study and then go back over the highlighted portions? Or do you type out notes of the important information? Or is it helpful to make flashcards that you can carry with you? Assemble the pens, index cards, highlighters, post-it notes, and any other materials you may need so you won't be distracted by getting up to find things while you study.

If you're having a hard time retaining the information or organizing your notes, experiment with different methods. For example, try color-coding by subject with colored pens, highlighters, or post-it notes. If you learn better by hearing, try recording yourself reading your notes so you can listen while in the car, working out, or simply sitting at your desk. Ask a friend to quiz you from your flashcards, or try teaching someone the material to solidify it in your mind.

STEP 4: CREATE YOUR ENVIRONMENT

It's important to avoid distractions while you study. This includes both the obvious distractions like visitors and the subtle distractions like an uncomfortable chair (or a too-comfortable couch that makes you want to fall asleep). Set up the best study environment possible: good lighting and a comfortable work area. If background music helps you focus, you may want to turn it on, but otherwise keep the room quiet. If you are using a computer to take notes, be sure you don't have any other windows open, especially applications like social media, games, or anything else that could distract you. Silence your phone and turn off notifications. Be sure to keep water close by so you stay hydrated while you study (but avoid unhealthy drinks and snacks).

Also, take into account the best time of day to study. Are you freshest first thing in the morning? Try to set aside some time then to work through the material. Is your mind clearer in the afternoon or evening? Schedule your study session then. Another method is to study at the same time of day that

245

you will take the test, so that your brain gets used to working on the material at that time and will be ready to focus at test time.

STEP 5: STUDY!

Once you have done all the study preparation, it's time to settle into the actual studying. Sit down, take a few moments to settle your mind so you can focus, and begin to follow your study plan. Don't give in to distractions or let yourself procrastinate. This is your time to prepare so you'll be ready to fearlessly approach the test. Make the most of the time and stay focused.

Of course, you don't want to burn out. If you study too long you may find that you're not retaining the information very well. Take regular study breaks. For example, taking five minutes out of every hour to walk briskly, breathing deeply and swinging your arms, can help your mind stay fresh.

As you get to the end of each chapter or section, it's a good idea to do a quick review. Remind yourself of what you learned and work on any difficult parts. When you feel that you've mastered the material, move on to the next part. At the end of your study session, briefly skim through your notes again.

But while review is helpful, cramming last minute is NOT. If at all possible, work ahead so that you won't need to fit all your study into the last day. Cramming overloads your brain with more information than it can process and retain, and your tired mind may struggle to recall even previously learned information when it is overwhelmed with last-minute study. Also, the urgent nature of cramming and the stress placed on your brain contribute to anxiety. You'll be more likely to go to the test feeling unprepared and having trouble thinking clearly.

So don't cram, and don't stay up late before the test, even just to review your notes at a leisurely pace. Your brain needs rest more than it needs to go over the information again. In fact, plan to finish your studies by noon or early afternoon the day before the test. Give your brain the rest of the day to relax or focus on other things, and get a good night's sleep. Then you will be fresh for the test and better able to recall what you've studied.

STEP 6: TAKE A PRACTICE TEST

Many courses offer sample tests, either online or in the study materials. This is an excellent resource to check whether you have mastered the material, as well as to prepare for the test format and environment.

Check the test format ahead of time: the number of questions, the type (multiple choice, free response, etc.), and the time limit. Then create a plan for working through them. For example, if you have 30 minutes to take a 60-question test, your limit is 30 seconds per question. Spend less time on the questions you know well so that you can take more time on the difficult ones.

If you have time to take several practice tests, take the first one open book, with no time limit. Work through the questions at your own pace and make sure you fully understand them. Gradually work up to taking a test under test conditions: sit at a desk with all study materials put away and set a timer. Pace yourself to make sure you finish the test with time to spare and go back to check your answers if you have time.

After each test, check your answers. On the questions you missed, be sure you understand why you missed them. Did you misread the question (tests can use tricky wording)? Did you forget the information? Or was it something you hadn't learned? Go back and study any shaky areas that the practice tests reveal.

Taking these tests not only helps with your grade, but also aids in combating test anxiety. If you're already used to the test conditions, you're less likely to worry about it, and working through tests until you're scoring well gives you a confidence boost. Go through the practice tests until you feel comfortable, and then you can go into the test knowing that you're ready for it.

Test Tips

On test day, you should be confident, knowing that you've prepared well and are ready to answer the questions. But aside from preparation, there are several test day strategies you can employ to maximize your performance.

First, as stated before, get a good night's sleep the night before the test (and for several nights before that, if possible). Go into the test with a fresh, alert mind rather than staying up late to study.

Try not to change too much about your normal routine on the day of the test. It's important to eat a nutritious breakfast, but if you normally don't eat breakfast at all, consider eating just a protein bar. If you're a coffee drinker, go ahead and have your normal coffee. Just make sure you time it so that the caffeine doesn't wear off right in the middle of your test. Avoid sugary beverages, and drink enough water to stay hydrated but not so much that you need a restroom break 10 minutes into the test. If your test isn't first thing in the morning, consider going for a walk or doing a light workout before the test to get your blood flowing.

Allow yourself enough time to get ready, and leave for the test with plenty of time to spare so you won't have the anxiety of scrambling to arrive in time. Another reason to be early is to select a good seat. It's helpful to sit away from doors and windows, which can be distracting. Find a good seat, get out your supplies, and settle your mind before the test begins.

When the test begins, start by going over the instructions carefully, even if you already know what to expect. Make sure you avoid any careless mistakes by following the directions.

Then begin working through the questions, pacing yourself as you've practiced. If you're not sure on an answer, don't spend too much time on it, and don't let it shake your confidence. Either skip it and come back later, or eliminate as many wrong answers as possible and guess among the remaining ones. Don't dwell on these questions as you continue—put them out of your mind and focus on what lies ahead.

Be sure to read all of the answer choices, even if you're sure the first one is the right answer. Sometimes you'll find a better one if you keep reading. But don't second-guess yourself if you do immediately know the answer. Your gut instinct is usually right. Don't let test anxiety rob you of the information you know.

If you have time at the end of the test (and if the test format allows), go back and review your answers. Be cautious about changing any, since your first instinct tends to be correct, but make sure you didn't misread any of the questions or accidentally mark the wrong answer choice. Look over any you skipped and make an educated guess.

At the end, leave the test feeling confident. You've done your best, so don't waste time worrying about your performance or wishing you could change anything. Instead, celebrate the successful

completion of this test. And finally, use this test to learn how to deal with anxiety even better next time.

> **Review Video: 5 Tips to Beat Test Anxiety**
> Visit mometrix.com/academy and enter code: 570656

Important Qualification

Not all anxiety is created equal. If your test anxiety is causing major issues in your life beyond the classroom or testing center, or if you are experiencing troubling physical symptoms related to your anxiety, it may be a sign of a serious physiological or psychological condition. If this sounds like your situation, we strongly encourage you to seek professional help.

Additional Bonus Material

Due to our efforts to try to keep this book to a manageable length, we've created a link that will give you access to all of your additional bonus material:

mometrix.com/bonus948/acsgenchem